THE SERIOUS SHOPPER'S GUIDE TO ITALY

Other titles available in THE SERIOUS SHOPPER'S series:

THE SERIOUS SHOPPER'S GUIDE TO LONDON
THE SERIOUS SHOPPER'S GUIDE TO LOS ANGELES
THE SERIOUS SHOPPER'S GUIDE TO PARIS

All published by Prentice Hall Press,
New York

THE SERIOUS SHOPPER'S
GUIDE TO
ITALY

ROBERT TINE

Photographs by Keri Pickett

Prentice Hall Press • New York

Copyright © 1988
by Robert Tine

Photographs Copyright © 1987
by Keri Pickett

Designed by Julie Linden

All rights reserved
including the right of reproduction
in whole or in part in any form

Published by Prentice Hall Press
A Division of Simon & Schuster, Inc.
Gulf + Western Building
One Gulf + Western Plaza
New York, NY 10023

Library of Congress Cataloging in Publication Data
Tine, Robert.
  The serious shopper's guide to Italy.

  Includes indexes.
  1. Shopping—Italy—Guide-books.   2. Italy—
Description and travel—1975-   —Guide-books.
I. Title.   II. Title: Guide to Italy.
TX337.I8T56   1988   381'.45'0002545   87-7195
ISBN 0-13-806894-1

Manufactured in the United States of America

CONTENTS

PART ONE
SHOPPING ITALY   1

Chapter I   An Introduction to Shopping Italy   3

Chapter II   Shopping Strategies   9
- What to Do Before You Go   9
- Comparison Shopping   10
- The ABCs of Shopping Italy   10

Chapter III   What to Buy   23
- Design   23
- Fashion   23
- Food   24
- Glass and Ceramics   24
- Lace   25
- Leather Goods   26
- Mosaics   27
- Paper Goods and Fine Bindings   27
- Prints and Engravings   27
- Religious Objects and Vestments   28
- Silk   28
- Wines   28

PART TWO
SHOPPING MILAN   31

Chapter IV   A Milan Overview   33
- Basic Orientation   33
- The ABCs of Shopping Milan   37

Chapter V Great Milan Shopping Strolls   40

   Monte Napoleone   40
   The Brera Area   50
   The Duomo Area   54
   Corso Buenos Aires   58

Chapter VI The Ultimate Milan Shopping Spree   60

   Antiques   60
   Art Galleries   66
   Books   68
   Clothing   69
     Childen's Fashions   69
     Maternity Wear   71
     Men's Fashions   72
     Women's Fashions   82
   Department Stores   103
   Discount Shopping   104
   Fabrics and Textiles   106
   Food   107
     Candy, Confectionery, Chocolate, and Pastries   107
     Cheese, Truffles, and Specialty Foods   108
     Ice Cream   110
   Furniture   111
   Furs   112
   Glass   114
   Hats   114
   Housewares   115
   Jewelry   119
     Antique   119
     Costume   119
     Precious   120
   Lace   123
   Leather Goods   123
   Linens   139
   Malls   140
   Porcelain   141

Prints and Engravings	142
Stationery Supplies	143
Toys	144
Wines	145

PART THREE
SHOPPING FLORENCE — 147

Chapter VII   A Florence Overview — 149
Basic Orientation	149
The ABCs of Shopping Florence	153

Chapter VIII   Great Florence Shopping Strolls — 156
The Heart of Florence	157
Across the River and into the Pitti	164
High-Fashion Florence	169

Chapter IX   The Ultimate Florence Shopping Spree — 173
Antiques	173
Books	179
Clothing	179
Children's Fashions	180
Men's Fashions	181
Women's Fashions	184
Food	195
Furniture	196
Housewares	196
Jewelry	198
Antique	198
Cameos	199
Costume	200
Precious	201
Lace	201
Leather Goods	202

Linens	209
Lingerie	210
Porcelain and Pottery	210
Prints and Engraving	211
Stationery Supplies	212
Wines	215

PART FOUR
SHOPPING VENICE — 217

Chapter X   A Venice Overview — 219

Basic Orientation	219
The ABCs of Shopping Venice	226

Chapter XI   Great Venice Shopping Strolls — 229

From San Marco to Campo Morosini	229
Piazza San Marco and the Frezzeria	233
The Mercerie and the Ruga Rialto	237

Chapter XII   The Ultimate Venice Shopping Spree — 241

Antiques	241
Clothing	243
Children's Fashions	243
Men's Fashions	244
Women's Fashions	246
Food	254
Furs	255
Glass	255
Lace	259
Leather Goods	261
Masks	269
Prints and Engravings	273
Stationery Supplies	274

PART FIVE
SHOPPING ROME — 275

Chapter XIII A Rome Overview — 277

Basic Orientation — 280
The ABCs of Shopping Rome — 283

Chapter XIV Great Rome Shopping Strolls — 286

The Shopping Triangle Around the Piazza di Spagna — 286
  Via Condotti and South — 288
  North from the Piazza di Spagna — 289
  Down Via del Corso — 291
  Above the Spanish Steps — 293
Via Cola di Rienzo — 296
The Heart of Old Rome — 299
Via Nazionale — 303

Chapter XV The Ultimate Rome Shopping Spree — 307

Antiques — 307
Art Galleries — 313
Books — 316
Clothing — 317
  Children's Fashions — 317
  Men's Fashions — 321
  Women's Fashions — 334
Department Store — 355
Discount Shopping — 356
Fabrics and Textiles — 357
Food — 359
  Chocolates — 359
  Ice Cream — 359
  Pastries — 360
  Specialty Foods — 361
Furniture — 363
Handcrafts — 365

Hats	366
Housewares	366
Jewelry	368
Antique	368
Costume	369
Precious	370
Lace	370
Leather Goods	371
Linens	389
Lingerie	390
Mosaics	391
Porcelain	392
Prints and Engravings	393
Records	394
Religious Articles and Vestments	394
Stationery Supplies	395
Toys	396
Walking Sticks	397
Wines	398

Index   401

General Information	403
Establishments	406
Products and Services	413
Designer and Other Prominent Names	416

MAPS

Italy	4–5
Milan	34–35
Florence	150–51
Venice	220–21
Rome	278–79
Piazza di Spagna Area	287
Old Rome Area	300

Acknowledgments

Obviously, a book of this scope could not have been assembled by one person. Therefore some heartfelt thanks are in order. Marilyn Wood, my editor in New York, is a demanding, conscientious, precise, but blessedly patient and understanding professional who helped me through every stage of this book.

In Italy the person who deserves the most thanks is Lucy Clink. She visited every store with me, read and reread the manuscript, and ventured into lingerie shops and asked a lot of questions I didn't have the courage to. This book is as much hers as it is mine.

I would also like to thank my parents, Harold and Rita Tine, old Italy hands who have lived here for years and have a deep knowledge of how the country works and where the bargains are to be found.

Dana Prescott gave an immense amount of time and thought to the book, and came up with vital and arcane information on Florence and Rome. I cannot thank her enough. I am also deeply grateful to Phoebe Natanson, who never turned down a plea for help and who always came up with the right answer.

I would also like to thank Cornelia McSheehy, who always said I would finish (and she was right), and Lenore Conroy, who put me on to the best chocolates in Rome, as well as some Valentino secrets.

I wish I could thank by name the Venetian glassmaker who gave me the low-down on fake Venetian glass, but as he requested anonymity, I must respect that. He said he would be ruined in the glass business if his "treachery" got around. But thank you, sir—you know who you are.

Finally, I would like to thank the hundreds of store managers and salespeople I have spoken to in the last year. They must have wondered why a young man was so interested in women's clothes, leather goods, and furs, but they were almost always too polite to ask and most of them answered every question cheerfully.

These are the thank yous. I acknowledge, of course, that mistakes are my own.

INFLATION ALERT: While the rate of inflation has declined over the past two years, we don't have to tell you that prices remain volatile. In researching this book we have made every effort to obtain up-to-the-minute prices, but even the most conscientious researcher cannot keep up with the ever-changing shop scene. However, as we go to press, we believe we have obtained the most reliable data possible.

A DISCLAIMER: All information in this book has been obtained from personal visits to each establishment. Because policies and managements change, we cannot be responsible for representations made or implied in this book. We suggest, therefore, that you check the policy of each establishment prior to any purchase.

PART ONE

SHOPPING ITALY

CHAPTER 1

AN INTRODUCTION TO SHOPPING ITALY

Shopping Italy is an adventure. The profusion of shops and markets and the huge variety of famous-name goods make Italy a shopper's paradise in which you're sure to come upon the perfect pair of boots, the ideal piece of Tuscan pottery, or a lovely piece of Venetian lace without doing much more than walking down the right street. Like the English, in Napoleon's famous phrase, the Italians are a nation of shopkeepers and they have been enthusiastic traders since before Christ. In Rome, one of the best-preserved ancient buildings is not a temple or a palace, but a market, built by the Emperor Trajan some 1,800 years ago. The rows of shops look much as they did when they were first erected—in fact it looks rather like an ancient version of a modern shopping center.

Venice was once the greatest commercial sea power in the world. Beginning with Venice's most famous son, Marco Polo, the Venetians controlled the trade with the East, bringing silks and spices back to a continent which had never imagined such exotic things existed.

Florence is the city which codified—invented, really—the banking and bookkeeping procedures that made international trade possible, handing down commercial practices that are still in use in our computerized age. That's not to mention the fact that the great Florentine family, the Medici, were such avid consumers that they almost single-handedly accounted for the gross national product of Tuscany.

Throughout history the Italians have known and appre-

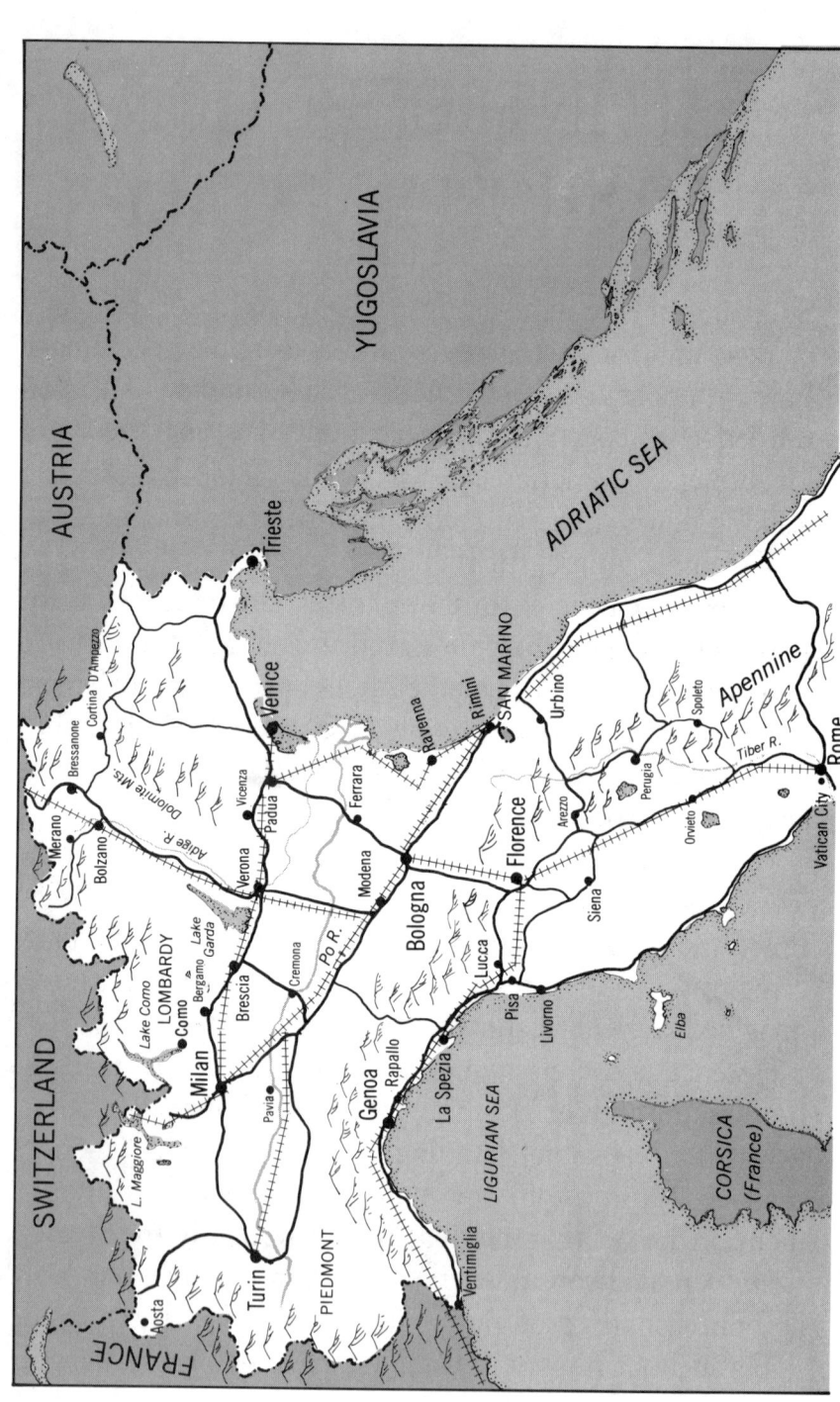

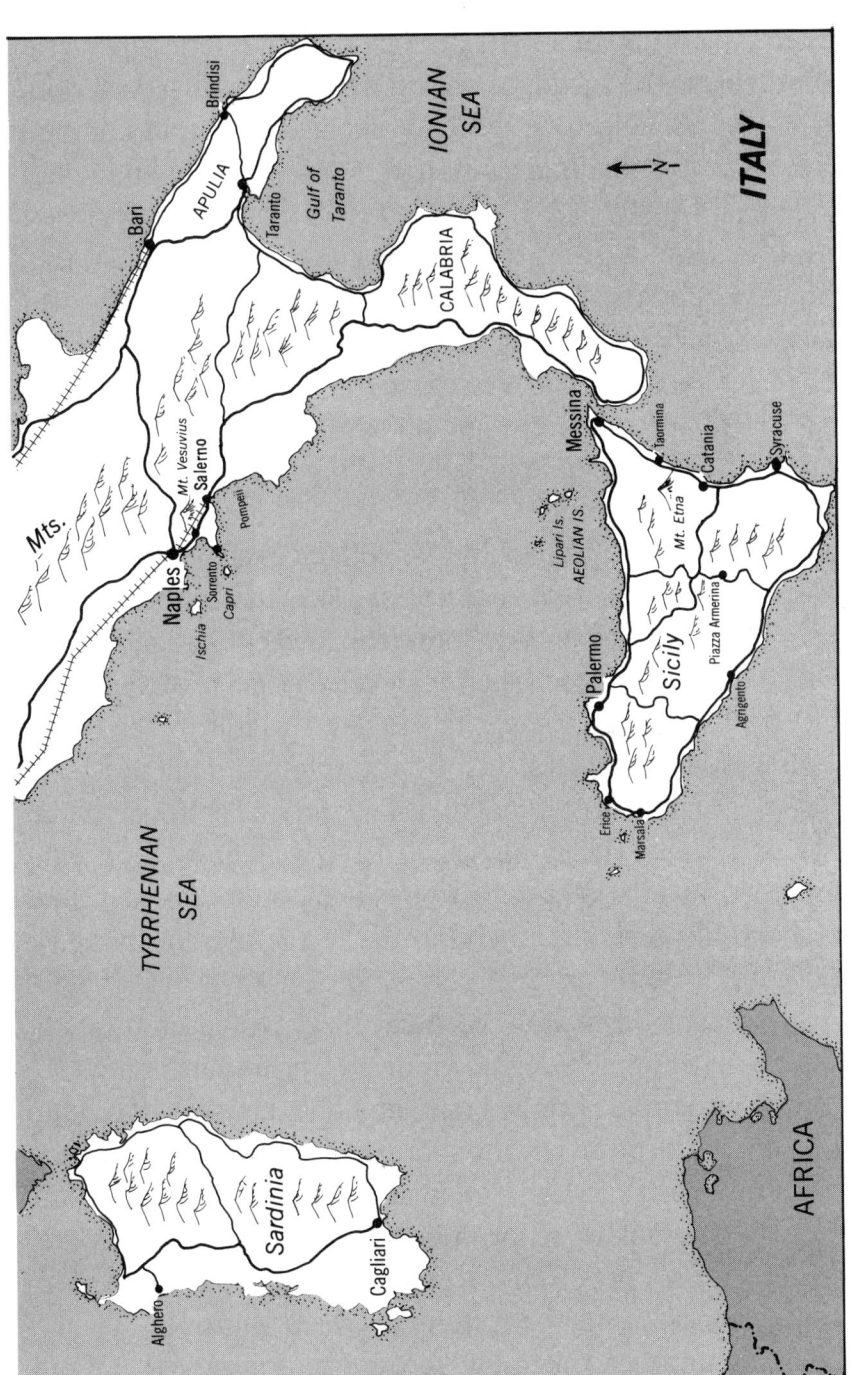

ciated quality. One of the reasons that the Venetians ventured east in the first place was because of their dissatisfaction with the poor cloths and dyes available to them in Europe. Their sense of quality remains to this day—Italians know and appreciate quality goods, and the rest of the world recognizes that "made in Italy" very often means "the best." When the Soviet Union threw in the towel and admitted that they just couldn't build a decent automobile, they looked not to Detroit for guidance or even to Japan—they turned to Fiat of Torino. The company built an entire town in Russia to produce Fiat cars and trucks—the town is named after an Italian: Togliattigrad.

The quality of Italian life is evident everywhere. Fresh pasta, fresh bread, fresh vegetables, good wines, and beautiful cuts of meat find their way onto the lowliest Italian tables. The corner *gelateria* sells better ice cream than the expensive ice-cream palaces of New York and Beverly Hills.

Italian lives are governed by the rules of *bruta* and *bella figura*. Italians will go out of their way to avoid cutting *la bruta figura* (literally "the ugly figure"). To be well dressed and well groomed at all times is extremely important: *bella figura* ("beautiful figure") is an end in itself, a reason for living. I have a private theory that punk and new wave styles never really caught on in Italy because they involved too much shoddy clothing, self-degradation: *bruta figura* personified.

Sit in Rome's Piazza Navona on a hot summer's day. The foreigners are dressed in the shortest of shorts, the skimpiest of T-shirts, and sandals—all in an attempt to beat the heat. The Italians look with horror on this kind of dress. They are wearing freshly pressed linen pants or cotton skirts, and look cool, composed, and the epitome of *la bella figura*.

That's not to say the Italians are any more reserved in their

AN INTRODUCTION TO ITALY

dress than they are in their driving, politics, or passion for soccer. They dress with style, panache, and color, yet somehow manage not to look outrageous or gauche. It is an innate sense of taste, style, elegance, and attention to detail which make Italian goods desirable, and that's the joy of shopping Italy.

Of course, nothing is perfect. Even if you've never been here before, you have no doubt heard that nothing in Italy is approached quite head-on and straightforwardly: the constantly shifting shoals of Italian business hours, long and rather chaotic lines in banks and sometimes in stores are nuisances which must be endured along with the normal difficulties of an unfamiliar language and foreign currency. But these things need not concern you unduly—Italy has played host to foreign visitors for 2,000 years and Italians have long since learned how to smooth the path for the shopper and the sightseer. *Pazienza*—patience—the Italians constantly admonish each other and foreigners, and it's not a bad motto to live by. Be patient in line and eventually you'll be served; look patiently through the thousands of stores in Rome, Florence, Milan, and Venice and in time you'll find what you are looking for. With *pazienza*, a healthy supply of good humor, and this book, your shopping trip to Italy should be nothing less than a triumph.

The Serious Shopper's Guide to Italy covers Italy as a whole —the nuts-and-bolts information that applies across the board in this country—suggests some ways to get the most out of your trip, and has some hints on which Italian goods you should be on the lookout for. Following that introductory section, you'll find the four most visited cities in Italy— Rome, Florence, Milan, and Venice—covered in depth. For each city there will be a short introductory chapter with special information particular to that city—what a Rome taxi costs, how to ride the vaporetto in Venice—followed by a chapter covering a series of strolls through the major shopping zones, highlighting stores which seemed to me to be the most interesting, unusual, had the best buys, or were just plain famous. Following that is a chapter listing, in alphabetical order by category, every store passed in the walks: here you'll find out what shops take which credit cards, their opening and closing hours, whether English is spoken, etc. Throughout the city chapters you'll find short descriptions of points of cultural interest and a brief rundown of bars, cafés, and restaurants you might want to try when your shopping day is done.

CHAPTER II

SHOPPING STRATEGIES

This chapter is designed to help you plan your trip and to answer questions pertaining to shopping in Italy. If you read this section closely, you'll never be at a loss when you want to make a phone call, mail a letter, or cash a traveler's check.

WHAT TO DO BEFORE YOU GO

Obviously, you want to arrive prepared in advance as shopping is so much easier when you know what you're looking for and have an idea where you can find it. Therefore I suggest that you read this book closely before you go to get an idea of how each of the four cities works and which is better for the merchandise you are looking for. That way, you'll know that you stand a better chance of getting a pair of Beltrami boots for less money in Florence than in Milan. Furthermore, there is another book which can help you. *All Italy: The Book of Everything Italian* (Columbus Books, $14.95) is a compendium of all the things Italy does best, her finest handcrafts, her most famous designers. It is not a shopper's guide, but a colorful celebration of Italian food, wine, clothing, art, crafts, and design.

On the more practical side, it is important to remember to bring certain pieces of information with you. If you are planning to buy Italian housewares or decorative goods—a Gaggia espresso maker for your kitchen, for example, or a 17th-century landscape to hang over your living room couch—take your measurements (the countertop, the wall space) in *centimeters* before you leave home. It's much easier to find metric rulers in the United States than it is to find an inch ruler in Italy.

Know your sizes and the sizes of those you will be buying for. The one piece of information you should have at your fingertips at all times is a U.S. size conversion chart (there is one on pages 19–20 of this book). Italian size designations bear no resemblance to American equivalents. A size 12 dress in the United States is a size 42 here; a woman's size 7 shoe in the U.S. is size 38 here. Waist and collar measurements are in centimeters: a trim 25-inch waist translates into an elephantine 63 centimeters here. The designations "small," "medium," and "large" are relatively rare—and if they do exist, they're in Italian: *piccolo* (small), *medio* (medium), and *grande* (large).

COMPARISON-SHOPPING

Although the dollar has declined substantially against the lire in the past year and a half (if you were last in Italy in 1984, for example, you'll find that your dollar buys 30% to 40% less now than it did then), Italian goods are still cheaper in Italy than they are in New York or Los Angeles—and what you lose in price you'll recover in quality. The two basic rules for comparison-shopping are obvious: know what you want and how much you would have to pay for it at home. Armed with these two pieces of information, comparison-shopping is that much easier. However, you should remember that not all Italian goods available in the United States are sold in Italy—and that not all Italian goods are to be had in the States. But even if you don't find exactly the Armani suit you saw in Beverly Hills, you are sure to find one similar—and if you can compare the American price to the Italian price, then you'll know if you have found a bargain or not.

The surest way to know what's available in Italy at the time of your trip is to buy the Italian fashion magazines and study them closely. *Vogue* alone publishes two huge spring and fall issues, as well as *Uomo Vogue*, *Vogue Leather*, *Vogue Jewelry*, *Vogue Bambini* (for children's clothes), *Casa Vogue* (housewares and home furnishings), *Vogue Sposa* (for those planning their weddings), *Vogue Uomo Mare* (dedicated exclusively to men's swimwear), and *Vogue Bellezza* (cosmetics and perfumes). If you bought all these magazines in the United States you would probably have spent over $100. The spring and fall *Vogues* alone are usually $14 or $15 each. If you have the time, wait until you reach Italy to look them over. The spring *Vogue* is just 6,000 lire (roughly $5) on the newsstand here. The ordinary monthly *Vogue* is only 5,000 lire ($4) and the specialized magazines are even cheaper.

In the best of all possible worlds, you should arrive on a Saturday evening, stock up on the various *Vogues* as well as other magazines like *Gran Bazaar* and *Moda*, and then spend Sunday in a sunny piazza with your magazines and a cappuccino. With some exceptions in Venice and Florence, no shops are open on Sundays or Monday mornings in Italy, so you'll have a day and a half to get to know the lay of the shopping land.

THE ABCs OF SHOPPING ITALY

AMERICAN EXPRESS

There are American Express offices in Milan, Venice, Rome, and Florence. Hours for all four offices are the same: Monday through Friday from 9 a.m. to 6 p.m. for travel arrangements, Monday through Friday from 9 a.m. to 5:30 p.m. for all financial transactions, and on Saturday from 9 a.m. to 1 p.m. for all services. The addresses for each office will be given in the appropriate city chapter.

AUCTIONS

These are not common in Italy, although the major international houses, Christie's and Sotheby's, have offices in Rome and in Milan. There are two, less formal, lesser-known auction houses in Rome—**Asta** (which is the Italian for "auction"), in the Palazzo Borghese on the Via Ripetta, at the corner of Via Tomacelli; and **Il Mercato Antiquario di Massimo Gelardini,** at Via Babuina 118A. The first tends to concentrate on paintings and other artworks, while the second specializes mainly in high-quality 18th-century furniture.

In Milan, try **Finarte,** Piazzetta Bossi 4; **Brerarte,** Piazza San Marco 1; **Manzoni Finarte,** Via Aless. Manzoni 38; and **Salamon Augustoni & Algranti,** Via Sant'Eufemia 25 (this last one is housed in a deconsecrated church and has the most unusual and beautiful premises of any auction house I've seen).

BANKING AND CURRENCY EXCHANGE HOURS

These vary from city to city, but not by very much. Generally speaking, most banks are open weekdays from 9 a.m. to 1:30 p.m. and 3 to 4 p.m. Some branches, however, open at 8:30 a.m. and close at 1 p.m., while others reopen from 2:45 to 3:45 p.m. Without exception, all banks in Italy are closed all day on Saturday and Sunday.

Exchange offices, marked *cambio,* are not affiliated with banks and they open and close more or less as they please, usually coinciding with shopping hours. They are not open on Saturday or Sunday either. Rates of exchange at the *cambios* range from the reasonable to the usurious, so if you're not in a hurry, you might want to visit a few of them and comparison-shop the rates of exchange before cashing your traveler's checks. Rates on American Express traveler's checks are always better at their own offices. Bank exchange rates are generally good—better than the *cambios*—and hotel exchange rates are always the least favorable.

BUSINESS HOURS

Each city has its own set of opening and closing hours. Not only do these vary by city, but in some cases they can also vary by business. You'll notice that the majority of shops in this book have the notation "closed Monday mornings." This means that they are closed right through the siesta hours, opening on Monday at the time they would normally open after lunch, usually sometime between 3:30 and 4:30 p.m.

Some clothing shops are open from 9 or 9:30 a.m. to 7:30 or 8 p.m. without a break. They usually have a sign in the window saying "Orario Non Stop." Shops that follow this practice are more common in Florence and Venice than they are in Milan or Rome.

Everything is open on Saturday afternoon except hardware stores and dry cleaners.

Sunday shopping is unheard-of in Rome and Milan, but is quite common during the tourist season in Florence and Venice. But even in those two cities schedules are not firm—sometimes the shops open, sometimes they don't. And if they do open, usually it's for a limited period—a few hours in the morning is the most common. So if you're going out of your way, clear across town, to shop a particular store, call first to make sure they'll be open.

CHAIN STORES

Leaving aside for a moment the enormous and enormously successful Benetton chain, the three major chain stores in Italy are Upim, Standa, and La Rinascente. **Upim** and **Standa** are the Italian equivalent of K-Mart or the five-and-dime. These are places where you might want to stock up on shampoo or soap, or even a cheap suitcase to cart home purchases made in tonier stores.

La Rinascente is a department store, but it has a way to go before it can compare itself to the American equivalent. La Rinascente has a shop in Milan and one in Rome. Of the two, the one in Milan is the more cosmopolitan, closer in design and purpose to the American stores. La Rinascente in Rome is smaller. Both shops are dependable sources of good-value-for-money clothing and costume jewelry, but there is little that's out of the ordinary. One point decidedly in La Rinascente's favor is that it offers excellent dollar-to-lire exchange rates—sometimes as much as 15 points higher than the banks.

Benetton is another matter altogether. In the past few years this chain selling quality knitwear and casual clothes for men, women, and children, has expanded greatly. As a rule, prices are reasonable, the standard of merchandise high, and the selection of goods enormous. There are also hundreds of branch stores. It would be just about impossible to visit and compare all of the Benetton shops, so they are mentioned in the text only if there is something truly exceptional about a particular store, like the one on Via Monte Napoleone in Milan or the Via Condotti shop in Rome. Overall, it's safe to say that if you are buying something at any Benetton outlet you are getting good value for your money.

CONSUMER COMPLAINTS

Italian stores do not have formal channels for lodging complaints. If you are lucky, your complaint will reach the right person and your grievance will be addressed immediately. If you don't receive satisfaction, ask to speak to *il direttore*—the boss. This usually brings results!

There is no Better Business Bureau type of organization in Italy and so redress is usually made through the police or the newspapers. It's unlikely that you would sit down and write a letter to a newspaper complaining about being overcharged or otherwise cheated—although *Il Messagero* in Rome is ever vigilant about this kind of thing—but you might want to file a *denuncia* with the police. Be warned—the process is cumbersome and you're likely to be back home long before anything comes of it.

SHOPPING STRATEGIES

CUSTOMS AND DUTIES

Most visitors arriving in Italy pass through Customs without having to open their suitcases. Italy does have restrictions on liquor (one liter per person), and cigarettes and cigars (two cartons or 100 cigars). If you are on your way to Italy after a shopping spree in Paris or London, you are not required to pay duty on goods purchased in other European Economic Community (EEC, or Common Market) countries.

When entering the United States, the Customs allowance for purchases made outside the country is $400. If you go over that you must declare all your purchases. If your purchases total less than $1,000, then there is a set 10% duty—pay your $100 and off you go. If you have gone over $1,000 then you must pay the set duty on each item, a percentage of the original purchase price. The percentages for duties paid on imported goods have been changed for 1987, for the most part in the traveler's favor. Here is a list of duties for which you are liable on goods you might have bought in Italy:

Antiques—If they are more than 100 years old there is no duty. You must have proof of age from the seller.

Automobiles—The Ferrari you bought new in Italy is subject to 2.5% duty.

Bags (leather)—5.3% to 10%.

China (other than tableware)—Bone, 6.6%; nonbone, 2.1% to 9%. Tableware: bone, 8%; nonbone and costing more than $56 a set, 26%.

Dolls—Stuffed dolls are free of duty at present, but U.S. Customs says this could change; nonstuffed, 12%.

Drawings—Duty-free.

Figurines—China, 9%; by a professional sculptor, 3.1%.

Fur—Wearing apparel, 5.3% to 7.4%; other, 3.4% to 7.4%.

Furniture—Wooden chairs, 3.4% to 7.4%; other than chairs, 2.5%; Bentwood, 6.6%.

Gloves—Fur, 4%; horse- or cowhide, 15%.

Jewelry—Precious metal (silver the chief value and not over $18 a dozen), 27.5%; other, 6.5%.

Leather—Flatgoods (wallets, etc.), 4.7% to 8%; other items, free to 5.3%.

Paintings—If done by hand, duty-free.

Perfume—4.9%.

Shoes (leather)—2.5% to 20%.

Sweaters (wool)—7.5% to 25.5%.

Toys—7% (see also "Dolls").

Wearing Apparel—embroidered or ornamented 8% to 35%

not embroidered or ornamented: cotton but not knit, cotton knit, linen but not knit 3%

man-made fiber, knit 3¢ per pound plus 19.2% to 13¢ per pound plus 32.5%

man-made fiber but not knit 3¢ per pound plus 15.1% to 14¢ per pound plus 27.5%

silk but not knit 7.5%

wool, knit 7.5% to 23%

wool but not knit 9.5% to 24¢ per pound plus 21%

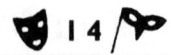

DISCOUNT SHOPPING

This is quite rare in Italy. There are a number of discount houses in Milan, one in Florence, and one in Rome. (Details are given in the appropriate chapters.)

DUTY-FREE SHOPS

Italy is trying, but the airport duty-free shops have a long way to go before they catch up with the facilities at Charles-de-Gaulle in Paris, Shannon in Ireland, or Schiphol in Amsterdam. The new duty-free shops at Leonardo da Vinci in Rome and Linate in Milan cater mostly to the alcohol/cigarettes/cigars buyer, but there are also some smaller "Made in Italy" shops where you can buy Italian leatherwork, handcrafts, and perfumes. Prices are lower, but the selection is limited.

EMBASSIES AND CONSULATES

Here is a list of addresses and phone numbers for the American, Canadian, and British government offices in Rome and Milan.

All of them keep open Monday through Friday from 9 a.m. to 5 p.m. During August the Canadian Embassy in Rome is open from 9 a.m. to 2 p.m., but a recording will give you an emergency number to call if you are in dire straits.

Rome: American Embassy
Via Veneto 121 (tel. 46-74)

British Embassy
Via Venti Settembre 80A (tel. 475-5441)

Canadian Embassy
Via Zara 30 (tel. 844-1841)

Milan: American Consulate
Piazza della Repubblica 32 (tel. 652-841)

British Consulate
Via San Paolo 7 (tel. 803-442)

Canadian Consulate
Via Vittor Pisani (tel. 669-7451)

SHOPPING STRATEGIES

ENGLISH SPOKEN

Many of the shops listed in this book have the note "English Spoken." The fluency, though, varies. In some shops you might encounter salespeople who speak English with the ease and command of Lord Olivier. Others sound like Chico Marx. Often, though, a little Italian on your part and a little English on their part bridges any gaps. It's always courteous to ask if someone speaks in English ("Parla inglese?") instead of just blasting off in your own language.

HOLIDAYS

Italy has a lot to celebrate, so Italians believe in holidays. Everything closes early the day before a holiday and things are shut tight as a drum on New Year's Day, Epiphany (January 6), Easter and Easter Monday, April 25 (Liberation Day), May 1 (Labor Day), June 2 (National Day), August 15 (Feast of the Assumption, also known as Feragusto), November 1 (All Saints' Day), November 4 (Victory Day), December 8 (Feast of the Immaculate Conception), December 25 (Christmas Day), and December 26 (Santo Stefano Day). Italy, generally, except for seacoast holiday towns, is closed in August when anyone who can goes on vacation.

A favorite Italian habit is the building of a *ponte* ("bridge") from one holiday to another. If, for example, Epiphany should fall on a Thursday, a lot of shops will be closed until Monday (bearing in mind that most things are closed Monday morning anyway...). So be prepared.

MAIL ORDER

The mail system in Italy is notoriously bad (though getting better) so mail order has never really caught on. Besides, Italians like to feel, fondle, and hold up to the light things they are buying. The Italian version of the Sears catalog is called *Postalmarket*. It's issued four times a year, with the advent of each season, and the magazine can be purchased at newsstands. Orders can be placed over the phone with a credit card (VISA, MasterCard), and while *Postalmarket* offers good-value-for-money merchandise, deliveries take four to six weeks and they do *not* mail outside Italy. So unless you plan a long stay or have a friend who will forward your purchase, *Postalmarket* is probably not the best way for you to shop.

MARKETS

Despite the growth of supermarkets, Italians would still rather shop at outdoor markets. These vary in size from four- or five-stall neighborhood markets to giants like the one in Piazza Vittorio in Rome, where you can buy everything from prosciutto to a complete wardrobe and a closet to keep it in. Italy also abounds in markets that sell things other than food and clothing: flea markets,

THE SERIOUS SHOPPER'S GUIDE TO ITALY

antiques markets, the famous straw market in Florence. There are markets that sell prints and drawings, automotive parts, or stamps and coins. You can bargain at any of them, except at the food markets.

METRIC WEIGHTS AND MEASURES

Weights
1 ounce = 28.3 grams
1 pound = 454 grams, or 4.5 etti
2.2 pounds = 1 kilogram, or kilo (1,000 grams)
1 etto = 100 grams
1 pint = 0.47 liter
1 quart = 0.94 liter
1 gallon = 3.78 liters

Measures
1 inch = 2.54 centimeters (cm)
1 foot = 0.3 meters (m)
1 yard = 0.91 m
1.09 yards = 1 m
1 mile = 1.61 kilometers (km)
0.62 mile = 1 k
1 acre = 0.40 hectare
2.47 acres = 1 hectare

MONEY MATTERS

Italians have no problem with the big figures that get bandied about: 1 million lire for this, 20 million for that, 100,000 for a meal for four. No one seems to mind this—except the government, which finds the numbers unwieldy and perhaps a little embarrassing. There has been much talk of introducing the *lira pesante*, the "heavy lire," whereby three zeroes will be knocked off each denomination. Thus 100,000 lire will become 100 lire and 100 lire will become 1 centesimo. This plan was due to be introduced early in 1987 but so far nothing has changed. That's not to say it couldn't happen overnight.

The unit of **currency** is the **lira** (plural: **lire**) and runs as follows. Coins are available in 10, 20, 50, 100, 200, and 500 lire. All are silver-colored except the 20- and the 200-lire coins, which are brass. The 500-lire coin is silver with a brass plug in the center. Banknotes are issued as 1,000, 2,000, 5,000, 10,000, 50,000, and 100,000 lire—all of different sizes and colors.

Warning: When the 500-lire coin was introduced, the 500-lire note was recalled. Some unscrupulous shopkeepers still try to palm these off on unsuspecting tourists. The 500-lire note is small, blue, and usually has the consistency of tissue paper. *Don't accept it!* Should you happen to find one in the middle of your change, you lose 38¢. There is a new 1,000-lire note as well. If someone tries to give you a purplish note with a picture of La Scala Opera House on one side and Giuseppe Verdi on the other, don't take it! The new note is pinkish and has a picture of Marco Polo on one side and the Doges' Palace in Venice on the other. If you get stuck with an old one, you are out approximately 80¢. Far more important is the new 50,000-lire note. It is pink and white and has a picture of Gian Lorenzo Bernini on one side and Bernini's statue of

SHOPPING STRATEGIES

The Florentine straw market sells a lot more than straw goods

Constantine and his design for the Scala Regia in the Vatican on the other. If you receive any other kind of 50,000-lire note, you are looking at a $40 loss.

Using **credit cards** can sometimes be a tricky proposition, mainly in Rome. Italian merchants don't like having to pay the credit-card companies their percentage and they object to the length of time the companies take to pay for charged merchandise. In Florence and Venice there is far less reluctance to take plastic, but you might encounter some. Obviously the larger, better-known shops don't mind taking credit cards, but smaller merchants are less appreciative. If they display a credit-card sign in the window they have to take the card—although sometimes they will offer a discount for cash. By the way, in Europe, MasterCard is called Access and you can use your MasterCard wherever the Access sign is displayed.

Traveler's checks are accepted everywhere, except in the smallest shops.

POST OFFICE

District post offices, as opposed to smaller, secondary post offices, are open from 8:30 a.m. to 8 p.m. Monday through Friday and from 8:30 a.m. to noon on Saturday. **Stamps** are sold at tobacconist shops, so you don't have to go to an Italian post office. But if you do, you'll find long, slow-moving lines, as Italian post offices do more than just sell stamps: residents can pay their tax, phone, electric, and water bills there as well.

Smaller, secondary post offices are open from 8:30 a.m. to 2 p.m.

If you decide to mail some of your purchases home, there are certain regulations you must follow. No **packages** weighing more than 2 kilos (4.4 pounds) can be sent. Packages must be wrapped in brown paper and tied with string. *But* leave one flap of the wrapping *unsealed* in case someone wants to inspect the contents further up the postal chain of command. You will have to fill out a form declaring what is inside, but this is not for insurance purposes. There is no provision for insurance on packages mailed to the United States and thus you send valuables at your own risk. Airmail to the United States takes about two to three weeks. Sea mail can take as long as three months.

RETURNS AND REPAIRS

Every shop sets its own policy on returns. In Italy this can generally be expressed as "no returns accepted." If you buy something that you are not absolutely sure you want, always obtain confirmation in advance that you can indeed return it. Needless to say, you must have the receipt with you when you come back. Sale merchandise can never be returned. Repairs are generally done without a murmur.

SALES

An Italian merchant cannot slap a *saldi* ("sale") sign in his window and price everything to go. There are government regulations covering sales, their duration and discount. The two sale periods allowed by law run from the middle of January to the end of February and during the entire month of July. A genuine, government-regulated *saldo* is usually an excellent time to buy. Prices are cut by as much as 50% and the goods on sale are of top quality. Italians love to shop during sales, and it's not unusual to find people crowded around the doorways of shops trying to get in. Frequently you'll find a doorman regulating the flow of shoppers in and out. Credit cards and traveler's checks are not usually accepted during sale periods, and as mentioned above, things bought on sale cannot be returned.

Stores at the upper end of the market have sales but frequently don't advertise them. Valentino and Maud Frizon, to name just two, have sales at the same time as everyone else, but you wouldn't know unless you called them up and asked. That's the rule with the fancy names: call ahead and make sure.

During nonsale times you might see shops with signs saying *sconti* ("discount") or *vendita promozionale* ("promotional sale") in their windows. These are nonregulated sales and the discounts are lower and the quality of goods not quite as high—but definitely worth a look.

SENIOR CITIZEN AND STUDENT DISCOUNTS

These discounts are not available to foreigners.

SHOPPING STRATEGIES

SHIPPING

There are many reputable shippers in Italy and a complete list would take up many pages. They handle all manner of goods and usually have a corresponding agent in the United States to clear your shipment when it arrives. Insurance is arranged through the shipper.

The best multilingual shipper servicing all of Italy is **Bolliger Transport**. The Rome office is at Via dei Buonvisi 61 (tel. 685-7161). This office handles shipments from Florence as well. In Milan, Bolliger is at Via Palmieri 46 (tel. 846-5741). This office handles Venice as well.

If you are bringing home a valuable work of art or an antique and wish to have a specialized fine arts shipper, then the best in the business covering the entire country is **Adami**, Via Francesco Carrara 30, Roma (tel. 361-1841, 361-1842, or 361-1843).

SIZES

The Italian for size is *taglia, misura,* or simply *numero.* The "small," "medium," "large," designations are rare.

SIZE CONVERSIONS

The accompanying charts should help you to find clothing sizes that fit. Italy uses the same sizes as the rest of the European continent; therefore, refer to the "Continental" column for the correct designations.

Women's Dresses, Coats, and Skirts

American	3	5	7	9	11	12	13	14	15	16	18
Continental	36	38	38	40	40	42	42	44	44	46	48
British	8	10	11	12	13	14	15	16	17	18	20

Women's Blouses and Sweaters

American	10	12	14	16	18	20
Continental	38	40	42	44	46	48
British	32	34	36	38	40	42

Women's Stockings

American	8	8½	9	9½	10	10½
Continental	1	2	3	4	5	6
British	8	8½	9	9½	10	10½

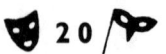

THE SERIOUS SHOPPER'S GUIDE TO ITALY

Women's Shoes

American	5	6	7	8	9	10
Continental	36	37	38	39	40	41
British	3½	4½	5½	6½	7½	8½

Children's Clothing

American	3	4	5	6	6X
Continental	98	104	110	116	122
British	18	20	22	24	26

Children's Shoes

American	8	9	10	11	12	13	1	2	3
Continental	24	25	27	28	29	30	32	33	34
British	7	8	9	10	11	12	13	1	2

Men's Suits

American	34	36	38	40	42	44	46	48
Continental	44	46	48	50	52	54	56	58
British	34	36	38	40	42	44	46	48

Men's Shirts

American	14½	15	15½	16	16½	17	17½	18
Continental	37	38	39	41	42	43	44	45
British	14½	15	15½	16	16½	17	17½	18

Men's Shoes

American	7	8	9	10	11	12	13
Continental	39½	41	42	43	44½	46	47
British	6	7	8	9	10	11	12

Men's Hats

American	6⅞	7⅛	7¼	7⅜	7½	7⅝
Continental	55	56	58	59	60	61
British	6¼	6⅞	7⅛	7¼	7⅜	7½

SHOPPING STRATEGIES

TAXES

The only tax a visitor to Italy need be concerned with is the **IVA**, Italy's version of the national sales tax. Everything in Italy is subject to the IVA, which runs from a negligible 2% up to an enormous 38% on super-luxury goods like a Maserati. The average, though, is 18%. Clothing (depending on the fabric) is reckoned on a sliding scale ranging from 10% to 25%.

This is made all the more confusing by the fact that most goods are sold "IVA inclusa," so a 10,000-lire purchase is rung up as 10,000 lire, leaving one in some doubt as to how much the item cost and how much is tax.

Italy does have a system for nonresident foreigners to claim an IVA rebate. Most shopkeepers will deny that the system exists, but it does. It applies to high-ticket purchases, usually $500 and up. In order to receive the *detasse*, as it's called, you must request it. If the shopkeeper does not immediately offer a *sconto* (discount) on your purchases, then you'll have to decide if it's worth the trouble of going through with the *detasse*. Any discount offered will be less than the IVA rebate, but it will be something in hand at least. Otherwise the application forms for the IVA rebate will be produced. In order to complete them you will need to have your passport with you and the address of your hotel. Take all the forms, plus an envelope with the name of the shop printed on it, and keep them along with a 500-lire stamp until you leave Italy.

Immediately upon arrival at the airport on the day of your departure, *before* you check in for your flight, ask for the Customs official handling the *detasse*. He has the right, rarely exercised, to examine the purchases you have made. Much rubber stamping will follow and you'll receive a set of forms, one set to be mailed back to the shop, the second for your files, and the third kept with the Customs man. Three to four months later you should receive a refund check in lire.

The best advice one can offer is to take the *sconto* if it's offered one and forget about the rebate.

TELEPHONES

A local call from an Italian pay phone costs 200 lire. There are two types of phones: the older models which only function with a copper telephone slug called a *gettone*, and the newer models which accept *gettoni*, one 200-lire coin, or two 100-lire coins.

Lift the receiver. A correct dial tone is one short beep followed by a longer one (a series of frenzied little pips means the phone is out of order, as does complete silence). Drop in the coins and dial the number. Italian phone numbers can have as few as four and as many as seven digits.

Sounds simple, doesn't it? It isn't. First of all, a large percentage of the public phones in Italy are broken (*guasto*). Many have a "guasto" sign on them but aren't *guasto* at all. This means that the bar or restaurant is (illegally) using a public phone as a business number. Curiously, it is an unwritten rule that a "guasto" sign is always accepted as valid, even if you know the proprietor knows that you know the phone works just fine.

The other problem is finding a *gettone*. These are usually purchased at tobacconists, newsstands, and bars that have phones in them, but the supply seems to ebb and flow like the tides. Sometimes everybody has them, but sometimes they can't be found anywhere. *Gettoni* are also used as currency, so don't be surprised if you get one in your change. You are free to pass them on when you buy things too.

For those who need to phone home, making long-distance and international from Italy calls is easy. Most countries can be dialed direct and connections with North America are usually good and clear. However, the six-hour time difference between the Italy and the United States and Canada makes getting a line between the hours of 3 and 7 p.m. Italian time a little difficult. During those four hours Italian and American business hours overlap, so there is heavy commercial traffic on the circuits as Italian banks and businesses talk to their American counterparts. It's not impossible to call during this time, but you might experience some delays.

Making a long-distance call from a pay phone, however, at any time is a hazardous operation. You will need huge numbers of gettoni and the coin box must be fed almost every second. Calling from your hotel is easy, but you should know that all hotels charge a substantial markup on long distance and international calls, sometimes as much as 100% over the phone company rate.

The best way to telephone is to go to one of the SIP (the Italian phone company) long-distance phone centers. These are modern, efficient offices and are found adjacent to the central post office in each city covered, as well as at airports and railway stations. The routine is pretty simple: You tell one of the operator/cashiers at the main desk what number you want to call and they assign you a booth. Sometimes they place the call for you, sometimes you have to dial it yourself. When you have finished your call, you return to the desk and pay your bill. Of course, they will arrange collect and person to person calls if requested.

If you are calling from your hotel or from a pay phone and wish to call collect, you must place the call through operators. If you are calling the United States or Canada, you dial 170 for the *servizi intercontinentali*. The operators (who speak English) will take the information, the party you wish to speak to, the number you are calling and the number you are calling from, and then call you back with the connection.

If you wish to call Great Britain or any other European country, you have to reach the *servizi internazionali,* by dialing 15. The procedure from then on is the same as that for intercontinental service.

The direct dial codes for the United States are: 001 + U.S. area code + U.S. phone number; Great Britain is 0044 + U.K. area code + U.K. phone number; Canada is 001 + Canadian area code + Canadian phone number.

CHAPTER III

WHAT TO BUY

Italy has broken through in recent years, establishing itself as a force to be reckoned with in new fields—fashion, design, fabrics—while maintaining a healthy regard for more traditional handcrafts and skills.

Italy's best buys run the gamut from ultra-traditional items like lace to products of the wilder design ateliers centered mostly in Milan. Here is a brief rundown of Italy's best, listed alphabetically:

DESIGN

The Italian studios of Memphis-Milano and Studio Alchimia are exerting great influence on the international design scene. The unabashed, vibrant oddity of the creations of both studios have taken the world by storm, putting Milan in a three-way tie with Paris and New York for the title of Design Capital of the World. The Memphis and Alchimia furniture is not to everyone's taste, but if you like it, Milan is the place for you. Both studios have showrooms, but you can also find out what's up by reading an Italian magazine called *Domus*. Published by Alessandro Mendini, one of the founders of Studio Alchimia, the magazine covers every aspect of the new Italian design scene.

FASHION

After the war there were signs that European fashion, so long dominated by the French, was about to acquire an Italian accent. First there were Pucci and Valentino, a Florentine and a Roman, who started Italian fashion on the road to prominence. They were joined by Mariuccia Mandelli, of Krizia, who centered Italian fashion in Milan. Today Milan remains the fashion capital of Italy, and the number of Italian designers clothing the rich and famous of the world is enormous. A few of the famous names are Fendi (the five Fendi sisters doing their own bit to put Italy on the fashion map in the 1950s with their stunning furs), Cappucci, Salvatore Ferragamo, Ferré, Giorgio Armani, Beltrami, Gianni Versace, Missoni, Laura Biagiotti, Gucci, Trussardi, etc.

It used to be that every year the fashion press looked for the new, young, daring French designer. Now they watch the Italian fashion scene very closely too, keeping a sharp lookout for a rising Milanese or Roman star. Giorgio Armani, for example, has been producing his own line of clothing now for a little more than ten years—and already he's part of the establishment.

In the end, Italian couture has had a little revenge on the high and mighty French. It's no secret that a lot of French fashion is produced and designed in Italy. It's not a fact the French try to hide. The other day I was looking at a very expensive Givenchy suit—is there any name more French?—and there, in the collar, was a label that proudly proclaimed "Made in Italy."

FOOD

Even the smallest *alimentari* (grocery store) in Rome, Milan, Florence, or Venice makes most Stateside "fine-food shops" look a little threadbare. While U.S. Customs might not appreciate your arriving home with an entire *porchetta* (an entire roast pig), there are some items you can take in freely. Cheeses are acceptable, so bring back some of the fine Italian cheeses, which are, by the way, far superior to the domestic American versions.

Consider taking home some of the delicious Italian chocolates and pastries as well, but remember that the goods are made fresh and without preservatives so they might not survive an extra-long flight home.

Packaged goods like extra-virgin olive oil and balsamic vinegar can be carried through Customs without any problem at all. Olive oil is an Italian staple and is therefore very inexpensive, although it's possible to pay as much as $25 or $30 a liter for the hand-pressed limited-edition oils from Tuscany. No matter what you pay, however, you'll find that Italian prices are much lower than American ones.

GLASS AND CERAMICS

Both are also traditional handcrafts. Pottery, particularly majolica, a type of earthenware which first became popular in the Renaissance (it is glazed and heavily ornamented with hand-painted designs) is centered in the town of Faenza in the Emilia-Romagna region. It is from Faenza that we get the other name for majolica—"faïence." Tuscany and Umbria have their own versions of earthenware pottery, and both can be found in abundance throughout the country.

Venetian glass is world famous and that city abounds in shops selling every conceivable glass item, ranging from the finely designed and delicately colored to the quite plainly grotesque. But you should be aware that a lot of Venetian glass is not made in Venice or even anywhere near Venice. Much of it comes from Czechoslovakia, West Germany, the Italian industrial town of Empoli, and Florence.

WHAT TO BUY

Vintage wines and fresh produce make Tuscany a food lover's dream

In addition, most of the "gold work" on some of the glass is not gold at all, but a mercury-based enamel that turns a gold color when fired. Virtually all "three-fire work," that is, glass with "gold" and enamel decoration, comes from Tuscany or Czechoslovakia.

To further dismay you, I must report that many of the glass factories on the island of Murano are not, in fact, glass factories at all. They are fronts for selling this imported "Venetian" glass. The true masters, so a glassmaker in Venice informs me, would never demonstrate their techniques in front of strangers. (See the "Venice" chapter, for the whole story.)

LACE

Lace has been produced in Italy for centuries and each region of the country has developed its own identifying stitch. From Florence, for example, where by tradition lace was made by cloistered nuns (less so now—still plenty of cloisters, not so many nuns), came the *punto Firenze*, the "Florentine stitch." Venice's lace products are famous the world over and have been for hundreds of years. Consequently, Venice has become the center of lace production for the entire country. You will find the entire array of regional specialties in that one city: *tombolo* (pillow lace), *chiacchierino* (a Venetian specialty), *fillet*, *macramé*, lace from Alpine Italy, and from the southern regions of the Abruzzi and Calabria.

It's easy to tell good handmade lace from the poorly worked machine-made stuff. Even an untrained eye can see the difference between intricate and finely

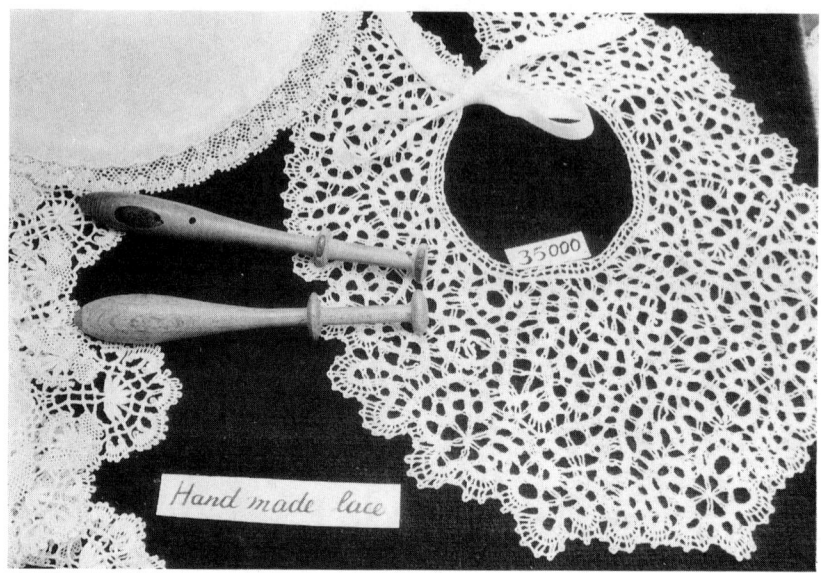

Trevisan, one of the finest names in Venetian lace

worked pieces and the shoddier examples of the art. There is an even simpler way of telling good from bad: price. A fine piece of 18th-century lace will cost a fortune. And a modern piece of high quality and substantial size, a bridal veil for example, can run into the millions of lire. This does not mean that quality lace cannot be had at reasonable prices. In Venice and Florence lovely lace pieces—collars, doilies, and handkerchiefs, for example—can be had for a few dollars.

LEATHER GOODS

Italian leather goods are considered the finest in the world, and each of the four cities in this book abounds with leather shops that sell everything from boots and shoes to wallets, luggage, and leather clothing. Most of the work is still done by hand, and while there is much substandard leather work around, Italian leather goods are probably the best value-for-money item to be had in the country. There's a good way to test for quality leather, but unfortunately few shopkeepers are likely to let you try it. Fold a tiny piece of the leather back on itself and press hard. If the finish cracks or splits, then you are holding a lemon. Look also at the unfinished side of the leather. If the fibers are coarse and long, the leather is no good; if they are of uniform length and smooth, almost like suede, then you have a good piece. Also, if the finishing work is good, the seams well cut and the stitching tight and regular, chances are the leather itself is of high quality. An easy way of checking good leather against bad is to go to any Salvatore Ferragamo shop and take a good hard look at any of their leather products. Keep the image in mind and try to conjure it up when looking at goods in less expensive, less well-known stores. If it remotely resembles the Ferragamo work—Ferragamo does the most beautiful leather work in Italy—then you're on to a good thing.

MOSAICS

Italy is still a center of mosaic production, and fine modern examples of the art can be found in the four cities covered. Some of the most famous mosaics in history are in the northern Italian city of Ravenna, and the tradition lives on there. Mosaic schools and studios in Ravenna export throughout Italy and the world.

PAPER GOODS AND FINE BINDINGS

These have always been an Italian specialty. Rome and Florence have hundreds of *legatori de libri*, where beautiful leather bindings and marbled boards are made. If you haven't brought your copy of *Anna Karenina* with you for rebinding, most of these shops also sell blank books, diaries, sketchbooks, and agendas off the rack. Florence is the home of beautiful stationery. Thick, creamy paper has been produced here by hand for centuries, as it is today. The prestigious stationer Pineider, based in Florence, has shops all over Italy.

PRINTS AND ENGRAVINGS

Since the 16th century Italy has been a center for prints and engravings. It seems that one cannot walk down a street in the historic centers of Rome or Florence without finding a shop stuffed to the rafters with copper engravings, wood engravings, etchings, woodcuts, and mezzotints ranging in size from miniatures to a *veduta* of the entire city of Florence that would cover a wall.

The thing to look for in buying a print is a faint, but tangible dimensionality —a lot of "genuine Piranesi" prints are in fact the product of offset and are as smooth as photographs. A Piranesi pulled from an actual plate should show the indentation of the plate itself and the lines that make up the etching should have a "tooth"—you should actually be able to feel where the paper has been "bitten" by the etched line.

Italy's vast reservoir of excellent—and inexpensive—prints is the result of Italy's popularity with foreign visitors for the last half millennium or so. While the rich travelers were picking up Raphaels and Roman antiquities by the wagonload, those less well heeled had to content themselves with inexpensive reproductions of the things they had seen to show the folks back home. As a result, there is not, it seems, an ancient or celebrated building, statue, view, church, or picture that has not been commemorated by Italian printmakers. The supply therefore is abundant, and the prices reasonable.

RELIGIOUS OBJECTS AND VESTMENTS

Until very recently the main industry in Rome was providing the Roman Catholic church and its churchmen with everything from artworks to vestments. Although the church doesn't dictate the financial well-being of the city anymore, there is still a small but flourishing religious-objects industry in Rome, centered mostly in the area around the ancient church of Santa Maria Sopra Minerva. In this neighborhood you'll find shops selling everything from rosary beads to cardinals' birettas. In the stores that sell nothing but religious objects, you'll find the selection so large as to be a little daunting. The merchants seem to have every religious base covered: pictures, statues, and reliefs of the Madonna, Jesus Christ, John the Baptist, prophets, saints, martyrs, popes, and angels ranging from tasteful to tacky.

SILK

Italian silk is the finest in the world and has been woven here for over 1,000 years. Although the industry was born in the south, silk production is now centered on the lake region in the north, particularly in the area around Lake Como. Silk quality is measured by the "mummy." One-mummy silk wrinkles easily, is very thin, tears easily, and cannot hold color well. The thing to look for is five- or six-mummy silk, which is heavy and smooth and can hold the most vibrant color with ease. Many people might want a Gucci scarf solely for the name, but Gucci's heavyweight Italian silks are some of the finest in the world.

WINES

It's hard to say just how many Italian wines there are, but experts put the number between 2,000 and 5,000. Some, of course, are the mass-produced equivalents of American jug wines bottled by the millions of liters every year, while others come from small vineyards producing only a few bottles a year. The *vino della casa* you'll get at the corner trattoria may have been made on the padrone's own plot of land or may come from the wine wholesaler who pulls his truck up in front of the restaurant once a week and pumps his wares into casks in the restaurant

WHAT TO BUY

basement. The wine, as you know, is generally good enough to accompany a plate of spaghetti al sugo but rarely so good that you'd want to take a liter of it home with you.

Until recently Italian wines have been considered the poor cousins to French vintages, but the discerning oenophile knows that Italian wines can hold their own with the best. Italian wine makers have their own version of the French *appellation contrôlée* designation denoting quality. It is the DOC, *denominazione di origine controllata*, a general indication of reputation and worth. The designation climbs to an even more august height in the DOCG, *denominazione di origine contrallata e garantita*, which is reserved for wines of special status produced under guaranteed quality control. In the DOCG category are the four finest Italian wines: barolo, barbaresco, vino nobile di Montepulciano, and brunello di Montalcino.

Barolo is produced in the Piedmont and is a full, rich red wine which needs to age about five years before drinking. Among the best producers are (to name a few) Aldo Conterno, Ceretto, Renato Ratti, and Vietti. The great years are 1982, 1981, 1979, and 1978. A bottle of '78 barolo Vietti costs about $25 in Italy. In the United States the same bottle would fetch $50 to $60.

The same is true of the barbaresco. A bottle of 1982 Barbaresco, from Gaja, perhaps the best of the vintners of this type, is $30 in Italy and about $60 in the United States.

Overall, you'll find that the wine prices in Italy are extremely reasonable—very good wine can be had for $5 or $10 a bottle. Collectors could add some very fine vintages to their cellar for little money, even including the duty imposed by Customs.

PART TWO

SHOPPING MILAN

CHAPTER IV

A MILAN OVERVIEW

The analogy goes like this: if Rome is the Washington of Italy, then Milan is the New York. With the exception of the fabulous Gothic Duomo (cathedral) in the center of the city, La Scala Opera House, and the Brera section of the city, there is little here that could be described as picturesque. Milan was bombed heavily during World War II and one of those raids set fire to the city center, which burned for several days. Consequently Milan, unlike virtually every other city in the country, looks new and modern, as if it should be someplace else. Milanese, like New Yorkers, are fast-on-their-feet, get-ahead types and they're convinced that they are the new aristocracy of Italy. They sneer at sleepy, southern Rome, and the climate in this northern city does not allow for sitting in a sunny piazza sipping wine and arguing about politics, religion, or most important of all, soccer.

BASIC ORIENTATION

Milan is a big, sprawling city but, again, as in Rome, the major shopping areas are all within walking distance of one another. For shopping purposes, the city can be divided into three main areas: the Monte Napoleone district, home to Milan's highest-ticket shopping, the area around the Brera Museum, and the area around the Piazza del Duomo.

Milan is a city of roughly two million inhabitants and, unlike other Italian cities, not many live in the downtown area. The city is ringed by large suburbs that are home to most Milanese. But it is the center of the city that concerns us, as it includes the major shopping areas, sights, and restaurants.

The geographic heart of the city is the vast Piazza Duomo, dominated by Milan's beautiful gothic cathedral. Radiating from this central point are major streets that lead out of the city in several directions. The most important streets that converge in the Piazza Duomo are the Corso Italia, the Corso Vittorio Emanuele, the Via Manzoni, and the Via Dante. The center is encircled by three concentric ring roads, each one with a greater circumference as they move away from the city center.

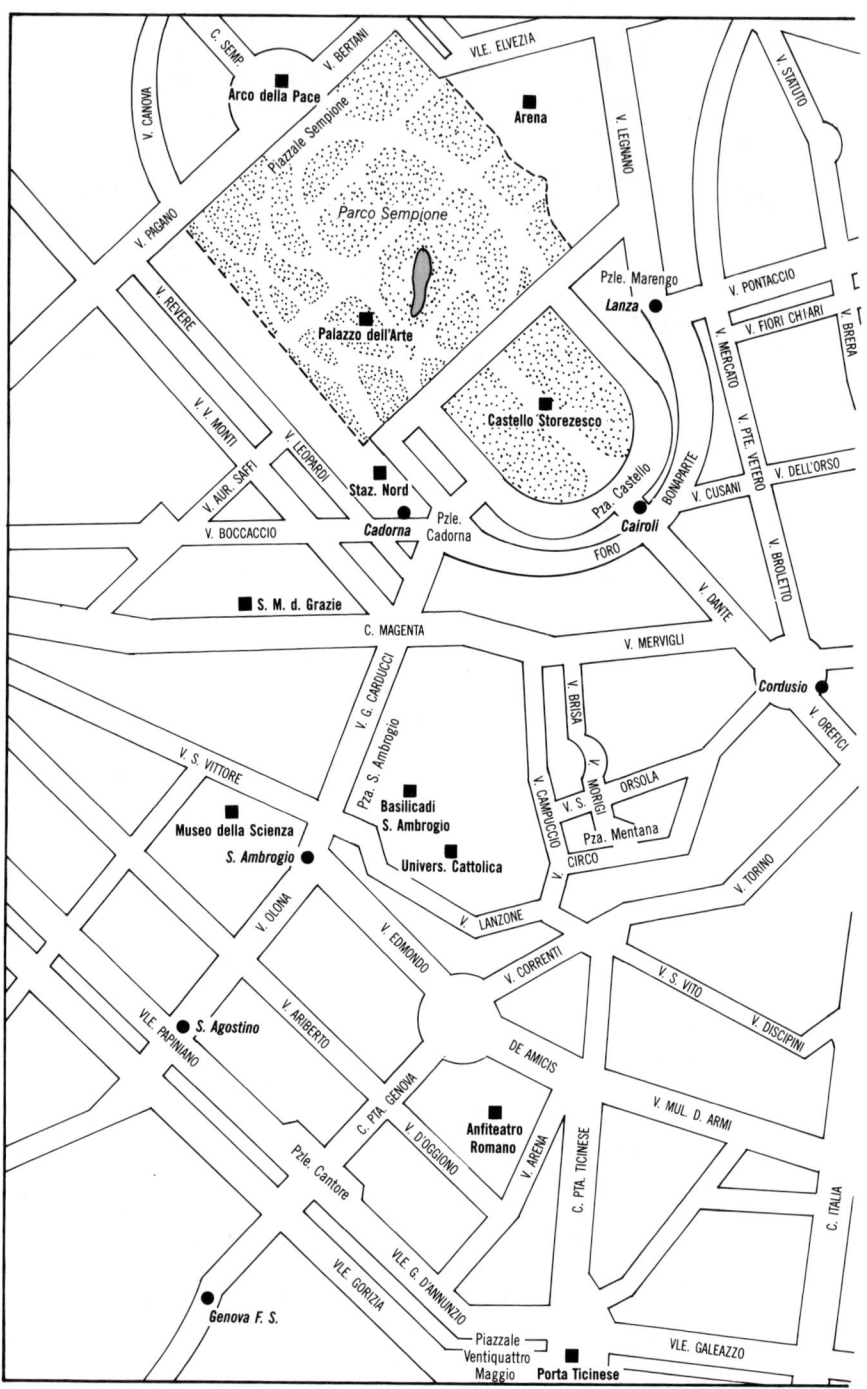

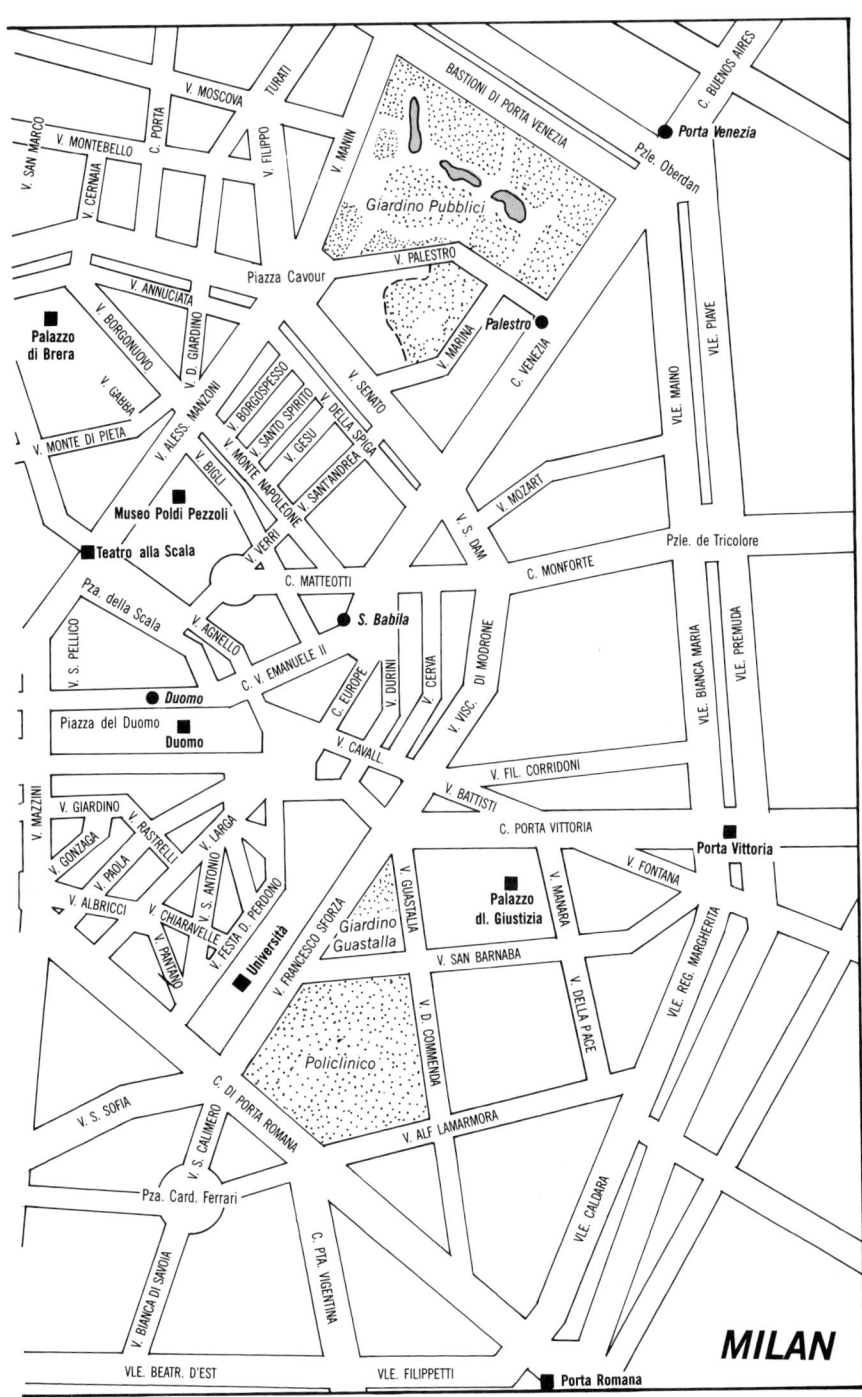

The innermost ring road is called the *Cerchia dei Navigli* and follows the path of the old medieval walls that once surrounded the city. The next ring out is the *Viali* or *Bastioni*, which is built on the site of fortifications constructed in the 16th century. The outermost highway, the newest and the longest, is called the *Circonvallazione Esterna*. Virtually all of the shops in this section are contained within the *Cerchia dei Navigli*.

GETTING FROM THE AIRPORT

Milan is served by two main airports, **Linate**, less than 10 km (6 miles) from the center of town, which handles all regularly scheduled international flights, and **Malpensa**, some 50 km (30 miles) out of town, which is the primary landing ground for charters.

There is a **bus service** serving both airports. The bus leaves from Linate every 20 minutes and deposits you at the main train station some 15 minutes later (it takes longer during rush hour). Tickets cost 5,000 lire and are purchased at the desk inside the arrivals terminal.

The bus from Malpensa meets flights as needed and also runs to the Stazione Centrale. Bear in mind that it takes at least 45 minutes to reach the center of Milan from Malpensa.

Taxis are available at both airports. From Linate to the center of town should cost about 20,000 lire. From distant Malpensa the price can be a whopping 90,000 lire to 120,000 lire.

GETTING AROUND

Milan has an excellent Metro system and one that you might find yourself using more than the one in Rome. There are two lengthy lines which criss-cross the city, MM1, the red line, and MM2, the green line. Of the two, MM1 is more likely to serve your needs, running as it does from the Piazza del Duomo and along the edge of the Monte Napoleone shopping area. Tickets are 700 lire and can be purchased in the subway stations, from magazine stands near a station, and from machines in the stations. While **buses** exist in Milan, the major form of surface transport is the excellent **trams**. Tickets for the trams are the same ones used for the Metro and can be purchased wherever you see the yellow "*vendita biglietti*" sign—the usual tobacconists, newsstands, and bars.

Trams are entered via the rear door, and once aboard, you cancel your ticket in the box near the rear door. From that moment on—the time has been stamped on your ticket—you have 75 minutes' worth of travel time. You can get off and on as many trams or buses as you please during your hour and a quarter, and it even entitles you to one ride on the Metro—within the allotted time, of course.

Taxis are available at ranks (there's a big one in Piazza del Duomo) or can be

MILAN: GENERAL INFORMATION

hailed on the street. The initial fee is 3,000 lire (although this may go up) and there are a host of new supplements waiting to be introduced. Every cab has a multilingual *tarriffe* displayed.

Milan is a city of wide streets and commodious sidewalks. Drivers obey the traffic rules and you don't have to play a game of chicken when crossing the street. Most of the streets covered in the shopping strolls are closed to traffic, so Milan is an excellent city to see on foot.

TOURIST INFORMATION

There are three efficient multilingual **EPT (Ente Provinciale per il Turismo)** tourist information offices in Milan. The central EPT office is at Via Marconi 1, on the edge of the Piazza del Duomo on the Palazzo Reale (Royal Palace—you can't miss it) side of the square. It's open Monday through Friday from 8:45 a.m. to 12:30 p.m. and 1:30 to 6 p.m., on Saturday from 9 a.m. to 12:30 p.m. and 1 to 5 p.m.; closed Sunday. There is another EPT office in the Stazione Centrale, on the first floor, open from 9 a.m. to 12:30 p.m. and 2 to 6 p.m. At Linate airport there is a third EPT office which is open as long as the airport is (except for unusually late flights) with half an hour off for lunch between 12:30 and 1 p.m.

WEATHER

Milan gets foggy: from November to March you are likely to go for weeks without seeing the sun. Winters are hard—snow is not unusual—with high temperatures hitting the 40s (if the sun can break through), dipping down to well below freezing at night. Spring is the nicest time to visit Milan, when skies are clear and temperatures range from the low 50s at night to the middle 70s during the day. The summers are not as bad as they are farther to the south. Temperatures rarely get much above 80.

THE ABCs OF SHOPPING MILAN

AMERICAN EXPRESS

The American Express office in Milan is at Via Brera 3 (tel. 85-571). It is open Monday through Friday from 9 a.m. to 6 p.m. for travel arrangements, Monday through Friday from 9 a.m. to 5:30 p.m. for financial transactions, and on Saturday from 9 a.m. to 1 p.m. for all services.

BANK HOURS

See "The ABCs of Shopping Italy" in Chapter II.

HOLIDAYS

December 7, the Feast of Saint Ambrose, Milan's patron saint, is celebrated as a holiday. Most shops are closed and a majority of restaurants. What is open is La Scala—the Feast of St. Ambrose is the traditional kick-off date for the opera season. For additional holidays, see "The ABCs of Shopping Italy" in Chapter II.

MARKETS

Every Saturday, the major flea market of the city opens up. Called the **Fiera di Senigallia,** it's located near the Piazza Vetra. An enormous market selling just about anything—furniture, clothing, antiques, bric-a-brac, artwork, and secondhand and new clothing—the fiera runs from early morning until dusk and is one of the better markets of its kind in Italy.

On Sunday mornings near the central post office is a market that sells only **stamps and coins.** The selection is large, and if you know your philately and/or numismatics, you might find a bargain here.

On the third Saturday of every month there is an **antiques fair** held in the picturesque Brera district on Via Madonnina and Via Fiori Chiari. Quality here is above average, and so are the prices. It lasts all day, but get there early for the good buys.

Of special interest to serious shoppers is the **clothing market** held on Saturday mornings in Viale Papiniano. Here you might find a lot of famous-maker seconds and rejects—and a lot of fakes. Prices are very low, but again, you have to get there early, and even then there's no guarantee you'll find a name you recognize. Supplies are erratic.

POST OFFICE

The Posta Centrale is very close to the Piazza del Duomo and is open from 8 a.m. to 8 p.m. The street address is Piazza Cordusio 4. The rules regarding packages and the like are explained in Chapter II.

SALES

See "The ABCs of Shopping Italy" in Chapter II.

SHOPPING HOURS

Milan, like the other three cities in this book, has its own set of business hours. You can count on finding all shops closed on Sunday and on Monday morning —except food shops, which are open Monday morning but closed Monday afternoon. Shops generally open between 9 and 10 a.m. and close at 12:30 or 1:30 p.m. for siesta. They tend to reopen earlier than their Roman counterparts, usually around 3 or 3:30 p.m., but they close earlier too, usually between 7 and 7:30 p.m. Milan has more "orario nonstop" shops than Rome, but far fewer than Venice or Florence. Virtually all stores are closed in August.

TAXES

See "The ABCs of Shopping Italy" in Chapter II.

CHAPTER V

GREAT MILAN SHOPPING STROLLS

When strolling the streets of Milan, you'll probably notice that the Milanese themselves don't stroll at all, they walk briskly and with purpose. Unlike their cousins to the south in Rome and Florence, who amble through their cities, the Milanese look like they are going somewhere, somewhere important, and that they *have* to be there on time. But that doesn't mean they'll elbow you out of the way. Quite the contrary—the Milanese are very courteous, if a bit serious, but they do have a job to do. As a Milanese would put it: They have to earn the money that the government spends (read: "wastes") in Rome. However, you should take your time, set your own pace, and take a good look at all the city has to offer.

MONTE NAPOLEONE

The place to begin a Milan shopping spree is, undoubtedly, the area around the Via Monte Napoleone, the "Montenapo" as it's known. On this street and the streets running parallel or at right angles to it, you'll find most of the finest Italian shopping names. You will also see some of the most beautifully designed shops in the world, and you could spend every cent you brought with you and run your credit cards up to stratospheric heights before you have gone a block in any direction.

The streets you'll be strolling are: Via Monte Napoleone, Via Alessandro Manzoni, Via della Spiga, Via Gesù, Via Pietro Verri, Via Borgospesso, Via Sant'Andrea, and Via Santo Spirito. Believe it or not, this only makes up little more than one square mile.

Let's start on the edge of the district, on the ultra-chic **Via della Spiga**. The first of many famous names you will encounter on this stroll is Prada, at no. 1, makers of classic leather goods, and at this location, bags and shoes in particular.

MILAN: GREAT SHOPPING STROLLS

A few steps away—and Via della Spiga is closed to traffic, by the way—is Lancetti, at no. 2. A newcomer to the neighborhood, this Roman designer has brought his high-fashion style to Milan. The shop is large, expensive, and just the place to sample the full range of Pino Lancetti's evening wear. At no. 4 is Gianni Versace, the flagship store in Milan for his distinctive clothing and accessories for women. Gio Moretti's striking two-story shop for women's clothes is at Via della Spiga 6. Gio Moretti's men's shop, also at no. 6, stocks clothes for men that range from the traditional to the wild. Here you'll find a wide array of colorful silks—shirts and ties particularly. At no. 5, El Vaquero is crammed full of their madcap, spangled, lamé, sequined, and silver-studded shoes and boots. Not for the faint-hearted or those who don't like having their feet stared at. Also at Via della Spiga 5, but light-years away in terms of style, is the only Bottega Veneta shop in Milan. Here you'll find their high-quality footwear, as well as accessories: bags, gloves, and even some items of menswear, notably ties and gloves. The Florentine leather goods fashioned by Gherardini are displayed on two cozy floors at Via della Spiga 8.

Cose, also at no. 8, lives up to its name—"things"—selling an eclectic selection of leather clothing, knitwear, and costume jewelry. The Fendi sisters weigh in at no. 11 with one of their two stores in Milan, this one selling the full range of Fendi clothes for women. Next door, another heavyweight, Gianfranco Ferré (also at no. 11), sports a full range of women's "architectural wear" as well as Ferré's elegant, distinctive footwear. Erreuno, at no. 15, features, in addition to their lovely line of women's clothing, some of the nicest salespeople I have encountered anywhere. Kashiyama, across the street at Via della Spiga

Flagship store of the Ferré fashion empire

19, sells baggy, black avant-garde clothing for men and women.

Francesca Ferrario's very upmarket (even for Via della Spiga) leather goods can be found at no. 20. This represents *alta moda* at its highest. Bags and shoes are handmade and beautifully designed.

The partially mosaic floors at Via della Spiga 20 indicate that you're in for something different—and you are. This is the Jean-Paul Gaultier shop for men and women in Milan. Adrianamode, at Via della Spiga 22, sells astonishingly expensive out-of-the-ordinary clothing for women. Diego della Valle, also at Via della Spiga 22, vends lovely, traditional-with-a-difference shoes for men and women. Maiuccia Mandelli's Krizia boutique occupies three floors at Via della Spiga 23. The shop carries the entire Krizia line, from dressy to their own-make jeans. Krizia's kids' line is also well represented.

At Via della Spiga 31 is Spiga 31, selling evening wear for women that is different and flamboyant but not avant-garde. Heavy use of ribbed gold lamé seems to be the trademark of this unusual shop. Baila, next door at no. 32, specializes in leather clothing for women. The marble and stainless-steel premises of Fontana, at Via della Spiga 33, is one of the most striking shops on the street. Clothing here is very high fashion and very modern in design, but unfortunately the help is a touch on the snooty side.

Michelle Mabelle/Milano Monamour has some of the wildest clothing on the street at Via della Spiga 36. Prices start low(ish) and then skyrocket. If you've got the guts, they've got the clothes. Armando Pollini's beautiful shoes are available at Via della Spiga 42. Pollini is now experimenting with his own version of western style (but not quite) boots. Beautiful suede goods too.

Gulp!!, at Via della Spiga 42, sells its own brand of clothing for the younger set, and carries a full range of accessories to go along with it.

Conti, at no. 50, offers high-quality knitwear at extremely reasonable prices. At no. 52, the end of Via della Spiga at the corner of Via Aless. Manzoni, Preattoni has an outstanding collection of cutlery and knives. Just next door, also at no. 52, Ivana Zanini offers classically tailored clothes for women.

You should now be standing at the corner of Via della Spiga and Via Aless. Manzoni. On **Via Allesandro Manzoni** there are a number of shops which deserve a look. Pennisi, Via Aless. Manzoni 29, is a treasure trove of precious and rare objects, Oriental antiques, and gems, as well as a large collection of art deco jewelry. Campana Coen, Via Aless. Manzoni 43, specializes in fine, rare Oriental carpets.

Next door at no. 46, is Pasini, where the adult Milanese elite dresses the miniature elite. This is where you'll find classic clothing for children.

Coppola & Toppo, Via Aless. Manzoni 20, is one of Milan's excellent creators of leather clothing and shoes. Giocatteli Noe, across the street at no. 38, is a vast toyshop, featuring toys and games from every country in Europe and for every age. Facing it is T&J Vestor, also at no. 38, part of the chain of fabric and linen shops.

The first floor at Via Aless. Manzoni 46 is the Memphis design showroom, where you can see all of the wild "New International Style" furniture, created in Milan.

MILAN: GREAT SHOPPING STROLLS

If you walk along Via Alessandro Manzoni toward La Scala and the center of town, you'll come to the intersection with Via Monte Napoleone.

Via Monte Napoleone begins with a quiet, discreet, and very expensive bang at Dal Vecchio, no. 29, the first of several world-class jewelers you'll encounter on this street. At the same address, Primizie, a colorful shop, sells maternity wear and clothes for children up to 6.

In a charming little arcade just off Via Monte Napoleone, at no. 27E, you'll find Luca, selling fine shoes and boots for women. Also at no. 27, but not in the arcade, is Galtrucco, featuring their own exclusive menswear, as well as being the Milan source for made-to-measure Brioni suits. Ungaro shares no. 27 as well.

At Via Monte Napoleone 22 is Mazzoleni, selling museum-quality Russian icons and jewelry. There is a lovely Pratesi shop a few steps away, selling the world-famous linens at Monte Napoleone 21. Cusi, at no. 21A, is another of the great Milanese jewel houses.

A few doors away at no. 24 is a large and (relatively—remember where you are) inexpensive ladies' shoe shop called Mortarotti—new to me, but definitely a find. As the name suggests, Lario 1898, at Via Monte Napoleone 21, has been around a while and sells classic leather goods for men and women.

The dramatic-looking Alberta Ferretti shop, at no. 21A, sells women's wear

Chic leather at Milan's Coppola and Toppo

ranging in price from the almost-reasonable to the out-of-sight. At no. 20 is one of two Salvatore Ferragamo shops on Via Monte Napoleone. This celebrated name has been making fine shoes and leather goods since the 1920s. This particular shop is devoted exclusively to menswear. The granite-framed doorway at Monte Napoleone 19 is the entrance to Alexander Nicolette, a shop which has a wide and distinctive selection of ladies' shoes and boots. The men's shop is right next door.

Beltrami takes up two whole floors of Via Monte Napoleone 16 with its collection of clothing, shoes, boots, and other leather goods for men and women. As a friend once remarked to me, "If I could buy that [$1,600 Beltrami leather jacket] my life would change." Here's the place to change your life—the selection is large and $1,600 will get you started. Eskenazi, at Via Monte Napoleone 15, deals in rare Orientalia, particularly carpets and sculptures.

If you aren't going to Venice this trip, don't miss your chance to check out one of the most famous names in Venetian lace at Monte Napoleone 14. Jesurum has a huge and high-quality selection of Venetian lace, embroidery, and linens.

Maybe I was just dazzled by the location, but the Benetton at Monte Napoleone 13—just one of more than three million Benetton shops in Milan alone—seems to have higher-quality merchandise than other branches and yet the prices don't seem to be any higher. Judge for yourself.

If you've had enough of clothes for the moment, step into Il Salumaio di Montenapoleone, at no. 12. This is one of the most elaborate fine-food shops I've ever seen in Italy. The place is always bustling with activity as the cooks make up the "working lunches" that are carried to the various palazzi in the neighborhood which house the main offices of the great design names. Here you'll find an immense selection of Italian delicacies: sauces, cheeses, wines, olive oils, vinegars, mushrooms. The day I was there the window was graced with a *half-pound* truffle.

David Colombo is a jeweler specializing in antique jewelry of the 18th and 19th centuries, but the master craftsmen of this exclusive shop will make modern pieces to order. The shop is at Via Monte Napoleone 12.

The large and lovely jewelry shop at Monte Napoleone 10 is Martignetti, and specializes in fine pearls, lapis lazuli, and jades. Exceptional antique French furniture is the specialty at the palatial showrooms of Maghenzani, Via Monte Napoleone 10.

Across the street at no. 9 are specialists of a different nature. G. Lorenzi has been making fine cutlery and knives since 1929. While the shop has expanded its range to include gourmet accessories (mother-of-pearl caviar spoons, that sort of thing), finely designed cutting implements remain their main stock in trade.

You should now be at the corner of Via Monte Napoleone and Via P. Verri. Here you'll find two famous names in menswear, but two that could not be more different in taste and temperament. There's Larusmiani, at no. 7, selling beautiful, traditional clothing for men (with prices quoted in dollars at a favorable rate) and nearby Gianni Versace, elegant, cool, and very expensive.

MILAN: GREAT SHOPPING STROLLS

At Monte Napoleone 9 you'll find Venini, a Milanese shop that carries the most tasteful Venetian glass products in the city. There's no question of fakes or corners cut here.

Time for a cappuccino, wouldn't you say? On the corner of Via Sant'Andrea (Via Pietro Verri becomes Sant'Andrea after crossing Monte Napoleone) at Via Monte Napoleone 8 is Cova. Since 1817 this palace of pastry has been serving the gentry who have always lived in this neighborhood. Here you are waited on by tuxedoed waiters and you can have anything you desire from a magnum of Mumm's to a pot of tea. Try some of their fabulous pastries and sweets—there's plenty of walking to be done yet. If you really know your designers, you might see a famous face here taking his or her after-lunch espresso.

Calderoni is one of the oldest names in Milanese jewelry and their exclusive premises are at Monte Napoleone 8. All the work for sale here is made in the Calderoni studios to their own designs.

The Serious Shopper's Guide Award for the nicest salespeople on Via Monte Napoleone goes to the folks at Enny, no. 8. This store features its own brand of leather goods, particularly gloves and luggage, and a peculiar compound of rubberized canvas called "nappa tevit" which makes for soft but very strong hand and shoulder bags and luggage. It sounds unusual and it is. And the people are charming!

Sable is the fur to shop for at Melegari and Costa, at Via Monte Napoleone 7A. This is one of Milan's newest and finest fur salons. Designs are sophisticated and the furs are the finest available. Bring money.

Also at no. 7A is a fabulous jeweler, Faraone. Designs here are decidedly out of the ordinary and the shop itself is astonishingly elegant, even for Via Monte Napoleone.

Donini, at Via Monte Napoleone 7, sells nothing but lingerie and other intimate apparel. Silks and satins predominate and they come in beautiful colors, particularly deep reds and soft pinks. Fredericks of Hollywood this ain't.

There are two Mila Schön shops on Via Monte Napoleone. The one at no. 6 features the full line of Mila Schön menswear. Also at no. 6 is Valeriano-Natale Ferrario, a shop featuring lovely suede clothing for women as well as a small selection of excellent traditional shoes for men.

Boutique Biki, Via Monte Napoleone 6, is a Milan institution. Ladies of Milan's aristocracy have been shopping here since the 1940s for Biki's high-fashion line. There is now a Biki-designed collection of menswear here too.

Gucci, at nos. 2 and 5, may be based in Florence, but I find it hard to believe that their Florence shop is any larger than this one. If they don't carry every Gucci item available in Italy at this location I would be very surprised. In this double-jointed shop—it connects with what appears to be another Gucci shop a few doors away, but in reality it's the same place—there is every imaginable product with the famous GG stamped on it.

An old, established, and world-famous jeweler, Buccellati, is at Via Monte Napoleone 4. Jewelry here is predominantly designed to the purchaser's specifications. There is also a selection of Buccellati's famous silver work, particularly the figures of animals.

There are good buys to be found on high-quality leatherwear, particularly ladies' shoes, at De Pietri, Via Monte Napoleone 4. At no. 3 is Tanino Crisci, famed makers of classic shoes and boots for men and women. Also at no. 3, but in a little courtyard off the street, is Silva, yet another high-quality jeweler. Salvatore Ferragamo for women is at no. 3 as well, offering the complete range of Ferragamo footwear, leather accessories, and clothing.

Mila Schön for men is at Via Monte Napoleone 6 (women's at no. 2). There's more Gucci clothing this time—at no. 2. Raimondi, also at no. 2, is the Hammacher-Schlemmer of the street. Look for an Armani-designed telephone or kitchenware by Krizia.

At Via Monte Napoleone 1 the street ends (or begins) with two of the best-known names in Milan. There is a large Missoni shop at no. 1 selling everything from raincoats to evening dress. And next door also at no. 1, is Pirovano, where the accent is classical. They have been dressing Milanese society women for decades.

The area might be known as "Montenapo," but there's certainly no disgrace in having a shop on one of the other streets in the neighborhood. **Via Sant'Andrea** is the next street we'll explore. It's quite a short stroll, in terms of distance, although it has a number of exciting, exclusive shops that will give you hours of shopping pleasure.

We start at the Guido Pasquali salon, at Via Sant'Andrea 1, where Pasquali's expert craftsmanship and timeless design are displayed in an exciting setting. Shoes here are for women (the men's line is available at Via Gesù 6, a couple of blocks away). Marisa is also at no. 1, and stocks a stunning line of knitwear, including some fabulous cashmere sweaters and dresses.

It would be hard to imagine a more exclusive fur salon than Pellegrini, Via Sant'Andrea 2. Pellegrini has been making classic furs since early in this century. It's another timeless, Milan tradition. Avagolf, at Via Sant'Andrea 3, is a knitwear shop of great charm and originality, specializing in comfortable, yet elegant clothes for women.

Trussardi, Via Sant'Andrea 5, makes some of the most original leather and vinyl accessories in Italy today. The ubiquitous greyhound head trademark is fast becoming as well known here as the Gucci double GG. Here, the only Trussardi shop in Milan carries the whole range of clothing and accessories for men, women, and children.

Cesare Paciotti's unusual shoes for men are sold from his tiny shop at Via Sant'Andrea 8. Styles here are chunky, heavy-soled—shoes, you might say, with a difference. Certainly not for everyone's taste.

Piva, at Sant'Andrea 8, has a fabulous collection of 17th- and 18th-century Italian art, sculpture, and furniture. Prices, like the quality, are high.

Given the neighborhood, you probably wouldn't expect to find any discount shopping in the vicinity, but you can, after a fashion, at Furs Bazaar, Sant'Andrea 8. Here you'll discover excellent buys on secondhand furs that might have been born a season or two back, from the ultra-expensive fur salons a few

MILAN: GREAT SHOPPING STROLLS

hundred yards away on Via Monte Napoleone or even on Via Sant'Andrea itself.

This leads us back to Giorgio Armani again, at Via Sant'Andrea 9. At no. 10A is Gianfranco Ferré's magnificent shop for menswear.

An exclusive shopping street in the Montenapo district

You don't have to look at the label to know you're looking at Armani

At the corner of Via Monte Napoleone and Via Sant'Andrea (no number) is Alma, one of the most celebrated of the smaller boutiques in the area. Clothing here promotes the work of younger, up-and-coming designers, men and women who haven't broken through yet, but will. Some goods are designed by giant names like Gianni Versace, who designs Alma's Spazio line.

Marcello Rubinacci, Via Sant'Andrea 10, is the place in Milan for the best-known names in French fashion. Here you'll find such icons as Chanel and Hermès. Prices are high—but you didn't come here to buy French stuff anyway.

Or Japanese, for that matter. But for those who want it, Kenzo is at Via Sant'Andrea 11. As the name suggests, Arte Antica, Via Sant'Andrea 11, sells artworks and furniture, mostly French and Italian, mostly from the 18th century.

The gravel floors (like a driveway) and the name of the shop spray-painted on the wall (like a New York subway car) lets you know that you're in for something a little different at Clara Antonini, Via Sant'Andrea 12. The clothes for women here are unabashedly eccentric.

Luciano Soprani, Via Sant'Andrea 14, makes fine shoes for ladies, updating traditional styles for a more modern look.

Fendi furs and leather are to be had in abundance at Via Sant'Andrea 16. The shop is large, the "one F up, one F down" logo is everywhere, and the salespeople speak every language under the sun.

Barba's, Via Sant'Andrea 21, offers unusual clothing for men. Also at no. 21 is Carrano, yet another shoe shop stocking excellent shoes for men and women, as well as other leather accessories.

Cross Via Monte Napoleone where Via Sant'Andrea changes its name to Via Pietro Verri. Here, at no. 3, is Ermenegildo Zegna, a fabulous three-floor men's shop offering fine traditional clothing, from casual to evening wear. While the Ermenegildo Zegna line is carried at other shops in Italy, this is the only location that bears the name.

Backtracking a bit, going up Via Monte Napoleone toward Via Alessandro Manzoni, there are a couple of side streets that deserve close attention from the serious shopper.

The first street to your right is **Via Gesù,** where you'll find the men's line of Guido Pasquali shoes at no. 6. Also on this tiny street is Giannetti, Via Gesù 3, which sells a wide and beautiful selection of antique Italian furniture, porcelain, and other objets d'art.

The next street up on the right is **Via Santo Spirito** and this is home to a number of Italian heavy hitters. Valentino is at no. 3 and needs, I guess, no introduction. Corrado Irioné, one of Milan's best-known furriers, is at no. 7. Paolo Canelli, at no. 14, specializes in Renaissance and Mannerist sculpture and some Italian furniture from the same period. Antonella Bensi is a fun, but expensive antique shop at Via Santo Spirito 15. The shop specializes in antique toys and games. Taccani, at no. 24, is another antique shop, this one devoted to fine European china and pottery of the 15th and 16th centuries. Tivoli, no. 26, is another fine furrier, and in an area where prices are high, Carlo Tivoli's just might be the highest—but worth it.

On the next street up, **Via Borgospesso,** there are two names that stand out. Roman designer Laura Biagiotti's shop for women (and more recently, men) is at Via Borgospesso 19. Across the street, at no. 18, is Sebastian, home to handmade and made-to-order shoes of the highest quality for men and women.

IN THE NEIGHBORHOOD

Near the Montenapo area, but not actually in it, are a couple of shops that might be of interest to the serious shopper.

For those who like to have designer everything, a quite ordinary-looking stationery shop, La Scrittura, at Via Filippo Turati 3 (the street which Via Alessandro Manzoni becomes as it runs away from the Montenapo area), stocks the entire line of Trussardi Scribe products. They have the elegant ring binders and notebooks at very reasonable prices.

On the same street, at Via Filippo Turati 2 and 5, is Sinig's, a vast housewares and ceramic shop which offers good buys on the lower end of the Richard Ginori line.

At the very end of Via Monte Napoleone is Piazza San Babila. Here is Valextra, at Piazza San Babila 1, a store selling a wide range of leather goods, particularly luggage. There are good buys to be had here.

Around the corner from Piazza San Babila is Corso Matteotti. Where the piazza and the corso meet stands Fratelli Rossetti, home to the famous line of Italian shoes for men and women.

Nearby, in a tiny side street called Via Morone, at no. 4, is Giusy Bresciani. In a shop that looks like a Kate Greenaway illustration come to life, you'll find modern updates of traditional, cute styles. Knitwear, particulary handmade cashmere goods, is a specialty of this lovely shop.

A SIGHTSEEING SUGGESTION

If the vigor and craziness of the Memphis "New International Style" at one end of Via Alessandro Manzoni left you with an urge to see something a little more traditional, then stop at the **Poldi Pezzoli Museum,** also on Via Manzoni.

The Poldi Pezzoli collection was assembled in the 19th century by Gian Giacomo Poldi Pezzoli, an extremely rich, and by all accounts, a very affable, art connoisseur. The building housing the collection was formerly the Poldi Pezzoli palazzo and it's a monument to the discerning eye of its former owner. Here are first-rate examples of such Renaissance masters as Mantegna, Giovanni Bellini, Piero della Francesca, Botticelli, and Perugino. There are also exceptional pieces from later periods, notably the 18th century. The collection, though, is quite small and makes a nice break from shopping. It is the kind of museum one browses in rather than undertaking a forced march through 500 years of European culture.

The Poldi Pezzoli feels very much like someone's home that just happens to be filled with masterpieces, rather similar to the Frick Collection in New York or the Isabella Stewart Gardner Museum in Boston.

The Poldi Pezzoli Museum is at Via Alessandro Manzoni 12. Hours are 9:30 a.m. to 12:30 p.m. and 2:30 to 5:30 p.m. Eleven months out of the year (August is the exception) the museum is also open every Thursday evening from 9 to 11 p.m. The museum is closed all day Monday throughout the year.

REFRESHMENTS

Dining in the Montenapo district is not easy. There are few restaurants and those are extremely expensive.

Bice, Via Borgospesso 12 (tel. 702-572); closed Monday. Credit cards: AE. This is an elegant restaurant, catering to the local princes and princesses of fashion (if they aren't dining in their private dining rooms in their palazzi). The tortellini is excellent, as are the roasts and other cuts of meat.

Don Lisander, Via Alessandro Manzoni 12A (tel. 790-130); closed Sunday. Credit cards: AE. Another elegant establishment at which you can dine in a lovely garden in the summertime. Fish is a specialty here.

St. Andrews, Via Sant'Andrea 23 (tel. 793-132); closed Sunday. Credit cards: AE. This is not so much an Italian restaurant as an international one. The food is excellent but extremely expensive.

Casanova Grill, in the Palace Hotel, Piazza della Repubblica 20 (tel. 650-803); closed Saturday and Sunday. AE. This is a little bit of a hike—a five-minute taxi ride—from Montenapo, but Casanova's is worth the trip. There is room for only 60 diners in this elegant establishment, but the food is without comparison in Milan. Since its opening in 1985, Casanova Grill has become *the* place to be seen.

THE BRERA AREA

The area around the Brera Museum, which is also Milan's most illustrious school of art, is the prettiest and most manageable of Milan's shopping districts. To draw on the New York analogy again, the Brera district, with its art students, antique shops, cafés, and shops selling all kinds of extraordinary goods, is Milan's Greenwich Village.

After undergoing some of the insufferable snootiness of the Montenapo, it's a relief to arrive in this neighborhood where the salespeople and the approach to selling itself are a lot more casual. Furthermore, there's a far more interesting mix of goods available here. If you're in the market for something odd or unusual, this is the area to shop.

The major streets we'll be strolling are Via Brera itself (on which, to be honest, there isn't much, but it is the main approach to the neighborhood), Via Fiori Chiari, Via Solferino, and Via Madonnina.

MILAN: GREAT SHOPPING STROLLS

Starting at La Scala Opera House, on the right as you face it is **Via Verdi.** A few blocks up, Via Verdi becomes **Via Brera.** Passing American Express at Via Brera 3, we come to the first stop on the stroll, the two Naj Oleari (Naj, by the way, is pronounced "nai") shops at nos. 5 and 8, on opposite sides of the street. Number 8 stocks clothes for children made from the almost-too-cute Naj Oleari fabrics. The shop across the street has all the Naj Oleari fabrics, notebooks, gardening sets, umbrellas, pillows, boxes, and bags.

Farther up Via Brera, at no. 16 is Piero Fornasetti, a shop cluttered with Fornasetti-designed furniture, lamps, fabrics, and ceramics.

Past the Brera Museum we come to **Via Fiori Chiari,** a cobbled pedestrians-only street running off Via Brera to the left. The first shop you encounter is Roberta e Basta, at Via Fiori Chiari 2, a gold-pillared store selling fine art deco and art nouveau furniture and bric-a-brac. Franco Sabetelli at no. 5 is chock full of fabulous old pictures and frames (more frames, actually than pictures), some 500 and 600 years old.

Via Fiori Chiari leads directly into another charming, traffic-free street, **Via Madonnina.** At no. 19 is a beautiful men's shop selling, as the name makes clear, shirts, ties, socks, and suits in Cashmere Cotton and Silk. Down the street a way at no. 11 is Angela Caputi, selling her playful line of clunky-funky costume jewelry and fun clothes for women.

Luisa Beccaria, Via Madonnina 10, is a charming little shop that sells clothing for children and their mothers. Next door is a well-known name in leather goods, Il Bisonte, which has a large selection of bags, shoes, and suede and leather clothing.

Naj Oleari handbags: Try just picking one

At no. 5 is L'Oro dei Farlocchi, an antique shop with the oddest selection of curiosities you are likely to encounter in Milan. Out of keeping with the charm of this little street, but nothing to complain about, is large, charmless shoe shop Alfonso Garlando—but, boy, do they have a lot of shoes! There are thousands of shoes for women here in every imaginable color and style. Prices range from practically nothing to not very much. Some orphans and seconds. The shop is at no. 2. If you walk up the **Corso Garibaldi,** the busy thoroughfare with which Via Madonnina connects, you'll be on your way to Via Solferino, another good shopping street in the Brera district. However, while on the Corso Garibaldi, you might want to stop at Surplus, Corso Garibaldi 7, an excellent secondhand clothing store—this is where young Milan shops for the latest styles in excellent condition. Excellent prices.

There is also a first-rate paper goods shop, I Giorni di Carta, at Corso Garibaldi 81.

At the corner of Via Pontaccio and Corso Garibaldi, turn right onto Via Pontaccio. Walk to the end of the block and you should be at the beginning of Via Solferino.

At the corner of Via Pontaccio and **Via Solferino** is Drogheria Solferino, which is not a drugstore—it was once, but no longer. Now it's a prime store for both men's and women's clothing. Also at the corner of Pontaccio and Solferino, at no. 2, is Spelta, a top-flight ladies' shoe shop selling its own colorful line of handmade shoes.

At Via Solferino 3, three completely different shops share the same number. There is Urrah, selling casual wear for young men and women; Merù, a jeweler whose original designs (and excellent prices) reflect the slightly offbeat character of the neighborhood; and Stationery, a fascinating gadget and toy shop that will enchant any child and most adults.

Guarda Roba, Via Solferino 9, is your stop for eye-catching, eccentric modern clothing—not the kind of thing you wear to opening night at La Scala.

Accademia, Via Solferino 11, is a menswear shop where the accent is on traditional clothing and hand-tailoring. Prices are reasonable, even on the made-to-measure suits.

Controbuffet, at no. 14, is a craft and design shop that sells objects designed with wit and verve. Nothing traditional about this place, but a lot of fun.

IN THE NEIGHBORHOOD

On **Via Palermo,** a street running parallel to Via Pontaccio, is La Carriola, at no. 11, a shop selling some of the most beautiful clothing for children in the city. Also on Via Palermo, at no. 5, is Legatoria Artistica, which offers a large selection of hand-painted paper products, boxes, blank books, and the like.

Cromo, on **Via Anfiteatro,** near the Corso Garibaldi, has a huge selection of antique and not-so-antique jewelry.

Roberto Dabbene, in Largo Treves 2, a small square at the end of Via Palermo, has lovely antique silver goods, mostly Italian and English.

MILAN: GREAT SHOPPING STROLLS

On the busy **Via Moscova** there are two design shops, both quite different. Arform, Via Moscova 22, stocks clean-lined Italian, Scandinavian, and Japanese objects: toys, cutlery, glass, and pottery. There's no telling what you'll find at Libri e Roba, Via Moscova 15. The name means "books and stuff"—the books might be rare, first editions, but perhaps not; the "stuff" is everything from secondhand clothes to antiques.

A SIGHTSEEING SUGGESTION

The **Brera Museum** is one of those marvelous museums in which you come face to face with a particular world-famous painting and say to yourself: "I didn't know that was here!" In the Brera's magnificent collection you'll see Piero della Francesca's Urbino Altarpiece, Mantegna's *Dead Christ*, *The Betrothal of the Virgin* by Raphael, Giovanni Bellini's *Pietà*, and Caravaggio's *Supper at Emmaus*.

The collection is vast and contains paintings by other great names like Giotto, Titian, Tintoretto, and Tiepolo. The Brera is by no means limited to Italian masters. The gallery includes masterpieces by El Greco, Rubens, Rembrandt, Van Dyke, and such 18th-century English masters as Joshua Reynolds and Thomas Gainsborough.

The Brera collection is at Via Brera 28, inside the Accademia di Brera (the art school) and is open from 9 a.m. to 2 p.m. weekdays, except for Monday when it's closed all day. The collection can be visited on Sunday and holidays from 9 a.m. to 1 p.m. On the portico overlooking the courtyard, next to the entrance to the gallery, is a very attractive open-air café serving light lunches and drinks. It's always crowded with students, but is open to all.

REFRESHMENTS EN ROUTE

The Brera district is a good place to get a snack, a drink, a pizza, or a full meal.

Bars

Bar Giamaica, Via Brera 26 (tel. 876-723); closed Sunday. This is by far the most famous bar/restaurant in the Brera district. Long the haunt of artists and art students, the Bar Giamaica serves good inexpensive lunches which you can eat outside when the weather is fine.

Caffè Resentin, Via Mercato 24 (tel. 875-923); closed Monday. Without the tradition of Bar Giamaica, this intimate little bar serves excellent wines and grappas. It's a fine place for lunch too.

Moscatelli, Corso Garibaldi 93 (tel. 655-4602); closed Monday. The most charming old bar in Milan, Moscatelli has excellent wines but not much to eat.

El Tumbun de San Marc, Via San Marco 20 (tel. 659-9507); closed Sunday. Whatever a tumbun may be, I can safely report that it's not something to eat. However, this charming, British pub-like place serves beer on tap and a nice selection of *stuzzichini* hot and cold snacks.

Restaurants

Franco il Contadino, Via Fiori Chiari 20 (tel. 808-153); closed Tuesday. Credit card: AE. A very good restaurant offering excellent Italian specialties, particularly pasta. Informal but expensive.

Vecchio Canneto, Via Solferino 56 (tel. 659-8498); closed Sunday and Monday. Credit card: AE. An excellent, moderately priced restaurant which specializes in fish. The grilled swordfish and spigola (sea bass) are particularly good.

Spaghetteria da Emilio, Via Solferino 3 (tel. 872-735); closed Monday. Credit card: AE. Dozens of different types of spaghetti. I liked the con melanzane and the particularly good carbonara. Moderately priced.

La Bricola, Via Solferino 25 (tel. 655-1012); closed Sunday and Monday. Chic, expensive, and serves excellent food. You must reserve a table, particularly at lunch.

La Libera, Via Palermo 21 (tel. 805-3603); closed Saturday. An expensive pizzeria, very au courant.

THE DUOMO AREA

If you can take your eyes off the magnificent Gothic cathedral, the Duomo, which dominates this area, you'll find yourself in the heart of an excellent shopping district. This is downtown Milan, the place where the Milanese shop for basics. That's not to suggest, of course, that you won't find an abundance of high fashion and famous names in this area also. Prices are lower in this neighborhood than in Montenapo and the merchandise isn't quite as offbeat as in the Brera.

The streets you'll be strolling are numerous and are not always contiguous. The most important of them are the Corso Vittorio Emanuele, which runs from Piazza del Duomo to Piazza San Bibila; the Galleria Vittorio Emanuele, a cruciform shopping "mall" built at the turn of the century; Via San Pietro all'Orto; and the Piazza del Duomo itself. Running off these streets, but usually retaining the street address, are smaller versions of the Galleria Vittorio Emanuele. Milan weather seems to have made off-street shopping a Milanese tradition.

In the **Piazza del Duomo** itself are two major shops. The largest of Italy's department stores, La Rinascente, is right there at no. 1. This department store is much more what an American visitor might expect of an emporium of this kind: there are several floors, it has been "boutiqued" featuring some well-known names, and there is a multilingual information center to help monolinguists shop.

Galtrucco, Piazza del Duomo 2, has been a landmark since the 1920s. It features its own brand of clothing for men and women as well as products by well-known Italian designers.

Although the **Galleria Vittorio Emanuele** itself, which fronts the piazza, has been largely given over to cafés and even a fast-food joint, there are a number

MILAN: GREAT SHOPPING STROLLS

of well-established old Milanese names to be found in this magnificent arcade.

As you enter the galleria from the Piazza del Duomo, you'll find a two-floor Prada shop, much larger than the one on Via della Spiga. It carries the full range of Prada luggage, handbags, wallets, and jewelry. Next door is B. Finzi, a shop that was founded in 1859 and has become something of a Milan institution. It specializes in lingerie and what the Italians call "biancheria intima"—underwear.

Across the hall, as it were, is a good Luisa Spagnoli shop, and next to that, another historic name, Borsalino, selling its distinctive hats for men.

Retracing your footsteps to the Piazza del Duomo, turn left and walk to the end of the cathedral. You will now be standing at the beginning of one of Milan's major streets, the **Corso Vittorio Emanuele**. At no. 1, next to Rinascente, is Fimar, featuring a large selection of clothing for men and women including many of Italy's most famous designer names: Valentino, Max Mara, and Krizia. This is not a bargain basement, but prices here do seem to be a little lower than at some other locations.

De Bernardi, at Corso Vittorio Emanuele 4, is stuffed floor to ceiling with women's hosiery—stockings, socks, leg-warmers, and the like—in every imaginable size, color, and design.

Another Borsalino shop, at Corso Vittorio Emanuele 5, offers Borsalino's newly introduced, but traditional style of clothing for men. At no. 7 is Avolio,

Valentino: The king of Italian fashion

an excellent shop for ties, handkerchiefs, and pajamas. Di Varese, at no. 9, is a chain shoe shop, selling everything from running shoes to dress shoes, for men and women. La Ragazzeria, Corso Vittorio Emanuele 13, is a huge, colorful, and reasonably priced children's clothing store, catering to kids 5 to 14 years old. Diana Due, next door at no. 15, is a good place to shop for handbags, wallets, and other leather goods—no footwear, though.

Stefanel, Corso Vittorio Emanuele 28, is the competition to Benetton, with similar high-quality, low-priced brightly colored knitwear for children and adults. Its neighbor is Cacharel, in the small gallery, Largo Corsiu dei Scrvi 11, running off the Corso Vittorio Emanuele.

They call it the Shit Shop (not me), and it too is in a gallery off the Corso, Galleria San Carlo. Here you'll find tough-looking, generally black clothing for Milan's new, or permanent, wave. Despite the off-putting name, the people who run it are quite friendly.

Bruno Magli has four far-flung shops in Milan. The one on the Corso Vittorio Emanuele, corner of Via San Paolo, is the largest and has the widest selection of the Magli line of shoes for men and women. Pollini, at Corso Vittorio Emanuele 30, is also a good place to shop for shoes, but ladies' only.

Zebedia, Corso Vittorio Emanuele 37 (in the Galleria del Toro) looks like an old-fashioned American diner, but is in fact a shirt shop for men. Styles range from the conservative to glow-in-the-dark wild.

A good shopping street intersecting with Corso Vittorio Emanuele is **Via San Pietro All'Orto.** On this short street at no. 9 you'll find Eve, another shop specializing in handbags, briefcases, and luggage. A few doors away at Via San Pietro all'Orto 11 is Coruzzi, one of the loveliest and most elegant tie shops I've ever seen. Coruzzi makes all its own products and the selection is large and timeless. Enrico Coveri, Via San Pietro all'Orto 12, can outfit the entire family in clothing with style and imagination.

Pomellato, at the corner of Via San Pietro all'Orto and Corso Matteotti, at no. 17, is a fine jeweler who also stocks beautiful items for the home like candlesticks, clocks, and silverware.

IN THE NEIGHBORHOOD

A side street behind the Palazzo Reale is the **Via Durini.** On this street you'll find two of Milan's newest shops. One is a giant and rather austere Emporio Armani, at Via Durini 24, the Giorgio Armani outlet for his casual wear. A few yards away is Caffè Moda, a very hip, three-floor shopping center that shelters a series of small boutiques with giant names in Italian fashion. There is Krizia Poi, Valentino Uomo, Enrico Coveri, Cacharel, Missoni accessories, and Gherardini, to mention a few. There is also a charming snackbar/restaurant on the ground floor. The Caffè Moda complex is at Via Durini 14.

Not far away, making your way back toward the Piazza del Duomo, at **Largo Augusto 3,** corner of Via Cavallotti, is La Porta Blu, a fabulous perfume and costume jewelry shop.

Near the Galleria Vittorio Emanuele, in **Piazza San Fedele** at no. 2, is Pellux, yet another excellent leather goods shop. Here you'll find everything from shoes for men and women to luggage. But there's more. Just around the corner is Nazareno Gabrielli, one of the most exclusive names in leather goods in Italy. It's at **Via Hoepli** 6.

Leaving fine leather goods, you can go a few streets away to **Via Visconti di Modrone** and Bramani, at no. 29, the place where "Vibram" soles for rock-climbing shoes were invented. The inventor, Brimani, has given his name to a superior sports-wear shop featuring the famous names: Fila, Ellesse, and Sergio Tacchino.

A SIGHTSEEING SUGGESTION

You've been walking by or around it all day. Now is the time to go into the **Duomo**. This is the most magnificent Gothic building in Italy, and is second only to St. Peter's in Rome in size. It was begun in 1386, the body of the apse having been finished in a scant 61 years. However, the finishing touches were not put on the building (there are, by the way, some 3,000 statues carved on or in the church, over 2,000 of them on the exterior) until 1813. Milanese used the phrase *"lungo come la fabbrica del Duomo"* to mean that something is never-ending.

The interior of the building is so vast that a lot of the decoration gets lost in space. Perhaps the best-known, and most impressive, work in the building is the Trivulzio Candelabrum, a seven-branched bronze candlestick almost 15 feet tall. It dates from the 13th or 14th century and the artist's name has been lost to time. The candelabrum stands in the left transept.

The Duomo is one of the few churches of note in Italy where you can go into the sanctuary of the altar (assuming there is no Mass being said, of course) and view the beautiful woodcarving of the choir stalls. These date from the 16th century and are some of the finest examples of baroque woodcarving in the country.

One of the great thrills of the Duomo is the fact that you can take the elevator to the roof and, if you have a head for heights, clamber around in the forest of pinnacles, getting a close-up look at how the building was constructed, as well as magnificent views of the city spread before you.

The Duomo is open every day from 8 a.m. until 7:30 p.m.

REFRESHMENTS EN ROUTE

Cafés

In the Galleria Vittorio Emanuele there must be a dozen open-air cafés. All are good, but the favorite seems to be **Il Salotto;** closed Tuesday. Here you'll get excellent service, cappuccino, and a view of the galleria. An excellent place to watch Milan walk by.

Biffi-Scala, Via Filodrammatici 2; closed Sunday. This is an old Milanese landmark, much frequented by off-duty personnel from La Scala, which is next door. Breakfasts and light lunches are served, as well as the usual Italian aperativi and coffees.

Restaurants

Savini, Galleria Vittorio Emanuele 11 (tel. 805-8343); closed Sunday. Credit cards: AE, DC, MC, V. Reservations are essential at this, perhaps Milan's most famous restaurant. Savini was founded in the 19th century and the old money of Milan still flocks here for risotto alla milanese, costoletta alla milanese, and the marvelous homemade tortellini.

El Toulà, Piazza Paola Ferrari 6 (tel 870-302); closed Sunday and Monday. Credit cards: AE, MC, V. This is another elegant restaurant, where one comes not just to dine but also to be seen dining by all the right people. The food, though, is excellent, particularly the gnocchetti in a truffle sauce, and a breast of duck served in a vinegar and apple sauce. For the experience of dining in one of Milan's most "in" restaurants and sampling this splendid food, expect to pay a very high price.

Da Luciano, Via Ugo Foscolo 1 (tel. 866-818); closed Saturday. Credit cards: AE, DC, MC, V. This is a lovely, flower-filled restaurant that features traditional Milanese cooking. Standouts on the menu are costolette alla milanese, liver in a butter-and-sage sauce, and a variety of fresh fish in season. In the summertime, try to get a table on the pleasant veranda. Expensive.

Al Mercante, Piazzetta Mercanti 17 (tel. 805-218); closed Sunday and lunchtime on Saturday. Credit cards: AE, V. This is a very pleasant restaurant in the heart of downtown Milan that has somehow managed to find one of the few medieval buildings in the area still in existence. Pasta here is particularly good, notably tagliolini ai funghi and gnocchetti alla Mercante. There is an excellent selection of grilled and roast meats, including a spiedino (shish kebab à la Italiana) of various meats and vegetables.

Allo Scudo, Via Mazzini 7 (tel. 805-2761); closed Sunday. Credit cards: AE, DC. This is a charming little restaurant and you can tell that the clientele is made up of regulars who come week after week knowing that they'll be served good food at a fair price.

Trattoria dell 'Angolo, Via Formentini 9 (tel. 805-8495); no credit cards. This is a modest, unassuming place that serves good no-nonsense Italian food. Excellent pastas and desserts.

CORSO BUENOS AIRES

No sightseeing on this trip! Corso Buenos Aires is all shopping—and there's plenty of it. To catalog the more than 400 shops along this three-mile stretch would take an entire volume in itself. What the strip in Las Vegas is to gambling, Corso Buenos Aires is to shopping in Milan. We are light-years away now from the plush and hush of Montenapo—this is the area where bargain-conscious

MILAN: GREAT SHOPPING STROLLS

Milanese come to shop for virtually everything. Prices are lower here than elsewhere and the selection of goods runs from used scuba-diving equipment to Richard-Ginori china.

Try to avoid the Corso Buenos Aires on Saturday—but if you hate crowds but love a bargain, you'll be in something of a quandary if you hit the Corso Buenos Aires during the two yearly sales periods. At that time prices plummet, but shopping at *saldi* time has all the charm of trench warfare.

Starting at the Piazza Oberdan end of the street, the end closest to the center of town, your first port of call might be Tincati, Piazza Oberdan 2, home to very traditional, good-quality Italian menswear.

Crossing the square—you're on Corso Buenos Aires proper now—there is another fine men's shop, this one a little more trendy, Diego, at Corso Buenos Aires 1. Lulu, at no. 3, is an upmarket shop for women's clothing that doesn't take itself too seriously. Nice casual wear. Barbara, also at Corso Buenos Aires 3, is an excellent shop stocking virtually every type of leather or soft luggage you can imagine. Good buys to be had here.

Buenos Sport, Corso Buenos Aires 4, is a good stop for lower than usual prices on sportswear. Fila and Ellesse dominate.

Mutinelli, at Corso Buenos Aires 5, has been selling hats for men and women at this location since the late 19th century.

At the corner of Corso Buenos Aires and Via Panfilo Castaldi is a large Richard-Ginori store at no. 42. Farther down Via Panfilo Castaldi at no. 29 is Top Sport, another discounter of the best Italian sportswear.

Back on the Corso Buenos Aires, at no. 7 is Mia, an excellent made-to-order shirt shop for men. There is also a large selection of ties. Darsena, Corso Buenos Aires 16, is a large clothing store for men and women. You'll recognize a lot of the brand names here, but even the less-than-famous goods are of high quality. Sogaro, Corso Buenos Aires 17, has two floors of excellent linens and materials. Ruggeri, Corso Buenos Aires 19, is another fine clothing shop for men. They offer first-rate bespoke and off-the-rack shirts and suits.

Mama Noel, Corso Buenos Aires 23, is a brand-new maternity wear and children's clothing shop. Good buys are to be had here on distinctive clothing for mothers and their newborns. Taufer, Corso Buenos Aires 24, is a hip, avant-garde clothing shop for women whose tastes run to the extravagant. In much the same vein is Il Drug Store, Corso Buenos Aires 28, although prices are lower here than at Taufer.

Reale, Corso Buenos Aires 30, is a clothing store for the entire family—the store is large, bustling, and always busy. Just up the street, at no. 42, is a family-run business, Sorelle Negri, a small shop selling lovely handmade ladies' lingerie and underwear.

Like its sister shop on Via Manzoni, the T&J Vestor at Corso Buenos Aires 52 offers good value on Missoni fabrics and linens. At the same number is Calzaturificio di Parabiago, an in-town factory outlet with spectacularly good buys on Italian men's and women's shoes.

Desart, Corso Buenos Aires 61, is an interesting, out-of-the-ordinary jeweler specializing in semiprecious stones.

CHAPTER VI

The Ultimate Milan Shopping Spree

While there is lots to buy in Rome, Venice, and Florence, the Romans, Venetians, and Florentines agree (reluctantly) that Milan has more of everything than all the other cities. Milan is not as much fun as Rome, its not as courtly as Florence, and it's not even in the same league as Venice when it comes to beauty, but Milan has something for every serious shopper, be it alarmingly expensive fashions on the Via Monte Napoleone or rock-bottom prices on discount merchandise. Herewith, then, is a list of the best, the rarest, the most expensive, and the cheapest Milan has to offer.

ANTIQUES

With very few exceptions, the antiques dealers in Milan sell extremely high-quality items. Prices are high—there is no range here such as one might find in London or Paris. Small, relatively inexpensive antique shops are rare. It's all top end of the market or nothing.

ARTE ANTICA
Via Sant'Andrea 11 (tel. 791-776)
Metro Stop: *San Babila*
Hours: *Monday through Saturday from 9:30 a.m. to 1:30 p.m. and 3:30 to 7 p.m. (closed Monday morning and Sunday; closed August)*
Credit Cards: *None*
English Spoken.

Despite the name, this exclusive, lavish shop sells not ancient art but furniture, mostly French and Italian, dating from the 18th century. The staff is extremely knowledgeable. Prices begin in the millions of lire for smaller, less intricate pieces and rocket up to the tens of millions for gilt and ormolu escritoire from the mid-1700s.

BRUNELLI
Corso Venezia 9, first floor (tel. 790-924)
Metro Stop: *San Babila*
Hours: *Monday through Saturday from 10 a.m. to 1:30 p.m. and 3:30 to 7:30 p.m. (closed Monday morning)*
Credit Cards: *None*

One of Milan's best-known antiques dealers, Brunelli specializes in Italian works of art and furniture from the 17th and 18th centuries. The store is quiet and the salespeople reserved until they realize you are there to buy not to browse.

CAMPANA COEN
Via Manzoni 43 (tel. 655-4617)
Metro Stop: *San Babila*
Hours: *Monday through Saturday from 9:30 a.m. to 1:30 p.m. and 3:30 to 7:30 p.m. (closed Monday morning)*
Credit Cards: *AE*

A large and beautiful shop with an outstanding collection of Persian and Oriental rugs. Expect lengthy and expert consultations with the salespeople who will overwhelm you with politeness and expertise. Prices on recent (19th-century) Persian carpets in good condition begin at 10 million lire. A large, intricately worked Persian carpet, ablaze with color despite its age, can cost between 100 million and 120 million lire.

CROMO
Via Anfiteatro at the corner of Corso Garibaldi (tel. 862-578)
Metro Stop: *Lanza or Moscova*
Hours: *Monday through Saturday from 10 a.m. to 1 p.m. and 3:30 to 7 p.m.*
Credit Cards: *None*
English Spoken.

This is a small excellent antique jewelry shop with items dating from the last century ranging up to the Swinging '60s.

ELIO CITTONE
Via Bigli 2 (tel. 701-745)
Metro Stop: *San Babila*
Hours: *Monday through Saturday from 10 a.m. to 1 p.m. and 3:30 to 7 p.m. (closed Monday morning)*
Credit Cards: *AE*
English Spoken.

This is another exclusive shop specializing in rugs, but it has a wide range of exquisite tapestries as well. They tend to be French and Italian in origin. Prices for a good 18th-century tapestry begin at approximately 10 million lire.

ESKENAZI
Via Monte Napoleone 15 (tel. 700-022)
Metro Stop: San Babila
Hours: Monday through Saturday from 10 a.m. to 1 p.m. and 3:30 to 7:30 p.m. (closed Monday morning)
Credit Cards: None
English Spoken.

More magnificent rugs, but Eskenazi's fabulous shop also has a wide selection of Oriental works of art, notably jade sculptures and Chinese porcelain.

FRANCO SABETELLI
Via Fiori Chiari 5 (tel. 805-2688)
Metro Stop: Lanza or Moscova
Hours: Monday through Saturday from 10 a.m. to 1:30 p.m. and 3:30 to 7 p.m. (closed Monday morning)
Credit Cards: None

This eccentric shop is crammed full of pictures and picture frames—more of the latter than the former. Some works date from as early as the 14th century.

GIANETTI
Via Gesù 3 (tel. 708-362)
Metro Stop: San Babila
Hours: Monday through Saturday from 9:30 a.m. to 1:30 p.m. and 3:30 to 7 p.m. (closed Monday morning)
Credit Cards: None
English Spoken.

Gianetti specializes in Italian antiques from the 16th century on. Here you'll find a large selection of polychrome Italian furniture, as well as Italian china and pottery.

LONGARI
Via Bigli 15 (tel. 780-322)
Metro Stop: San Babila
Hours: Monday through Saturday from 10 a.m. to 12:30 p.m. and 3:30 to 7 p.m., or by appointment
Credit Cards: AE
English Spoken.

The rarefied air of this lavish shop reflects the esoteric nature of the objects it sells: musuem-quality 15th- and 16th-century art objects with an emphasis on Renaissance and baroque sculpture.

L'ORO DEI FARLOCCHI
Via Madonnina 5 (tel. 860-589)
Metro Stop: Lanza or Moscova

MILAN SHOPS: ANTIQUES

At Franco Sabetelli you'll find 500 years' worth of beautiful frames

Hours: *Monday through Saturday from 10 a.m. to 1 p.m. and 3:30 to 7 p.m. (closed Monday morning)*
Credit Cards: *AE*
English Spoken.

Here at Milan's old curiosity shop the emphasis is on the odd and frankly bizarre. Items can be a century old or a decade or two.

MAURO BRUCOLI
Via della Spiga 42 (tel. 793-767)
Metro Stop: *San Babila*
Hours: *Monday through Saturday from 10 a.m. to 1:30 p.m. and 3:30 to 7 p.m. (closed Monday morning)*
Credit Cards: *AE*
English Spoken.

An intimate shop specializing in 19th-century objects, clocks, bric-a-brac, and jewelry.

MAZZOLENI
Via Monte Napoleone 22 (tel. 780-348)
Metro Stop: *San Babila*
Hours: *Monday through Saturday from 10 a.m. to 1:30 p.m. and 3:30 to 7 p.m., or by appointment (closed Monday morning)*
Credit Cards: *AE*
English Spoken.

An odd mixture of items in this, one of the most exclusive antique dealers on Via Monte Napoleone. Mazzoleni specializes in Russian icons and jewelry as well as primitive and pre-Columbian art. Prices for a small, 18th-century icon begin at approximately 50 million lire.

MENGHENZANI
Via Monte Napoleone 10 (tel. 790-085)
Metro Stop: *San Babila*
Hours: *Monday through Saturday from 10 a.m. to 1 p.m. and 3 to 7 p.m. (closed Monday morning)*
Credit Cards: *None*
English Spoken.

Extremely high-quality furniture, exclusively French, and dating from Louis XIV to Empire.

PAOLO CANELLI
Via Santo Spirito 14 (tel. 702-124)
Metro Stop: *San Babila*
Hours: *Monday through Saturday from 10 a.m. to 1 p.m. and 3:30 to 7 p.m. (closed Monday morning)*
Credit Cards: *None*
English Spoken.

Beautiful Renaissance and baroque sculptures. There is also a large selection of Italian furniture of the 15th and 16th centuries.

PIVA
Via Sant'Andrea (tel. 700-678)
Metro Stop: *San Babila*
Hours: *Monday through Saturday from 9:30 a.m. to 12:30 p.m. and 3 to 7 p.m., or by appointment*
Credit Cards: *None*
English Spoken.

A lovely shop specializing in Italian furniture, paintings, and objets d'art from the 18th century.

ROBERTA E BASTA
Via Fiori Chiari 2 (tel. 861-593)
Metro Stop: *Lanza or Moscova*
Hours: *Monday through Saturday from 9:30 a.m. to 1 p.m. and 3:30 to 7:30 p.m. (closed Monday morning)*
Credit Cards: *None*

A dramatic-looking gold-pillared shop that specializes in art deco and art nouveau furniture, pictures, objects, lamps, and frames.

ROBERTO DABBENE
Largo Treves 2 (tel. 655-4406)
Metro Stop: *Lanza or Moscova*
Hours: *Monday through Saturday from 10 a.m. to 1 p.m. and 3 to 7 p.m. (closed Monday morning)*
Credit Cards: *None*
English Spoken.

A small, exclusive shop specializing in Italian and English silver, both tableware and objects, of the 17th and 18th centuries.

TINO BELLINI
Via Madonnina 17 (tel. 872-963)
Metro Stop: *Lanza or Moscova*
Hours: *Monday through Saturday from 10 a.m. to 1 p.m. and 3:30 to 7 p.m. (closed Monday morning)*
Credit Cards: *None*
English Spoken.

Lovely polychrome furniture, figures, and reliquaries from the Renaissance to the baroque. There is also a wide selection of Italian tapestries.

Art deco furniture and artwork is the specialty at Roberta e Basta

ART GALLERIES

Milan has overtaken Rome as the center of contemporary Italian art. The city now abounds in galleries—there is no central gallery district—which feature already world-famous 20th-century Italian artists like De Chirico and Morandi, and works by artists who have become world famous only in the last few years such as Sandro Chia, Francesco Clemente, and Enzo Cucchi.

BRUNA SOLETTI
Piazza Sant'Alessandro 6 (tel. 860-789)
Metro Stop: *Duomo*
Hours: *Monday through Saturday from 10 a.m. to 1:30 p.m. and 3:30 to 7 p.m. (closed Monday morning)*
Credit Cards: *None*
English Spoken.

This is where a lot of the new art in Italy is shown first. Bruna Soletti has a good eye for unknown and up-and-coming artists and isn't afraid of taking a chance on a complete newcomer.

GALLERIA ANNUCIATA
Via Manzoni 44 (tel. 796-026)
Metro Stop: *San Babila*
Hours: *Monday through Saturday from 10 a.m. to 1 p.m. and 3:30 to 7 p.m. (closed Monday morning)*
Credit Cards: *None*
English Spoken.

Like Gian Ferrari, Galleria Annuciata was one of the first galleries to show the pioneers of 20th-century Italian art, the modern, metaphysical Giorgio Morandi and the futurist Carlo Carrà.

GALLERIA BERGAMINI
Corso Venezia 16 (tel. 702-346)
Metro Stop: *San Babila*
Hours: *Monday through Saturday from 10 a.m. to 12:30 p.m. and 3:30 to 7 p.m.*
Credit Cards: *None*
English Spoken.

An important gallery for post–World War II Italian art. Galleria Bergamini was the Milan home of the recently deceased Roman artist Renato Guttuso.

GALLERIA LORENZELLI
Via Sant'Andrea 19 (tel. 783-035)

MILAN SHOPS: ART GALLERIES

Metro Stop: *San Babila*
Hours: *Monday through Saturday from 10 a.m. to 1 p.m. and 4 to 7 p.m. (closed Monday morning)*
Credit Cards: *None*
English Spoken.

This is the soup-to-nuts gallery in Milan. Here you can look for 18th-century landscapes by painters famous in their day but largely forgotten today, as well as the biggest names in old masters, 19th-century ground-breakers, and the finest of Italian postwar modernists.

GIAN FERRARI
Via Gesù 19 (tel. 705-250)
Metro Stop: *San Babila*
Hours: *Monday through Saturday from 10 a.m. to 12:30 p.m. and 3:30 to 7 p.m. (closed Monday morning)*
Credit Cards: *None*
English Spoken.

One of the shrines to the Milanese art movements of the 1920s and 1930s, futurism, and novecento. Works by Arturo Martini, who was so highly thought of by collectors like Peggy Guggenheim, are available here.

SALVATORE ALA
Piazza Umanitaria 2 (tel. 548-5245)
Hours: *Monday through Saturday from 10 a.m. to 1 p.m. and 3:30 to 7 p.m. (closed Monday morning)*
Credit Cards: *None*
English Spoken.

Along with its New York branch, Salvatore Ala is keeping the world informed about the latest developments in Italian art. Nonfigurative and abstract dominate here.

STUDIO CARLO GROSSETTI
Via dei Piatti 9 (tel. 805-3532)
Metro Stop: *Duomo*
Hours: *Monday through Saturday from 10 a.m. to 1 p.m. and 3:30 to 7 p.m. (closed Monday morning)*
Credit Cards: *None*
English Spoken.

Owned by the same people who run the Galleria Annuciata, this newer gallery keeps a close watch on the Italian avant-garde. You might not recognize the names shown here, but you very well might in the future.

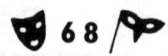

BOOKS

ALGANI
Piazza Scala, corner Galleria Vittorio Emanuele (facing La Scala Opera House) (no phone)
Metro Stop: *Duomo*
Hours: *Monday through Saturday from 8 a.m. to 7 p.m. (closed Monday morning)*
Credit Cards: *None*

This tiny book and magazine store, the size of a walk-in closet, has every American magazine you can think of from *Biker Babes* to *Artforum*. One wall is given over to English-language paperbacks, a haphazard collection in which you'll find Judith Krantz alongside Emmanuel Kant. There is also a large selection of Milan maps, guidebooks, and postcards, as well as guides to the rest of Italy. English newspapers (from England) are available on the day of publication. There are no American newspapers except for the *International Herald Tribune* and the European edition of *USA Today*.

THE AMERICAN BOOKSTORE
Largo Cairoli 16 (facing the Castello) (tel. 870-944)
Metro Stop: *Cairoli*
Hours: *Monday through Saturday from 9:30 a.m. to 1:30 p.m. and 3:30 to 7 p.m. (closed Monday morning)*
Credit Cards: *None*
English Spoken.

Although not in one of the main shopping areas, the American Bookstore is close enough to two major sights (the Castello Sforzesco) and the Church of Santa Maria delle Grazie, which houses Leonardo's *The Last Supper* (closed indefinitely, unfortunately, for a last-ditch restoration effort), to warrant a look. If you crave something to while away the hours on the flight back home or want a scholarly guide to Italian sights yet to be seen, then you should shop here.

THE INTERNATIONAL BOOKSHOP
Via Senato 28 (tel. 545-6436)
Metro Stop: *San Babila*
Hours: *Monday through Saturday from 9:30 a.m. to 1:30 p.m. and 3:30 to 7:30 p.m. (closed Monday morning)*
Credit Cards: *AE*
English Spoken.

You have to go into the courtyard of number 28 Via Senato, up a flight of steps and then down another, to get to the three or four large subterranean rooms which make up this, one of the finest English-language bookstores in all of Italy. The International caters to all literary tastes, from light reading to learned, with a fine selection of novels, nonfiction, children's books, and guidebooks.

MILAN SHOPS: BOOKS/CLOTHING

CLOTHING

CHILDREN'S FASHIONS

Italians not only dress their children well, but with a degree of sophistication. There are clothes for 10-year-olds that look like, and almost cost as much as, the designer wear that their parents may have bought for themselves. That's not to say that all Italian kids are little clothes horses or that there is no rough-and-tumble clothing to be had—just don't be surprised when you happen to find a dinner jacket for a 7-year-old boy with satin lapels costing 500,000 lire.

BENETTON 0-12
Via Monte Napoleone 13 (tel. 794-973)
Metro Stop: *San Babila*
Hours: *Monday through Saturday from 10 a.m. to 7 p.m. nonstop (closed Monday morning)*
Credit Cards: AE, DC, MC, V
English Spoken.

There are dozens of Benetton 0-12s in the city—there are five on the Corso Buenos Aires alone—but this one in the swankest part of town is representative of all of them. And prices at this particular outlet seem no higher than at any other Benetton. For example, a red wool pleated skirt for ages 5 to 7 with a matching red sweater is 75,000 lire. A hooded corduroy jacket for a little boy is 80,000 lire.

CACHAREL
In Caffè Moda, Via Durini 14 (tel. 665-781) and Corso Vittorio Emanuele II, at Largo Corsia dei Servi II (tel. 784-211)
Metro Stop: *Duomo*
Hours: *Monday through Saturday from 10 a.m. to 7 p.m. nonstop (at the Corso Vittorio Emanuele II shop, to 7:30 p.m., but closed Monday morning)*
Credit Cards: AE, DC, MC, V
English Spoken.

See "Women's Fashions" and "Malls."

KRIZIA: see "Women's Fashions"

LA CARRIOLA
Via Palermo 11 (tel. 866-715)
Metro Stop: *Lanza or Moscova*
Hours: *Monday through Saturday from 9:30 a.m. to 1:30 p.m. and 3:30 to 7:30 p.m. (closed Monday morning)*
Credit Cards: None
English Spoken.

La Carriola handmakes its beautiful clothes for children so prices are high. However, the clothes themselves are lovely. A Glen plaid belted jumper with a kick pleat is 240,000 lire. A silk dress, just the thing if your daughter is going to be a train bearer at the next royal wedding, is 520,000 lire.

LUISA BECCARIA
Via Madonnina 10 (tel. 805-6258)
Metro Stop: *Lanza or Moscova*
Hours: *Monday through Saturday from 9:30 a.m. to 1 p.m. and 3:30 to 7:30 p.m. (closed Monday morning)*
Credit Cards: *AE, DC, MC, V*
English Spoken.

Luisa Beccaria has a line of babies' clothing. A christening gown in silk and lace is 400,000 lire. A pair of velvet trousers in dark blue is 85,000 lire.

MAMA NOEL: see "Maternity Wear"

NAJ OLEARI
Via Brera 8 (tel. 800-633)
Metro Stop: *Lanza or Moscova*
Hours: *Monday through Saturday from 10 a.m. to 1:30 p.m. and 2:30 to 7 p.m. (closed Monday morning)*
Credit Cards: *AE*
English Spoken.

This shop has all the clothing for babies and toddlers in the whimsical, printed fabrics Naj Oleari is famous for. A sun dress for ages 2 to 6 is 90,000 lire. A sun hat to go with it is a further 35,000 lire.

PASINI
Via Manzoni 46 (tel. 700-935)
Metro Stop: *San Babila*
Hours: *Monday through Saturday from 9:30 a.m. to 1:30 p.m. and 3:30 to 7 p.m. (closed Monday morning)*
Credit Cards: *AE*
English Spoken.

Pasini sells very traditional, high-quality clothing for babies and young children. A loden coat in green wool is 250,000 lire. A black velvet dress with a white lace collar is 160,000 lire.

PRIMIZIE
Via Monte Napoleone 29 (tel. 701-731)
Metro Stop: *San Babila*
Hours: *Monday through Saturday from 9:30 a.m. to 1:30 p.m. and*

3:30 to 7:30 p.m. (closed Monday morning)
Credit Cards: AE, V

This shop specializes in relatively inexpensive clothing for newborns and kids up to the age of 7 or 8. A matching hat and coat for spring in peach linen with dark-green piping costs 175,000 lire.

STEFANEL
Corso Vittorio Emanuele II 28 (tel. 780-721)
Metro Stop: *Duomo*
Hours: *Monday through Saturday from 10 a.m. to 7 p.m. nonstop (closed Monday morning)*
Credit Cards: AE
English Spoken.

Stefanel does not have a separate set of stores for kids like the Benetton 0–12s, but each store in the chain does include a children's department. Prices are reasonable: a knit cardigan in kelly-green wool is 37,500 lire. A heavy crew-necked sweater for a boy 7 to 9 costs 45,000 lire.

MATERNITY WEAR

MAMA NOEL
Corso Buenos Aires 23 (tel. 279-655)
Metro Stop: *Porta Venezia*
Hours: *Monday through Saturday from 10 a.m. to 1:30 p.m. and 3:30 to 7 p.m. (closed Monday morning)*
Credit Cards: None

Mama Noel is a great store for maternity wear and children's wear. An Italian woman insists on looking her best even when in her third trimester—hence stylish shops like this one. A pretty summer maternity dress costs about 75,000 lire to 100,000 lire.

PRIMIZIE
Via Monte Napoleone 29 (tel. 701-731)
Metro Stop: *San Babila*
Hours: *Monday through Saturday from 9:30 a.m. to 1:30 p.m. and 3:30 to 7:30 p.m. (closed Monday morning)*
Credit Cards: AE, V

This is a fashionable, yet reasonably priced maternity-wear shop. A summer-weight maternity dress in linen, with an embroidered collar, is 250,000 lire. The staff doesn't speak English, but they cheerfully go out of their way to make shopping easy, despite a language barrier.

MEN'S FASHIONS

In a survey of member countries of the European Economic Community conducted recently, it was discovered that the Italian male spent more money on his own clothing than any other nationality in Europe. Italian men, the survey discovered, also outbought most European women—including the Italian women. Looking good, cutting the *bella figura,* is just as important for an Italian man as it is for any Italian woman. And the process begins at an early age—children's clothing here is as stylish, and often just as expensive, as clothing for adults. By the time an Italian man has reached maturity and can play in the big leagues of men's fashion, he will find an enormous selection of clothes in all styles to suit the national mania for dressing well.

ACCADEMIA
Via Solferino 11 (tel. 870-370)
Metro Stop: *Lanza or Moscova*
Hours: *Monday through Saturday from 9:30 a.m. to 1 p.m. and 3 to 7 p.m. (closed Monday morning)*
Credit Cards: *None*

A pleasant store which specializes in traditional outerwear and overcoats. This is one of the few shops in the city that offers men's clothing in those hard-to-find sizes, extra large and very small. If they can't fit you, then they'll make up one of their items in a size to fit. This service, however, takes about two weeks.

AVOLIO
Corso Vittorio Emanuele II 7 (tel. 709-772)
Metro Stop: *Duomo*
Hours: *Monday through Saturday from 9:30 a.m. to 1:30 p.m. and 3:30 to 7:30 p.m. (closed Monday morning)*
Credit Cards: *None*

This shop specializes in ties, but there is a selection of shirts and pajamas too. A silk tie here costs 35,000 lire; pajamas in dark-blue silk with white piping, 150,000 lire.

BARBA'S
Via Sant'Andrea 21 (tel. 701-426)
Metro Stop: *San Babila*
Hours: *Monday through Saturday from 9:30 a.m. to 1:30 p.m. and 3:30 to 7 p.m. (closed Monday morning)*
Credit Cards: AE, MC, DC, V
English Spoken.

Barba's specializes in decidedly different clothes for men: baggy, dark colored, distinctive, just this side of avant-garde. While Barba's clothing is different, there is a certain elegance to it, so much so that a Barba's suit would not seem out

MILAN SHOPS: CLOTHING

of place in a corporate boardroom—but only if the corporation is one of the more artistic type: motion pictures, advertising, publishing, that sort of thing. If you work for a bank or on Wall Street, you might want to save a Barba's suit for the weekends.

Single-breasted two-piece suits have wide, indented lapels, and sometimes feature a chalk pinstripe that's wider and more widely placed than a similar offering from a more traditional house. A Barba's suit is not cheap: for the one described here, expect to pay about 1¼ million lire.

Barba's also features a wide selection of outerwear for men. A full-length gabardine raincoat, in dark gray, is 950,000 lire. A beautifully finished black shearling hip-length jacket is 1 million lire. There is also a Barba's line of knitwear, ties, and shirts.

BORSALINO
Corso Vittorio Emanuele II 5 (tel. 869-0805)
Metro Stop: *Duomo*
Hours: *Monday through Saturday from 9:30 a.m. to 1:30 p.m. and 3:30 to 7:30 p.m. (closed Monday morning)*
Credit Cards: AE
English Spoken.

This is the shop that sells the new Borsalino clothing line. As you might expect, the clothes tend toward the traditional, like the famous Borsalino hats, but there's nothing old-fashioned or dated about them. The store's casual wear is particularly nice. A blue cotton crew-necked sweater with raglan sleeves is 175,000 lire. A pure-linen shirt is 100,000 lire, and a pair of blue-black pants made out of softened canvas is 150,000 lire.

BUENOS SPORT
Corso Buenos Aires 4 (tel. 271-5295)
Metro Stop: *Porta Venezia*
Hours: *Monday through Saturday from 9:30 a.m. to 1:30 p.m. and 3:30 to 7 p.m. (closed Monday morning)*
Credit Cards: None

Buenos Sport is a good place to buy your Fila sportswear. Tennis shirts by Fila, for example, are 45,000 lire.

CACHAREL
Corso Vittorio Emanuele II, at Largo Corsia dei Servi II (tel. 784-211)
Metro Stop: *Duomo*
Hours: *Monday through Saturday from 10 a.m. to 7:30 p.m. nonstop (closed Monday morning)*
Credit Cards: AE, DC, MC, V
English Spoken.

See "Women's Fashions."

CAFFÈ MODA: see "Malls"

CASHMERE COTTON AND SILK
Via Madonnina 19 (tel. 805-7426)
Metro Stop: *Lanza or Moscova*
Hours: *Monday through Saturday from 10 a.m. to 1 p.m. and 3:30 to 7:30 p.m. (closed Monday morning)*
Credit Cards: AE

As the name suggests, this is a shop specializing in items—mainly shirts, ties, and sweaters—in these three fabrics. One of their classically tailored cotton shirts in a variety of colors costs 140,000 lire. A silk shirt, also their own brand, is 200,000 lire. Cashmere sweaters begin at 350,000 lire.

CLAN
Via Pontaccio 19 (tel. 875-759)
Metro Stop: *Lanza or Moscova*
Hours: *Monday through Saturday from 9:30 a.m. to 1:30 p.m. and 3 to 7 p.m. (closed Monday morning)*
Credit Cards: None

This is a small shop catering to Milanese who want to dress à la preppy. There's a nice selection of gabardine and twill trousers, beginning at about 100,000 lire. Also a large choice of knit and silk ties from 40,000 lire.

CORUZZI
Via San Pietro all'Orto (tel. 792-284)
Metro Stop: *Duomo*
Hours: *Monday through Saturday from 9:30 a.m. to 1:30 p.m. and 3:30 to 7 p.m. (closed Monday morning)*
Credit Cards: None
English Spoken.

Coruzzi is an elegant and expensive tie shop (Milan seems to have more shops dedicated to men's neckwear than anywhere else in Italy) and they come in every imaginable and classical style. Prices for silk knits begin at 40,000 lire, a rep tie, also in silk, is 60,000 lire.

DARSENA
Corso Buenos Aires 16 (tel. 272-532)
Metro Stop: *Porta Venezia*
Hours: *Monday through Saturday from 9:30 a.m. to 1 p.m. and 3 to 7:30 p.m. (closed Monday morning)*
Credit Cards: AE
English Spoken.

There is quite a bit of good-quality menswear to be found in this large shop.

MILAN SHOPS: CLOTHING

There's some designer wear, but the bulk of the merchandise carries the name of the shop. Prices are reasonable. A lightweight blue blazer in cotton is 250,000 lire.

EMPORIO ARMANI
Via Durini 24 (tel. 709-030)
Metro Stop: *Duomo*
Hours: *Monday through Saturday from 10 a.m. to 7 p.m. nonstop (closed Monday morning)*
Credit Cards: AE
English Spoken.

The Emporio Armanis springing up all over Italy, and the world, carry Giorgio Armani's line of casual wear. This rather imposing shop seems to have it all. For summer you'll find Armani bermuda shorts, swimwear, and striped sweatshirts, as well as Armani's version of a canvas-topped boat shoe with white rubber soles. It might be casual and fun, but the prices are not. The shorts are 100,000 lire, the sweats are 120,000 lire, and the shoes run 75,000 lire.

ERMENEGILDO ZEGNA
Via Pietro Verri 3 (tel. 795-521)
Metro Stop: *San Babila*
Hours: *Monday through Saturday from 9:30 a.m. to 1 p.m. and 3 to 7 p.m. (closed Monday morning)*
Credit Cards: AE, DC, MC, V
English Spoken.

This large, modern shop sells some of the most beautiful traditional-style Italian menswear in the country. The accent here is very much on clothes for the professional man who wants to cut a bit of a dash at the office but still keep within the bounds of classic styling. A traditional double-breasted two-piece suit with an understated check pattern, in wool, is 990,000 lire. Ermenegildo Zegna's shirts in cotton or silk are extremely well made and run the gamut from formal for evening wear to something suitable for the weekend. This is the only Ermenegildo Zegna shop in Italy — so far.

GALTRUCCO
Via Monte Napoleone 27 (tel. 702-978)
Metro Stop: *San Babila*
Hours: *Monday through Saturday from 9 a.m. to 1 p.m. and 3 to 7:30 p.m. (closed Monday morning)*
Credit Cards: AE, DC, MC, V
English Spoken.

While Galtrucco is perhaps better known for marvelous fabrics (sold at the Piazza del Duomo outlet) and ladies' wear, this shop devoted exclusively to menswear is a good find. One of Galtrucco's lightweight checked suits, in wool,

In downtown Milan is the striking new Emporio Armani

is 1¼ million lire. This shop is also the Milan outlet for made-to-measure Brioni suits, but there is also some off-the-rack Brioni here, a suit costing approximately 1.3 million lire. The bespoke clothing is much more expensive and the price is based on the choice of fabric and style. If you're in the market for Brioni and you're going on to Rome, it might be better to visit the flagship store there.

GIANFRANCO FERRÉ
Via Sant'Andrea 10A (tel. 700-385)
Metro Stop: *San Babila*
Hours: *Monday through Saturday from 9:30 a.m. to 1:30 p.m. and 3:30 to 7 p.m. (closed Monday morning)*
Credit Cards: *AE, DC, MC, V*
English Spoken.

The men's line of Gianfranco Ferré's empire reflects the same philosophy he has brought to women's clothing. While the clothes for men aren't quite as "architectural" as those for women, the men's line has the same streamlined, out-of-the-ordinary look. The colors are somber: dark greens, earthy browns, blacks, and grays. Ferré's clothes are not for everybody, but those who can wear them always look very stylish. At this shop you'll find the entire Ferré line, including his leisurewear, Oaks by Ferré. There are also suits, jackets, ties, and sleepwear. Prices are high, although considerably less than you'd pay in the United States. You can expect a savings of some 15% to 20%. A bathrobe in black silk costs 490,000 lire here. It would be a good $100 more in New York. See also "Malls."

MILAN SHOPS: CLOTHING

GIANNI VERSACE
Via Pietro Verri 9 (tel. 790-281)
Metro Stop: *San Babila*
Hours: *Monday through Saturday from 9:30 a.m. to 1 p.m. and 3:30 to 7 p.m. (closed Monday morning)*
Credit Cards: *AE, MC, V*
English Spoken.

Not being content to leave the detail work to minions, Gianni Versace maintains total control over every item that carries his name. This might be obvious from his women's line of clothing, but the men's line is just as well thought-out and designed. His shop for men on Via Pietro Verri is a beautiful place, stocking his entire line of menswear and accessories for men. Prices here are high—of course—but again represent a significant savings over the same line available in the United States. A loose-cut blue blazer in linen, ideal for summer wear, is 750,000 lire.

GIO MORETTI
Via della Spiga 6 (tel. 702-172)
Metro Stop: *San Babila*
Hours: *Monday through Saturday from 10 a.m. to 1:30 p.m. and 2:30 to 7 p.m. (closed Monday morning)*
Credit Cards: *AE, DC, MC, V*
English Spoken.

The menswear at Gio Moretti covers all the bases, ranging from the traditional to the wild. The traditional wear is, well, traditional: well-cut two-button suits in cotton or wool are 1.2 million lire and up. The less-traditional clothing is brightly colored and tends to be more for casual wear. There is a huge selection of very nice, colorful silk ties and other neckwear. None of it is cheap. A wool print scarf here costs 100,000 lire.

GIORGIO ARMANI
Via Sant'Andrea 9 (tel. 792-757)
Metro Stop: *San Babila*
Hours: *Monday through Saturday from 10 a.m. to 1:30 p.m. and 3:30 to 7 p.m. (closed Monday morning)*
Credit Cards: *AE, DC, MC, V*
English Spoken.

In the years since Giorgio Armani blew into the men's fashion scene his unstructured clothes, devoid of padding and lining, have become world famous. His clothes continue to be loose and lightweight, but the early Armani has passed on to a more "mature" style. His clothes for men now are a little more structured than before. At this elegant shop you'll find a beautiful double-breasted full-length man's overcoat in heavy, almost military-style wool, for 1,160,000 lire. A racetrack plaid three-button jacket is 980,000 lire.

GUCCI
Via Monte Napoleone 2 (tel. 799-955)
Metro Stop: San Babila
Hours: Monday through Saturday from 10 a.m. to 7 p.m. nonstop (closed Monday morning)
Credit Cards: AE, DC, MC, V
English Spoken.

This shop houses both the men's and women's line of Gucci clothing. The men's department is on the second floor. Here you'll find everything Gucci makes for the man: ties, beginning at 45,000 lire; shirts in a variety of fabrics, from 100,000 lire; double- and single-breasted suits begin at 800,000 lire and zoom up from there.

LARUSMIANI
Via Pietro Verri 7 (tel. 706-957)
Metro Stop: San Babila
Hours: Monday through Saturday from 10 a.m. to 1:30 p.m. and 3 to 7:30 p.m. (closed Monday morning)
Credit Cards: AE
English Spoken.

This is one of the most expensive men's clothiers in Milan. Larusmiani caters to the traditional dresser with costly clothes that are British in inspiration but with a very slight Italian accent. This is also a Milan outlet for Burberry. Materials and workmanship are of extremely high quality, but you certainly pay for it! Larusmiani's lovely cable-knit sweaters in wool begin at 300,000 lire. A two-piece suit can cost 2 million lire or more. Cashmere sweaters for men with a wide ribbed weave are 400,000 lire. Prices here are also quoted in dollars—to give you a clear idea of what you could be spending—but the exchange is quite favorable.

MILA SCHÖN
Via Monte Napoleone (tel. 701-803)
Metro Stop: San Babila
Hours: Monday through Saturday from 10 a.m. to 1 p.m. and 3 to 7 p.m. (closed Monday morning)
Credit Cards: AE, DC, MC, V
English Spoken.

The distinctive Mila Schön line for men is available here in all types of clothing. The standout, though, is the casual wear. There are some nice sport jackets in a linen and cotton with an understated check. These cost 750,000 lire. Men's white pleated trousers are 200,000 lire. There is a large selection of Mila Schön ties, beginning at 45,000 lire.

The ultimate: Clothing and accessories by Gucci

REALE
Corso Buenos Aires 30 (tel. 276-657)
Metro Stop: *Porta Venezia*
Hours: *Monday through Saturday from 9:30 a.m. to 1:30 p.m. and 3:30 to 7:30 p.m. (closed Monday morning)*
Credit Cards: AE
English Spoken.

This department store on a small scale stocks clothes for men, women, and children. The menswear department is large, and while there are no surprises here, prices are reasonable and the quality of the clothing is first rate.

RUGGERI
Corso Buenos Aires 19 (tel. 273-202)
Metro Stop: *Porta Venezia*
Hours: *Monday through Saturday from 9:30 a.m. to 1:30 p.m. and 3 to 7 p.m. (closed Monday morning)*
Credit Cards: AE
English Spoken.

This small, elegant shop is an excellent place to buy Ruggeri's own brand of shirts. A striped cotton shirt with a button-down collar costs 60,000 lire off the rack, but Ruggeri is better known for made-to-measure shirts. A tailor-made white silk shirt for evening wear is approximately 250,000 lire.

SALVATORE FERRAGAMO
Via Monte Napoleone 20 (tel. 706-660)
Metro Stop: *San Babila*
Hours: *Monday through Saturday from 10 a.m. to 7 p.m. nonstop (closed Monday morning)*
Credit Cards: *AE, DC, MC, V*
English Spoken.

Although Ferragamo is better known for his leather goods, particularly shoes, there is a line of men's clothing here. Ferragamo has put his distinctive stamp on beautiful shirts in cotton, for day and evening wear. These begin at 100,000 lire. Very nicely finished jackets in heavyweight tweed go for 500,000 lire and up. Ties, belts, and sweaters too.

TINCATI
Piazza Oberdan 2 (tel. 204-2220)
Metro Stop: *Porta Venezia*
Hours: *Monday through Saturday from 9:30 a.m. to 1:30 p.m. and 3:30 to 7 p.m. (closed Monday morning)*
Credit Cards: *AE*
English Spoken.

One of the oldest men's outfitters in Milan, Tincati has no time for what's in and what's out in the fashion world. This is a Brooks Brothers sort of store—it has sold and continues to sell the same traditional men's clothing it has for years. A pair of line whipcord trousers here costs 200,000 lire.

TOP SPORT
Via Panfilo Castaldi 29 (tel. 279-653)
Metro Stop: *Porta Venezia*
Hours: *Monday through Saturday from 9:30 a.m. to 1:30 p.m. and 3:30 to 7 p.m. (closed Monday morning)*
Credit Cards: *None*

Here you'll find a large selection of the top names in Italian sportswear for men and women. A man's Fila warmup jacket is 150,000 lire.

URRAH
Via Solferino 3 (tel. 870-370)
Metro Stop: *Lanza or Moscova*
Hours: *Monday through Saturday from 10 a.m. to 1:30 p.m. and 3:30 to 7 p.m. (closed Monday morning)*

Credit Cards: AE
English Spoken.

Casual clothing for young people is the stock in trade of this shop. There is swimwear, T-shirts, and roughwear jackets by Belfe, and sports jackets by Paul Smith and Henry Lloyd. Everything here is modern looking and a little out of the ordinary. Not for the traditional dresser.

VALENTINO UOMO
Via Santo Spirito 3 (tel. 706-478)
Metro Stop: *San Babila*
Hours: *Monday through Saturday from 10 a.m. to 1:30 p.m. and 3:30 to 7 p.m. (closed Monday morning)*
Credit Cards: AE
English Spoken.

The men's line of Valentino shares its quarters with the women's clothes in the huge Valentino shop on Via Santo Spirito. While prices are high here, they are much lower than in the United States. Expect Valentino formal wear, as well as Valentino shirts, suits, shoes, and more casual items like swimwear. A gray-check two-piece double-breasted suit is 1.65 million lire. The casual wear is cheaper—a striped or wide-checked short-sleeve shirt is 140,000 lire. See also "Malls."

VERRI UOMO
Via Pietro Verri, at the corner of Via Monte Napoleone (tel. 792-817)
Metro Stop: *San Babila*
Hours: *Monday through Saturday from 10 a.m. to 1 p.m. and 3 to 7 p.m. (closed Monday morning)*
Credit Cards: AE, DC, MC, V
English Spoken.

A very stylish men's shop offering some truly lovely clothes, which though a little different from the norm, are nonetheless elegant and understated. A lightweight overcoat for spring wear in blue tropical-weight wool is 1 million lire. A shirt with wide stripes in cotton is 150,000 lire. There is also a nice selection of ties. A blue silk crêpe tie, for example, is 50,000 lire.

ZEBEDIA
Corso Vittorio Emanuele II 37 (tel. 792-078)
Metro Stop: *Duomo*
Hours: *Monday through Saturday from 9:30 a.m. to 1 p.m. and 3:30 to 7 p.m. (closed Monday morning)*
Credit Cards: AE

This store looks like an old-fashioned American diner but it serves nothing but men's shirts. The range is vast but the scales are tilted somewhat toward the weird and wonderful. Many of the shirts are brightly colored fun-in-the-sun–type Hawaiian or dark new-wave type. Prices are quite good. They begin at about 40,000 lire and don't go up much from there.

WOMEN'S FASHIONS

ADRIANAMODE
Via della Spiga 22 (tel. 708-458)
Metro Stop: *San Babila*
Hours: *Monday through Saturday from 10 a.m. to 1 p.m. and 3:30 to 7 p.m. (closed Monday morning)*
Credit Cards: *None*
English Spoken.

Extremely nice, attentive people run this expensive shop. The merchandise, all of it Italian, tends to be a little on the out-of-the-ordinary side of the fashion world. There are unusually tailored jackets and dresses in a variety of combinations: cashmere with silk trim; hats fashioned in Persian lamb and shaped like the ones the doges of Venice used to wear. In all, a shop for those who aren't quite ready yet for the plunge into the avant-garde, but who aren't content to look like everybody else. If you shop at Adrianamode, be prepared to spend freely. The little hat I mentioned was priced at 850,000 lire.

ALBERTA FERRETTI
Via Monte Napoleone 21A (tel. 709-095)
Metro Stop: *San Babila*
Hours: *Monday through Saturday from 10 a.m. to 1:30 p.m. and 2:30 to 7 p.m. (closed Monday morning)*
Credit Cards: *AE*
English Spoken.

This lovely, low-key shop sells everything from its own brand of blue jeans at 79,000 lire a pair, to outerwear like a long, flaring rather dramatic lady's overcoat in finely woven wool for 836,000 lire. The shop also boasts an extremely accommodating staff.

ALMA
Via Sant'Andrea (tel. 791-446)
Metro Stop: *San Babila*
Hours: *Monday through Saturday from 10 a.m. to 1 p.m. and 3 to 7 p.m. (closed Monday morning)*
Credit Cards: *AE, DC, MC, V*
English Spoken.

One of the nicest shops in Milan and a fine one-stop shopping place if you're pressed for time. The Alma group, now world famous, has shops in New York and Toronto as well, but this is the headquarters and prices are good here. It's no secret that Alma's Spazio line was designed by Gianni Versace, so if you can't afford the name brand a couple of blocks away, you can stock up on real Versace at a much lower price here.

ANGELA CAPUTI
Via Madonnina 11 (tel. 807-384)
Metro Stop: *Lanza*
Hours: Monday through Saturday from 10 a.m. to 1 p.m. and 2:30 to 7:30 p.m. (closed Monday morning)
Credit Cards: AE, DC, MC, V
English Spoken.

This is the Milan outpost of an excellent Florentine designer who is quickly becoming famous for her quirky, playful leisure and swim wear, as well as for her chunky, clunky-but-nice costume jewelry. This little shop seems to stock more jewelry than anything else, but there are some clothes: her breathtaking swimsuits, ranging from 80,000 lire to 150,000 lire, and lesser-priced items like red woolen scarves with rhinestone accents.

AVAGOLF
Via Sant'Andrea 3 (tel. 706-307)
Metro Stop: *San Babila*
Hours: Monday through Saturday from 9:30 a.m. to 1:30 p.m. and 3:30 to 7 p.m. (closed Monday morning)
Credit Cards: AE
English Spoken.

Comfortable, stylish knitwear is the main attraction of this pleasant shop. Prices are not exactly bargain basement, but as the merchandise comes directly from a factory just outside Milan, prices are lower here than at some of the more famous shops in the neighborhood. Expect to pay 250,000 lire for a sweater, more of course if it's cashmere. A sweater-dress costs approximately 400,000 lire and up.

BAILA
Via della Spiga 32 (tel. 798-170)
Metro Stop: *San Babila*
Hours: Monday through Saturday from 10 a.m. to 1:30 p.m. and 2 to 7 p.m. (closed Monday morning)
Credit Cards: AE, DC, MC, V
English Spoken.

An intimate shop where the accent is on leather clothing, particularly skirts and pants. A beautifully made red-and-white leather dress costs 780,000 lire, which isn't a bad price considering the quality of the garment.

BELTRAMI
Via Monte Napoleone 16 (tel. 702-975)
Metro Stop: *San Babila*
Hours: *Monday through Saturday from 10 a.m. to 1 p.m. and 3:30 to 7 p.m. (closed Monday morning)*
Credit Cards: *AE, MC, V*
English Spoken.

While Beltrami may have started off as a shoe store, the two floors of this magnificent shop have enough clothing as well as leather goods to raise it out of the shoes-only category. Beltrami offers the latest in top-drawer clothing design, as well as their world-famous leather goods. A Beltrami evening dress, black and no frills, is likely to cost upward of 1 million lire.

BENETTON
Via Monte Napoleone 13 (tel. 794-973)
Metro Stop: *San Babila*
Hours: *Monday through Saturday from 10 a.m. to 7 p.m. nonstop (closed Monday morning)*
Credit Cards: *AE, DC, MC, V*
English Spoken.

This prestigious location for Benetton doesn't seem to have turned their heads in the least. You'll still find a wide assortment of the colorful, quality woolens that have made Benetton famous. A nice bulky cable-knit sweater in pure wool, just the thing for a cold winter morning, is 89,000 lire. Lined, soft corduroy pants in dark brown are a lowly 44,900 lire.

B. FINZI
Galleria Vittorio Emanuele (tel. 872-345)
Metro Stop: *Duomo*
Hours: *Monday through Saturday from 9:30 a.m. to 1 p.m. and 3:30 to 7:30 p.m. (closed Monday morning)*
Credit Cards: *None*

Finzi has been a Milan institution since 1859, selling fine-quality ladies' underwear and lingerie designed to keep the cold, damp Milan winters at bay. Prices for merchandise as high quality as this are much lower here than in the United States. For example, silk and wool camisoles, warm but lightweight and with satin ribbing, cost just 30,000 lire.

BIKI
Via Monte Napoleone 6 (tel. 709-693)
Metro Stop: *San Babila*
Hours: *Monday through Saturday from 9:30 a.m. to 1 p.m. and 3:30 to 7 p.m. (closed Monday morning)*
Credit Cards: *AE*
English Spoken.

MILAN SHOPS: CLOTHING

Beltrami's window displays only hint at the treasures within

Biki has been a Milan landmark since after the war. Then, and now, Milanese society has flocked to this elegant little shop to buy the latest in Milan high fashion.

BUENOS SPORT
Corso Buenos Aires 4 (tel. 271-5295)
Metro Stop: *Porta Venezia*
Hours: *Monday through Saturday from 9:30 a.m. to 1:30 p.m. and 3:30 to 7 p.m. (closed Monday morning)*
Credit Cards: *None*

A great place to stock up on sportswear by Fila. A *tutta da footing*, in other words, a running suit, will cost less than 200,000 lire here, and that's a good price anywhere.

CACHAREL
Corso Vittorio Emanuele II at Largo Corsia dei Servi 11 (tel. 784-211)
Metro Stop: *Duomo*
Hours: *Monday through Saturday from 10 a.m. to 7:30 p.m. nonstop (closed Monday morning)*
Credit Cards: *AE, DC, MC, V*
English Spoken.

Milan seems to have taken to Cacharel in a big way if the size of this shop is anything to go by. Here you'll find three floors of Cacharel everything: women's wear, menswear, and clothing for children, as well as the full line of accessories and perfumes. Prices here are very good and much less than you might pay in the United States. A black T-shirt with the Cacharel logo is only 38,000 lire here, and a lovely, soft wool white or navy-blue pullover is 168,000 lire.

CAFFÈ MODA: see "Malls"

CLARA ANTONINI
Via Sant'Andrea 12 (tel. 780-788)
Metro Stop: *San Babila*
Hours: *Monday through Saturday from 10 a.m. to 1 p.m. and 3:30 to 7:30 p.m. (closed Monday morning)*
Credit Cards: AE, DC, MC, V
English Spoken.

This is one of the more peculiar shops on Via Sant'Andrea. The selling floor appears to be an indoor parking lot—there's gravel on the floor and the name of the shop is spray-painted raggedly on one wall. The clothing is decidedly different. Flimsy, daring leopard-print dresses seem to predominate. Not for the faint-hearted. Prices begin at 650,000 lire.

CONTI
Via della Spiga 50 (tel. 798-508)
Metro Stop: *San Babila*
Hours: *Monday through Saturday from 9:30 a.m. to 1 p.m. and 3:30 to 7:30 p.m. (closed Monday morning)*
Credit Cards: AE, DC, MC, V
English Spoken.

This is a small, one-person operation offering some of the best prices on no-name goods on the Via della Spiga. Casual wear is the stuff to shop for here. There are baskets of good Italian knitwear with prices starting at 50,000 lire, and racks of lined, pearled cotton pants for summer. These cost a mere 80,000 lire.

COSE
Via della Spiga 8 (tel. 790-703)
Metro Stop: *San Babila*
Hours: *Monday through Saturday from 10 a.m. to 1:30 p.m. and 2:30 to 7 p.m. (closed Monday morning)*
Credit Cards: AE, DC, MC, V
English Spoken.

Cose means "things" in Italian and there are a number of interesting items in this shop. There is an electric selection of sweaters, hats, some costume jewelry, and a wide selection of leather clothing. Prices vary. Nicely finished wool sweaters cost between 150,000 lire and 300,000 lire. A lovely navy-blue leather jacket, hip length, is an expensive 1,860,000 lire.

DARSENA
Corso Buenos Aires 16 (tel. 272-532)
Metro Stop: *Porta Venezia*
Hours: *Monday through Saturday from 9:30 a.m. to 1 p.m. and 3 to 7:30 p.m. (closed Monday morning)*
Credit Cards: AE
English Spoken.

This huge shop on several floors offers excellent prices on no-name and on some designer wear. All the merchandise is of good quality and the store attempts to keep up with the styles and trends that originate in the high-rent districts downtown. On the casual side, but plainly a lot of thought has gone into the large selection of sweaters, sportswear, trousers, and skirts to be found here. Reasonable prices.

DE BERNARDI
Corso Vittorio Emanuele II 4 (tel. 872-130)
Metro Stop: *Duomo*
Hours: *Monday through Saturday from 9:30 a.m. to 1:30 p.m. and 3:30 to 7 p.m. (closed Monday morning)*
Credit Cards: AE

This is a tiny shop which sells every imaginable type of stocking: hundreds of colors, designs, and designers. A pair of Valentino stockings will cost 20,000 lire.

DONINI
Via Monte Napoleone 7 (tel. 702-568)
Metro Stop: *San Babila*
Monday through Saturday from 10 a.m. to 2 p.m. and 3 to 7 p.m. (closed Monday morning)
Credit Cards: AE, DC, MC, V
English Spoken.

This is a beautiful little shop devoted to the finest in handmade and hand-embroidered ladies' lingerie and intimate apparel. A handmade fuschia silk camisole will cost about 120,000 lire.

DROGHERIA SOLFERINO
Via Solferino, at the corner of Via Pontaccio (tel. 878-740)
Metro Stop: *Lanza or Moscova*
Hours: *Monday through Saturday from 10 a.m. to 1:30 p.m. and 3:30 to 7:30 p.m. (closed Monday morning)*

Credit Cards: *None.*
English Spoken.

Sophisticated clothes for young women. Particularly fine are the knitwear and blouses in cotton or silk. One of these will cost around 100,000 lire. The staff is excellent and helpful.

EMPORIO ARMANI
Via Durini 24 (tel. 709-030)
Metro Stop: *Duomo*
Hours: *Monday through Saturday from 10 a.m. to 7 p.m. nonstop (closed Monday morning)*
Credit Cards: *AE*
English Spoken.

Once you've visited the Caffè Moda just down the street, drop in at this new Armani outlet, selling the casual end of the Armani line. The shop itself is striking, with sunken floors, mezzanines, and beautifully displayed merchandise. But, this being Armani-land, prices are steep, although perhaps cheaper than you might expect. A full-length check ladies' skirt in wool is 128,000 lire; a half-length shearling jacket is 1,350,000 lire. Black flat shoes are 98,000 lire.

Slinky, satiny lingerie from Donini

MILAN SHOPS: CLOTHING

ENRICO COVERI
Via San Pietro all'Orto 12 (tel. 701-624)
Metro Stop: *Duomo*
Hours: *Monday through Saturday from 9:30 a.m. to 1:30 p.m. and 3:30 to 7:30 p.m. (closed Monday morning)*
Credit Cards: AE
English Spoken.

A large, elegant shop full of the youthful, colorful Coveri evening, day, and roughwear. See also "Malls."

ERREUNO
Via della Spiga 15 (tel. 795-575)
Metro Stop: *San Babila*
Hours: *Monday through Saturday from 9:30 a.m. to 1 p.m. and 3 to 7 p.m. (closed Monday morning)*
Credit Cards: AE, MC, V
English Spoken.

There is a rumor which I can neither confirm nor deny that a lot of Erreuno's playful high-fashion clothes are designed by Gianfranco Ferre. If your eye is good enough, maybe you'll be able to tell. What is known, however, is that Erreuno is the brainchild of Graziella Ronchi. She has brought her distinctive look to the forefront of Milanese fashion recently, and her shop here is filled with quirky delights like a long, black velvet evening skirt with a bit of paisley thrown in. This item costs 790,000 lire.

FENDI
Via della Spiga 11 (tel. 799-544)
Metro Stop: *San Babila*
Hours: *Monday through Saturday from 9:30 a.m. to 1 p.m. and 3 to 7:30 p.m. (closed Monday morning)*
Credit Cards: AE, DC, MC, V
English Spoken.

The five Fendi sisters first made their name in furs in the 1950s, but it seems that they now sell just about anything you can think of with the distinctive "one F up and one F down" logo, designed for them by Karl Lagerfeld. It's an open secret that Lagerfeld still contributes to the Fendi line. The shop on Via della Spiga specializes in clothing. Prices are high, much as you would expect them to be, but they're no lower at the other Fendi locations in Italy. Be prepared to spend 400,000 lire to 500,000 lire for a skirt here, or 1,040,000 lire for a full-cut belted coat in soft green wool.

FIMAR
Corso Vittorio Emanuele II 1 (tel. 806-342)
Metro Stop: *Duomo*

THE SERIOUS SHOPPER'S GUIDE TO ITALY

Hours: *Monday through Saturday from 9 a.m. to 7:30 p.m. nonstop (closed Monday morning)*
Credit Cards: AE, DC, MC, V
English Spoken.

Firmar is like a small department store. It stocks its own brand of clothing, but the real discovery here is that they have a good selection of major design names as well. Valentino, Max Mara, and Krizia are the best-known labels found here. Prices seem a bit lower than at the flagship stores of those names, but of course the selection is much smaller. A Valentino striped blouse in cotton cost 154,000 lire. A gray wool embroidered top by Krizia is 165,000 lire.

FONTANA
Via della Spiga 33 (tel. 705-372)
Metro Stop: *San Babila*
Hours: *Monday through Saturday from 10 a.m. to 1:30 p.m. and 3:30 to 7 p.m. (closed Monday morning)*
Credit Cards: AE, DC, MC, V
English Spoken.

This is an extremely striking marble and stainless-steel shop, catering exclusively to the upper, upper end of the high-fashion market. Prices are stratospheric and the designs themselves are very elegant but very modern. Prices for just about anything here begin around 1 million lire.

GALTRUCCO
Piazza del Duomo 2 (tel. 861-674)
Metro Stop: *Duomo*
Hours: *Monday through Saturday from 9:30 a.m. to 1 p.m. and 3 to 7 p.m. (closed Monday morning)*
Credit Cards: AE
English Spoken.

While Galtrucco is best known for its lovely fabrics, this shop also offers designer name clothing for women. There are two stories to this large old store (it was built in 1924) with the bulk of the clothing on the first floor. The best known names here are Krizia, Armani, and Miss V. However, while prices are lower than at the flagship stores in the Montenapo, they are not bargain-basement. If the Galtrucco name is good enough—and it ought to be—you'll find some exceptionally beautiful evening wear and blouses made from the store's own fabulous silks.

GIANFRANCO FERRÉ
Via della Spiga 11 (tel. 794-864)
Metro Stop: *San Babila*
Hours: *Monday through Saturday from 10 a.m. to 1 p.m. and 3:30 to 7 p.m. (closed Monday morning)*

MILAN SHOPS: CLOTHING

Credit Cards: AE, DC, MC, V
English Spoken.

Ferré's shop in Milan is his flagship store and it's quite a place to see. The shop is beautiful, the salespeople are beautiful, and the clothes are beautiful (if you like that kind of thing). The prices are not beautiful—although I am assured they're lower here than in the United States. Still, 1.9 million lire for a moiré silk jacket in a lovely shade of peach does seem high. Here, though, you might find some Ferré footwear in a more reasonable price category. There are lovely black evening slippers with a gold stripe at 250,000 lire, and a similar high-heel for 380,000 lire.

GIANNI VERSACE
Via della Spiga 4 (tel. 705-451)
Metro Stop: *San Babila*
Hours: *Monday through Saturday from 9:30 a.m. to 1 p.m. and 3:30 to 7 p.m. (closed Monday morning)*
Credit Cards: AE, MC, V
English Spoken.

The Versace store for women in Milan stocks more than just clothes. Here you'll also find a wide range of Versace accessories, like a leather-and-vinyl briefcase at

The cool, spare elegance of Gianfranco Ferré's Milan shop

400,000 lire. The clothes in Versace's autumnal colors are soft, sensuous, and cost a lot. A polo-neck cashmere sweater sells for 700,000 lire.

GIO MORETTI
Via della Spiga 6 (tel. 702-172)
Metro Stop: *San Babila*
Hours: *Monday through Saturday from 10 a.m. to 7 p.m. nonstop (closed Monday morning)*
Credit Cards: *AE, MC, V*
English Spoken.

A fabulous store on two levels, Gio Moretti sells beautiful clothes to the younger set who have a lot of money and perfect figures. For example, a lamb's leather skirt, cut very tight in the hips, is 990,000 lire.

GUARDAROBA
Via Solferino 9 (tel. 805-8987)
Metro Stop: *Lanza or Moscova*
Hours: *Monday through Saturday from 9:30 a.m. to 1:30 p.m and 3:30 to 7:30 p.m. (closed Monday morning)*
Credit Cards: *AE*
English Spoken.

A store that looks like a factory, with metal shelves, exposed ventilation pipes, etc.—this is the place to find some of the more avant-garde but comfortable clothing for Milan's young artsy set. There are T-shirts and pants that are out of the ordinary, as well as a large selection of shoes—you'll have to work hard to find a traditional brown or black pair as bright colors predominate.

GUCCI
Via Monte Napoleone 2 (tel. 545-6621)
Metro Stop: *San Babila*
Hours: *Monday through Saturday from 10 a.m. to 7 p.m. nonstop (closed Monday morning)*
Credit Cards: *AE, DC, MC, V*
English Spoken.

This is the clothing shop for both men and women. The women get the entire downstairs selling floor, the men are sent upstairs. The women's line is traditional—well tailored and beautifully finished. A woolen skirt with belt to match will cost 350,000 lire.

GUISY BRESCIANI
Via Morone 4 and 8 (tel. 708-655)
Metro Stop: *San Babila*
Hours: *Monday through Saturday from 9:30 a.m. to 1 p.m. and 3:30 to 7:30 p.m. (closed Monday morning)*

Credit Cards: AE
English Spoken.

This is a charming, cluttered shop, furnished with old wooden display cases, roll-top desks, and brass runners and hooks. Everywhere you look there seems to be a bunch of dried flowers. In and among this cute profusion are some lovely handmade clothes for women. Handmade cashmere cardigans range from a low of 280,000 lire to 820,000 lire. Shoes can cost as little as 79,000 lire up to 550,000 lire for crocodile. Everything is designed in a style that is best described as sophisticated Laura Ashley, old-fashioned styles updated à la Italiana. I can't help but speculate that we'll be hearing more from Guisy Bresciani.

GULP!!
Via della Spiga 42 (tel. 704-818)
Metro Stop: San Babila
**Hours: Monday through Saturday from 9:30 a.m. to 1 p.m. and 3:30 to
   7 p.m. (closed Monday morning)**
Credit Cards: AE, DC, MC, V
English Spoken.

Gulp!!'s own brand of clothing is very much for the young. Wherever a bit of kitsch or glitter fits—or doesn't fit—on a wide selection of belts, pants, and jackets, bang it goes on. The clothes are funny and unusual, but not for everybody.

IL DRUG STORE
Corso Buenos Aires 28 (tel. 272-532)
Metro Stop: Porta Venezia
**Hours: Monday through Saturday from 10 a.m. to 7 p.m. non stop
   (closed Monday morning)**
Credit Cards: None
English Spoken.

Nonstop hours and nonstop rock music blaring through the store might make you think you're back in the States, but you aren't. This cheap, trendy shop is an excellent place to get some younger-style knits and dresses. A sweater "embroidered or ornamented" (as the U.S. Customs Service refers to sweaters with sequins, rhinestones, bits of fur, beads, or lamé) costs about 60,000 lire, depending on the ornamentation.

IVANA ZANINI
Via della Spiga 52 (tel. 795-287)
Metro Stop: San Babila
**Hours: Monday through Saturday from 9:30 a.m. to 12:30 p.m. and 3:30
   to 7:30 p.m. (closed Monday morning)**
Credit Cards: AE, MC, V
English Spoken.

This small, intimate shop caters to those who want classic clothing that will never go out of style. The cut and materials are faintly reminiscent of Chanel. Soft colors and fabrics abound, with an accent on gray and peach cashmere and wool. Prices are not low: a spectacular three-quarter-length coat in pale pink was 1.2 million lire.

JEAN-PAUL GAULTIER/KASHIYAMA
Via della Spiga 19–20 (tel. 781-469)
Metro Stop: *San Babila*
Hours: *Monday through Saturday from 10 a.m. to 1 p.m. and 3:30 to 7 p.m. (closed Monday morning)*
Credit Cards: *AE, DC, MC, V*

These two shops are side by side and under the same management. Both shops look wonderful, particularly Jean-Paul Gaultier, which has partially mosaiced floors, as if you were walking on the site of a Roman ruin. The clothes are avant-garde, black, baggy, and expensive.

KRIZIA
Via della Spiga 23 (tel. 708-429)
Metro Stop: *San Babila*
Hours: *Monday through Saturday 9:30 a.m. to 12:30 p.m. and 3:30 to 7 p.m. (closed Monday morning)*
Credit Cards: *AE, DC, MC, V*
English Spoken.

Very chic, very French, and in the heart of Milan: Fashions by Jean-Paul Gaultier

Maiuccia Mandelli's flagship shop. On several floors you'll find every Krizia product you could ever want, from dressy to jeans to clothing for kids. The prices aren't as high as you might expect. Krizia jeans are 100,000 lire; a sweater with the famous Krizia logo is 170,000 lire. A plastic hat in the shape of a geodesic dome—and I defy anyone to wear one without feeling self-conscious—is a mere 60,000 lire.

LANCETTI
Via della Spiga 2 (tel. 795-883)
Metro Stop: *San Babila*
Hours: *Monday through Saturday from 10 a.m. to 7 p.m. nonstop (closed Monday morning)*
Credit Cards: *DC, MC, V*
English Spoken.

Lancetti is a Roman designer specializing in classic evening wear. His talents do not come cheap, however. A red wool suit trimmed in black velvet is 1 million lire.

LAURA BIAGIOTTI
Via Borgospesso 19 (tel. 799-659)
Metro Stop: *San Babila*
Hours: *Monday through Saturday from 10 a.m. to 1:30 p.m. and 3:30 to 7 p.m. (closed Monday morning)*
Credit Cards: *AE, MC, V*

Krizia's trademark black panther

Biagiotti is a Roman fashion star, but her designs have caught on throughout the country in a big way. (After her first big success a few years ago she had enough confidence in the future that she immediately went out and bought herself a 70-room castle.) Her clothes, made from everything from linen to cashmere, are much cheaper here than in the United States—but they are not cheap. In the giant selection in this Milan shop you'll find items for 400,000 lire or 500,000 lire, but the big time begins at 900,000 lire for cashmere and more luxurious fabrics.

LUCIANO SOPRANI
Via Sant'Andrea 14 (tel. 798-327)
Metro Stop: *San Babila*
Hours: *Monday through Saturday from 9:30 a.m. to 1 p.m. and 3:30 to 7:30 p.m. (closed Monday morning)*
Credit Cards: *AE, DC, MC, V*
English Spoken.

Luciano Soprani is one of the latest names to emerge in Italian fashion, his first collection having been unveiled as recently as 1981. The name, along with the Basile line from the same house, is well known in Italy, less so in the United States. There is no Basile shop in Milan (that I could find, anyway) so you'll have to wait for Rome for that. However, there are excellent buys here on Soprani casual wear: a wool dress for 450,000 lire and evening wear that's 720,000 lire and up. Don't overlook his shoes, either. A brown leather day shoe, a sort of 19th-century update, is a remarkably low 180,000 lire. If I had to guess, there will come a day when we look back and realize Soprani was affordable once, like Missoni and Laura Biagiotti.

LUISA BECCARIA
Via Madonnina 10 (tel. 805-6258)
Metro Stop: *Lanza or Moscova*
Hours: *Monday through Saturday from 9:30 a.m. to 1 p.m. and 3:30 to 7:30 p.m. (closed Monday morning)*
Credit Cards: *AE, DC, MC, V*
English Spoken.

There are clothes for women and children here. Some maternity wear, but very little. The Luisa Beccaria line for women tends toward beautifully cut, distinctive, but tasteful high fashion. There is a full range of accessories, like hats, gloves, bags, and costume jewelry. Prices are a little on the high side, such as 260,000 lire for a striped silk blouse. The salespeople are some of the nicest in Milan. Luisa Beccaria might be another name to watch for in the future.

LUISA SPAGNOLI
Galleria Vittorio Emanuele 69 (tel. 863-225)
Metro Stop: *Duomo*

MILAN SHOPS: CLOTHING

Hours: *Monday through Saturday from 9:30 a.m. to 7:30 p.m. nonstop (closed Monday morning)*
Credit Cards: *AE, DC, MC, V*
English Spoken.

The Luisa Spagnoli shop in the Galleria Vittorio Emanuele is well stocked and well staffed. Prices are disarmingly low. A finely made gray flannel skirt which you could wear for day or evening is only 75,000 lire.

LULU
Corso Buenos Aires 3 (tel. 204-6074)
Metro Stop: *Porta Venezia*
Hours: *Monday through Saturday from 9:30 a.m. to 1:30 p.m. and 3:30 to 7:30 p.m. (closed Monday morning)*
Credit Cards: *None*

Geographically not far from the drugstore, but light-years away in style, Lulu offers tailored, low-key colored clothing at an excellent price. That's not to suggest that the clothing here is drab or dull—far from it, but it doesn't have the zing of Il Drug Store. A pleated silk crêpe skirt is an inexpensive 100,000 lire.

MARCELLO RUBINACCI
Via Sant'Andrea 10 (tel. 701-605)
Metro Stop: *San Babila*
Hours: *Monday through Saturday from 9:30 a.m. to 1:30 p.m. and 3:30 to 7 p.m. (closed Monday morning)*
Credit Cards: *AE, MC, V*
English Spoken.

This large, elegant store is your stop if you suddenly decide that you've had it with Italian goods and want something "foreign." You'll find Hermès, Chanel —even Calvin Klein—all at prices higher than in their home countries.

MARISA
Via Sant'Andrea 1 (tel. 799-225)
Metro Stop: *San Babila*
Hours: *Monday through Saturday from 9:30 a.m. to 1 p.m. and 3:30 to 7 p.m. (closed Monday morning)*
Credit Cards: *AE, DC, MC, V*
English Spoken.

An excellent knitwear shop with some excellent buys on woolens and cashmere. A cashmere sweater-dress will cost you 860,000 lire.

MICHELLE MABELLE/MILANO MONAMOUR
Via della Spiga 36 (tel. 701-309)
Metro Stop: *San Babila*

Hours: *Monday through Saturday from 9:30 a.m. to 1 p.m. and 3:30 to 7:30 p.m. (closed Monday morning)*
Credit Cards: AE
English Spoken.

Baggy, loose clothing, some of it rubberized. This is the outer edge of the Milan fashion scene. They have their own line of accessories and shoes, including a pair of black and clear vinyl flats that are certainly out of the ordinary. These cost 65,000 lire.

MILA SCHÖN
Via Monte Napoleone 2 (tel. 701-333)
Metro Stop: *San Babila*
Hours: *Monday through Saturday from 10 a.m. to 1 p.m. and 3 to 7 p.m.*
Credit Cards: AE, DC, MC, V
English Spoken.

Here is the full complement of the Mila Schön line—the shirt-dresses, long coats, and exquisitely tailored suits. The price for a Mila Schön accessory, like one of her famous cashmere shawls, is approximately 400,000 lire.

MISSONI
Via Monte Napoleone 1 (tel. 700-906)
Metro Stop: *San Babila*
Hours: *Monday through Saturday from 9:30 a.m. to 1:30 p.m. and 3:30 to 7 p.m. (closed Monday morning)*
Credit Cards: AE, DC, MC, V
English Spoken.

The Missoni shop here is smaller than you might expect, perhaps in inverse proportion to the prices, which are extremely high. Missoni sweaters start at 450,000 lire and zoom up from there. Missoni ensembles, suits, and the like are priced at 1 million and up. See also "Malls."

NAJ OLEARI
Via Brera 5–8 (tel. 800-633)
Metro Stop: *Lanza or Moscova*
Hours: *Monday through Saturday from 10 a.m. to 1:30 p.m. and 2:30 to 7 p.m. (closed Monday morning)*
Credit Cards: AE
English Spoken.

Italy's answer to Pierre Deux and Laura Ashley. The clothes for women here run to cute cotton prints: skirts, blouses, shorts, and sweaters in the pale greens, yellows, and pinks that seem to be the house colors of these stores. A blouse starts at 79,000 lire and up, skirts at 150,000 lire, with sweaters about the same.

MILAN SHOPS: CLOTHING

Michelle Mabelle/Milano Monamour: If you've got the guts, they've got the clothes

PIROVANO
Via Monte Napoleone 1 (tel. 702-473)
Metro Stop: *San Babila*
Hours: *Monday through Saturday from 9:30 a.m. to 1:30 p.m. and 3:30 to 7 p.m. (closed Monday morning)*
Credit Cards: AE
English Spoken.

This is one of the best-known names among old Milanese society. Here you are likely to encounter a contessa buying something to wear to an opening night at LaScala. She will be paying upward of 800,000 lire for her gown.

REALE
Corso Buenos Aires 30 (tel. 276-657)
Metro Stop: *Porta Venezia*
Hours: *Monday through Saturday from 9:30 a.m. to 1:30 p.m. and 3:30 to 7:30 p.m. (closed Monday morning)*
Credit Cards: AE
English Spoken.

A good shop for every member of the family, but a particularly good place for women's casual wear. A lovely linen skirt for summer, front buttoned and tapered at the waist, is 150,000 lire.

SALVATORE FERRAGAMO
Via Monte Napoleone 3 *(tel. 700-054)*
Metro Stop: *San Babila*
Hours: *Monday through Saturday from 10 a.m. to 7 p.m. nonstop (closed Monday morning)*
Credit Cards: *AE, MC, V*
English Spoken.

Ferragamo is in much the same boat as Beltrami. While it's best known for shoes and leather goods, there is now a whole range of women's clothing available at this Milan store. Like the shoes that made Ferragamo famous, the clothing is of excellent quality and high priced.

SHIT SHOP
Galleria San Carlo, off Corso Vittorio Emanuele *(no phone)*
Metro Stop: *Duomo*
Hours: *Monday through Saturday from 9:30 a.m. to 1:30 p.m. and 3:30 to 7 p.m. (closed Monday morning)*
Credit Cards: *None*

If you'd rather be Joan Jett than Princess Di, your favorite color is black, and your hobby is frequenting rock clubs that the normal people haven't discovered —and ruined—yet, then the Shit Shop is for you. The clothes here are almost uniformly black, studded, and zipped. A pair of Levi 501s dyed black is 62,000 lire. A vinyl jacket with studs and zips is 94,000 lire.

SPIGA 31
Via della Spiga 31 *(tel. 793-502)*
Metro Stop: *San Babila*
Hours: *Monday through Saturday from 10 a.m. to 1:30 p.m. and 3:30 to 7 p.m. (closed Monday morning)*
Credit Cards: *AE, DC, MC, V*
English Spoken.

Here you'll find evening wear that is different and flamboyant but still manages to be elegant. An evening dress in silk, ribbed with gold lamé, is 1.2 million lire.

STEFANEL
Corso Vittorio Emanuele II 28 *(tel. 780-721)*
Metro Stop: *Duomo*
Hours: *Monday through Saturday from 10 a.m. to 7 p.m. nonstop (closed Monday morning)*
Credit Cards: *AE*
English Spoken.

This is the big competition to Benetton. Sometimes it's hard to tell them apart. Stefanel sells good-quality knitwear at reasonable prices. A pair of brightly colored, well-made gloves will cost only 11,900 lire, and a heavy cable-knit sweater, 59,900 lire.

MILAN SHOPS: CLOTHING

They (not I) chose the name; it's in the Galleria San Carlo

Spiga 31's fashions are avant-garde
—but still chic

SURPLUS
Corso Garibaldi 7 (tel. 803-696)
Metro Stop: Moscova or Lanza
Hours: Monday through Saturday from 10 a.m. to 1:30 p.m. and 3:30 to 7:30 p.m. (closed Monday morning)
Credit Cards: None

This is the best secondhand-clothing shop in Milan. Of course, in any shop of this nature stocks and supplies vary, but the clothes are always interesting and the condition generally excellent. Prices are low.

TAUPER
Corso Buenos Aires 24 (tel. 209-590)
Metro Stop: Porta Venezia
Hours: Monday through Saturday from 10 a.m. to 1:30 p.m. and 3:30 to 7:30 p.m. (closed Monday morning)
Credit Cards: AE
English Spoken.

This small shop specializes in the women's wear aimed at the outer limits of the avant-garde. Designs are extravagant, flamboyant, and decidedly different. Not to everyone's taste, or pocketbook. A geometric, oversize jacket with sharp shoulders and thin lapels in silk and cotton is 300,000 lire.

TOP SPORT
Via Panfilo Castaldi 29 (tel. 279-653)
Metro Stop: Porta Venezia
Hours: Monday through Saturday from 9:30 a.m. to 1:30 p.m. and 3:30 to 7 p.m. (closed Monday morning)
Credit Cards: None

A good shop for women's sports wear. Once again the major names predominate. A tennis dress and top by Ellesse costs 175,000 lire.

UNGARO
Via Monte Napoleone 27 (tel. 784-256)
Metro Stop: San Babila
Hours: Monday through Saturday from 10 a.m. to 1 p.m. and 3:30 to 7 p.m. (closed Monday morning)
Credit Cards: AE, DC, MC, V
English Spoken.

The Ungaro merchandise available at this chic, elegant shop varies considerably from the Ungaro in Rome and the Ungaro sellers in Venice and Florence. One thing all the shops have in common is the high price. At this shop a simple double-breasted four-pocket jacket in pink wool with a matching gray silk blouse will cost 1.8 million lire.

URRAH
Via Solferino 3 (tel. 864-385)
Metro Stop: *Lanza or Moscova*
Hours: *Monday through Saturday from 9:30 a.m. to 1:30 p.m. and 3 to 7 p.m. (closed Monday morning)*
Credit Cards: *AE*
English Spoken.

Good-quality, well-designed no-name fashions. Styles are on the casual side with an eye for new trends in up and coming Milanese fashion. Prices are reasonable.

VALENTINO
Via Santo Spirito 3 (tel. 706-478)
Metro Stop: *San Babila*
Hours: *Monday through Saturday from 10 a.m. to 1:30 p.m. and 3:30 to 7 p.m. (closed Monday morning)*
Credit Cards: *AE*
English Spoken.

If there is one name that sums up the entire Italian fashion industry, it must be Valentino—honored by the Metropolitan Museum of Art in New York and hailed around the world as the foremost Italian designer of the age. It's always something of a shock to realize that Valentino's creations are for sale—they're for anybody who can afford them. That might narrow the field a bit, but remember, you can always save up—something you can't do for a Michelangelo. Admittedly, you might have to save a while. A silk evening dress at Valentino, something suitable for meeting royalty, is likely to cost in the region of 7 million lire.

DEPARTMENT STORES

LA RINASCENTE
Piazza del Duomo (tel. 88-521)
Metro Stop: *Duomo*
Hours: *Monday through Saturday from 9:30 a.m. to 7:30 p.m. nonstop (closed Monday morning)*
Credit Cards: *AE, DC, MC, V*
English Spoken.

La Rinascente in Milan, the first and largest of this nationwide chain, is a department store with a history. Founded in the late 1800s and christened La Rinascente by the flamboyant Italian poet Gabriele D'Annunzio, the shop is now a Milan institution. The store has burned down and been leveled by bombs, but demand for La Rinascente in Milan was such that each time disaster struck, the owners cleared away the rubble and began building again.

The present building consists of six floors of Italian goods—clothing for men, women, and children, jewelry, accessories, housewares, toys, linens, luggage, and leather. The store offers services that are common in the United States but still quite rare in Italy: deliveries to your hotel, an easy returns policy (returns must be made within one week of purchase), and payment in dollars if you run out of lire.

La Rinascente's prices are reasonable but not bargain basement. The house design label "Elle Erre" (L.R.) is a good-quality line, particularly in women's woolens and knits. A three-quarter-length wool overcoat costs 275,000 lire and will keep out the most biting Milan cold. A cardigan in pure wool is just 65,000 lire. Summer fashions are good-value-for-the-money as well. An Elle Erre skirt in cool linen is 85,000 lire.

Menswear is a bargain here also. A pair of black cords is 79,500 lire, a three-piece suit in cotton is 375,000 lire, and pure-wool socks are just 12,000 lire a pair.

Other departments that are particularly good are stockings and ladies' hosiery (the selection is vast and the prices low: 4,500 lire for basic black stockings), handbags and purses, toys, sportswear, and perfumes.

La Rinascente boasts what must be the only department-store restaurant with a stupendous view. Situated on the sixth floor of the building, the restaurant brings you to eye level with the upper reaches of the Duomo, just across the street. Shoppers with an interest in Gothic architecture should stop in for a cappuccino and a good look at the cathedral.

DISCOUNT SHOPPING

Virtually every big Italian designer—even Valentino—consigns the previous season's clothing to discount houses. The trick is finding them—they don't advertise, they don't front onto a street (they're usually in a courtyard or *vicolo*, a cross between a side street and an alley), and they don't put out signs. However, even if they did, the chances that a casual visitor to Milan would find them are slim. Most discounters, or *blocchisti*, as they are called in Italian, are far from the tourist routes, usually in the more anonymous parts of the city—that's why they were not included in the "shopping strolls" chapter. Despite all this, you should not get the idea that the *blocchisti* are clandestine set-ups operating without the designer's knowledge or approval. The grand names and the lowly discounters work closely together (although a big name or two has been known to deny it); however, the names do tend to impose rules on the *blocchisti*. For example, more often than not the clothing is sold without the designer label. This shouldn't put you off these places though, as the garments are of the same quality as the ones sold in the Montenapo. If you have an eye for fashion, you'll be able to tell the Valentinos from the Armanis.

Supplies to the various discount houses are erratic. Therefore it's a little difficult to forecast exactly which *blocchisto* is going to have which designer's

MILAN SHOPS: DISCOUNT SHOPPING

goods available. All that can be said is that the names available are the most fashionable in Italian clothing for men and women. I can name some names with certainty. Clothes by Valentino, Ferré, Fendi, Krizia Poi, Gianni Versace, Giorgio Armani, and Mila Schön have been spotted in the discount shops on a fairly regular basis. Because supply is a problem, the best way to find what you are looking for is to browse these stores fortnightly or even weekly. Unfortunately, if you are pressed for time you won't have that option—all you can do is hope they have what you're looking for.

Of course, the best reason to shop the *blocchisti* is for the amazing discounts they offer. They range from a minimum of 40% to a high of about 75%. A Gianfranco Ferré wool suit, for example, which once sold for 2 million lire on Via della Spiga, might go for as little as 500,000 lire at a discount house.

Finally, if you are visiting all four cities covered in this book, you should know that discount houses are peculiar to Milan. Florence and Rome have one each. There are none in Venice.

In every shop mentioned below, credit cards are not accepted. English is not spoken, and merchandise cannot be returned.

FALZONE
Via de Amicis 51 (no phone)
Metro Stop: None near
Hours: Monday through Saturday from 3:30 to 7:30 p.m. (closed every morning of the week)

Falzone is said to have the finest prices on cashmere goods in Italy. Prices for a ladies' sweater range from 90,000 lire. There is some clothing for men, but the bulk of the stock is given over to women's wear.

FRATELLI RECCHIA
Via della Forze Armate 11 (no phone)
Metro Stop: Bande Nere
Hours: Monday through Saturday from 9:30 a.m. to 1:30 p.m. and 3:30 to 7:30 p.m. (closed Monday morning)

This is another good source of cashmere and woolens. The clothes here tend to be more on the casual side than elsewhere. The prices, of course, are very good. A lady's angora sweater costs about 49,000 lire.

IL SALVAGENTE
Via Fratelli Bronzetti 16 (no phone)
Hours: Monday through Saturday from 9:30 a.m. to 1:30 p.m. and 3:30 to 7:30 p.m. (closed Monday morning)

This is the best-known discounter in Milan—selections for men and women are large, but because of Salvagente's fame this vast store is more likely to be crowded and/or picked-over than the others mentioned here. This is not to suggest that you shouldn't take a look. Prices are very low and some of the clothes still carry the designer label.

LEUCE
Via B. Panizza 6 (no phone)
Metro Stop: Cadorna
Hours: Monday through Saturday from 3:30 to 7:30 p.m. (closed every morning of the week.)

A huge selection of clothes for both men and women. Here you'll find just about everything from casuals to evening dress. A suede skirt was priced at 220,000 lire.

MODASTOCK
Viale Premuda 2 (no phone)
Hours: Monday through Saturday from 10 a.m. to 1 p.m. and 3 to 7 p.m. (closed Monday morning)

A good selection of clothes for men and women. Prices begin at 60,000 lire for a cotton blouse.

MONITOR
Viale Monte Nero 78 (no phone)
Hours: Monday through Saturday from 9:30 a.m. to 1:30 p.m. and 3:30 to 7:30 p.m. (closed Monday morning)

Women's clothing only. Silk is a specialty here. Silk blouses cost from 40,000 lire to 100,000 lire. Dresses start at 175,000 lire.

FABRICS AND TEXTILES

GALTRUCCO
Piazza del Duomo 2 (tel. 861-674)
Metro Stop: Duomo
Hours: Monday through Saturday from 9:30 a.m. to 1 p.m. and 3 to 7 p.m. (closed Monday morning)
Credit Cards: AE
English Spoken.

Galtrucco has branched out into fashions for men and women, but fabrics remain the cornerstone of the Galtrucco reputation. At this store, right next to La Rinascente, you'll find bolts of cotton, wool, and linen in dozens of patterns and weights. There are fabrics for upholstery and home furnishings as well as for clothing. However, the fabric Galtrucco is famous for is silk, and this particular store is one of the best sources of silk in Italy. Silk chiffon is 50,000 lire to 85,000 lire a meter; raw silk in a beautiful deep indigo is 87,000 lire a meter; delicate silk brocades are 80,000 lire to 100,000 lire a meter.

T&J VESTOR
Via Manzoni 38 (tel. 709-530)
Metro Stop: *San Babila*
Hours: *Monday through Saturday from 9:30 a.m. to 1 p.m. and 3:30 to 7 p.m. (closed Monday morning)*
English Spoken.
   and
Corso Buenos Aires 52 (tel. 273-492)
Metro Stop: *Porta Venezia*
Hours: *Monday through Saturday from 9:30 a.m. to 1 p.m. and 3:30 to 7 p.m. (closed Monday morning)*
Credit Cards: AE, DC, MC, V

The Italian fabric chain, T&J Vestor, markets its own make fabrics and sells a large selection of Missoni-designed textiles. A meter of Missoni wool in the famous multicolored zigzag pattern is 95,000 lire.

FOOD

CANDY, CONFECTIONERY, CHOCOLATE, AND PASTRIES

The Italian sweet tooth is incurable and insatiable. A single sweet shop, usually the extension of a café, is likely to sell dozens of varieties of candies, pastries, chocolates, and ice cream. Most *pasticcerie* are open throughout the day (although pickings can get a little slim toward early evening) and on Sunday mornings when Italians buy pastries and sweets to accompany their large Sunday lunches. If there's a bar attached to a pastry shop you can satisfy your own sweet tooth standing at the counter or at a table. Any kind of confectioner will wrap up your purchase (often quite elaborately—pastries and other sweets are frequently given as gifts) and you can sneak it back to your hotel room to feast in quiet and comfort.

CAFFÈ ALEGMENA
Via Manzoni, at the corner of Via Giardino (no phone)
Metro Stop: *San Babila*
Hours: *Daily from 8 a.m. to 8 p.m.*
Credit Cards: None
   and
Galleria Vittorio Emanuele (no phone)

Metro Stop: *Duomo*
Hours: *Daily from 8 a.m. to 8 p.m.*
Credit Cards: *None*

There are several of these big, bustling café/pastry shops in Milan, but the two listed here are near the shopping trails. Each has a dining area (the one on Via Manzoni is more elegant) and pastry and sweet counters that seem to stretch for 100 yards. Try the creamy napoleone, the butter-smooth chocolate cake, or marzipan in every shape and variety (cakes, candies, pastries); cookies are in plentiful supply also. There are chocolate-dipped butter cookies, nut-flavored bruti ma buoni (it means "ugly but good"), macaroons, and biscotti made with pignoli nuts.

COVA
Via Monte Napoleone 8 (tel. 700-578 or 793-187)
Metro Stop: *San Babila*
Hours: *Monday through Saturday from 8 a.m. to 7 p.m.*
Credit Cards: *None*

This is a very upmarket café and confectionery right in the heart of Milan's most exclusive neighborhood. There is a good selection of *biscotti* and other baked goods, but chocolate is the real specialty here. Cherries covered in rich dark chocolate can be purchased loose, by the *etto* (100 grams, about 3½ ounces), or in ornate gift boxes in which the candies are set like jewels. An *etto* is 6,500 lire; a gift box is 25,000 lire. Other chocolate goodies are the Cova truffles, candies with a hazel-nut center, and chocolate-dipped apricots, mandarins, and plums.

TAVEGGIA
Via Visconti di Modrone 2 (tel. 791-257)
Metro Stop: *Duomo or San Babila*
Hours: *Monday through Saturday from 8 a.m. to 7 p.m. nonstop (closed Monday afternoon)*
Credit Cards: *None*

One of the best pastry shops in Milan. The millefoglie are as light as air and have chocolate or cream fillings. If you happen to be in Milan at Christmastime, try some of Taveggia's traditional Milanese sweet bread, panetone. Shaped like a chef's hat, they are packed with pieces of fruit, nuts, and raisins. In March, around carnival time, look for bigne di San Giuseppe, a big, sweet creampuff eaten, for some reason lost to time, in honor of Saint Joseph.

CHEESE, TRUFFLES, AND SPECIALTY FOODS

An ordinary Italian grocery store can be a gold mine for American gastronomes —and the luxury food shops are even more magnificent. There are several generic names for food shops, all more or less interchangeable. The corner grocery and the highest-priced specialty store might both be called *alimentari, salumeria,* or *gastronomia.*

CASA DEL FORMAGGIO
Via Speronari 3 (tel. 800-858)
Metro Stop: *Cordusio or Duomo*
Hours: *Monday through Saturday from 9 a.m. to 1 p.m. and 2:30 to 7 p.m. (closed Monday afternoon)*
Credit Cards: *None*

This is the largest cheese shop in the city, with cheeses too numerous to count. The long counter is always crowded with Milanese buying delicious bel paese, ricotta that's fresh or baked in a little paper envelope, parmesans not just from Parma but from all over the parmesan-producing province of Emilia, and the very strong gorgonzola that comes neat or mixed with an Italian cream cheese called mascarpone. The mozzarella di bufalo ranges from grape-size nuggets called *ovalini* up to round cheeses the size of a man's fist. Provolone is available in a number of varieties: *dolce* (sweet) and spicy, and for those who really like cheese to have a *piccante* kick to it, there is provolone shot through with bits of Italian hot pepper.

GASTRONOMIA PECK
Via Spadari 9 (tel. 871-737)
Metro Stop: *Duomo or Cordusio*
Hours: *Monday through Saturday from 9 a.m. to 1 p.m. and 3:30 to 7 p.m. (closed Monday afternoon)*
Credit Cards: *None*

This famous old food shop is in the same neighborhood as the Casa del Formaggio. It has a vast assortment of hams and other cold cuts, with particularly good prosciutto, as well as a number of prepared items like seafood salads, lobster tails, veal tonné, and roasted game (quail, pheasant, and guinea fowl). The selection of olive oils ranges from the mass-produced Bertoli and Monini, which can be purchased in giant two-liter cans (25,000 lire) to select extra-vergine olive oils which come from small producers in Tuscany. These are often bottled like rare wines and production is limited. A bottle of Ligostro, a representative brand, is 30,000 lire for a liter.

IL SALUMAIO DI MONTE NAPOLEONE
Via Monte Napoleone 12 (tel. 701-123)
Metro Stop: *San Babila*
Hours: *Monday through Saturday from 9:30 a.m. to 7 p.m. nonstop (closed Monday afternoon)*
Credit Cards: *None*

A lavish food extravaganza, Il Salumaio displays food the way the designers on Via Monte Napoleone show off their *alta moda* fashions. On one side of this always-crowded shop is a counter displaying cheeses and cold cuts. Facing it is the prepared-food counter where they sell everything from a lowly stuffed pepper to more exotic offerings like a wild boar and olive salad at 70,000 lire a kilo. Il Salumaio is also famous for its truffles. A truffle of a few grams, about the size of a garlic bulb, is priced at 180,000 lire. The traffic-stopping truffles which weigh a kilo or more, and always occupy a prominent place in the shop window, cost a whopping 1.9 million lire.

ICE CREAM

The number of neighborhood *gelaterias* in any Italian town is large, and in a city the size of Milan they are beyond counting. Any of the confectioners mentioned above sell luscious ice cream in a variety of flavors. However, there are two ice cream parlors that should be mentioned by name.

GRASSO
Viale Andrea Doria 17 (no phone)
Metro Stop: *Stazione Centrale*
Hours: *Tuesday through Sunday from 10 a.m. to midnight nonstop*
Credit Cards: *None*

This is a *gelateria* dating back to the 1920s. It has exceptional ice cream, made on the premises—the chocolate and strawberry are particularly good. In the summertime, enjoy your ice cream treat on a large sunny terrace.

Il Salumaio di Monte Napoleone: Where the elite meet to buy meat

POZZI
Piazza le G. Cantore 4 (no phone)
Metro Stop: *Genova*
Hours: *Thursday through Tuesday from 9:30 a.m. to 1 a.m. nonstop*
Credit Cards: *None*

This place has been serving fine homemade ice cream since the turn of the century. Pistacchio, lemon, and plain old vanilla—which comes in three subtly different flavors: crema, vanilla, and French vanilla—are the standouts here. Like Grasso, Pozzi has a terrace.

FURNITURE

MEMPHIS
Via Alessandro Manzoni 46 (tel. 798-955)
Metro Stop: *San Babila*
Hours: *Monday through Saturday from 10 a.m to 1:30 p.m. and 3:30 to 7 p.m. (closed Monday morning)*
Credit Cards: *None*
English Spoken.

Love it or hate it, the furniture created by the Memphis group of designers, headed by Ettore Sottsass, is certainly an attention getter. When Memphis burst onto the international design scene in the late 1970s, some critics dismissed the irrational, crazily colored and patterned furniture as nothing more than a joke or a publicity stunt—this nonsense would be over in a matter of months. They were wrong! Memphis has proven that it's here to stay and manic Memphis furniture now graces homes in the United States from Boston to Beverly Hills.

It's certainly not to everyone's taste. In this, the showroom for the Milan-based group, you'll get a clear picture of what it's all about and you'll be able to decide if you could live with some of the items. The fabrics and plastic laminates adorning the Memphis furniture sort of harken back to the 1950s, but it's more than that—although exactly what, no one has as yet been able to say. See for yourself—you'll either get sick to your stomach or fall in love.

Either way, you won't be able to buy anything as this is a "to the trade" showroom only. You'll have to wait until you return to the United States and buy the furniture through an interior decorator.

POLTRONA FRAU
Via Alessandro Manzoni 20 (tel. 796-865)
Metro Stop: *San Babila*
Hours: *Monday through Saturday from 10 a.m. to 1 p.m. and 2:30 to 7 p.m. (closed Monday morning)*
Credit Cards: *None*
English Spoken.

Poltrona Frau has been making fine furniture since before World War I. It's hard to decide whether their 1920s styling is deliberately retro or if they just kept on doing what they did best and waited for their work to come into fashion again. Poltrona Frau does believe in quality. The furniture is almost all handmade, using the finest woods and leathers, which helps explain why the famous, bulbous Poltrona Frau armchair, while incredibly comfortable, costs 5 million lire.

FURS

CORRADO IRIONÉ
Via Santo Spirito (tel. 795-630)
Metro Stop: *San Babila*
Hours: *Monday through Saturday from 9:30 a.m. to 1 p.m. and 3:30 to 7:30 p.m.*
Credit Cards: *AE*
English Spoken.

One of the best-known furriers in Milan, Irioné was established and thriving by the early 1960s. His designs tend to keep up more with the latest trends than the older, more conservative furriers, but that's not to say that his creations are "in" one season and "out" the next. Prices begin at about 15 million lire for a short mink jacket.

FENDI
Via Sant'Andrea 16 (tel. 791-617)
Metro Stop: *San Babila*
Hours: *Monday through Saturday from 10 a.m. to 1:30 p.m. and 3:30 to 7:30 p.m. (closed Monday morning)*
Credit Cards: *AE, DC, MC, V*
English Spoken.

Furs are what made Fendi famous and they remain a mainstay of the firm despite the explosion of Fendi clothes, accessories, luggage, perfume, etc. The famous Fendi fur-lined raincoat is here at 5.8 million lire. More lavish items, of course, have larger pricetags attached.

FURS BAZAAR
Via Sant'Andrea 8 (tel. 702-452)
Metro Stop: *San Babila*
Hours: *Monday through Saturday from 9:30 a.m. to 1:30 p.m. and 3:30 to 7 p.m. (closed Monday morning)*
Credit Cards: *None*
English Spoken.

This is a wonderful store for bargains in this expensive area. Prices on second-

MILAN SHOPS: FURS

hand furs are dramatically lower than on furs purchased new from the great and grand furriers in the neighborhood. Furs Bazaar is no bargain-basement operation, however. The premises are nice, though not lavish, and the salespeople treat you as if you were buying a new fur, not a used one. The furs themselves are high quality (no ratty old pelts here!) and the prices are good. They begin at 1.5 million lire.

MELEGARI E COSTA
Via Monte Napoleone 7 A (tel. 794-785)
Metro Stop: *San Babila*
Hours: *Monday through Saturday from 10 a.m. to 1 p.m. and 3:30 to 7:30 p.m. (closed Monday morning)*
Credit Cards: AE, DC, MC, V
English Spoken.

Beautifully designed furs, sable and mink in particular, are the best-known wares of this newer fur salon. Prices on a featherweight sable jacket begin at approximately 30 million lire.

PELLEGRINI
Via Sant'Andrea 2 (tel. 701-605)
Metro Stop: *San Babila*
Hours: *Monday through Saturday from 9:30 a.m. to 1 p.m. and 3:30 to 7:30 p.m. (closed Monday morning)*
Credit Cards: *None*
English Spoken.

If you can afford furs from Melegari e Costa you are among the very lucky few

An exceptional fur house, and has been since its foundation at the turn of the century. The showroom is lavish and hushed. The simplest item sold here is likely to begin in the millions of lire.

TIVOLI
Via Santo Spirito 26 (tel. 701-490)
Metro Stop: *San Babila*
Hours: *Monday through Saturday from 10 a.m. to 1 p.m. and 3:30 to 7 p.m. (closed Monday morning)*
Credit Cards: *None*
English Spoken.

Perhaps the most expensive furrier in Milan. Carlo Tivoli's rich, luxurious furs are beyond the reach of most. Prices begin at 10 million lire.

GLASS

VENINI
Via Monte Napoleone 9 (tel. 700-539)
Metro Stop: *San Babila*
Hours: *Monday through Saturday from 9:30 a.m. to 1:30 p.m. and 3:30 to 7 p.m. (closed Monday morning)*
Credit Cards: *AE, MC, V*
English Spoken.

If you aren't going to make it to Venice this trip you can still shop for some of the finest Murano glass at Venini, the Milan branch of one of Venice's best-known names. The elegant shop is a blizzard of glass products, ranging from simple *murrine*, glass paperweights with a colored design in the center, to elaborate and multicolored lamps and chandeliers. Prices are a little higher here than they are in Venice. A blown-glass decanter with a gentle green-and-yellow swirl pattern is 300,000 lire. Perfume bottles etched with a floral design and blown so thin you think they'll break if you even look at them are 120,000 lire. The larger chandeliers can cost in the tens of millions of lire.

HATS

A number of the women's-wear shops in the Monte Napoleone district sell hats in addition to their other products, notably **Cose** (Via della Spiga 8), **Adrianamode** (Via della Spiga 22), **Krizia** (Via della Spiga 23), and **Guisy Bresciani** (Via Morone 4). Here, however, are some shops which deal primarily in millinery.

MILAN SHOPS: GLASS/HATS/HOUSEWARES

BORSALINO
Galleria Vittorio Emanuele 9 (tel. 874-244)
Metro Stop: *Duomo*
Hours: *Monday through Saturday from 9:30 a.m. to 1:30 p.m. and 3:30 to 7:30 p.m. (closed Monday morning)*
Credit Cards: *AE*

The world-famous Borsalino hats are available at this small, wood-paneled shop at the end of the galleria facing La Scala Opera House. While predominantly for men, there are some hats for women, and some for men that a woman could wear. Prices are good. A classic Borsalino snap-brim fedora is 240,000 lire, a green felt driving cap is 75,000 lire, and a scarlet trilby with a red silk hatband is 175,000 lire.

MELEGARI
Via Paolo Sarpi 19 (tel. 312-094)
Metro Stop: *Moscova*
Hours: *Monday through Saturday from 9:30 a.m. to 1:30 p.m. and 3:30 to 7 p.m. (closed Monday morning)*
Credit Cards: *None*

This milliner stocks very traditional hats for women. Much of the decoration and veil work is done by hand. A pillbox in dark-blue satin costs 145,000 lire. A simple cloche or turban costs about the same. A more extravagant creation with a floral decoration or a gossamer veil will cost 200,000 lire and up.

MUTINELLI
Corso Buenos Aires 5 (tel. 273-492)
Metro Stop: *Porta Venezia*
Hours: *Monday through Saturday from 9:30 a.m. to 1:30 p.m. and 3:30 to 7:30 p.m. (closed Monday morning)*
Credit Cards: *AE*

Mutinelli is a very old, very traditional hat shop for men and women. A panama hat for a woman costs 350,000 lire; a man's cloth driving cap in checked tweed costs 125,000 lire.

HOUSEWARES

ARFORM
Via Moscova 22 (tel. 655-4691)
Metro Stop: *Moscova*
Hours: *Monday through Saturday from 10 a.m. to 1 p.m. and 3 to 7 p.m. (closed Monday morning)*
Credit Cards: *AE, DC, MC, V*

This is a housewares shop specializing in the clean, spare Scandinavian-type designs in cutlery, kitchenware, lamps, glass, and china. A set of square-ish, chunky, informal knives, forks, and tea- and tablespoons (four of each) with a wall or table mount is 25,000 lire. A polished stainless-steel pasta pot with brass handles and built-in colander holds about three liters of water and costs 95,000 lire. A hand-operated pasta maker—the kind with the old-fashioned crank handle—is 35,500 lire.

CONTROBUFFET
Via Solferino 14 (tel. 655-4934)
Metro Stop: *Moscova or Lanza*
Hours: *Monday through Saturday from 10 a.m. to 1 p.m. and 3:30 to 7:30 p.m. (closed Monday morning)*
Credit Cards: *None*

The ecletic selection of products here is almost exclusively Italian and has some of the Memphis quirkiness about it. An end table made from black enamel stainless steel decorated in a brightly colored confetti design, with a built-in ashtray, costs 150,000 lire. There are magenta-colored clocks with ultramarine-blue hands costing 95,000 lire and equally brightly colored coffee mugs, plates, and vases.

G. PREATTONI
Via della Spiga 52 (tel. 701-059)
Metro Stop: *San Babila*
Hours: *Monday through Saturday from 9:30 a.m. to 1 p.m. and 3:30 to 7:30 P.M. (closed Monday morning)*
Credit Cards: *AE, MC, V*

This is another excellent knife shop, stocking everything from hunting to kitchen knives. It's not as large as Lorenzi nor as expensive. A mushroom knife with a ruler on one side and a blade and a brush for cleaning at either end costs just 24,000 lire. (*Note:* While the address is Via della Spiga, the entrance is actually on Via Alessandro Manzoni.)

LORENZI
Via Monte Napoleone 9 (tel. 790-593)
Metro Stop: *San Babila*
Hours: *Monday through Saturday from 9 a.m. to 12:30 p.m. and 3 to 7:30 p.m. (closed Monday morning)*
Credit Cards: *AE, DC, V*
English Spoken.

Lorenzi has been a Milan institution since the late 1920s. Gourmets and those who love to cook will find a marvelous array of items for cooking and eating. Lorenzi's knives are almost works of art. A highly polished bread knife with a

MILAN SHOPS: HOUSEWARES

beautiful teak handle that fits one's hand perfectly costs 90,000 lire. A simple double-bladed jackknife covered in leather is 45,000 lire. Steak knives with bone handles cost 250,000 lire for a set of six. An oyster knife with a slip-guard and a perfectly shaped lip costs 75,000 lire. A chain mail glove to hold the mollusc while you pry it open is 200,000 lire. A nutcracker with a horn handle costs 90,000 lire.

PIERO FORNASETTI
Via Brera 16 (tel. 805-0321)
Metro Stop: *Duomo or Moscova*
Hours: *Monday through Saturday from 10:30 a.m. to 1 p.m. and 3:30 to 7 p.m. (closed Monday morning)*
Credit Cards: *None*

This is a one-man design workshop a few hundred yards from the Brera Museum. It's hard to get into this small shop, so cluttered is it with Signor Fornasetti's eccentric swinging-'60s type furniture, trompe l'oeil wallpapers, and fabrics. He borrows freely from the past. Opera enthusiasts will love the mugs, ashtrays, and pencil boxes decorated with copies of original posters advertising the opening nights of famous operas at La Scala. A china ashtray with the *La Bohème* poster is 40,000 lire.

Since the twenties Lorenzi has been supplying the needs of gourmets and gourmands

RAIMONDI
Via Monte Napoleone 2 (tel. 700-682)
Metro Stop: San Babila
Hours: Monday through Saturday from 10 a.m. to 1 p.m. and 3 to 7 p.m. (closed Monday morning)
Credit Cards: AE, DC, V
English Spoken.

Raimondi is a very large store selling all kinds of kitchen gadgets, patio furniture, and designer housewares. An espresso maker, in copper and stainless steel and converted to U.S. current, by Gaggia, costs 300,000 lire. More complicated models with a steamer attachment for heating milk for cappuccino and two coffee spigots are 750,000 lire. There are some newly introduced Krizia-designed china and cookware. A heavy casserole dish with a lid is 180,000 lire. If you don't mind having things shipped (the store will arrange shipping) there are some extremely nice pieces of outdoor furniture. A beautiful *basilica*, the square wood-and-canvas umbrellas that shade market stalls all over Italy (and honored by inclusion in the New York Museum of Modern Art's design collection) costs 850,000 lire.

A Pavoni espresso machine at Raimondi, the finest housewares shop in Milan

JEWELRY

ANTIQUE

CROMO
Via Anfiteatro, at the corner of Corso Garibaldi (tel. 862-578)
Metro Stop: *Moscova or Lanza*
Hours: *Monday through Saturday from 10 a.m. to 1 p.m. and 3:30 to 7 p.m. (closed Monday morning)*
Credit Cards: *None*
English Spoken.

The jewelry in this small shop dates back only to the last century and very little of it showcases gemstones, but Cromo is definitely worth a visit, particularly if you have a taste for quality art nouveau, art deco, and 1940s broaches, bracelets, and necklaces. There is also a lot of costume jewelry from the '50s and '60s. Prices are reasonable.

COSTUME

ANGELA CAPUTI
Via Madonnina 11 (tel. 807-348)
Metro Stop: *Lanza or Moscova*
Hours: *Monday through Saturday from 10 a.m. to 1 p.m. and 3:30 to 7:30 p.m. (closed Monday morning)*
Credit Cards: *AE, DC, MC, V*
English Spoken.

Costume jewelry is the specialty of this Florentine designer. In this delightful little shop in the Brera district you'll find all of the Angela Caputi chunky, geometrical, brightly colored plastic and rhinestone jewelry. A choker of braided strands of red, blue, and yellow beads with a rhinestone center costs 150,000 lire. A Caputi watch with a white face and a black case with a bright-red tied strap is 130,000 lire. Rhinestone-studded gloves in black suede are 140,000 lire.

LA PORTA BLU
Largo Augusto 3, at the corner of Via Cavallotti (tel. 700-407)
Metro Stop: *Duomo*
Hours: *Monday through Saturday from 9:30 a.m. to 1 p.m. and 2:30 to 7:30 p.m. (closed Monday morning)*
Credit Cards: *None*

A small shop near the Duomo, La Porta Blu stocks a large and very inexpensive collection of zircon and rhinestone rings and broaches, as well as dozens of different types of barettes and combs. A large simulated tortoise-shell comb with rhinestone accents cost 20,000 lire. One with less decoration can cost as little as 10,000 lire or they can be as expensive as 60,000 lire. A black velvet bow with silver sparkles is 15,000 lire. A gold lamé bow costs the same.

PRECIOUS

Milan has a number of very expensive, exclusive jewelers, centered, as you might expect, in the Monte Napoleone area. All these houses are world class in terms of quality and cost: prices ascend effortlessly into the hundreds of millions of lire. Few encourage casual browsing and often you must be dressed for the part just to get in the door.

CALDERONI
Via Monte Napoleone 8 (tel. 701-293)
Metro Stop: San Babila
Hours: Monday through Saturday from 10 a.m. to 1:30 p.m. and 3 to 7:30 p.m. (closed Monday morning)
Credit Cards: AE
English Spoken.

A very old jewelry house, Calderoni does fine work in silver and gold. A necklace with 80 small diamonds carrying a huge diamond pendant is beyond price—they weren't saying.

CUSI
Via Monte Napoleone 21A (tel. 791-977)
Metro Stop: San Babila
Hours: Monday through Saturday from 9:30 a.m. to 1:30 p.m. and 3:30 to 7 p.m. (closed Monday morning)
Credit Cards: None
English Spoken.

Like Calderoni, Cusi is another long-established Milanese jeweler. Diamonds and goldwork are the specialties here. A ring with two small diamonds flanking a large one, a total of approximately five karats, in a very simple setting is 40 million lire. Cusi also sells watches by Blancpain and Gerald Genta.

DAL VECCHIO
Via Monte Napoleone 29 (tel. 708-740)
Metro Stop: San Babila
Hours: Monday through Saturday from 9:30 a.m. to 1:30 p.m. and 3:30 to 7:30 p.m. (closed Monday morning)
Credit Cards: AE
English Spoken.

A smaller shop than the others listed so far, Dal Vecchio has a lovely selection of jewelry from its own workshops. Design tends toward the traditional, with goldwork predominating. A small emerald in a diamond setting is 75 million lire.

FARAONE
Via Monte Napoleone 7A (tel. 545-6256)
Metro Stop: *San Babila*
Hours: *Monday through Saturday from 10 a.m. to 1 p.m. and 3 to 7 p.m. (closed Monday morning)*
Credit Cards: AE
English Spoken.

Faraone is one of the most interesting sources of fine gemstone jewelry in the city. Far less traditional than the other houses in the neighborhood, Faraone has gone outside of its own design atelier and hired designers from among the more progressive Italian design groups. Bepe Modenese has designed a decidedly different set of broaches in crystal and gold using colors and shapes based on the human eye. This sort of thing, characteristic of Faraone's daring, but still elegant, approach to high-fashion jewelry, is definitely not for everyone, but those who have a taste for objects that are graceful but unusual need look no further. Prices at Faraone are high. The piece described above is 1.2 million lire.

GUCCI
Via Monte Napoleone 5 (tel. 545-6621)
Metro Stop: *San Babila*
Hours: *Monday through Saturday from 10 a.m. to 7 p.m. nonstop (closed Monday morning)*
Credit Cards: AE DC, MC, V
English Spoken.

One of the Gucci daughters has introduced a line of jewelry more expensive than the more informal typical Gucci jewelry. The results are modern, striking, and don't have a GG in sight. A gold choker with a zigzag line of diamonds at the throat is 6.5 million lire. A matching bracelet is 4.5 million lire. The "ordinary" Gucci jewelry is also available at this location. A Gucci watch with the famous Gs and bridle costs 850,000 lire, although there are more expensive models costing in the millions.

MARIO BUCCELLATI
Via Monte Napoleone 4 (tel. 702-153)
Metro Stop: *San Babila*
Hours: *Monday through Saturday from 10 a.m. to 1 p.m. and 3 to 7 p.m. (closed Monday morning)*
Credit Cards: AE
English Spoken.

Buccellati is famous for his silver work, particularly for figures of animals cast in sterling. Prices on these vary according to the size and the complexity of design, but a small figure of a bird or cat is 1.5 million lire. Of course, Buccellati has some beautiful gemstone jewelry as well. An exceptional white-gold bracelet, so finely worked it looks like lace, studded with tiny diamonds and set with half a dozen larger ones, costs 175 million lire. A large, rectangular aquamarine ring, also set in white gold, is 85 million lire.

MARTIGNETTI
Via Monte Napoleone 10 (tel. 798-113)
Metro Stop: *San Babila*
Hours: *Monday through Saturday from 9:30 a.m. to 1:30 p.m. and 3:30 to 7:30 p.m. (closed Monday morning)*
Credit Cards: AE
English Spoken.

This is the largest jeweler on Via Monte Napoleone. While there is a large selection of just about every kind of gem and setting, the specialties here are pearls, lapis lazuli, coral, and jade. A long, three-strand coral necklace in deep crimson costs 1.95 million lire. A lapis ring in a gold setting is 2 million lire. Pearls, depending on size, can vary between 1.35 million lire (for a very small, set pearl) and the sky's the limit.

MERU
Via Solferino 3 (tel. 871-595)
Metro Stop: *Lanza or Moscova*
Hours: *Monday through Saturday from 10 a.m. to 1 p.m. and 3 to 7 p.m. (closed Monday morning)*
Credit Cards: None

We are back in the Brera area now, and a world away from the formal jewelers of that district. Meru deals exclusively in semiprecious stones like tiger's eye, amethyst, rose quartz, turquoise, amber, coral, and the like. Settings of the offbeat designs at this casual shop can be in gold, but more frequently in enamels, even leather. Most of the styles seem to have been inspired by primitive art, particularly from Oceania and Africa. A heavy necklace in rough coral, leather, and enamel is 450,000 lire. The "micro-jewelry," very small pieces of enamel assembled into a large piece like a necklace or bracelet, range from 150,000 lire to 600,000 lire. The work done here is of a very high standard and the shop does invite you to browse. Isabelle Rossellini and Natassia Kinski are said to have bought Meru pieces.

POMELLATO
Via San Pietro all'Orto 17, at the corner of Corso Matteotti (tel. 706-068)
Metro Stop: *Duomo*
Hours: *Monday through Saturday from 9:30 a.m. to 1 p.m. and*

3 to 7 p.m. (closed Monday morning)
Credit Cards: AE, MC, V
English Spoken.

With extravagant designs in a "post modern" style, Pomellato is more than just a jeweler. In addition to modern gold and silver work there is an exceptional selection of out-of-the-ordinary luxury items. In the jewelry department, however, an asymetrical diamond ring in a gold setting (the stone is about half of a karat) is 3.5 million lire. The gift items, though, are really interesting, and are as finely made as any piece of jewelry. The Pomellato game box, in heavy black Chinese lacquer, containing a beautiful chess set and board, decks of cards, and poker chips, all stored in small drawers, costs 1.2 million lire.

LACE

JESURUM
Via Monte Napoleone 14 (tel. 799-965)
Metro Stop: San Babila
Hours: Monday through Saturday from 9:30 a.m. to 1:30 p.m. and
  3:30 to 7:30 p.m. (closed Monday morning)
Credit Cards: AE, DC, MC, V
English Spoken.

One of the oldest and best-known names in Venetian lace, the Jesurum in Milan is no more expensive than the Venice flagship store. Although smaller than the head office, this shop on Via Monte Napoleone has a full selection of Jesurum handmade lace and embroidered linens, as well as the Jesurum line of swimwear. A simple lace doily costs 55,000 lire. A tablecloth for a fairly large round table costs 1.4 million lire—but the workmanship is exquisite. A one-piece Jesurum bathing suit, too nice to actually swim in, runs 200,000 lire.

LEATHER GOODS

It seems that every other shop in Milan—in Italy—is a dealer in fine leather goods. Italy's reputation as the leather capital of the world has been a fact of fashion for decades now and there is hardly a designer who doesn't have leather products to complement the clothing line. Some, like Ferragamo and Beltrami, started out in leather and diversified into clothes. Others, like Armani and Versace, went the other way, coming up with leather fashions after they had established names in the clothing field.

There is also a great deal of crossover in the types of merchandise offered. A single shop might sell shoes, luggage, handbags, and leather clothing. Because of this, leather goods are grouped under a single heading. Specialties and the particular range of items stocked in a store are, of course, pointed out in the text.

ALEXANDER NICOLETTE
Via Monte Napoleone 19 (tel. 701-886)
Metro Stop: *San Babila*
Hours: *Monday through Saturday from 10 a.m. to 1 p.m. and 3:30 to 7 p.m. (closed Monday morning)*
Credit Cards: *AE, DC, MC, V*
English Spoken.

Back to the "unreal" world on Via Monte Napoleone. Alexander Nicolette is an elegant, refined, expensive shop where a pair of knee-high shearling-lined boots for a woman costs 430,000 lire. The men's shop is right next door. Black wingtips are 280,000 lire.

ALFONSO GARLANDO
Via Madonnina 2 (tel. 874-665)
Metro Stop: *Lanza or Moscova*
Hours: *Monday through Saturday from 10 a.m. to 7:30 p.m. non-stop (closed Monday morning)*
Credit Cards: *AE, DC, MC, V*

For once we start off with bargains. Alfonso Garlando occupies two large whitewashed rooms—no attempt at classy decoration here—with a huge supply of extremely inexpensive shoes set out on the floor or just stacked in boxes on top of one another. Every style and color imaginable is available, and the shoes seem to be orphans, seconds, and no-names. If they were once famous-designer products, the labels have been removed. The fact that the shop accepts so many credit cards and keeps such convenient hours suggests that this is not a *blocchisto* (see "Discount Shopping") for shoes. Even if it isn't, Garlando is sure to have something you want in a price you can afford. Prices begin at 10,000 lire and don't exceed 130,000 lire.

ARMANDO POLLINI
Via della Spiga 42 (tel. 795-081)
Metro Stop: *San Babila*
Hours: *Monday through Saturday from 10 a.m. to 1 p.m. and 3 to 7:30 p.m. (closed Monday morning)*
Credit Cards: *AE, V*
English Spoken.

High fashion and prices that won't kill you are the hallmarks of this elegant, tasteful shop. Boots and shoes for women are the specialty (no men's shoes), and they come not only in leather but in a variety of fabrics as well. A pair of western-style boots à la Italiana, in black suede with a lambswool lining, cost 175,000 lire, a much lower price than you'd expect to pay back home. A pair of black velveteen flats for evening wear is 118,000 lire.

MILAN SHOPS: LEATHER GOODS

BAILA
Via della Spiga 32 (tel. 798-170)
Metro Stop: San Babila
Hours: Monday through Saturday from 10 a.m. to 1:30 p.m. and
2 to 7 p.m. (closed Monday morning)
Credit Cards: AE, DC, MC, V
English Spoken.

While the accent here is on women's clothes generally, there are some particularly interesting garments in leather. Multicolored, hand-sewn form-fitting leather jackets and skirts cost from 780,000 lire for a skirt to 1.5 million for a jacket.

BARBARA
Corso Buenos Aires 3 (tel. 200-971)
Metro Stop: Porta Venezia
Hours: Monday through Saturday from 9:30 a.m. to 1:30 p.m. and
3:30 to 7:30 p.m. (closed Monday morning)
Credit Cards: AE, MC, V

Barbara is a large shop which sells handbags and luggage only. A large black hard-vinyl suitcase with leather trim costs 525,000 lire. A soft leather mid-size shoulder bag with a button flap in brown leather is 145,000 lire.

Exquisite footwear by Armando Pollini

BELTRAMI
Via Monte Napoleone 16 (tel. 702-975)
Metro Stop: San Babila
Hours: Monday through Saturday from 10 a.m. to 1:30 p.m. and 3:30 to 7 p.m. (closed Monday morning)
Credit Cards: AE, DC, MC, V
English Spoken.

One of the biggest names in Italian leather wear, this two-story shop in the heart of Monte Napoleone has clothing for men and women in leather, as well as shoes. Prices are extremely high, only about 10% less than you'll find at Beltrami on Fifth Avenue in New York. A pair of fur-lined, white leather boots costs 650,000 lire. Of course, the workmanship and quality of the hides couldn't be any better. If you aren't going to Florence, where Beltrami prices are generally lower (and where I have a big surprise for you), then this is the place to shop.

BOTTEGA VENETA
Via della Spiga 5 (tel. 791-651)
Metro Stop: San Babila
Hours: Monday through Saturday from 10:00 a.m. to 1 p.m. and 3 to 7 p.m. (closed Monday morning)
Credit Cards: AE, DC, MC, V
English Spoken.

A small, intimate, wood-paneled shop, this Bottega Veneta stocks leather goods—shoes, bags, briefcases—and some silk. Although the company is based in Venice, the Milan shop offers prices equal to those at the home store and *much* cheaper than in the United States. An ultramarine-violet shoulder bag with a tie mouth is 130,000 lire in a small size and 235,000 lire for the largest. The traditional Bottega Veneta dark-red leather briefcases are 450,000 lire and up. A pair of classic knee boots with a low heel is 360,000 lire.

BRUNO MAGLI
Corso Vittorio Emanuele II, at the corner of Via San Paolo (tel. 865-695)
Metro Stop: Duomo
Hours: Monday through Saturday from 9:30 a.m. to 1 p.m. and 3 to 7:30 p.m. (closed Monday morning)
Credit Cards: AE, DC, MC, V
English Spoken.

The Bruno Magli in the heart of Milan is one of the largest shops in the chain. The selection, as you might expect from a shop this size, is large. There are shoes for men and for women, and in every style from casual to dressy. Prices are a good 25% to 30% less than you'll pay in the United States. A ladies' suede flat in green, red, or black is just 50,000 lire. A pair of dark-blue leather high heels is 150,000 lire. Calf-length boots in smooth cordovan leather are 145,000 lire. A top-of-the-line knee boot costs about 450,000 lire. Men's shoes are good buys as well. A fine pair of wingtips is 280,000 lire. A pair of traditional loafers in dark brown or black is 175,000 lire.

CALZATURIFICIO DI PARABAIGO
Corso Buenos Aires 52 (tel. 271-6851)
Metro Stop: Porta Venezia
Hours: Monday through Saturday from 9:30 a.m. to 1:30 p.m. and 3:30 to 7 p.m. (closed Monday morning)
Credit Cards: AE, DC, MC, V

Parabaigo is one of the main shoe-manufacturing areas in Italy. This large shop in Milan's lower-priced neighborhood is an in-town factory outlet with shoes for men and women. Manufacturers who send their products here might be the same ones who produce shoes for the great designer lines. If they are, though, it's a secret. Prices for ladies' shoes begin at about 35,000 lire for a simple flat and don't stray far beyond 200,000 lire. Men's shoes start at 50,000 lire.

CESARE PACIOTTI
Via Sant'Andrea 8 (tel. 701-164)
Metro Stop: San Babila
Hours: Monday through Saturday from 10 a.m. to 1 p.m. and 3:30 to 7 p.m. (closed Monday morning)
Credit Cards: AE, DC, MC, V
English Spoken.

The store's small mirrored interior is encircled with black leather banquettes. The shoes, for men only, tend to be black too, most of them with thick rubber soles and unusual styling—not the kind of thing you'd wear to the office. Shoes like this range between 130,000 lire and 400,000 lire. There are some equally distinctive dress shoes. An elastic-sided loafer in blue leather, with a bulbous rubber toe, costs 560,000 lire.

COLOMBO
Via della Spiga 9 (tel. 700-184) and Via Filippo Turati 7 (tel. 659-7607)
Metro Stop: San Babila
Hours: Monday through Saturday from 10 a.m. to 7 p.m. nonstop
Credit Cards: AE, DC, MC, V
English Spoken.

Colombo is a luggage and handbag shop, selling not just leather goods but vinyl and nylon as well. Prices are not low on the beautifully made Colombo products. For example, the traditional paisley-print suitcases with leather trim are 420,000 lire for a medium-sized one and 523,000 lire for the larger model. There are toilet kits and accessory bags in leather at 250,000 lire and 350,000 lire respectively.

COPPOLA AND TOPPO
Via Alessandro Manzoni 20 (tel. 791-459)
Metro Stop: San Babila
Hours: Monday through Saturday from 9:30 a.m. to 1 p.m. and 3:30 to 7 p.m. (closed Monday morning)
Credit Cards: AE, MC
English Spoken.

A name that is becoming better and better known in Italy. This small shop on Via Alessandro Manzoni has shoes for men and women, as well as women's skirts, pants, and jackets. A pair of butter-smooth black leather pants, lined with silk, is 950,000 lire. Black leather boots to match are 325,000 lire.

DE PIETRI
Via Monte Napoleone 4 (tel. 793-421)
Metro Stop: San Babila
Hours: Monday through Saturday from 9:30 a.m. to 1 p.m. and 3:30 to 7:30 p.m. (closed Monday morning)
Credit Cards: AE, DC, MC, V
English Spoken.

De Pietri is proof that fine shoes for women in Monte Napoleone district need not be all that expensive. There's a very large selection of the their own-name products in everything from boots to flats, and while it's possible to spend a lot of money here, a pair of blue high heels for day or evening wear costs just 89,000 lire. The craftsmanship and leather used are of very high quality.

DIANA DUE
Corso Vittorio Emanuele II 15 (tel. 795-623)
Metro Stop: Duomo
Hours: Monday through Saturday from 9:30 a.m. to 1:30 p.m. and 3:30 to 7:30 p.m. (closed Monday morning)
Credit Cards: AE, DC, MC, V
English Spoken.

A first-rate shop packed to the rafters with all kinds of leather accessories for women. Bags are the specialty though, and there is an endless, or so it seems, variety of shoulder bags, evening bags, clutches, and change purses. A small silk-lined braided-leather bag in blue or deep red is 80,000 lire. A larger version of the same is 150,000 lire.

DIEGO DELLA VALLE
Via della Spiga 22 (tel. 702-423)
Metro Stop: San Babila
Hours: Monday through Saturday from 10:00 a.m. to 1:30 p.m. and 3 to 7:30 p.m. (closed Monday morning)
Credit Cards: AE
English Spoken.

MILAN SHOPS: LEATHER GOODS

High fashion and high prices are the trademarks of the Diego della Valle, a very elegant shop which has shoes for men and women. A pair of flats in either leather or black velvet with a cameo-adorned bow cost 170,000 lire. A pair of black lace-up shoes for men, with slim leather soles and a low heel, is priced at 220,000 lire.

DI VARESE
Corso Vittorio Emanuele II 9 (tel. 708-774)
Metro Stop: *Duomo*
Hours: *Monday through Saturday from 9:30 a.m. to 1:30 p.m. and 3:30 to 7:30 p.m. (closed Monday morning)*
Credit Cards: AE, MC, V
English Spoken.

This is part of a chain that you'll find throughout Italy. The primary business of the various Di Vareses is in selling foreign shoes (Reeboks, Topsiders, Timberland) to Italians at very high prices, but there are good buys to be had here on Di Varese's own Italian shoes. A ladies' tasseled loafer is 90,000 lire; the same item for a man is 120,000 lire. There are also boots (for women only) and dress shoes.

EL VAQUERO
Via della Spiga 5 (tel. 795-694)
Metro Stop: *San Babila*
Hours: *Monday through Saturday from 10 a.m. to 1:30 p.m. and 2 to 7 p.m. (closed Monday morning)*
Credit Cards: AE, DC, MC, V
English Spoken.

El Vaquero's crazy, spangled, studded, bejeweled shoes are not for everyone, but as they're sold in a dozen shops around the world, from San Tropez to Bar Harbor, there must be plenty of interest in them. Although the shoes are manufactured in Italy the prices here seem no lower than anywhere else. A pair of relatively tame bronze lamé high heels costs 300,000 lire. A pair of boots with all the trimmings is 500,000 lire.

ENNY
Via Monte Napoleone 8 (tel. 793-349)
Metro Stop: *San Babila*
Hours: *Monday through Saturday from 9:30 a.m. to 1 p.m. and 3:30 to 7:30 p.m. (closed Monday morning)*
Credit Cards: AE
English Spoken.

Enny is a small shop, staffed by extremely pleasant people, selling a series of leather goods for women. A pair of black leather gauntlets, which would look great behind the wheel of a Rolls or on a Harley Davidson, costs 104,000 lire. A green suede shoulder bag with the brass Enny nameplate is 188,000 lire. The "nappa tevit" process of rubberized canvas is applied to Enny's roughwear bags for women. A soft shoulder bag with leather trim is strong, light, and very soft (and waterproof, of course). It costs 98,000 lire.

EVE
Via San Pietro All'Orto 9 (tel. 706-450)
Metro Stop: *Duomo*
Hours: *Monday through Saturday from 9:30 a.m. to 1:30 p.m. and 3:30 to 7 p.m. (closed Monday morning)*
Credit Cards: *AE, MC*
English Spoken.

An excellent source of handbags for women. They come in every size, shape, and color, from clutch purses in green leather (125,000 lire) to suitcases large enough to pack your entire wardrobe (700,000 lire). Smaller items—change purses, key cases, credit-card holders—are reasonably priced. A key case, for example, is 45,000 lire.

FENDI
Via della Spiga 11 (tel. 799-544)
Metro Stop: *San Babila*
Hours: *Monday through Saturday from 10 a.m. to 1 p.m. and 3 to 7 p.m. (closed Monday morning)*
Credit Cards: *AE, DC, MC, V*
English Spoken.

The entire Fendi line of leather and vinyl goods can be found in this large, elegant shop. Prices seem to be a little higher here than in the flagship store in Rome. However, if you aren't going to be in the Eternal City this time around, you can shop here knowing that prices are lower in Milan than they are in the United States. A simple Fendi key chain, with the logo, in chrome and leather is just 30,000 lire. An elegant black leather clutch is 195,000 lire; a vinyl cosmetic case, 420,000 lire.

FRANCESCA FERRARIO
Via della Spiga 20 (tel. 782-475)
Metro Stop: *San Babila*
Hours: *Monday through Saturday from 9:30 a.m. to 1 p.m. and 3:30 to 7:30 p.m. (closed Monday morning)*
Credit Cards: *AE, DC, V*
English Spoken.

This is an extremely upmarket, *alta moda* source of women's shoes and bags. Prices are very high, as befits the beautiful, traditional-with-a-difference designs and the exceptional quality of the leather and workmanship. Those seeking some of the finest Italian leather goods around would do well to look here. Prices on bags begin at about 250,000 lire (for a small, red leather clutch purse) and rise sharply from there.

FRATELLI ROSSETTI
Via Monte Napoleone 1 (tel. 791-650)
Metro Stop: *San Babila*
Hours: *Monday through Saturday from 10:00 a.m. to 1 p.m. and 3 to 7 p.m. (closed Monday morning)*
Credit Cards: AE, MC, V
English Spoken.

The street address is Via Monte Napoleone, but an easier way of finding this shop is to go to Piazza San Babila. The shop is located where the Corso Matteotti and Montenapo meet in the piazza itself. Make sure you find it because this Fratelli Rossetti shop is a first-rate source of this excellent line of shoes for men and women. The Rossetti brothers make their beautiful wares in a variety of leathers and fabrics, and the designs are always right up-to-date but with a timeless quality as well. A pair of walking shoes made out of grainy calfskin in brown or black, with a tassel, is 188,000 lire. A shoulder bag to match is 265,000 lire. A satiny-smooth pair of high heels in rose or kelly-green leather is 142,000 lire. A rubber-soled desert boot for a man in chestnut-colored leather is 270,000 lire. A lizard-skin loafer, jet black, is 490,000 lire.

GHERARDINI
Via della Spiga 9 (tel. 700-171)
Metro Stop: *San Babila*
Hours: *Monday through Saturday from 10 a.m. to 1 p.m. and 2 to 7 p.m. (closed Monday morning)*
Credit Cards: AE, MC
English Spoken.

Gherardini began in Florence as a maker of leather goods, particularly luggage, but has since branched out to include pieces in vinyl, satin, and crocodile. Prices begin low for the smaller items, but shoot up quickly when one gets to larger things like luggage. A simple key chain in chrome and leather is 24,000 lire. A money clip is 23,500 lire. Round or triangular evening bags in satin cost 230,000 lire. A cosmetic case, not much bigger than a lunch pail, made from vinyl and leather is 1.14 million lire. See also "Malls."

GIANFRANCO FERRÉ
Via della Spiga 11 (tel. 794-864)
Metro Stop: *San Babila*
Hours: *Monday through Saturday from 10 a.m. to 1 p.m. and 3:30 to 7 p.m. (closed Monday morning)*
Credit Cards: AE, DC, MC, V
English Spoken.

While Ferré is not best known for his leather clothing for women, his shop on Via della Spiga does have some stunning creations. For example, a severely cut, "architectural" three-quarter-length sleeveless black leather jacket with white lapels costing 3.5 million lire. A brown leather jacket and skirt—all one piece, with a zip running from collar to hem—is about the same.

GIANNI VERSACE
Via della Spiga 4 (tel. 705-451)
Metro Stop: *San Babila*
Hours: *Monday through Saturday from 9:30 a.m. to 1 p.m. and 3:30 to 7 p.m. (closed Monday morning)*
Credit Cards: AE, DC, MC, V
English Spoken.

Gianni Versace has leather and vinyl accessories at this store, as well as some leather clothing for women. A lady's briefcase in vinyl with leather trim is 400,000 lire. A butter-smooth white suede shift with a plunging V-neck is 3 million lire.

GIORGIO ARMANI
Via Sant'Andrea 9 (tel. 792-757)
Metro Stop: *San Babila*
  and
EMPORIO ARMANI
Via Durini 24 (tel. 709-030)
Metro Stop: *Duomo*
Hours: *10 a.m. to 1 p.m. and 3:30 to 7 p.m. (closed Monday morning)*
Credit Cards: AE, DC, MC, V
English Spoken.

The Armani flagship store on Via Sant'Andrea has some sensational leather items for men and women. A slinky, silky soft woman's skirt in black leather is 1.95 million lire. A purse for day use, also in black leather, is 450,000 lire. A man's leather jacket, cut loose in the shoulders, is 1.8 million lire.

The Emporio Armani, in the downtown district, has leather for men and women as well, but for casual wear. A three-quarter-length shearling jacket for a woman is 1.35 million lire; a pair of black leather flats costs 98,000 lire. A waist-length shearling coat for a man is 1.6 million lire.

GUCCI
Via Monte Napoleone 5 (tel. 545-6621)
Metro Stop: *San Babila*
Hours: *Monday through Saturday from 10 a.m. to 7 p.m. nonstop (closed Monday morning)*
Credit Cards: AE, DC, MC, V
English Spoken.

MILAN SHOPS: LEATHER GOODS

It's actually quite difficult to know in which category to put Gucci. Its reputation is based on leather goods, but the selection of merchandise available at all of the shops goes far beyond that. I have covered Gucci ready-to-wear clothing for men and women in other categories (there is a separate shop for that at Via Monte Napoleone 2); this is the "everything else" location. On two floors and a mezzanine are Gucci products for very little money, like a coffee mug with the Gs and bridle motif for 16,000 lire, or a felt tote bag with leather trim, again with the trademark, for 20,000 lire. There are also items costing a lot of money: a black leather vanity case is 720,000 lire (add an extra 10,000 lire to that figure if you want it with the Gucci red-and-green stripe); a vinyl-and-leather overnight bag is 195,000 lire; a pair of Gucci loafers for women costs 240,000 lire; silk and wool shawls begin at 140,000 lire and go up to 175,000 lire. The selection of goods goes on and on. Of course, the prices go up and up as well.

GUIDO PASQUALI
Via Sant'Andrea 1 (tel. 701-645 for women) and
  Via Gesù 6 (tel. 783-508 for men)
Metro Stop: *San Babila*
Hours: *Monday through Saturday from 9:30 a.m. to 1 p.m. and*
  4 to 7:30 p.m. (closed Monday morning)
Credit Cards: AE, DC, MC, V
English Spoken.

Pasquali's high-fashion boots and shoes are famous throughout Italy. At the intimate, luxurious women's shop on Via Sant'Andrea, a pair of brown kidskin pumps are beautifully crafted and cost 190,000 lire. A pair of knee-high boots in fabulous black suede is 320,000 lire. The Guido Pasquali line for men at the Via Gesù shop is equally distinguished. A pair of black tasseled loafers is 200,000 lire.

IL BISONTE
Via Madonnina 10 (tel. 805-8467)
Metro Stop: *Lanza or Moscova*
Hours: *Monday through Saturday from 10 a.m. to 1 p.m. and*
  2:30 to 7:30 p.m. (closed Monday morning)
Credit Cards: AE, DC, MC, V
English Spoken.

The very attractive, casual Il Bisonte line of leather shoes and clothing is represented here in full force, although the shop itself is quite small. A cute suede jacket in dark green with red fur trim is a not-so-cute 1.7 million lire. Calf-height boots, also in suede, with a stacked heel, are a more reasonable 275,000 lire.

LARIO 1898
Via Monte Napoleone 21 (tel. 702-641)

Metro Stop: *San Babila*
Hours: *Monday through Saturday from 10 a.m. to 7 p.m. nonstop (closed Monday morning)*
Credit Cards: *AE, DC, MC, V*
English Spoken.

Lovely traditional shoes and leather accessories for men and women. A classic pair of oxfords in brown suede is 220,000 lire. A large lady's wallet with a change purse in grainy brown leather is 60,000 lire.

LUCA
Via Monte Napoleone 27E (tel. 791-115)
Metro Stop: *San Babila*
Hours: *Monday through Saturday from 9:30 a.m. to 1:30 p.m. and 3:30 to 7:30 p.m. (closed Monday morning)*
Credit Cards: *AE, DC, MC*
English Spoken.

Situated in a charming little arcade just off Via Monte Napoleone, Luca stocks shoes and boots for women only. There are excellent buys to be had here, particularly Luca brand-name leather boots. A pair of black or brown knee boots with tassels costs only 150,000 lire.

LUCIANO SOPRANI
Via Sant'Andrea 14 (tel. 798-327)
Metro Stop: *San Babila*
Hours: *Monday through Saturday from 9 a.m. to 1 p.m. and 3:30 to 7:30 p.m. (closed Monday morning)*
Credit Cards: *AE, DC, MC, V*
English Spoken.

Although predominantly a shop for women's clothing, there are some leather goods. A brown leather day shoe that updates a traditional design is 180,000 lire. A suede loafer is 195,000 lire.

MORTAROTTI
Via Monte Napoleone 24 (tel. 709-839)
Metro Stop: *San Babila*
Hours: *Monday through Saturday from 9:30 a.m. to 1:30 p.m. and 3 to 7:30 p.m. (closed Monday morning)*
Credit Cards: *AE, DC, MC, V*
English Spoken.

If the great designers leave you cold and their prices give you chills—but you still want to buy shoes on Via Monte Napoleone—then you probably cannot do better than Mortarotti. This is a sensational wellspring of women's shoes at prices that won't make you faint. There is an abundance of styles, and not just in fine-quality leather, either. A pair of very elegant black satin high heels is 100,000 lire. The same item in black lambskin is 145,000 lire. A calf-height boot in a delicate shade of dove gray will cost 180,000 lire.

NAZARENO GABRIELLI
Via Hoepli 6 (tel. 805-2769)
Metro Stop: *Duomo*
Hours: *Monday through Saturday from 10 a.m. to 1 p.m. and 3:30 to 7 p.m. (closed Monday morning)*
Credit Cards: **AE**
English Spoken.

Do Italian leather goods come any more elegant than the marvelous wares at Nazareno Gabrielli? The short answer is "maybe," but you'd have to work hard to find them. There is an excellent selection of women's bags, briefcases, and other accessories here, and you have to expect to pay at least one arm and one leg for them. A mid-sized suitcase, silk lined, is 780,000 lire. A large, flat clutch, sort of a leather envelope in smooth, satiny dark-brown braided leather, is 325,000 lire. An agenda in scarlet—remember, it's only good for a year—is 65,000 lire.

PELLUX
Piazza San Fedele 2 (tel. 864-104)
Metro Stop: *Duomo*
Hours: *Monday through Saturday from 10 a.m. to 1:30 p.m. and 3:30 p.m. to 7 p.m. (closed Monday morning)*
Credit Cards: **AE, MC, V**
English Spoken.

Leather goods for men and women in every shape and form. There are shoes, bags, accessories, and luggage, all designed with taste and with an eye to quality. Pellux is cheaper than the better-known names on Via Monte Napoleone, but not by much.

POLLINI
Corso Vittorio Emanuele II 30 (tel. 794-912)
Metro Stop: *Duomo*
Hours: *Monday through Saturday from 9:30 a.m. to 1:30 p.m. and 3:30 to 7 p.m. (closed Monday morning)*
Credit Cards: **AE, DC, V**
English Spoken.

Not to be confused with Armando Pollini, this Pollini stocks women's shoes in all types of hides and colors. Prices vary from the disarmingly low—75,000 lire for plain black flats—to quite high. A pair of gold leather high heels with a jeweled back are 249,000 lire.

PRADA
Galleria Vittorio Emanuele and Via della Spiga 1 (tel. 876-979)
Metro Stop: *Duomo*
Hours: *Monday through Saturday from 9:30 a.m. to 1 p.m. and 2:30 to 7 p.m. (closed Monday morning)*
Credit Cards: *AE*
English Spoken.

Ultra-traditional and ultra-elegant leather goods for men and women, the Prada name is a byword for fabulous quality as well. The small shop on Via della Spiga has just a small selection of the vast line of products. There are shoes (like a suede and crocodile flat in dark brown, for 190,000 lire), gloves, bags, and odds and ends; a pack of Prada playing cards, for example, in a leather case is 55,000 lire. A Prada key chain—an enamel facsimile of the Prada label and a chrome loop—is 30,000 lire. The Prada downtown in the galleria is a two-story shop which has everything this famous name produces. Downstairs, in a showroom that looks like it hasn't changed since the 1930s, is a wonderful selection of luggage. Prices are high. A medium-size black leather suitcase costs 670,000 lire. A vinyl-and-leather attaché case is 290,000 lire. A steamer trunk—just the thing for the old *Normandie* or the *Queen Mary*—is 850,000 lire.

SALVATORE FERRAGAMO
Via Monte Napoleone 3 (tel. 700-054 for women) and Via Monte Napoleone 20 (tel. 706-660 for men)
Metro Stop: *San Babila*
Hours: *Monday through Saturday from 10 a.m. to 7 p.m. nonstop (closed Monday morning)*
Credit Cards: *AE, DC, MC, V*
English Spoken.

Salvatore Ferragamo is one of the most illustrious family-run leather dynasties in Italy. Salvatore Ferragamo, the founder of the firm, designed shoes that were worn by everyone from the Duchess of Windsor to Greta Garbo. Today the company still thrives under a younger generation of Ferragamos. The two Ferragamo shops in Milan, one for women, one for men, have all the Ferragamo leather goods. Ornate gold or silver high heels, with a sling or closed back, range from 200,000 lire to 300,000 lire. A pair of creamy-white leather flats with a black patent-leather toe-cap costs 195,000 lire. There is also extremely elegant luggage. A set of black leather suitcases with brass fittings and hardware, including a small, square cosmetic case, a briefcase, two mid-size suitcases, and a large one, is approximately 15 million lire. Of course, pieces can be bought individually and prices on smaller pieces begin at 1.2 million lire. Ferragamo makes leather clothing as well. Jackets begin at 1 million lire.

The Ferragamo for men is just as well stocked. A magnificent pair of black lace-ups for men, in leather so smooth it feels as though it will melt, costs 300,000 lire. A Ferragamo belt, also in black leather, with a small brass buckle is

MILAN SHOPS: LEATHER GOODS

The Galleria Vittorio Emanuele

125,000 lire. Calf-height boots begin at 450,000 lire, and leather jackets at 850,000 lire. Despite the prices on Ferragamo's goods, which are not low, you can't beat the style and longstanding tradition of quality behind each item.

SEBASTIAN
Via Borgospesso 18 (tel. 780-532)
Metro Stop: *San Babila*
Hours: *Monday through Saturday from 10 a.m. to 1 p.m. and 3 to 7 p.m. (closed Monday morning)*
Credit Cards: AE
English Spoken.

This is another excellent shop in the Monte Napoleone district selling extremely well-made shoes for men and women. The Sebastian products come from the shop's own workshops and they are just about handmade (only the cutting is done by machine). Despite this, they will hand-make a pair of shoes for you (it takes about two months) and the shop will ship them. A pair of off-the-rack shoes for women, pale-pink high heels with an open toe, are 350,000 lire. A man's black dress shoe is about the same. Made-to-measure shoes cost considerably more, depending on style, size, and type of hide.

SPELTA
Via Pontaccio 2, at the corner of Via Solferino (tel. 805-2592)
Metro Stop: *Lanza or Moscova*

Hours: *Monday through Saturday from 10 a.m. to 1 p.m. and 3:30 to 7 p.m. (closed Monday morning)*
Credit Cards: *None*

Casual shoes for young women in a wide variety of colors and styles. There is a particularly large selection of sandals and boots. Prices are low. A pair of flat sandals which tie at the ankle is only 20,000 lire. A pair of kidskin boots with tassels and silver studs in a blinding shade of red costs 100,000 lire.

TANINO CRISCI
Via Monte Napoleone 3 (tel. 791-264)
Metro Stop: *San Babila*
Hours: *Monday through Saturday from 9:30 a.m. to 1 p.m. and 3:30 to 7:30 p.m. (closed Monday morning)*
Credit Cards: *AE, MC*

Very traditional handcrafted shoes for men and women. The specialty at Crisci is boots. A classic woman's knee boot in lightweight black leather costs 300,000 lire. A man's buckled chukka boot costs 360,000 lire.

TRUSSARDI
Via Sant'Andrea 5 (tel. 781-878)
Metro Stop: *San Babila*
Hours: *Monday through Saturday from 10 a.m. to 2:30 p.m. and 3:30 to 7:30 p.m. (closed Monday morning)*
Credit Cards: *AE, DC, MC, V*
English Spoken.

Trussardi is another name which found fame and fortune as a maker of leather goods—but the name is now showing up on everything from children's clothing to their own brand of blue jeans. The trademark greyhound head is somewhere on every item. On the two floors of this shop you'll find leather goods, of course, as well as the other things in the Trussardi line. A fleece-lined, three-quarter-length leather coat for a woman is 864,000 lire. A black leather matching jacket and skirt costs 1,872,000 lire. A quilted silk winter coat for a little girl is 213,000 lire. A Trussardi sweater to go with it is 97,000 lire. There are also leather accessories. A light-brown tobacco pouch with the greyhound head stamped on it costs 84,000 lire. A large agenda bound in green leather is 232,000 lire.

VALERIANO-NATALE FERRARIO
Via Monte Napoleone 6 (tel. 790-928)
Metro Stop: *San Babila*
Hours: *Monday through Saturday from 9:30 a.m. to 1 p.m. and 3:30 to 7:30 p.m. (closed Monday morning)*
Credit Cards: *AE*
English Spoken.

A very elegant, intimate shop, Valeriano-Natale Ferrario sells leather goods and shoes for women mostly, although there are some items for men too. Traditional styles predominate and prices are average for the neighborhood. A beautifully made short suede jacket in scarlet costs 1.35 million lire. A pair of classic gray suede flats with a buckle front is 170,000 lire. A pair of traditional loafers for a man, in an ox-blood-colored leather, costs 175,000 lire.

VALEXTRA
Piazza San Babila 1 (tel. 705-024)
Metro Stop: *San Babila*
Hours: *Monday through Saturday from 9:30 p.m. to 1:30 p.m. and 3:30 to 7:30 p.m. (closed Monday morning)*
Credit Cards: AE, DC, MC, V
English Spoken.

Since 1938 Valextra has been selling sturdy, high-quality luggage at this very large shop on Piazza San Babila. The Valextra line encompasses everything from a tiny change purse to a large suitcase, and the products come in vinyl and fabrics as well. A good size man's attaché case in black leather with brass corners costs 325,000 lire. A black portfolio with a brass lock is 185,000 lire. A lightweight garment bag in nylon with leather trim is 295,000 lire. A slim wallet for a woman, in patterned nylon, again with leather trim, is 55,000 lire.

LINENS

PRATESI
Via Monte Napoleone 21 (tel. 701-551)
Metro Stop: *San Babila*
Hours: *Monday through Saturday from 10 a.m. to 1:30 p.m. and 3:30 to 7:30 p.m. (closed Monday morning)*
Credit Cards: AE, MC, V
English Spoken.

The merchandise is displayed in lovely oak cabinets in this beautiful, refined shop. The Pratesi name is well known all over the world for high-quality linens, and this particular shop is one of the best I've seen in Italy. There are luxurious thick towels in a selection of soft pastel colors with prices beginning at 45,000 lire for a hand towel and going up to 175,000 lire for a large bath-towel. Cotton or linen sheets with delicate flower designs are 145,000 lire for a single flat and about 200,000 lire for a double. Prices here are much lower than in the United States, although Pratesi in Milan, while very pretty, is a little more expensive than the shops in Rome and Florence.

T&J VESTOR
Via Alessandro Manzoni 39 (tel. 709-530)
Metro Stop: *San Babila*
English Spoken.
   and
Corso Buenos Aires 52 (tel. 273-492)
Metro Stop: *Porto Venezia*
Hours: *Monday through Saturday from 9:30 a.m. to 1 p.m. and 3:30 p.m. to 7 p.m. (closed Monday morning)*
Credit Cards: *AE, DC, MC, V*

The famous Missoni linens are for sale at all T&J Vestor stores, as well as Missoni and Vestor fabrics (see "Fabrics and Textiles"). While a Missoni sheet for a single bed costs 90,000 lire (180,000 lire for a double) at either of these two shops, this is a good 20% less than you'd pay in the United States.

LUGGAGE (see "Leather Goods")

MALLS

CAFFÈ MODA
Via Durini 14
Metro Stop: *Duomo*
Hours: *Monday through Saturday from 10 a.m. to 7 p.m. nonstop, although some of the shops in the complex close for half an hour for lunch.*
Credit Cards: *Varies from store to store*
English Spoken: *Throughout*

This small three-story shopping mall, crammed with shops, has become the "in" place to shop in Milan (the day I was there, so was Jay McInerney) for the young, hip, well-dressed set. Prices here are generally lower than at the shops' other branches. Among the shops here are Krizia Poi (women's wear), Missoni (accessories, costume jewelry, and notebooks on the top floor), Enrico Coveri (on the second floor, with casual clothing in the "Young You" line for both men and women), Cacherel (children's clothing), Oaks by Ferré (cheaper men's casual wear), and Henry Cotton and Gherardini (for handbags).

PAPER AND PAPER GOODS
(see "Stationery Supplies")

MILAN SHOPS: LINENS/MALLS/PORCELAIN

PORCELAIN

RICHARD-GINORI
Van Panfilo Castaldi 42 (tel. 206-611)
Metro Stop: Porta Venezia
   and
Corso Matteotti 1 (tel. 700-361)
Metro Stop: San Babila
Hours: Monday through Saturday from 9:30 a.m. to 1:30 p.m. and
   3:30 to 7:30 p.m. (closed Monday morning)
Credit Cards: AE, MC, V
English Spoken.

Richard-Ginori's porcelain was born in Milan in the 19th century (it was called Richard then) and the original factory still stands. The two stores in Milan sell much more than the oven-proof porcelain—the Ginori line has expanded to include silverware and glassware, as well as dealing in other brand names like Baccarat. One of the two shops listed here, the larger is on Corso Matteotti, but the prices seem a little less on Corso Buenos Aires and the merchandise a little less "formal." At the latter store a dinner set of simple white porcelain with a fine black-stripe rim containing place settings for 12 (dinner plate, salad plate, soup bowl) plus a large platter, casserole, and salt and pepper shaker, is 570,000 lire. A porcelain vase in a glossy black glaze is 37,000 lire. A sleek, modern sauce boat is 42,000 lire. A huge coffee cup and saucer with a naïf painting of country

Take time out to enjoy a glass of tea, served Italian style

scenes (sort of like Grandma Moses) is 16,500 lire. On Corso Matteotti, prices are much, much higher. A large casserole with a floral design is 480,000 lire. A 12-person dinnerware set is 3.4 million lire.

SINIGS
Via Filippo Turati 2 and 5 (tel. 659-9359)
Metro Stop: *San Babila*
Hours: *Monday through Saturday from 9:30 a.m. to 1:30 p.m. and 3:30 to 7 p.m. (closed Monday morning)*
Credit Cards: *None*

The Sinigs shops on Via Filippo Turati, an extension of Via Alessandro Manzoni, are good china and glass outlets which stock the lower end of the Richard-Ginori line. Prices are very low, but of course the merchandise is not terribly delicate and hardly ornamented at all. However, a 21-piece set of china, with plates, soup bowls, and desserts bowls for six, plus a large pasta bowl and two large platters (one round, one oval), is just 120,000 lire.

VALENTINO PIU
Via Santo Spirito 3 (tel. 706-478)
Metro Stop: *San Babila*
Hours: *Monday through Saturday from 10 a.m. to 1:30 p.m. and 3:30 to 7 p.m. (closed Monday morning)*
Credit Cards: *AE*
English Spoken.

The Valentino Piu china and housewares shop is part of the Valentino complex on Via Santo Spirito. While Valentino-anything is likely to be expensive, the smaller things at this store can be had for little money—much less than you'd pay in the United States. A simple white porcelain vase with red accents is 105,000 lire. A large Valentino platter with an elaborate floral design is 320,000 lire.

PRINTS AND ENGRAVINGS

PETTINAROLI-RAIMONDI
Corso Venezia 6 (tel. 702-412)
Metro Stop: *San Babila*
Hours: *Monday through Saturday from 9:30 a.m. to 1 p.m. and 3:30 to 7:30 p.m. (closed Monday morning)*
Credit Cards: *None*

Close to, but not actually in, the Monte Napoleone district, this grand old print shop is the finest in Milan. There are beautiful hand-colored views of old Milan (it was a very picturesque city before the Industrial Revolution and World War II) as well as high-quality art prints and drawings of the 18th and 19th century. A

MILAN SHOPS: PRINTS & ENGRAVINGS/STATIONERY

small view of the Duomo is 25,000 lire. Prices on rarer items can go into the millions.

SHOES (see "Leather Goods")

STATIONERY SUPPLIES

I GIORNI DI CARTA
Corso Garibaldi 81 (tel. 655-2514)
Metro Stop: *Lanza or Moscova*
Hours: *Monday through Saturday from 9:30 a.m. to 1:30 p.m. and 3:30 to 7 p.m. (closed Monday morning)*
Credit Cards: *None*

A charming store in the Brera district, I Giorni di Carta ("Days of Paper") features paper goods in all kinds of designs and weights. The handmade objects include items you might expect—like diaries, address books, and lampshades—and things that you don't, like picture frames and clocks.

LA SCRITTURA
Via Filippo Turati 3 (tel. 652-763)
Metro Stop: *San Babila*
Hours: *Monday through Saturday from 9 a.m. to 1 p.m. and 3 to 7 p.m. (closed Monday morning)*
Credit Cards: *AE, DC, MC, V*

This is an otherwise ordinary *cartoleria* (stationery shop) which has the full line of Trussardi Scribe products—things that you won't find at Trussardi on Via Sant'Andrea. A large ring binder in red vinyl is 20,000 lire. A smaller version is 10,000 lire. A large lined notebook, bound in red or blue vinyl, is 20,000 lire; the smaller version is 12,500 lire. All the Scribe products carry the Trussardi seal.

LEGATORIA ARTISTICA
Via Palermo 5 (tel. 861-113)
Metro Stop: *Lanza or Moscova*
Hours: *Monday through Saturday from 9:30 a.m. to 1:30 p.m. and 3:30 to 7:30 p.m. (closed Monday morning)*
Credit Cards: *None*

A traditional binder of books in leather, this store also stocks lined notebooks and sketchbooks filled with 100% rag paper in various finishes. Some have bevelled or straight edges. The marbled boards enclosing the paper are colorful and very traditional. A blank sketchbook is 25,000 lire, but prices can rise to 100,000 lire depending on size.

TOYS

ANTONELLA BENSI
Via Santo Spirito 15 (tel. 793-007)
Metro Stop: *San Babila*
Hours: *Monday through Saturday from 10 a.m. to 1 p.m. and 3:30 to 7 p.m. (closed Monday morning)*
Credit Cards: *AE*
English Spoken.

This is a fascinating antique shop selling fabulous antique toys at high prices, but they are the kind of mechanical toys and games that are hard to find anywhere at any price. It's not devoted exclusively to antique toys, but collectors will find lots to interest them here. Mechanical toys from Germany and Switzerland from the late 19th century cost 800,000 lire and up, but can cost many millions of lire if they are complicated and in pristine condition.

CITTA DEL SOLE
Via Meravigli 7 (tel. 805-5991)
Metro Stop: *Cairoli or Cordusio*
Hours: *Monday through Saturday from 9:30 a.m. to 1:30 p.m. and 3:30 to 7 p.m. (closed Monday morning)*
Credit Cards: *None*

If you are on your way to Santa Maria delle Grazie to see Leonardo da Vinci's *Last Supper* only to find out that it has been closed for restoration (sadly, closed indefinitely while scientists and restorers work against the clock to find a way to save it before is disappears completely), you might want to stop in at this toy shop in the neighborhood. Citta del Sole has beautifully wooden jigsaw puzzles, conundrums, and games, as well as odd, new mechanical toys from Italy, Germany, and the Far East. It is the kind of shop that all children and most adults will be able to browse in for hours.

NOÈGIOCATTOLI
Via Alessandro Manzoni 40 (tel. 792-971)
Metro Stop: *San Babila*
Hours: *Monday through Saturday from 10 a.m. to 1 p.m. and 3 to 7 p.m. (closed Monday morning)*
Credit Cards: *AE, DC, MC, V*
English Spoken.

This is a huge toy shop in the Montenapo district, much like the huge toy stores found in the States, but with a European accent. There is something here to suit boys and girls of every age.

STATIONERY
Via Solferino 3 (tel. 805-2562)
Metro Stop: *Lanza or Moscova*
Hours: *Monday through Saturday from 10 a.m. to 1 p.m. and 3:30 to 7 p.m. (closed Monday morning)*
Credit Cards: *AE, MC*
English Spoken.

This is an adult toy shop—as in grownup, as opposed to X-rated—that kids will love too. In addition to things like the British Filofax diaries, there are mechanical toys and slot machines from the Far East, kites, models of antique cars and trains, and lovely old-fashioned-style notebooks and drawing blocks.

WINES

ENOTECA COTTI
Via Solferino 42 (tel. 655-5736)
Metro Stop: *Moscova or Lanza*
Hours: *Monday through Saturday from 10 a.m. to 1 p.m. and 3:30 to 8 p.m. (closed Monday morning)*
Credit Cards: *None*

This fine old wine shop has a giant selection of the best Italian wines. Following the "When in Rome rule," you should buy wines from Lombardy here (Milan is the capital of Lombardy), notably Franciacorta, a dry white Pinot which leads the pack of Lombardian whites. It comes in two varieties: the sparkling white and the non-*frizzante*. The sparkling is one of the best spumantes available in Italy.

PROVERA
Corso Magenta 7 (tel. 805-0523)
Hours: *Monday through Saturday from 10 a.m. to 7 p.m. (no lunch closing) (closed Monday morning)*
Credit Cards: *None*

At Provera you present yourself at the bar and have a taste of a number of wines before you decide which you want to buy (you have to pay for each glass you sip, though). Its a fine old Ca' de vin, though, and you'll enjoy yourself here. As one might expect it is an excellent place to buy Lombard wines, notably the Franciacorta (mentioned above) and the excellent Lombard reds, like Riviera del Garda Bresciano, which comes in a red or rosé.

PART THREE
SHOPPING FLORENCE

CHAPTER VII

A FLORENCE OVERVIEW

Florence is the ideal city for combined shopping and sightseeing in Italy. The city is small, it has a large but manageable number of shops, and the pace of life is slower than in Milan or Rome. Added to this, Florentines are a generally courteous and accommodating lot and their beautiful city boasts some of the most spectacular cultural attractions in Europe.

BASIC ORIENTATION

Florence is divided into two halves by the River Arno. The northern bank, the side of the river with the Duomo, the Piazza Signoria, and the Uffizi museum, also contains the major high-priced shopping streets. Nearest the river, the streets are Via dei Tornabuoni, Via del Parione, and Via della Vigna Nuova; around the Duomo and the Piazza della Signoria the streets to look out for are Via dei Calzaiuoli, Via Strozzi, and the street which connects Piazza della Repubblica to the Ponte Vecchio. This street changes its name three times: the end closest to the Ponte Vecchio is called Via Por Santa Maria; the Piazza della Repubblica end is Via Calimala; and the part closest to the Duomo is Via Roma.

On the southern bank, in the area around the Pitti Palace, the major shopping streets are Borgo San Jacopo, Via dei Guicciardini, and Via Maggio.

The streets running along the Arno on either side of the river are all prefixed with "Lungarno" and change their name every few blocks. Thus the Lungarno Vespucci and the Lungarno della Zeccha Vecchia are different names for the same street.

The Ponte Vecchio is a sightseeing attraction and a shopping street rolled into one: this beautiful old bridge was built in 1345 and is lined with small jeweler's shops.

GETTING FROM THE AIRPORT

Although there has been talk for years about building a Florence airport, a plan has yet to be adopted. The nearest airport to Florence is Galileo Galilei Airport, near Pisa, about 95 km (60 miles) from Florence. There is no regular bus service running from the airport to Florence. In order to get from Galileo to Florence you have to go into Pisa and then take a train across Tuscany to Florence—a time-consuming and awkward way of getting to the city. A taxi from the airport to Florence will cost a great deal of money, probably somewhere around 200,000

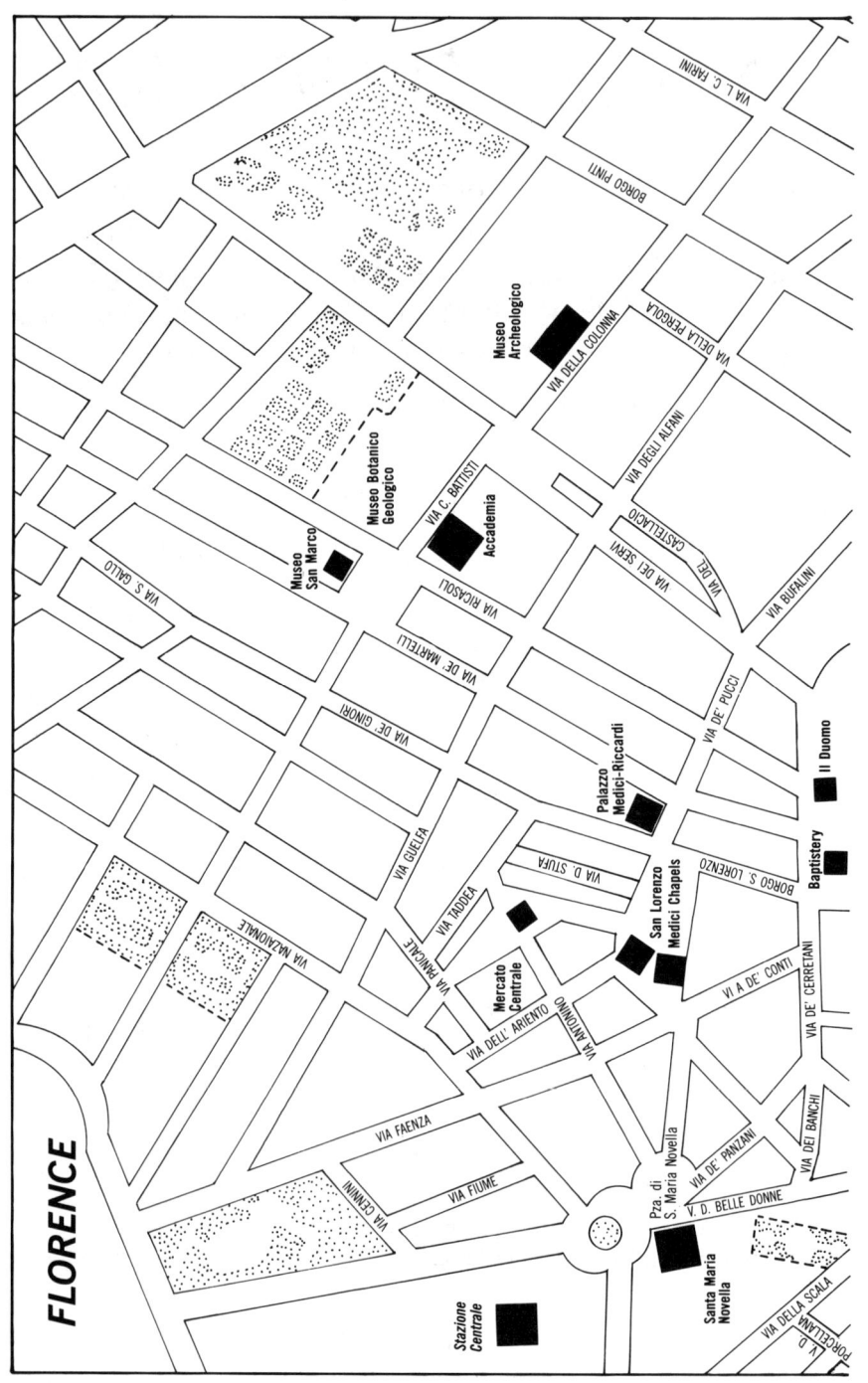

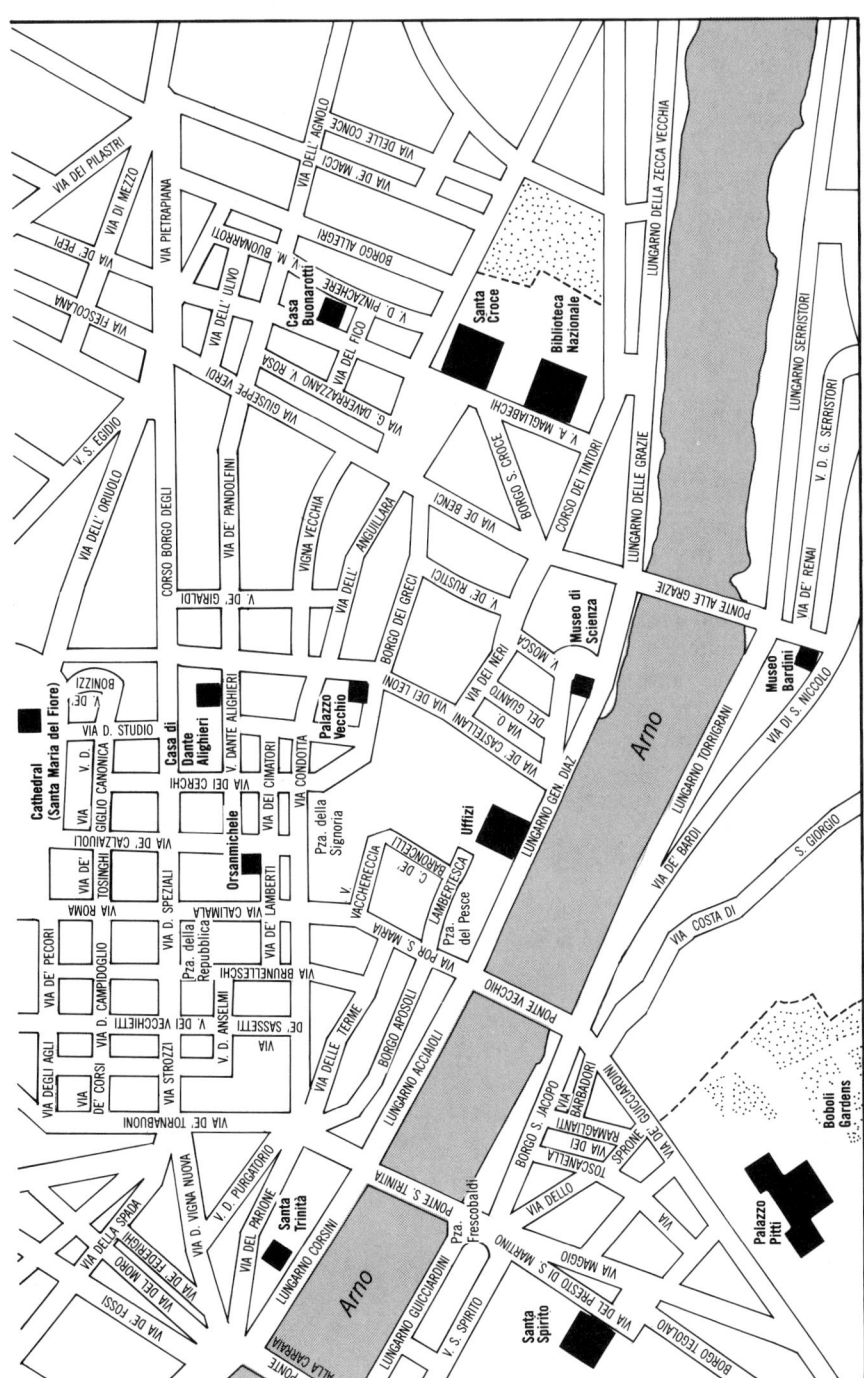

THE SERIOUS SHOPPER'S GUIDE TO ITALY

lire. As your driver is likely to be Pisan, you'll probably have to pay his way back to his hometown.

It's quite rare for visitors to fly to Pisa to get to Florence as the city is connected to all major Italian cities by direct and frequent train service. The station, called the Stazione di Santa Maria Novella, is in the piazza of the same name, at the end of Via Nazionale. There is an enormous bus stop just outside the station, with the no. 7 bus being the most handy. It runs from the station to the heart of the city, around the Duomo.

GETTING AROUND

The **bus** service in Florence is fast and the buses frequent. As in Rome and Milan, bus riding is on the honor system. You purchase your ticket at shops or newsstands displaying the ATAF sign and cancel them in the time-stamp box at the rear of the bus. From the moment you cancel your ticket you can get on and off as many buses as you like for the next 60 minutes. Tickets cost 700 lire.

The most noticiable thing about **taxis** in Florence is that they are white, not yellow. Other than that, they're perfectly normal. They cost 3,500 lire on the drop of the flag and turn over in 350-lire increments every minute. There is a 2,000-lire surcharge for Sunday and holidays, and a 2,500-lire surcharge for night service after 9 p.m. In keeping with their Milanese cousins, the Florentine taxi drivers are agitating for a rate change, so prices will probably rise.

But that's not really a worry. The best way to see Florence is **on foot**. The city is small and compact, and apart from a trip from the station to your hotel when you arrive, you probably won't need a taxi at all. Many streets have been closed to traffic, and Florentines are far more mannerly about parking and pedestrians' rights than in Rome.

There is no metro in Florence and there are no plans to build one.

TOURIST INFORMATION

There are three **EPT** government tourist information offices in Florence. One is just outside the main entrance to the train station in the Piazza di Santa Maria Novella, open Monday through Saturday from 9 a.m. to 1 p.m. and 3 to 7 p.m. (closed Sunday); English is spoken. The other office, the largest of the three, is inconveniently located at Via Alessandro Manzoni 16 (walk past the Duomo and keep on going for about half a mile). The hours are the same as above, and English is spoken here also. The telephone number is 678-841. The most convenient location is at Via dei Tornabuoni 15 (tel. 216-544), same hours.

WEATHER

The general rule of thumb for Florentine weather is that whatever happens in Rome happens worse in Florence. Summers are hotter, with a high of 90° in August. Winters are cold and snow is far more frequent here than in Rome. Fog often blankets the city and doesn't disperse easily because it cannot get over the mountains surrounding the city. There is usually a morning fog all year round, which does burn off in the summer; but the morning fogs have a way of becoming all-day fogs on cold winter days. Spring and fall are the best times to visit Florence. Days are generally clear and still warm enough for lunch out of doors in late September and October. There is a rainy season in February and early March. Late March to June is lovely.

THE ABCs OF SHOPPING FLORENCE

AMERICAN EXPRESS

The Florence branch of American Express is at Via dei Guicciardini 49R (tel. 278-781). It's open Monday through Friday from 9 a.m. to 6 p.m. for travel arrangements, Monday through Friday from 9 a.m. to 5:30 p.m. for financial transactions, and on Saturday from 9 a.m. to 1 p.m. for all services.

BANKING HOURS

Banking hours are a little different in Florence than elsewhere in Italy. Banks are open Monday through Friday from 8:20 a.m. to 1:20 p.m. and 2:45 to 3:45 p.m. (closed Saturday and Sunday). The day before major holidays banks are open from 8:20 to 11:20 a.m.

BUSINESS HOURS

Hours are more or less the same as Rome, Milan, and Venice. Shops open around 9 a.m., close for lunch at 1 or 1:30 p.m., and reopen at 3 or 3:30 p.m. Stores close Monday mornings, except for food shops which are closed on Wednesday afternoon. Unlike Milan and Rome (but like Venice) many shops in Florence open all or part of the day on Sunday—there's no hard-and-fast rule though. Sometimes a shop is open on Sunday; other times it isn't—it's up to the whim of the shopkeeper. Finally, Florence closes in August and goes to the beach.

HOLIDAYS

Florence celebrates the same holidays as the rest of the country. The feast of the patron saint of Florence, Saint John the Baptist, falls on August 29. Falling as it does during the quietest time of Florence's hottest and most moribund month few stores which were open anyway bother to close.

MARKETS

The major market in Florence is the **Mercato Centrale**, in the piazza of the same name, near the church of San Lorenzo. It is open mornings only, every day of the week except Monday, and the vendors in the piazza and the nearby side streets sell leather goods, clothing, sunglasses—everything, in fact, except food. There are bargains to be had here on "genuine" famous-make Italian designers. Actually, the Gucci and Bottega Veneta labels might be (probably are) fake, but none of the vendors will say. Fake or not, a lot of the stuff for sale, particularly knitwear, is of good quality and the prices are low.

The **straw market** is officially called the Mercato Nuovo, although it's not new at all. The covered marketplace, on Via Por Santa Maria, was built in 1547 as a market for gold and silk. Now it sells inexpensive straw goods and some leather, every morning except Monday. Baskets, hats, raffiawork, and household goods like placemats are very cheap and woven in Florence.

Payment in these markets is a lot more sophisticated than anywhere else in Italy. There is no mistrust of credit cards here—even the smallest vendor is likely to accept the major cards.

If you time your trip to Florence correctly, you can find one of the best **antiques markets** in the country in nearby Arezzo, a beautiful walled town 81 km (50 miles) to the south. Trains leave Florence for Arezzo regularly. The market only functions on the first Sunday of every month, but on that day all of Arezzo seems to turn into one giant market. There are stands selling junk and there are stands selling high-quality antiques; some stands are devoted exclusively to jewelry, others to furniture (shipping is your problem, unfortunately), but most have a weird and wonderful selection of oddments. Bargaining is certainly allowed, but you are dealing with masters of the art so prices don't come down much.

POST OFFICE

Hours are standard throughout Italy, as are shipping regulations (see "The ABCs of Shopping Italy" in Chapter II). The main post office in Florence is at Via Pellicceria 1, right at the corner of the Piazza della Repubblica in the center of town. Hours are 8:30 a.m. to 8 p.m. Monday through Friday, on Saturday to noon.

SALES

See "The ABCs of Shopping Italy" in Chapter II.

TAXES

See "The ABCs of Shopping Italy" in Chapter II.

FLORENCE: GENERAL INFORMATION

On the first Sunday of every month, Arezzo hosts the largest antiques market in Italy

CHAPTER VIII

GREAT FLORENCE SHOPPING STROLLS

During the Renaissance Florence had half the population of Milan but twice—perhaps three times—the power of the great city to the north. The reason was simple: trade. Florentine merchants had financial interests throughout Italy, in Spain, France, Germany, England, the Middle East, even in faraway Russia. The foundation of this economic strength lay in the Florentine's single-minded pursuit of money, achieved primarily through banking and the leather and wool trade. They were the founders of something which would later be called the "Protestant work ethic"—although the merchants were devoutly Catholic to a man. It is not surprising that an enterprising Florentine merchant used to inscribe the first page of each of his heavy ledgers "In the name of God and of profit."

The Florentines are no longer as powerful as the Milanese—Milan finally abandoned the sword in favor of the account sheet—but the trading spirit of the city has never died. The streets one walks today still bear the names of the trades which were once carried on there. Via Calimala recalls the great Florentine wool traders; Via Calzaiuoli harkens back to the days when the street was the home of the shoemakers and leatherworkers. Make no mistake, there is still profit to be made in Florence—but there are bargains to be found as well.

FLORENCE: GREAT SHOPPING STROLLS

THE HEART OF FLORENCE

This stroll begins in the **Piazza della Signoria**, right across the street from the Palazzo Vecchio, and ends at the Ponte Vecchio. The streets covered are Via dei Calzaiuoli, Via Strozzi, Via Roma, Via Calimala, and Via Por Santa Maria—remember, the last three streets are all different names for the same thoroughfare. Some of the shops included are at the upper end of the price range, but most are moderate or inexpensive. This stroll has a little bit of everything: Florentine handcrafts, high fashion, household goods, and of course, leather and shoes.

We begin at Pineider, world-famous stationers at Piazza della Signoria 1, right at the beginning of **Via dei Calzaiuoli**. Next comes Ribot, at Via de Calzaiuoli 1, a fine but small shop for women's fashion. Next door at Via dei Calzaiuoli 3 is more ladies' clothing as well as shoes at Franco Rizzo.

Across the street, on the corner of Via Condotta, at Via dei Calzaiuoli 10 is G. Clemente, a large luggage and leather-goods shop, with a giant selection of everything except shoes. Next comes Marina Rinaldi, at Via dei Calzaiuoli 14, a very elegant shop for high-fashion women's wear.

The first of many Beltrami shops we'll see in Florence is at Via dei Calzaiuoli 31 (for clothing) and across the street at no. 44 (for shoes). A. Ugolini & Figli is another clothier for women and it's just down from Beltrami at Via dei Calzaiuoli 65. Conservative, traditional styles predominate here.

Cellini's statue of Perseus (that's the head of the Gorgon he's clutching) in the majestic Piazza Signoria

Make a detour onto **Via dei Tosinghi.** Just around the corner from Via dei Calzaiuoli is Casa dello Sport, a large shop which has a huge selection of summer and winter sportswear for every member of the family. The street address is Via de' Tosinghi 8-10.

Return to Via dei Calzaiuoli and head for the Duomo, turning left in the piazza. With the bapistry on your right, you should be standing at the corner of a busy intersection. If you turn left again you'll be on Via Roma, the main drag of this stroll. But before you do, walk straight across Via Roma to **Via dei Pecori.** This street is only two blocks long but there are a couple of interesting shops on it. At Via dei Pecori 14 is an excellent Max Mara shop, stocking high-quality clothes for women. Next door at no. 16 is another Beltrami. Farther down the street is the menswear branch of Ugolini e Figli, at no. 68 (we saw the women's wear shop of the same name on Via dei Calzaiuoli).

Returning to **Via Roma** and turning right, toward the river away from the Duomo, you come to Luisa Via Roma, at no. 21, a women's wear shop which stocks numerous designer labels. Raspini is at Via Roma 25 and is one of two Raspini shoe shops (for men and women) we'll see on this route.

Entering the giant **Piazza della Repubblica,** you'll find clothes for men and women at Mantelassi, Piazza della Repubblica 21. Also in the piazza, at the corner of Via degli Speziali, is a shoe and bag shop, Romano.

Crossing the piazza, head down **Via Strozzi,** on the edge of Florence's high-priced area. The first shop you'll encounter is Neuber, at no. 32, an expensive shop for designer clothing for women only. Gherardini Uomo, at no. 25, is a leather-goods shop for men devoted exclusively to the Florentine leather house Gherardini. In the same building (but at no. 21) is Principe, the closest thing that Florence has to a department store.

Retrace your steps toward the Piazza della Repubblica to Via Roma and turn right. You're not on Via Roma anymore, you're on **Via Calimala.**

Calderai, at Via Calimala 19, is a fabulous food shop, one of the oldest and best in the city. Just down the street is our third Beltrami of the day, Beltrami Junior, at Via Calimala 9. A very nice linen shop, Ferrini Firenze, is at Via Calimala 5, just across from the straw market.

Via Calimala is short and changes its name to Via Por Santa Maria at the straw market.

Pause for a moment to secure some good luck by rubbing the nose of *Il Porcellino,* a bronze fountain crowned by a statue of a wild boar (which still thrive in Tuscany) that is the Florentine equivalent of the Blarney Stone. His nose has been worn smooth by countless generations of shoppers before you.

You are now on Via Por Santa Maria. We encounter another Raspini shoe shop at Via Por Santa Maria 72. The comes Cirri, at no. 38-40, a great source of beautiful lace. Scarabeo, where you'll find excellent buys on leather wear for men and women, is at Via Por Santa Maria 23.

There's more lace and embroidery at Taf, Via Por Santa Maria 22.

This brings you to the foot of the **Ponte Vecchio,** where this stroll ends and the next one begins.

FLORENCE: GREAT SHOPPING STROLLS

The Ponte Vecchio, a Florentine marketplace since the 14th century

IN THE NEIGHBORHOOD

Just where this stroll ends, to your left as you face the Ponte Vecchio, is the **Piazza del Pesce.** At no. 2 in this small square is Menegatti, an excellent shop for Italian pottery and majolica.

Across the street from the straw market is a street called **Via Vacchereccia**, which leads you back to the Piazza della Signoria. Before you reach the piazza, however, at Via Vacchereccia 6 is Mujer, an elegant Florence-based shop specializing in silk clothing for women.

On the far side of the Duomo, running parallel to Via Camillo Cavour is **Via Ricasoli.** On it, at no. 53, is Vice Versa, one of the finest stores for beautifully designed Italian house and kitchen wares.

Nearby is I Nomi, at Corso 27, which has extremely attractive clothes for young women at reasonable prices. Intersecting with the Corso is a little side street, **Via dello Studio**, which leads to the Duomo. At no. 26 is Pegna, which must be the most beautiful supermarket in Italy. Lots of delicacies are stocked.

Another excellent food shop is Granna Market, at Via dei Tavolini 11. You'll find that street intersects with Via dei Calzaiuoli.

Emilio Pucci's Florence address is easy to remember. It's at Via dei Pucci 6, near the Duomo.

Behind the Palazzo Vecchio on **Borgo dei Greci** you'll find the largest and best glove shop in Florence—Casa del Guanto, at Borgo dei Greci 11.

There is an Ellesse shop on **Via del Proconsolo**, another street near the Duomo. It has everything in the Ellesse line and is at Via del Proconsolo 5.

SIGHTSEEING SUGGESTIONS

In this short stroll you have passed or been within shouting distance of some of Florence's most famous cultural attractions. If you had decided to take just a little look at the **Uffizi** gallery, a few yards from the Palazzo Vecchio, chances are that you didn't take the stroll at all.

The Uffizi palace was built by Vasari in the 1560s and 1570s for Cosimo dei Medici to house the city government offices and the Medici collections of painting and sculpture. With that kind of endowment, it's not surprising that the Uffizi is the finest art gallery in Italy, topped only by the Vatican museums in Rome.

It's hard to know exactly where to begin to describe this vast collection. Of course, the great names of Tuscan painting of the late Middle Ages and Renaissance predominate, although there are also exceptional classical sculptures and paintings from the mannerist and baroque periods as well.

Virtually the first sight you encounter is three huge paintings jointly called *La Maestá*. Together these three altarpieces showing the Virgin Enthroned, by Duccio, Cimabue, and Giotto, provide a historical overview of Tuscan painting. The first, by Cimabue, is the last of the old order painted as the Middle Ages waned, while the panels by Giotto and Duccio display the new sense of perspective and form that were to characterize the Renaissance—although there are still traces of the old school in Duccio's *Ruccelai Madonna*.

You can get an idea of the development of painting in the region by looking at Fra Angelico's *Coronation of the Virgin*, painted 100 years later. The figures are

Imperial Roman busts at the Galleria dell'Accademia

alive, but calm, serene, and dignified. Little wonder that the Good Friar is the unofficial patron saint of Italian artists to this day.

Of course the most famous works in the Uffizi are the two great Botticellis, *La Primavera* and *The Birth of Venus*. People tend to cluster around these two paintings the way they do around the *Mona Lisa* in the Louvre, but it's worth elbowing your way to the front to get a good look. *La Primavera*, "whom the graces deck with flowers denoting spring," is Venus in another guise. The painting has recently been restored and looks, so the experts say, just as it must have when it left Botticelli's studio in the 1480s.

The rooms of the Uffizi roll on and on, and the famous painters represented read like an honor roll in the history of art. Raphael, Leonardo da Vinci, Michelangelo, Titian, Tintoretto, Caravaggio remind us of a time when Italy was as famous for her art as she is for her wines.

It's possible to spend all day in the Uffizi, but if you just want to duck in and see a few of the masterworks, then you should begin with *La Maestá* (Room 1), *La Primavera* and *The Birth of Venus* (Room 10), Michelangelo's tondo of the Holy Family (Room 25), Raphael's *Portrait of Leo X*, the first Medici pope (Room 26), and Titian's *Venus of Urbino* (Room 28).

Those used to the North American and British style of museum shops will be disappointed. None of the museums in Italy has the quality or variety of museum gift shops as elsewhere. All they offer are slides, guidebooks, postcards, and larger reproductions.

The Galleria Uffizi is open Tuesday to Saturday from 9 a.m. to 7 p.m., with no break for lunch. On Sunday it's open from 9 a.m. to 1 p.m. (very crowded it is too). It's closed all day Monday.

Returning to the Piazza della Signoria, you might want to go inside the **Palazzo Vecchio**, a fortress-palace built in the late 1200s to house the administrators of the Florentine republic. The Medici took it over in the 1500s and immediately set about transforming the austere interior into a palace more fitting for the Grand Dukes of Tuscany.

It's open from 9 a.m. to 7 p.m. daily except Saturday (on Sunday from 8 a.m. to 1 p.m.).

The fabulous **Duomo** and the magnificent Bapistry facing it stand in the Piazza del Duomo. The Duomo was begun in 1296 but the dome wasn't erected until 1435 when Brunelleschi figured out how to build it. The interior is very spare and is a perfect atmosphere in which to summon up faint echoes of the Pazzi conspiracy of 1478. Lorenzo Medici, "The Magnificent," was set upon by assassins as he attended Mass in the Duomo. His brother, Giuliano, was killed at the foot of the altar, but Lorenzo escaped through the transept door to the left. The plot to rid Florence of the Medici failed, but Lorenzo, in fine Renaissance style, exacted a terrible and painful revenge on his would-be killers.

There isn't much decoration in the church. The most famous piece is Paolo Uccello's monument to Sir John Hawkwood, a famous English soldier of fortune of the 1500s, often employed by Florence to fight its battles. The monument is painted on canvas, but the trompe l'oeil is so cunning you'd swear it's three-

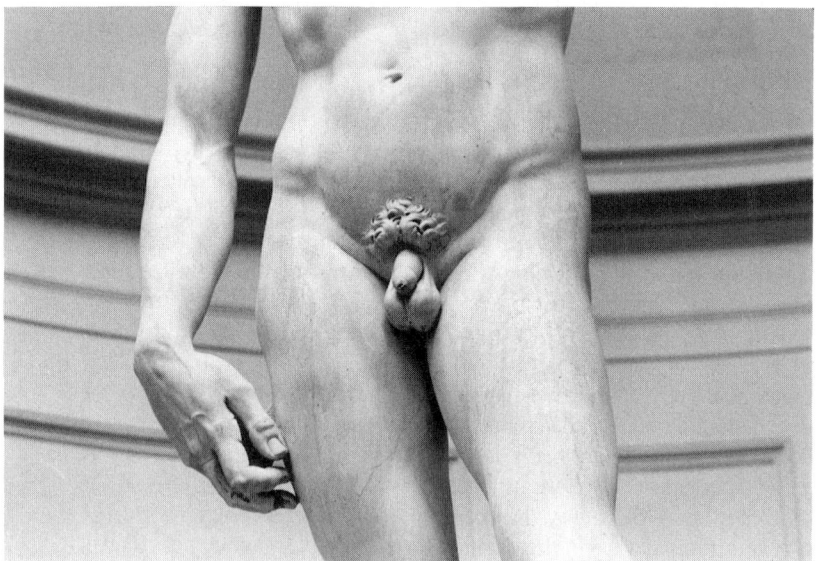

The Michelangelo David in all his glory, the Galleria dell'Accademia

FLORENCE: GREAT SHOPPING STROLLS

dimensional. It can be found on the inside wall of the façade, above you as you enter.

The Duomo is open from 7 a.m. to noon and 3:30 to 6 p.m. daily.

Facing the Duomo is the **Baptistery,** with its famous bronze doors by Ghiberti and Andrea Pisano. The Pisano doors, showing the life of John the Baptist, are on the south side. They date from 1335. On the north and east sides are the Ghiberti doors. These are approximately 100 years older and depict the Annunciation, the Nativity (north side), and scene from the Passion (east side).

REFRESHMENTS EN ROUTE

As one might expect, Florence has dozens of little bars serving espresso, cappuccino, soft drinks, and sandwiches. Facing the Palazzo Vecchio, **Bar Signoria,** a door or two down from Pineider, is a welcoming old-fashioned bar, which is open daily except Monday morning.

In the **Piazza della Repubblica** there are three huge bars all with enormous numbers of tables outside. At any one of the three you can get anything from a full meal to a bottle of champagne, but the prices are the highest in town. **Gilli** is the most famous, and the oldest, of the three.

Dining

This part of Florence does not have a very large selection of restaurants, but because the city is so small, a good restaurant is never much more than a 15-minute walk, or 5-minute taxi ride, away. There are four places, however, you might want to make note of.

Il Barrino, Via dei Biffi 2 (tel. 215-180); closed Sunday and Monday. No credit cards. This is a very good family-run restaurant in the heart of town. Tuscan dishes are, naturally enough, a specialty, with very good roasts and fresh fish taking the honors. Whatever is in season is on the menu. Prices are high. Dinner for two with one of Il Barrino's fine selection of Tuscan wines will cost approximately 170,000 lire.

Al Campidoglio, Via del Campidoglio 8 (tel. 287-770); closed Thursday. Credit Cards: AE, DC, MC, V. Just off Via Strozzi, this fine old Tuscan restaurant serves hearty local food in a relaxed, informal atmosphere. There are delicious robust soups—just the thing if you happen to be in Florence in the dead of winter—with the minestrone being the best. Pastas are also very good. In the summertime Al Campidoglio serves homemade ice cream. Prices here used to be very low, but they have climbed considerably in the last few years. Dinner for two is about 125,000 lire.

Paoli, Via dei Tavolini 12 (tel. 216-215); closed Tuesday. Credit Cards: AE, DC, MC, V. You'll find this *catteristico* Tuscan restaurant just off Via dei Calzaiuoli. It is elegant and old-fashioned, and serves some of the best food in the center of town. Try the rich cannelloni as a first course. The bistecca a la fiorentina is an excellent second course, as is the scampi marinara. Dinner for two can cost as much as 200,000 lire, depending on your choice of wine.

Giovacchino, Via dei Tosinghi 34 (tel. 213-276); closed Monday morning. No credit cards. This is a no-nonsense cafeteria-style *tavola calda*. You can choose from two or three pastas or sandwiches. The food is not world class of course, but Giovacchino is a perfect place for a quick and inexpensive lunch a stone's throw from the Duomo.

ACROSS THE RIVER AND INTO THE PITTI

This walk crosses the Ponte Vecchio and explores the area around the Palazzo Pitti. Once again, the stores are a mixture—fine handmade paper, clothing, and antiques. The major streets covered are Borgo San Jacopo, Via dei Guicciardini, and Via Maggio, with detours down a number of side streets for notable shops just off the beaten track.

There are so many tiny jewelry shops on the **Ponte Vecchio** that it gets a little bit difficult to tell them apart. In many cases you don't have to: many shops with different names and different owners sell nearly identical goods. There is something a little tacky about many of them, and plainly touristy about all of them. The stores are good for small souvenir items like a silver or gold charm of the Duomo or inexpensive enamel earrings, but the days when bargains were to be had over the Arno are gone. In a lot of the shops the constant tourist traffic has worn some of the jewelers' nerves a little thin and the size of the shops doesn't allow for extended browsing. These places are so small they're crowded when there are three people in them.

Of course, there are a couple of shops you should see. That's not to say the others are bad, of course; it just seems that these three stand out a bit. The first of two Rudolfo Fallaci shops is located at the beginning of the bridge on the Uffizzi side, at Ponte Vecchio 10, and sells new and antique gold, silver, and enamel jewelry. Melli, at Ponte Vecchio 46, specializes in antique jewelry only. Across the street from that is the other Rudolfo Fallaci, at no. 51. Facing it at no. 54 is Burchi, the smartest and most expensive jeweler on the bridge.

The major street dead ahead of you as soon as you have crossed the bridge is Via dei Guicciardini. To your right is Borgo San Jacopo. We are going to have a good look at both of these streets, but not yet. First, detour off Via dei Guicciardini, taking the turn to your left, onto **Via dei Bardi.** About a block in, after the movie theater, is Terre di Tuscia, at Via dei Bardi 63, one of the best shops for painted Tuscan pottery in the city.

Back on Via Guicciardini, make another detour, this time to your right down **Via Barbadori.** About halfway down the block at no. 10 is Dodo, a small, charming shop which sells clothing, furniture, toys, and odds and ends for young children.

Now proceed down **Via dei Guicciardini.** The street is not as long as it looks

FLORENCE: GREAT SHOPPING STROLLS

on a map as over half of it is taken up by the Pitti Palace.

Quaglia & Forte, at Via dei Guicciardini 12, is the most famous store in the city for cameos of every shape and description. Just down the street is the house in which Machiavelli used to live, and in it is Galleria Machiavelli, which sells fine Tuscan pottery. This is at Via dei Guicciardini 18/104 (numbers are a little odd on this street).

At Via dei Guicciardini 114 is Umberto, a vast leather shop selling everything in leather except shoes. Next door is Macel, Via dei Guicciardini 128, an elegant but reasonably priced boutique for women's wear.

Detour off Via dei Guicciardini to your right, making the turn onto **Via dello Sprone**. At no. 25 is La Casa Abitata, the best source in Florence of Italian housewares and cooking utensils.

Once back on Via dei Guicciardini, go straight to the **Piazza Pitti** itself. Facing the palazzo, at Piazza Pitti 37, is Giulio Giannini e Figlio, which has been hand-making paper in this location since the mid-19th century.

Via dei Guicciardini meets Via Maggio in a small piazza. We are going to walk the length of Via Maggio (heading back toward the river), but before we do, cross Via Maggio and walk 50 yards down a street called **Via Mazzetta,** to no. 22, Vainio, another maker of fine paper. Unlike Guilio Giannini, there is nothing traditional about the designs here.

Via Maggio is absolutely *the* antiques street in Florence, so if you are not in the market for them, then you might as well skip the whole street. Except that you'd miss Soluzioni, at Via Maggio 82, a fun, interesting, and just plain weird shop which sells eccentrically designed housewares, purses, clocks—anything, in fact, that struck the owner's fancy. Even if you don't want to buy anything, you can still spend an hour here just marveling at the oddness of it all.

On Via Maggio, the odd numbers are on the right-hand side of the street and the even numbers on the left. However, no. 2 does not face no. 3, for example. You'll have to keep on changing sides of the street as you work your way down. The shops are in this zigzag order, even though it doesn't appear that way from the order of the numbers.

Artstudio, Via Maggio 41, has beautiful antique porcelains and Orientalia. Il Maggiolino, on the other side of the street at Via Maggio 80, sells fine antique jewelry, particularly from the last century.

There's furniture of recent vintage, art deco particularly, at Bottega San Felice, Via Maggio 39. Gallori Turchi, Via Maggio 14, has an exceptional collection of Italian antiques of the 17th and 18th centuries: furniture, tapestries, paintings, even arms.

Antique fabrics and embroidery are the specialty at Mirella Piselli, Via Maggio 23. There's more high-quality furniture and objets d'art at Giovanni Pratesi, Via Maggio 13. A few doors away at Via Maggio 28, Adriana Chelini, has more 18th-century furniture and porcelain.

Paolo Paoletti, Via Maggio 30, has beautiful silver and art objects of the Italian Renaissance and baroque periods. Guido Bartolozzi, Via Maggio 18, has later works of Italian origin, particularly furniture and paintings. There are 18th-century clocks, glass, and furniture at Antichita Lorena, Via Maggio 10.

At Via Maggio 9, 16th-century European objects are the specialty at Lo Stipo. A more recent past is recalled at Fantasie del Passato, Via Maggio 7, which goes in for art nouveau and art deco bric-a-brac and porcelain.

At the very end—or beginning—of Via Maggio is Mary Pavan, Via Maggio 1, which had beautiful and specifically Florentine or Tuscan antiques from the 16th and 17th centuries.

This brings us to **Piazza Frescobaldi** and the bank of the Arno, where the Ponte San Trinità crosses the river. In this small piazza there is another antique shop of note—Kolligian Franceschi, Piazza Frescobaldi 2, selling exceptional carved and painted wood figures and dolls from the last four centuries.

Across the piazza, and very contemporary, is Parfums-Bijoux, Piazza Frescobaldi 11, a small but excellent source of costume and silver jewelry. There are also some perfumes.

Where Via Maggio meets Piazza Frescobaldi, **Borgo San Jacopo** begins, marking the last leg of this stroll. The street is old and charming, and has everything from designer goods to one of the best restaurants in town.

Angela Caputi has two shops on Borgo San Jacopo, right next to one another at nos. 82 and 78. The first is tiny but offers a great selection of the Caputi Giuggiù costume jewelry. Look for the Caputi casual wear in the larger store next door.

Picarda, Borgo San Jacopo 58, has beautiful blouses in various fabrics. La Casa delle Stampa, a quality print shop, is at Borgo San Jacopo 54. Across the street you'll find good values on women's knitwear at Glamour, Borgo San Jacopo 49.

On the corner of Borgo San Jacopo and Via Toscanella, stop at The Corner, Borgo San Jacopo 29B, for prime fashions for young women. Next door, at Borgo San Jacopo 29A, is Giachi, an excellent shoe and bag shop. Across the street at no. 44, Duvet possesses both a lovely view of the Arno and high-quality woolens and cashmere for men and women.

Crossing the street again, take a moment to browse at Cose del'900, "Things of the 1900s," an antique shop specializing in glass objects from the century. The address is Borgo San Jacopo 45.

As you near the end of this street, approaching the intersection of Via dei Guicciardini and the Ponte Vecchio, there are two shops of note. One is Cinzia, Borgo San Jacopo 22, a worthwhile stop for brightly colored, handmade casual knitwear. And right at the corner of Borgo San Jacopo and Via dei Guicciardini is a fabulous leather shop, Mannelli, at Via Borgo San Jacopo 3.

A SIGHTSEEING SUGGESTION

Work began on the vast **Palazzo Pitti** in 1458, commissioned by a merchant named Luca Pitti. He was a bitter and implacable rival of the Medici, but as usual, things turned out to the Medicis' advantage and they moved into it in the 1560s. They are largely responsible for its current look and collection of paintings.

FLORENCE: GREAT SHOPPING STROLLS

Fashions on Borgo San Jacopo

The Pitti collection is hung in a succession of magnificent rooms, notably those named after Roman gods. The Sala di Marte (Mars), the Sala di Venere (Venus), and the Sala di Saturno (Saturn) are all lavishly frescoed and decorated. These rooms rival the paintings hung frame-to-frame on the walls. For the most part the artworks are later than those in the Uffizi (to which the Pitti is connected by the covered corridor on the upper level of the Ponte Vecchio), with many pieces by the greatest baroque masters. There are works by Rubens, Breughel, and Guido Reni (thought by the Victorians to be the greatest painter of all time—"The Divine Guido," they called him), as well as paintings by Van Dyck and Tintoretto. The great painters of the Renaissance are represented by Raphael, Andrea del Sarto, and Filippo Lippi.

The Pitti also houses the **Museo degli Argenti**, a series of rooms devoted to jewelry from the 15th to the 18th century owned by the Medici, or collected by one of the last Medici princesses, Anna Maria, in the 18th century. Those with an interest in the evolution of jewelry design should take a look here.

The Palazzo Pitti is open Tuesday through Saturday from 9 a.m. to 2 p.m., and on Sunday from 9 a.m. to 1 p.m. It is closed all day Monday.

REFRESHMENTS EN ROUTE

The most refreshing thing you can do in this neighborhood is to relax in the tranquil Boboli Gardens behind the Pitti Palace. First laid out in 1550, they have miles of walks, acres of flowers, and many beautiful fountains. If you want something to drink and a bite to eat, this neighborhood can provide both.

Bars

Bar Santa Trinità, Via Maggio 2 (no phone), open from 8 a.m. to 7:30 p.m.; closed Sunday. No credit cards. An attractive place with whitewashed walls and a polished-wood bar, the Bar Santa Trinità couldn't be better situated. It's right at the corner of Borgo San Jacopo and Via Maggio in the Piazza Frescobaldi. This is a nice, quiet spot for a mid-morning cappuccino, a good sandwich at lunchtime, or an afternoon tea.

Cennini, Borgo San Jacopo 2 (no phone), open from 8 a.m. to 1:30 p.m. and 2:30 to 7 p.m.; closed Sunday and Wednesday afternoons. No credit cards. Cennini is a pastry shop which has a small area with tables and chairs. Come here in the afternoon for coffee and some of their delicious bignes (cream-filled pastries), chocolate cake, or a selection of biscuits. If breakfast at your hotel wasn't enough, stop in first thing in the morning for a croissant or ciambella (an Italian doughnut).

Ringo, Borgo San Jacopo 19 (tel. 704-173), open from 9 a.m. to 7 p.m.; closed Sunday. No credit cards. Ringo's is a shiny, chrome and pale-wood bar which gets crowded with younger Florentines who look in for an aperitivo at the end of the day. There is some hot food served at lunchtime.

Vera, Piazza Frescobaldi (no phone), open from 10 a.m. to 7 p.m. daily. No credit cards. A bustling, noisy, no-frills tavola calda. Vera serves a variety of baked pastas at lunchtime. The food is good, fast, and cheap, but there is little time to linger over it.

Restaurants

Osteria del Cinghiale Bianco, Borgo San Jacopo 43 (tel. 215-706), open from 12:30 to 3 p.m. and 7:30 to 10:30 p.m. Credit Cards: AE. This is one of the newest restaurants in Florence and it has quickly become one of the best. There are two simply decorated rooms, moderate to expensive prices, and a very imaginative menu. As the name suggests (Cinghiale means "wild boar"), game dishes predominate. There is exceptionally good papardelle alle leppre, wide flat noodles in a meat sauce—the meat is hare—and excellent risotto alla cacciatora. Second courses include pheasant, quail, and of course, cinghiale, usually accompanied by polenta and fresh greens, depending on what's in season.

Cammillo, Borgo San Jacopo 57 (tel. 212-427), open from 1 to 2:30 p.m. and 7:30 to 10:30 p.m.; closed Wednesday and Thursday. Credit Cards: AE, DC, MC, V. This is a good old-fashioned Italian trattoria which serves lunches in portions large enough to call it dinner and end your day's shopping at midday. The food—particularly the pasta, the grilled meats and the desserts—is extremely good. Despite the consistent quality of the menu, Cammillo is not a temple of gastronomy with white-gloved waiters and the like. The atmosphere is casual and relaxed. Dinner for two with a good bottle of chianti costs about 75,000 lire to 120,000 lire.

FLORENCE: GREAT SHOPPING STROLLS

HIGH-FASHION FLORENCE

This walk covers the most exclusive shopping streets in Florence, encompassing just about all the big names in Italian design. Although this is the most expensive neighborhood in the city, we'll also visit a discount outlet for one of the priciest names in Italian leather, Beltrami.

The streets are: Via dei Tornabuoni, Via della Vigna Nuova, Via del Parione, Lungarno Amerigo Vespucci, Lungarno Corsini, and Borgo Ognissanti.

The walk begins at the end of **Via dei Tornabuoni** farthest from the river at the corner of Piazza Antinori. You'll encounter two big names immediately. The smaller of the two Pineider stationery shops is at Via dei Tornabuoni 76. Across the street is Gucci's home base at Via dei Tornabuoni 73.

Heading toward the river, stop next at Mario Valentino, a shoe store at Via dei Tornabuoni 67. There's more leather at Roberta di Camerino, Via dei Tornabuoni 47. Next door, at no. 43, is the exclusive jeweler Mario Buccellati.

Giorgio Armani for men and women is at Via dei Tornabuoni 35-37. There's more menswear at Contemporaneo, Vie dei Tornabuoni 36. The beautiful Casadei shop, one of *the* places to shop for ladies' shoes, is at Via dei Tornabuoni 33.

Across the street at no. 32 is Bijoux Cascio, with a wonderful selection of quality costume jewelry. You have to cross the street again to see Florence's only Fendi shop, at no. 27. Casa di Hogg, at Via dei Tornabuoni 26, looks like an upmarket Benetton, but that's because it's owned by Benetton.

The flagship Salvatore Ferragamo, with leather and clothing for men and women, is at Via dei Tornabuoni 16. Across the street is another giant name: Gianni Versace, at nos. 13-15.

Just before you reach the river you'll pass the Cesari store in Florence, at Via dei Tornabuoni 2. If you are shopping for linens or fabrics, this store is a must.

As you come down Via dei Tornabuoni, you pass two streets on your right. The one closest to the Arno is Via del Parione; a block farther inland is Via della Vigna Nuova. Retrace your footsteps and head down **Via del Parione.** There are two shops on this short, narrow street you should see, both famous makers of leather goods: *Trussardi* at no. 15, and Il Bisonte at no. 35.

At the bottom of Via del Parione is a busy square, Piazza Carlo Goldoni. Here Via del Parione and Via della Vigna Nuova meet. Unfortunately, if you head up Vigna Nuova, you'll be heading back the way you've come, toward ground you've covered already on Via dei Tornabuoni. But it can't be helped—**Via della Vigna Nuova** has to be seen, even though it means doubling back. You'll get to know the street well because you'll have to come down it again to explore a major antiques street, Borgo Ognissanti.

But first Vigna Nuova itself. Right at the corner of Via del Parione and Via della Vigna Nuova are two &C (ampersand-C is shorthand for "et cetera"), fabulous modern stationery stores. The street addresses are Via della Vigna Nuova 82 and 91.

Next comes Lord Brummell, an exceptional men's clothier, at Via della Vigna Nuova 79. Next to it, at no. 75, is Giovanni Baccani, a print and fine stationery shop.

One of two Gherardini leather shops is at Via della Vigna Nuova 57. At no. 47 is another heavyweight: Valentino. Cross the street to look at the clothing for women at Mattolini, Via della Vigna Nuova 44. There's more clothing at Giulia Carla Cecchi, at no. 40.

All the cute and casual Naj Oleari products are in the shop of the same name at Via della Vigna Nuova 35.

Alex, Via della Vigna Nuova 19, has clothes for women by a dozen different famous names, the majority of them French. Happy Jack, next door at Via della Vigna Nuova 7, has clothes for men.

Return to Piazza Carlo Goldoni and walk up **Borgo Ognissanti.** This is another great antiques street, but the first shop you'll encounter is Loretta Caponi, at no. 12, which sells exquisite lingerie. Then comes Alberto Pierini, Borgo Ognissanti 22, an antiques dealer specializing in quality 18th-century furniture. At no. 16 is Paola Ventura, a shop dealing in rare porcelain and majolica, particularly from the early 20th century. Palloni is next door, at no. 19, and has rare crystal and furniture. Its neighbor, Fallani Best, Borgo Ognissanti 15, sells paintings from the last three centuries.

At Paola Romano, across the street at Borgo Ognissanti 20, antique ceramics are the stock in trade. At the corner of Borgo Ognissanti and Via del Porcellana (Borgo Ognissanti 43), Giampaolo Fioretto has Italian furniture, objects, and paintings of the 16th, 17th, and 18th centuries.

You are now in Piazza Ognissanti, the home of the two best hotels in Florence. On one side of the square is the Grand Hotel and facing it is the Excelsior. On the Grand side of the piazza is Bottega Veneta, at no. 3.

Cross the square and walk down **Lungarno Amerigo Vespucci** toward the Ponte Vecchio. First you'll come to Pratesi, Lungarno Amerigo Vespucci 8, home to fine fabrics and linens; the next stop is Mila Schön, at Lungarno Amerigo Vespucci 26-28.

At about this point the lungarno changes its name to **Lungarno Corsini.** At Lungarno Corsini 24 is Ducci, a huge furniture, print, and knickknack shop. At Lungarno Corsini 38-40 is Bottega del Artigiana del Libro, a great place to shop for Florentine decorated paper.

IN THE NEIGHBORHOOD

Two blocks from where this stroll began (Piazza Antinori) is **Via dei Panzani.** At no. 1—which, due to the fiendish Florentine street-numbering system, is right in the middle of the street, not at one end—is Beltrami Spa, a discount outlet for the famous leatherware.

Cellerini, at no. 37 on **Via del Sole,** which is a couple of blocks off Via della Vigna Nuova (go down Via della Spada), is a wonderful luggage shop.

Nearby, on **Via del Moro** at no. 44, is Casalini, a minute shop selling leather-covered boxes and other small leather furnishings.

Genni, at **Via dei Cerretani** 29, has stylish lingerie and sleep wear. You'll find the street between the Duomo and Via dei Panzani.

SIGHTSEEING SUGGESTION

The **Church of Santa Maria Novella** is not far from the path just described. This beautiful old church was begun in the 13th century but not finished until the 16th, which is why there is a fusion of Renaissance and Florentine Gothic in its design.

The interior of the church is lavishly decorated with frescoes and panel paintings. The oldest frescoes date from the 14th century and are by Nardo di Cione. There are also frescoes by Ghirlandaio, Filippino Lippi, and in the cloister, scenes of the Old Testament by Paolo Uccello.

The most celebrated work in this church, however, is Masaccio's fresco of the *Holy Trinity with the Madonna*. It is considered one of the most revolutionary works of the Renaissance for its masterful use of perspective. The frescoes are on the right as you enter.

Santa Maria Novella is open every day, but from 9 a.m. to 2 p.m. only.

REFRESHMENTS EN ROUTE

Giacosa, Via dei Tornabuoni 83 (tel. 632-127), open from 10 a.m. to 7:30 p.m.; closed Sunday. No credit cards. A Florentine landmark, Giacosa is right on Via dei Tornabuoni. There is a tearoom serving excellent English-style afternoon teas, a cocktail bar, and a section where you can get a quick meal at midday.

Il Cestello, in the Hotel Excelsior, Piazza Ognissanti 3 (tel. 294-301), open from 1 to 3 p.m. and 7 to 10:30 p.m. daily. Credit Cards: AE, DC, MC, V. Situated on the roof of one of Florence's finest hotels, Il Cestello serves food as good as the view—and the view is stupendous. Looking out across the Arno and downstream to the Ponte Vecchio, terrace dining at Il Cestello is a treat. The pasta e fagioli and the crab-and-artichoke salad are the best first courses, along with linguine in a white truffle sauce. Bistecca fiorentina is an exceptional second. In the summer there is a buffet table at lunchtime and it groans with excellent salads, cold meats, and cheeses. The view and the food do not come cheap. Dinner for two can easily cost 200,000 lire.

Doney, Via dei Tornabuoni 46 (tel. 214-348), open from 7 to 11 p.m., closed Monday. Credit Cards: AE, DC. As one might expect for an eatery founded in 1822, Doney is an old-fashioned, extremely elegant restaurant serving traditional French and Italian dishes. Begin with the pennette in an olive sauce, the tortelli with a grating of fresh white truffles, or the delicious cannelloni. If it's winter, minestrone soup is an excellent and warming first course. The second courses are uniformly good, especially the fish. Service is impeccable and the prices are high. Dinner for two will cost in the region of 175,000 lire.

Harry's Bar, Lungarno Amerigo Vespucci 22 (tel. 296-700), open from 1 to 5 p.m. and 7:30 p.m. to midnight; closed Sunday. Credit Cards: AE, DC, MC, V. You can have a cocktail, a hamburger, or a full meal in this facsimile of the famous Venetian Harry's. The crowd is chic, multilingual, and always dressed to the nines. Prices are high—but consider the neighborhood, the clientele, and the cachet of the name. A light lunch for two is about 100,000 lire.

CHAPTER IX

THE ULTIMATE FLORENCE SHOPPING SPREE

No matter what the Milanese and the Romans think, all Italy agrees that the real aristrocrats of the country are Florentines (the Venetians, however, dissent from this). An Italian with a Tuscan accent is deferred to much in the same way as an Englishman who speaks "Oxbridge" commands respect. As one might expect, these *gente per bene* (roughly translated as "the upper crust") expect to be able to buy the best in clothing, in antiques, and furnishings for their homes. The following section tells you where the Florentine gentleman and woman shop.

ANTIQUES

ADRIANA CHELINI
Via Maggio 28 (tel. 213-471)
Hours: *Monday through Saturday from 10 a.m. to 1:30 p.m. and 4 to 7 p.m. (closed Monday morning)*
Credit Cards: *None*
English Spoken.

This is a very elegant shop with silk-covered walls and parquet floors, offering furniture and objets d'art from the 17th and 18th centuries. The high-quality pieces are beautifully displayed and the staff is extremely knowledgeable. They will also assist with shipping. A pair of beautifully gilded Tuscan console tables dating from the 1700s, elaborately carved and in very good condition, costs 18 million lire.

ALBERTO PIERINI
Borgo Ognissanti 22 (tel. 298-138)
Hours: *Monday through Saturday from 10 a.m. to 1 p.m. and 4 to 7 p.m. (closed Monday morning)*

Credit Cards: *None*
English Spoken.

This lovely shop on Borgo Ognissanti caters to collectors of painted and decorated Tuscan country furniture of the 1600s and 1700s. A very unusual 18th-century version of the murphy bed, which folds out from what appears to be a secretary desk, was 15.5 million lire.

ANTICHITA LORENA
Via Maggio 10 (tel. 211-426)
Hours: *Monday through Saturday from 10 a.m. to 1 p.m. and 3:30 to 7 p.m. (closed Monday morning)*
Credit Cards: *None*
English Spoken.

Furniture, paintings, glass, and art objects of the 18th century are the stock in trade of this fine antiques shop. A burled briarwood commode with three large and two smaller drawers, from the second half of the 1700s, is 24 million lire.

ARTSTUDIO
Via Maggio 41 (tel. 282-978)
Hours: *Monday through Saturday from 10 a.m. to 1 p.m. and 4 to 7 p.m. (closed Monday morning)*
Credit Cards: *None*
English Spoken.

This small shop on Via Maggio specializes in fine porcelain, from Europe and the Far East. A porcelain plate of the Chien-Lung era (1736–1796) with a multicolored floral design—the colors are very bright and the brushwork very skillful—costs 25 million lire.

BOTTEGA SAN FELICE
Via Maggio 39 (tel. 215-479)
Hours: *Monday through Saturday from 9:30 a.m. to 1 p.m. and 3:30 to 7 p.m. (closed Monday morning)*
Credit Cards: *None*
English Spoken.

Fanciers of 20th-century furniture, particularly of the art deco period, will be fascinated by this shop. Collected in two rooms are examples of the style, all of them in superb condition. A wood vanity table from the 1930s, covered in mother-of-pearl celluloide (it looks like it belongs in Joan Crawford's dressing room at Metro) and designed by Meroni and Fossati, is 19.5 million lire.

COSE DEL '900
Borgo San Jacopo 45 (tel. 283-491)

Hours: **Monday through Saturday from 10 a.m. to 1 p.m. and 3:30 to 7:30 p.m. (closed Monday morning)**
Credit Cards: **AE, DC, MC, V**
English Spoken.

This tiny little shop is crammed full of small objects, most of them in glass, dating from 1900 to 1940. Prices are reasonable. A small art nouveau picture frame in bronze costs 40,000 lire. A deco-style clock in top working order is 240,000 lire.

FALLANI BEST
Borgo Ognissanti 15 (tel. 214-986)
Hours: **Monday through Saturday from 10 a.m. to 1 p.m. and 4 to 7 p.m. (closed Monday morning)**
Credit Cards: **None**
English Spoken.

Italian paintings of the 18th and 19th centuries, as well as some sculpture and bric-a-brac can be found here. Prices on paintings range from one to many millions of lire.

FANTASIE DEL PASSATO
Via Maggio 7 (tel. 217-744)
Hours: **Monday through Saturday from 9:30 a.m. to 1:30 p.m. and 3:30 to 7:30 p.m. (closed Monday morning)**
Credit Cards: **None**
English Spoken.

The specialty of this small shop is glassware and pottery, largely of Italian manufacture, some of it dating from the 18th century but most of it from the 19th and early 20th centuries. A piece of 18th-century majolica can cost as much as 10 million lire; newer glass items are less. There are also some oddments which have low prices. An ivory-handled buttonhook, for example, is just 20,000 lire. What you'd do with it, however, is another question.

GALLORI TURCHI
Via Maggio 14 (tel. 282-279)
Hours: **Monday through Saturday from 10 a.m. to 1:30 p.m. and 4 to 7 p.m. (closed Monday morning)**
Credit Cards: **None**
English Spoken.

This is a large, excellent gallery with a marvelous collection of antiques: inlaid and gilded Italian furniture from the 17th and 18th centuries; art objects, like polychrome figures in wood and gesso from the 1500s; tapestries, paintings, and a selection of carved and engraved weapons, particularly pistols, from Italy and France.

Gallori Turchi: Antique collector's heaven

GIAMPAOLO FIORETTI
Borgo Ognissanti 43 (tel. 214-927)
Hours: *Monday through Saturday from 10 a.m. to 1 p.m. and 4 to 7 p.m. (closed Monday morning)*
Credit Cards: *None*
English Spoken.

An elegant antique shop with paintings, objets d'art, and some surprises, like a beautifully decorated birdcage produced in Florence at the end of the 16th century.

GIOVANNI PRATESI
Via Maggio 13 (tel. 296-568)
Hours: *Monday through Saturday from 10 a.m. to 1 p.m. and 4 to 7 p.m. (closed Monday morning)*
Credit Cards: *None*
English Spoken.

High-quality furniture, paintings, and objects are offered, predominantly Italian pieces from the 17th and 18th centuries.

GUIDO BARTOLOZZI
Via Maggio 18 (tel. 215-602)
Hours: *Monday through Saturday from 10 a.m. to 1 p.m. and 3:30 to 7 p.m.*

Credit Cards: *None*
English Spoken.

The accent here is on Florentine antiques from the 1500s through the 1900s, everything from tapestries to furniture. The qualilty of the works shown here is exceptionally high—as are the prices.

IL MAGGIOLINO
Via Maggio 80 (tel. 216-660)
Hours: *Monday through Saturday from 10 a.m. to 1:30 p.m. and 3:30 to 7:30 p.m.*
Credit Cards: *None*
English Spoken.

This small shop sells nothing but stunning jewelry and watches from France and Italy, and mostly from the late 19th century to the 1940s.

KOLLIGIAN FRANCESCHI
Piazza Frescobaldi 2 (tel. 282-756)
Hours: *Monday through Saturday from 10 a.m. to 1 p.m. and 3:30 to 7:30 p.m. (closed Monday morning)*
Credit Cards: *None*

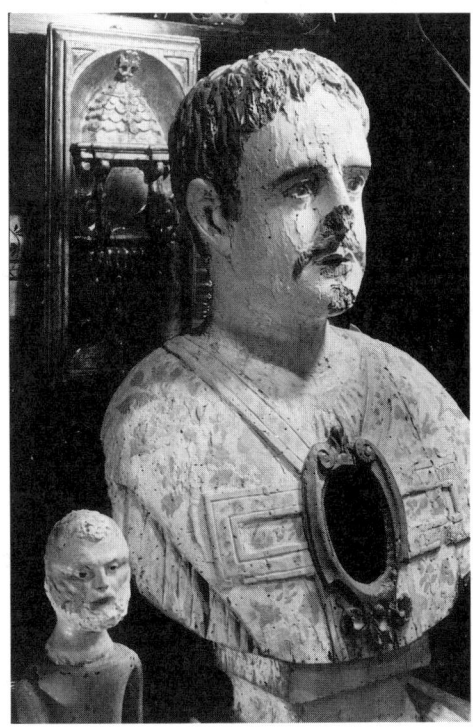

The treasures at Kolligian Franceschi include lovely polychrome carved reliquaries of the 16th century

As you cross the Piazza di Santa Trinità, you'll find this charming, cluttered antique shop on the left. Items here are almost exclusively painted, carved, wooden figures and Italian objects from the 16th century. There are exquisite articulated figures of saints, priced from about 400,000 lire for a very small one. An ornate carved frame is 1.8 million lire. A painted reliquary in wood and ivory is also 1.8 million lire.

LO STIPO
Via Maggio 9 (tel. 292-398)
Hours: *Monday through Saturday from 10 a.m. to 1 p.m. and 3:30 to 7:30 p.m. (closed Monday morning)*
Credit Cards: *None*
English Spoken.

Lo Stipo carries late Renaissance furniture. The selection is large and of a very high standard. All the paintings, particularly those of the 16th century, have scrupulously researched provenances.

MARY PAVAN
Via Maggio 1 (tel. 263-302)
Hours: *Monday through Saturday from 10 a.m. to 1:30 p.m. and 3:30 to 7 p.m. (closed Monday morning)*
Credit Cards: *None*

Exclusively Tuscan antiques of impeccable quality are to be found here, including ceramic glazed reliefs from the Della Robbia school, 17th-century furniture, and some decidedly different pieces like marquetry games and gaming boards.

PALLONI
Borgo Ognissanti 19 (tel. 298-709)
Hours: *Monday through Saturday from 10 a.m. to 1 p.m. and 4 to 7 p.m. (closed Monday morning)*
Credit Cards: *None*
English Spoken.

Beautiful antique crystal and glass, as well as some furniture and smaller art objects.

PAOLO PAOLETTI
Via Maggio 30 (tel. 214-728)
Hours: *Monday through Saturday from 10 a.m. to 1 p.m. and 3:30 to 7 p.m. (closed Monday morning)*
Credit Cards: *None*
English Spoken.

Rare and beautiful antiques dating from the 15th and 16th centuries, centered

mostly on Florence. There are fine examples of painted stucco reliefs and works in silver, some from the 1400s.

PAOLO ROMANO
Borgo Ognissanti 20 (tel. 293-294)
Hours: Monday through Saturday from 10 a.m. to 1:30 p.m. and 3:30 to 7 p.m. (closed Monday morning)
Credit Cards: None
English Spoken.

Paolo Romano specializes in 18th-century ceramics and porcelains, ranging from small, delicate pieces to large, rare items like a magnificently decorated ceramic heating stove dating from the baroque era.

PAOLA VENTURA
Borgo Ognissanti 16 (tel. 210-914)
Hours: Monday through Saturday from 10 a.m. to 1:30 p.m. and 3:30 to 7 p.m. (closed Monday morning)
Credit Cards: None
English Spoken.

Antique porcelains and other ceramics are sold exclusively here. There are some superb examples of work from all parts of the world and from various periods, but the 20-th century work is remarkably fine. A 1928 coffee service in faience, designed by Giacomo Balla is particularly stunning. It costs 3.5 million lire.

PISELLI
Via Maggio 23 (tel. 298-029)
Hours: Monday through Saturday from 10 a.m. to 1 p.m. and 4 to 7 p.m. (closed Monday morning)
Credit Cards: None
English Spoken.

Piselli sells antique embroidery and tapestries and some smaller art objects. The selection and quality of some of the embroidered work is exceptional, particularly the vestments and other religious works from the 16th and 17th centuries.

BOOKS

BM BOOKSHOP
Borgognissanti 4 (tel. 294-575)
Hours: Monday through Saturday from 10 a.m. to 1:30 p.m. and 4 to 7:30 p.m. (closed Monday morning)
Credit Cards: None
English Spoken.

You'll find the largest selection of English-language books at this pleasant shop on the Duomo/Uffizi side of the River Arno, not far from Florence's finest hotels, the Excelsior and the Grand. The stock comes from both American and British publishers, and there are always the bestsellers of both countries on hand, as well as a huge selection of guides to Florence in particular and Italy in general.

CLOTHING

CHILDREN'S FASHIONS

CASA DELLO SPORT
Via dei Tosinghi 8–10 (tel. 212-344)
Hours: Monday through Saturday from 9:30 a.m. to 1:30 p.m. and 3:30 to 7:30 p.m. (closed Monday morning)
Credit Cards: AE, MC

It's back to Casa dello Sport again, this time for children's play and sportswear. A Fila parka for a boy or girl 8 to 11 years old is 95,000 lire. There are shorts, snowsuits, and polo shirts for girls and boys by Fila, Ellesse, and Kappa.

CIRRI
Via Por Santa Maria 38–40 (tel. 296-593)
Hours: Monday through Saturday from 9 a.m. to 1 p.m. and 3:30 to 7:30 p.m. (closed Monday morning)
Credit Cards: AE, DC, MC, V
English Spoken.

Lovely, old-fashioned hand-embroidered clothes for children from infants to 10 years old. The kind of thing on sale here looks as though it stepped out of an illustrated volume of *Alice in Wonderland* or from Christopher Robin's closet. Sailor suits for a boy or a girl are 250,000 lire. A little girl's party dress with a lace collar is 275,000 lire.

DODO
Via Barbadori 10 (tel. 296-933)
Hours: Monday through Saturday from 9:30 a.m. to 1 p.m. and 3:30 to 7:30 p.m. (closed Monday morning)
Credit Cards: AE

Lots of cute things for kids, and not just clothes either. If your 8-year-old is wearing earrings already, you can buy pair of Peter Rabbit clip-ons for 15,000 lire. There are playsuits, overalls, and shorts in pastel colors from 55,000 lire up, suitable for newborns and toddlers.

NAJ OLEARI
Via della Vigna Nuova 35 (tel. 210-443)
Hours: *Monday through Saturday from 9:30 a.m. to 1 p.m. and 3:30 to 7:30 p.m. (closed Monday morning)*
Credit Cards: AE, MC, V

"Adorable" is the appropriate word for the Naj Oleari line of clothes for children. A pair of overalls in pale yellow or green made from the Naj Oleari patterns, for ages 2 to 4, is 95,000 lire. A skirt for a little girl in the same age range is 95,000 lira.

TAF
Via Por Santa Maria 22 (tel. 213-190)
Hours: *Monday through Saturday from 9 a.m. to 1 p.m. and 3:30 to 7:30 p.m. (closed Monday morning)*
Credit Cards: None
English Spoken.

Beautiful embroidered clothes for newborns and tots. A three-piece silk christening gown, with lace collar, cuffs, and hem, is 365,000 lire. It will be in your family for years.

MEN'S FASHIONS

CASA DELLO SPORT
Via dei Tosinghi 8–10 (tel. 212-344)
Hours: *Monday through Saturday from 9:30 a.m. to 1:30 p.m. and 3:30 to 7:30 p.m. (closed Monday morning)*
Credit Cards: AE, MC

Great prices are to be found in this sportswear supermarket, with the best-known Italian names and some foreigners like Lacoste. A complete Fila running suit is 220,000 lire. A Fila parka in maroon with the stripes on the sleeves and the black and red Fs on the breast is 275,000 lire. There is also some casual wear.

CONTEMPORANEO
Via dei Tornabuoni 36 (tel. 213-741)
Hours: *Monday through Saturday from 10 a.m. to 1:30 p.m. and 3:30 to 7:30 p.m. (closed Monday morning)*
Credit Cards: AE
English Spoken.

A good men's shop with Italian fashions ranging from the traditional to the unusual. Here you'll find all the standards—blazers, sports jackets, ties, twill and wool trousers—as well as some trendier leather jackets. There is excellent knitwear too. A bulky cable-knit sweater with a lozenge pattern in one of a dozen colors is 235,000 lire. A pair of heavy gray cords is 260,000 lire. The leather jackets, short or three-quarter-length, cost between 700,000 lire and 1 million lire.

ELLESSE SPA
Via del Proconsolo 5 and Corso 1–11 (tel. 213-780)
Hours: *Monday through Saturday from 9:30 a.m. to 1:30 p.m. and 3:30 to 7 p.m.*
Credit Cards: AE, DC, MC, V
English Spoken.

Two different addresses for the same shop. This is the head office of Ellesse in Florence, and because it's a company-supervised outlet prices do not include the usual store markup. A tennis shirt with a collar is 60,000 lire; with a V-neck, 55,000 lire. The Ellesse running gear is favorably priced. Sweatsuits in a dozen different colors and patterns range from 175,000 lire to 300,000 lire.

GIANNI VERSACE
Via dei Tornabuoni 13–15 (tel. 296-167)
Hours: *Monday through Saturday from 9:30 a.m. to 1 p.m. and 3:30 to 7:30 p.m. (closed Monday morning)*
Credit Cards: AE
English Spoken.

A beautiful but not very large store with a good selection of menswear nonetheless. A two-piece suit in black or a small check is 1.45 million lire to 1.8 million lire. More casual wear—a pair of pleated pants, say—is 400,000 lire.

GIORGIO ARMANI
Via dei Tornabuoni 35–37 (tel. 213-819)
Hours: *Monday through Friday from 9:30 a.m. to 1:30 p.m. and 3:30 to 7:30 p.m. (closed Monday morning)*
Credit Cards: AE, DC, MC, V
English Spoken.

Modern men's clothes by one of Italy's masters, the Armani line here is all on the high-ticket end of the price range—there is no Emporio Armani shop in Florence, not yet anyway. A suit with a wide pinstripe is 950,000 lire. There is also a selection of leather jackets, in the 850,000-lire to 1.5-million-lire range.

HAPPY JACK
Via della Vigna Nuova 7 (tel. 217-331)
Hours: *Monday through Saturday from 9:30 a.m. to 1:30 p.m. and 3:30 to 7:30 p.m. (closed Monday morning)*
Credit Cards: AE, DC, MC, V
English Spoken.

A high-quality menswear shop. If you aren't going to Rome, this is the Florence

Giorgio Armani style

shop for ready-to-wear Brioni. You'll also find Valentino Uomo, Basile, and Les Copains.

LORD BRUMMELL
Via della Vigna Nuova 79 (tel. 265-302)
Hours: *Monday through Saturday from 9:30 a.m. to 1:30 p.m. and 3:30 to 7:30 p.m. (closed Monday morning)*

Except for the fact that the salespeople speak Italian, you'd swear you were in St. James at men's clothier Lord Brummell

Credit Cards: AE
English Spoken.

This two-story shop looks more like the smoking room of a venerable old club than a store for menswear. (There's even a pool table upstairs.) The clothes have their roots in traditional styles, but with a little Italian zing added. Casual wear for winter and summer are the best things to shop for here. A pair of pleated linen pants costs 280,000 lire. A roomy winter coat in kelly-green wool is 520,000 lire.

MANTELASSI
Piazza della Repubblica 21 (tel. 212-334)
Hours: *Monday through Saturday from 10 a.m. to 1 p.m. and 3:30 to 7:30 p.m. (closed Monday morning)*
Credit Cards: AE, DC, MC, V
English Spoken.

English clothes and knits, cheaper than in the States but more expensive than in London. An excellent selection of Shetland sweaters for 90,000 lire and up.

UGOLINI E FIGLI
Via dei Calzaiuoli 65–68 (tel. 214-439)
Hours: *Monday through Saturday from 9:30 a.m. to 1 p.m. and 3:30 to 7:30 p.m. (closed Monday morning)*
Credit Cards: AE
English Spoken.

More traditional English clothing, but at higher prices than Mantelassi (see above). A gray tweed hacking jacket costs 750,000 lire.

WOMEN'S FASHIONS

ALEX
Via della Vigna Nuova 19 (tel. 214-952)
Hours: *Monday through Saturday from 10 a.m. to 7:30 p.m. nonstop*
Credit Cards: AE, DC, MC, V
English Spoken.

This very chic shop has gathered a dozen or so of the best-known designers under one elegant roof. Only a few of them are Italian, notably Byblos and Romeo Gigli. The best-known names are French: Jean-Paul Gaultier, Claude Montana, Thierry Mugler, for example. The accent here is on more formal clothing and prices are not bargain basement by any means. A two-piece black suit in fine Italian silk by Martine Sitbon costs 880,000 lire. Clothes by Byblos begin at about 400,000 lire.

ANGELA CAPUTI
Borgo San Jacopo 78 and 82 (tel. 212-972)
Hours: *Monday through Saturday from 9 a.m. to 1 p.m. and 4 to 8 p.m. (closed Monday morning)*
Credit Cards: *AE, DC, MC, V*

You'll find the fun, eccentric Angela Caputi shops side by side on Borgo San Jacopo. Number 78 is a small shop with all the amusing Caputi line of costume jewelry. Next door is a larger establishment with all of the Angela Caputi clothing. It's mostly casual wear, a touch on the avant-garde side, but not so strange as to be conspicuous. Bright colors predominate, particularly red, usually paired with black, and the funny Carmen Miranda–style fruit prints can be found on everything from lingerie to swimwear. Prices are modest. A summer-weight smock, with the fruit, is 150,000 lire. A red knit scarf with a rhinestone pattern is 50,000 lire.

Fun and inexpensive fashions at Angela Caputi

BELTRAMI
Via dei Calzaiuoli 31 and 44 (tel. 212-418)
Hours: *Monday through Saturday from 9:30 a.m. to 7:30 p.m. nonstop (closed Monday morning)*

Credit Cards: AE, DC, MC, V
English Spoken.

Although justly famed for leatherwork, the Beltrami line of clothing maintains the same high quality, high fashion, and high prices as the boots and shoes Beltrami is best known for. Much of the clothing in this shop is leather (to be dealth with in the "Leather Goods" section), but there are some things that are not. Beltrami silk scarves, not as elaborately patterned as their Gucci counterparts, but of excellent heavyweight silk, begin at about 175,000 lire. The very dressy and very elaborate Beltrami evening clothes cost in the millions of lire. Beltrami is Florence based, so prices are lower here than elsewhere in Italy, but not by much. There are, however, significant savings to be had here as opposed to shopping for Beltrami in the States.

CASA DI HOGG/BENETTON
Via dei Tornabuoni 26 (tel. 293-060)
Hours: Monday through Saturday from 10 a.m. to 1:30 p.m. and 3:30 to 7:30 p.m. (closed Monday morning)
Credit Cards: AE, DC, MC, V

Benetton acquired this venerable name recently and has maintained its high-quality line of knits and blouses. The styles are slightly more reserved than the usual Benetton product, and it looks as though Casa di Hogg might become the "traditional" end of the Benetton line. Sweaters in wool begin at about 75,000 lire. A lighweight cotton-and-linen sweater, perfect for spring in Florence, is 145,000 lire.

CASA DELLO SPORT
Via Tosinghi 8–10 (tel. 212-344)
Hours: Monday through Saturday from 9:30 a.m. to 1:30 p.m. and 3:30 to 7:30 p.m. (closed Monday morning)
Credit Cards: AE, MC

This giant sportswear shop has a large selection of the top names in Italian sports fashion, like Fila, Ellesse, Sergio Tacchini, and Kappa. Prices are very good. Fila tennis gear, a tennis shirt, for example, with a V-neck, is 45,000 lire. A pleated tennis skirt is 85,000 lire. Tacchini warmup suits are 145,000 lire for a top and pants; a warmup jacket is 89,000 lire. (Tacchini, by the way, usually has American size labels sewn into their products.)

CINZIA
Borgo San Jacopo 22 (tel. 298-078)
Hours: Monday through Saturday from 9 a.m. to 1 p.m. and 3:30 to 7:30 p.m. (closed Monday morning)
Credit Cards: AE, DC, MC, V
English Spoken.

FLORENCE SHOPS: CLOTHING

Extremely colorful, handmade knits are the only items carried at this shop on the Pitti Palace side of the river. The colors run from bright red to violet, and there are lots of patterns too. There are even some with entire pictures knitted into them. A basic heavy cardigan, handmade and decorated in any one of a dozen colors, is 189,000 lire.

DUVET
Borgo San Jacopo 44 (tel. 284-497)
Hours: Monday through Saturday from 9 a.m. to 1 p.m. and 3:30 to 7:30 p.m. (closed Monday morning)
Credit Cards: AE, DC, MC, V
English Spoken.

This striking, modern store, with a beautiful view of the River Arno, has sensational cashmere goods. The designs are as cool and sleek as the store itself. A soft knee-length cashmere skirt in common or garden-variety gray, is 230,000 lire. Also beautiful cashmere sweaters (320,000 lire) and scarves (120,000 lire).

FRANCO RIZZO
Via dei Calzaiuoli 3 (tel. 284-881)
Hours: Monday through Saturday from 9:30 a.m. to 1 p.m. and 3:30 to 7:30 p.m. (closed Monday morning)
Credit Cards: AE, DC, MC, V

Fashions for the younger set, just a few yards from the Palazzo Vecchio. The Franco Rizzo–designed clothing is a little out of the ordinary—leopard-skin prints and dramatic black are the favorite themes. A belted one-piece knit dress with a deep V neckline is 345,000 lire. There are Rizzo shoes as well. A pair of demure embroidered flats in green, red, or black is 90,000 lire.

GENNI
Via dei Cerretani 29 (tel. 210-413)
Hours: Monday through Saturday from 9:30 a.m. to 1:30 p.m. and 3:30 to 7:30 p.m. (closed Monday morning)
Credit Cards: MC, V

There are excellent buys to be had here on lingerie. A full-length cotton nightdress with a V-neck and a matching bed jacket is 200,000 lire. A sleek silk camisole is 85,000 lire.

GIANNI VERSACE
Via dei Tornabuoni 13–15 (tel. 296-167)
Hours: Monday through Saturday from 9:30 a.m. to 1 p.m. and 3:30 to 7:30 p.m. (closed Monday morning)
Credit Cards: AE
English Spoken.

The unmistakeable look of Gianni Versace

Gianni Versace has taken an old Florentine building and modernized it beautifully. The ceilings are still ancient and vaulted, but the furnishings, and the clothes, of course, are strictly late 20th century. The store is not very large, however, so if you are going on to Milan or Rome you might want to wait until the bigger stores where you'll find everything you might want. Prices don't differ much. What the Italians call a "pull," a longer-than-average sweater, in basic black, very severe looking but very chic, is 590,000 lire. A tight gray knee-length skirt is 480,000 lire.

GIORGIO ARMANI
Via dei Tornabuoni 35–37 (tel. 213-819)
Hours: Monday through Saturday from 9:30 a.m. to 1:30 p.m. and 3:30 to 7:30 p.m. (closed Monday morning)
Credit Cards: AE, DC, MC, V
English Spoken.

This is another dramatic-looking shop for one of the great names of Italian fashion design. Armani prices seem to be a little lower here than in Milan—which is odd because Milan is the home base of the empire (the Florence shop is just a small outpost). A fawn-colored silk blouse is 350,000 lire. A beautiful black velvet evening dress is 1.4 million lire.

GIULIA CARLA CECCHI
Via della Vigna Nuova 40 (tel. 264-367)
Hours: Monday through Saturday from 10 a.m. to 1 p.m. and 3:30 to 7:30 p.m. (closed Monday morning)
Credit Cards: None
English Spoken.

FLORENCE SHOPS: CLOTHING

Giulia Carla Cecchi is where old aristocratic Florence shops for evening wear. Styles are frilly-conservative, and lovely silks and organdy are the most favored materials. Expect to pay upward of 1.5 million lire for a creation from the grande dame of Florence fashion.

GLAMOUR
Borgo San Jacopo 49 (tel. 210-334)
Hours: Monday through Saturday from 9 a.m. to 1 p.m. and 3:30 to 7:30 p.m. (closed Monday morning)
Credit Cards: AE, MC, V

This is a great place to shop for Italian clothing that's in style but won't put you in the poorhouse. Knits, blouses, and skirts are here in a variety of materials, all of them well made and fashionable. You won't find any famous names, but you will find good buys. Sweaters are in the 50,000-lire to 100,000-lire range. Cotton blouses are 50,000 lire to 145,000 lire.

GUCCI
Via dei Tornabuoni 73 (tel. 264-011)
Hours: Monday through Saturday from 9:30 a.m. to 1:30 p.m. and 3:30 to 7:30 p.m. (closed Monday morning)
Credit Cards: AE, DC, MC, V
English Spoken.

The little Gucci store at no. 73 is kept open for sentimental reasons. This is the mother of all Guccis everywhere. The place to shop is right next door, also at no. 73, a giant store with a modern interior and lighting which has every Gucci item you could name. Gucci shawls in wool and silk are 135,000 lire to 175,000 lire, a little cheaper than in Milan and a lot cheaper than in the United States. Overall, this is the place to shop for Gucci in Italy.

I NOMI
Corso 27 (tel. 212-415)
Hours: Monday through Saturday from 9 a.m. to 1 p.m. and 3:30 to 7:30 p.m. (closed Monday morning)
Credit Cards: AE

I Nomi stocks fashionable, relatively inexpensive, upscale clothing for young women. A tailored lightweight full-length coat in gray wool is just 400,000 lire. The selection of casual wear is large and colorful. Expect to pay 85,000 lire and up for a blouse and 145,000 lire for a dress.

LORETTA CAPONI
Borgo Ognissanti 12 (tel. 264-155)
Hours: Monday through Saturday from 10 a.m. to 1 p.m. and 4 to 7 p.m. (closed Monday morning)

Credit Cards: AE, DC, MC, V
English Spoken.

A marvelous shop for beautiful silk, cotton, or linen lingerie. Most everything is decorated with embroidery or Sangallo lace. Prices vary according to the amount of ornament. One of the plainer nightdresses in linen, with a lace collar and hem, is 265,000 lire.

LUISA
Via Roma 21 (tel. 234-798)
Hours: *Monday through Saturday from 10 a.m. to 1:30 p.m. and 3:30 to 7 p.m. (closed Monday morning)*
Credit Cards: AE, MC, V
English Spoken.

Luisa is a very large store which carries its own Luisa line, as well as a number of well-known designers from Italy and elsewhere. Byblos, Moschino, and Tarlazzi are joined by Claude Montana, Maud Frizon, and Gaultier from France, and Miyake, Kenzo, and Matsuda among the Japanese. Prices are not rock-bottom, but they are lower than at the full-blown big-name boutiques. A Moschino dress in dove gray with a wide belt with the Moschino logo in brass is 450,000 lire. One of the store's own crêpe de chine blouses is 135,000 lire.

MACEL
Via dei Guicciardini 128 (tel. 287-355)
Hours: *Monday through Saturday from 9 a.m. to 7:30 p.m. nonstop (closed Monday morning)*
Credit Cards: AE

A few steps from the Pitti Palace, Macel, has up-to-the-minute fashions for young women. There are some designer names, like Miss V from Valentino. A nice silk blouse in dark blue costs 175,000 lire. There are some designer knockoffs too. A double-breasted blue blazer with razor-sharp styling, in wool, is 270,000 lire. Macel's own label clothing is quite reasonable. One of their silk blouses is 139,000 lire. A full skirt in cotton or lightweight wool is 220,000 lire.

MANTELASSI
Piazza della Repubblica 21 (tel. 212-334)
Hours: *Monday through Saturday from 10 a.m. to 1 p.m. and 3:30 to 7:30 p.m. (closed Monday morning)*
Credit Cards: AE, DC, MC, V
English Spoken.

A very traditional store selling goods largely of English manufacture: Shetland sweaters and the like. The clothing is of very high quality, but the tweeds and knits are unlikely to be much different from anything you've seen in the United States. Prices are higher than London, but lower than back home. A rich red Shetland sweater is 85,000 lire.

FLORENCE SHOPS: CLOTHING

MARINA RINALDI
Via dei Calzaiuoli 14 (tel. 292-360)
Hours: Monday through Saturday from 9 a.m. to 1 p.m. and 3:30 to 7:30 p.m. (closed Monday morning)
Credit Cards: AE, DC, MC, V
English Spoken.

There are Marina Rinaldi shops all over Italy and Europe, but none in the States yet. As the store in Florence is one of the best, you might want to stock up here. Marina Rinaldi makes everything from jeans in soft gray denim (100,000 lire a pair) to accessories like knit scarves (80,000 lire), gloves (45,000 lire), and brightly colored, high-quality silk scarves (125,000 lire to 185,000 lire). There is also some very elegant evening wear. A three-quarter-length deep-purple silk top with a black stripe and a long black skirt cost 880,000 lire. A silver lamé top with a black geometric design is 450,000 lire.

MATTOLINI
Via della Vigna Nuova 44 (tel. 210-631)
Hours: Monday through Saturday from 9:30 a.m. to 1:30 p.m. and 3:30 to 7:30 p.m. (closed Monday morning)
Credit Cards: AE

This one room and a loft store on Via della Vigna Nuova sells the Iceberg line of ready-to-wear casuals and roughwear, as well as its own line of rich-looking, but informal, clothing. A quilted silk jacket, heavy enough to keep out a very cold wind, but delicate nonetheless, is 620,000 lire. There's a small discount rack on the upper level where you might find a bargain or two.

MAX MARA
Via dei Pecori 14 (tel. 212-907)
Hours: Monday through Saturday from 9:30 a.m. to 1 p.m. and 3:30 to 7:30 p.m. (closed Monday morning)
Credit Cards: AE, MC, V
English Spoken.

Classic elegance with a touch of flamboyance, Max Mara sells high-quality clothes for less than the really big names and more than unknowns. This particular shop, while not large, has everything Max Mara: hats, sweaters, coats, skirts, slacks.

MILA SCHÖN
Lungarno Amerigo Vespucci 26–28 (tel. 294-977)
Hours: Monday through Saturday from 9:30 a.m. to 1 p.m. and 3:30 to 7 p.m. (closed Monday morning)
Credit Cards: AE
English Spoken.

This is quite a small Mila Schön, selling clothes for both men and women, so the selection is quite limited. The styling is the sharply tailored look people have come to expect from this name and, as always, the fabrics are chosen with care. A two-piece wool suit is 1.2 million lire. A blazer is 575,000 lire.

MUJER
Via Vacchereccia 6 (tel. 779-905)
Hours: Monday through Saturday from 10 a.m. to 1 p.m. and 3:30 to 7 p.m. (closed Monday morning)
Credit Cards: AE, MC, V

This is a lovely little store just a few yards from the Palazzo Vecchio. All the clothing sold here is of Florentine manufacture and designed by the store's stylists. Velvet, lace, and silk are the most commonly used fabrics, making for lush and "feminine" fashions. A black velvet jacket for evening wear is 450,000 lire. A silk top to wear under it is 300,000 lire.

NAJ OLEARI
Via della Vigna Nuova 35 (tel. 210-443)
Hours: Monday through Saturday from 9:30 a.m. to 1 p.m. and 3:30 to 7:30 p.m. (closed Monday morning)
Credit Cards: AE, MC, V

Lots of blond wood and hundreds of things made from or decorated with the busy, colorful Naj Oleari patterns make up this store. Out of keeping with Florence, this Naj Oleari is bigger than the two in Milan and about the same size

Naj Oleari fabrics—Italy's answer to Pierre Deux and Laura Ashley

as the one in Rome. Although this is by no means a clothing shop exclusively, there are some sundresses and skirts, all in the cheerful Naj Oleari materials. A simple smock is 245,000 lire; a wide-brimmed hat, 85,000 lire.

NEUBER
Via Strozzi 32 (tel. 210-056)
Hours: Monday through Saturday 10 a.m. to 1 p.m. and 3:30 to 7:30 p.m. (closed Monday morning)
Credit Cards: AE
English Spoken.

This is your source for French designer names in Florence, particularly Hermès and Dior. Prices are higher than Paris but less than New York—but not less than the exclusively Hermès shop in Rome. A Hermès scarf is 260,000 lire.

PICCARDA
Borgo San Jacopo 58 (tel. 262-311)
Hours: Monday through Saturday from 9:30 a.m. to 1:30 p.m. and 3:30 to 7:30 p.m. (closed Monday morning)
Credit Cards: AE, MC, V
English Spoken.

If you're in the market for a silk blouse, then you couldn't do better than to head for Piccarda, on the Pitti Palace side of the Arno—that's all they sell. There is silk in every size and style, from casual to dressy. Prices begin at about 145,000 lire and go up to 450,000 lire.

PRINCIPE
Via Strozzi 21 (tel. 212-680)
Hours: Monday through Saturday from 9:30 a.m. to 1:30 p.m. and 3:30 to 7:30 p.m. (closed Monday morning)
Credit Cards: AE, DC, MC, V
English Spoken.

This is almost a department store, except that all the departments sell clothing—men's, women's, and children's. The women's clothing is aimed mostly at the younger end of the market, but things are traditionally styled, rather than flashy. A pleated three-quarter-length tweed skirt is 350,000 lire. There is also a huge selection of blouses, trousers, knits, and jackets, and some evening wear.

PUCCI
Via dei Pucci 6 (tel. 212-331)
Hours: Monday through Saturday from 10 a.m. to 1 p.m. and 3:30 to 7 p.m. (closed Monday morning)
Credit Cards: AE
English Spoken.

Emilio Pucci broke into the fashion scene just after the war (about the same time as Valentino) and his name has become a byword for sleek, traditional elegance. His shop here is much smaller than the flasgship store in Rome, but prices are about the same. A tasteful Pucci skirt costs 650,000 lire. His colorful evening wear, mostly in silk or satin, costs many millions of lire.

RIBOT
Via dei Calzaiuoli 1 (tel. 214-959)
Hours: *Monday through Saturday from 9:30 a.m. to 1:30 p.m. and 3:30 to 7:30 p.m. (closed Monday morning)*
Credit Cards: *AE, DC, MC, V*
English Spoken.

This tiny shop has beautiful blouses and tops for women. A sensational silk blouse in a series of pastel colors is 225,000 lire.

SALVATORE FERRAGAMO
Via dei Tornabuoni 16 (tel. 292-123)
Hours: *Monday through Saturday from 9:30 to 1:30 p.m. and 3:30 to 7:30 p.m. (closed Monday morning)*
Credit Cards: *AE, DC, MC, V*
English Spoken.

The head office of the Ferragamo empire is just down the street at no. 2, and this is their premier store. It's a beautiful place, occupying two floors of the Palazzo Spini-Ferroni, built in 1289. The present store, a series of large and small rooms, incorporates elements of the original building: vaulted ceilings, ancient brick and stone work, and stained glass.

Of course, leather is the thing to shop for here, but there is a lot of prêt-à-porter clothing as well. Knitwear with a silver lamé and white geometric pattern is the latest Ferragamo design. A three-quarter-length sweater in this style, a touch on the dressy side, is 555,000 lire. A waist-length sweater in the same pattern is 325,000 lire. A muted plaid in white and pale-green stripes is another new design—a skirt and pair of loose-fitting pants are 425,000 lire and 400,000 lire respectively.

THE CORNER
Borgo San Jacopo 29B (tel. 256-344)
Hours: *Monday through Saturday from 9:30 a.m. to 7:30 p.m. nonstop (closed Monday morning)*
Credit Cards: *DC*
English Spoken.

This small and informal shop caters to those looking for trendy Italian clothing at reasonable prices. You don't have to pay much, particularly for casual wear. A straight-cut, square-shouldered wool sweater-dress in 100% wool is only 119,000 lire. Prices don't get much higher than that.

UGOLINI E FIGLI
Via dei Calzuaioli 65–68 (tel. 214-439)
Hours: Monday through Saturday from 9:30 a.m. to 1 p.m. and 3:30 to 7:30 p.m. (closed Monday morning)
Credit Cards: AE
English Spoken.

Very conservative English or English-style clothing for women. The range of merchandise here tends to run to tailored blue blazers with brass buttons, tartan skirts, and tweeds. Prices are very high—a wool blazer costs 850,000 lire, slightly less for a summer-weight linen or cotton version. A tweed suit with a muted check is 1.45 million lire.

VALENTINO
Via della Vigna Nuova 47 (tel. 215-180)
Hours: Monday through Saturday from 10 a.m. to 1:30 p.m. and 3:30 to 7 p.m. (closed Monday morning)
Credit Cards: AE
English Spoken.

This is the smallest of the Valentinos in the four cities covered in this book, and, naturally enough, has the least in the way of selection. However, like all Valentino shops everywhere, there's always something to catch the eye of the fashion conscious. A beautiful black three-piece wool-and-cashmere suit, with a knee-length skirt, a short jacket, and a sweater, is 1.9 million lire. Casual gray wool-and-silk-blend pleated pants cost 400,000 lire. A crêpe blouse with a finely worked paisley-ish pattern is 520,000 lire.

FOOD

CALDERAI
Via Calimala 19 (no phone)
Hours: Monday through Saturday from 9 a.m. to 1:30 p.m. and 3:30 to 7:30 p.m. (closed Wednesday afternoon)
Credit Cards: None

This is your stop for Tuscan delicacies: cured hams made from cinghiale (wild boar), pâtés, Parma hams, and truffles. If you're in the market for olive oil, then you'll find virtually every Tuscan brand here, from the mass produced to the handmade.

GRANNA MARKET
Via dei Tavolini 11 (no phone)
Hours: Monday through Saturday from 9:30 a.m. to 1:30 p.m. and 3:30 to 7 p.m. (closed Wednesday afternoon)
Credit Cards: None

A huge selection of cheeses—you name it and they have it. There are also mouthwatering cold cuts and salads.

PEGNA
Via dello Studio 26 (tel. 212-333)
Hours: Monday through Saturday from 9:30 a.m. to 1:30 p.m. and 3:30 to 7 p.m. (closed Wednesday afternoon)
Credit Cards: None

Even if you aren't hungry, you should stop in at this delightful grocery store a few yards away from the Duomo, toward the river. The store displays food the way Armani or Valentino displays clothes, with tiled floors, walnut doors, skylights, and classical music piped in. On top of this, there is every kind of Italian delicacy you can think of at ordinary grocery-store prices.

FURNITURE

DUCCI
Lungarno Corsini 24 (tel. 214-550)
Hours: Monday through Saturday from 9:30 a.m. to 1 p.m. and 3:30 to 7:30 p.m. (closed Monday morning)
Credit Cards: AE, DC, MC, V
English Spoken.

Furniture is just one of the many interesting things that this shop offers. In a series of rooms, you'll find inlaid coffee tables, marble-top end tables, and carved dining tables, all of new manufacture but designed with an eye to the past. There are also objects and pictures, including such hard-to-find items as a persimmon sculpted from rose-colored marble (40,000 lire). One of the beautiful marquetry coffee tables is 1.6 million lire. Ducci will arrange shipping for an extra charge.

HOUSEWARES

LA CASA ABITATA
Via dello Sprone 25 (tel. 295-300)
Hours: Monday through Saturday from 9:30 a.m. to 1:30 p.m. and 3:30 to 7:30 p.m. (closed Monday morning)
Credit Cards: AE, DC, MC, V

One of the nicest cookware and furnishings stores you can find in Florence. This brightly lit, functional-looking shop has the latest in Italian design. A stark, modern espresso maker by Girmi, converted to American current, is 458,000 lire. There is also cutlery and kitchenware. A stainless-steel pasta pot by Alessi costs 98,000 lire.

FLORENCE SHOPS: FURNITURE/HOUSEWARES

SOLUZIONI
Via Maggio 82 *(tel. 298-270)*
Hours: *Monday through Saturday from 10 a.m. to 1:30 p.m. and 3:30 to 7 p.m. (closed Monday morning)*
Credit Cards: *None*

Laughing at the design world while contributing to it, Soluzioni has some of the most peculiar, but still functional, housewares, implements, and accessories around. The store is filled with eccentrically designed things like an enamel-and-silver cocktail-bar set that conjures up the 1950s and 1980s Memphis (344,000 lire) or a perfectly designed set of scissors and paper knife that fits your hand and its tiny carrying case (12,000 lire), and the plainly strange, like a black patent-leather woman's purse which has a doorknob lock instead of an ordinary clasp (80,000 lire).

Ultra-modern housewares at Soluzioni

VICE VERSA
Via Ricasoli 53 *(tel. 298-281)*
Hours: *Monday through Saturday from 9 a.m. to 1 p.m. and 3:30 to 7:30 p.m. (closed Monday morning)*
Credit Cards: *AE, DC, MC, V*

This store has only Italian-designed housewares. The selection of clocks, cooking utensils, and other items for the home is huge, and the prices reason-

The Alessi tea kettles, stunning examples of the new Italian design

able. The famous Alessi tea kettle, in a rounded or triangular form (with a whistle that sounds like a harmonica), a 105,000 lire. The cylindrical Alessi coffee pot, in stainless steel, is 125,000 lire.

JEWELRY

ANTIQUE

IL MAGGIOLINO
Via Maggio 80 (tel. 216-660)
Hours: *Monday through Saturday from 10 a.m. to 1:30 p.m. and 3:30 to 7:30 p.m. (closed Monday morning)*
Credit Cards: *None*
English Spoken.

The most beautiful antique jewelry in the city can be found in this small shop in the heart of the Florence antiques district. The pieces tend to date from the late 19th century to the 1940s and come mostly from France and Italy.

MELLI
Ponte Vecchio 46 (no phone)
Hours: *Monday through Saturday from 9:30 a.m. to 7:30 p.m. nonstop (closed Monday morning)*
Credit Cards: *AE, MC, V*
English Spoken.

Fine antique jewelry at more affordable prices than Il Maggiolino (see above).

FLORENCE SHOPS: JEWELRY

This is one of the best shops on the Ponte Vecchio for fine cameos and medallions of the last two centuries.

RUDOLFO FALLACI
Ponte Vecchio 10 and 51 (tel. 294-981)
Hours: Monday through Saturday from 9:15 a.m. to 7:15 p.m. nonstop (closed Monday morning)
Credit Cards: None
English Spoken.

There are two Rudolfo Fallaci stores on the Ponte Vecchio with some antique jewelry, but the one at no. 51 (on the Pitti Palace end of the bridge) specializes in old silver and gold work. There are lovely enameled silver boxes from the 19th and 20th centuries, priced in the 800,000-lire to 2-million-lire range, depending on age, size, and condition. Also cameos, earrings, and brooches using a variety of stones and settings.

Just one of the Ponte Vecchio jewelers

CAMEOS

QUAGLIA & FORTE
Via dei Guicciardini 12 (tel. 294-534)

Hours: *Monday through Saturday from 9:30 a.m. to 7:30 p.m. nonstop (closed Monday morning)*
Credit Cards: *AE, DC, MC, V*
English Spoken.

Quaglia & Forte have been selling cameos since the first decade of this century—the first products were handmade by Quaglia senior and the tradition is now being carried on by his son. The jewelry comes in a variety of shapes and sizes, secular and religious. A small button-size cameo broach will cost 200,000 lire, but prices run up to 4 million lire for the large pieces. Some are literally priceless: the Quaglia cameo of Botticelli's *La Primavera* is not for sale.

COSTUME

ANGELA CAPUTI
Borgo San Jacopo 78–82 (tel. 212-972)
Hours: *Monday through Saturday from 9 a.m. to 1 p.m. and 4 to 8 p.m. (closed Monday morning)*
Credit Cards: *AE, DC, MC, V*

Caputi's own line of *giuggiù* costume jewelry is brightly colored, glitzy, and so clunky it's striking. Black and red plastics combined with rhinestones are the basic materials used, and Caputi puts them into earrings, broaches, necklaces, and accents on her own line of trendy clothing (the clothing shop is next door). A Caputi wristwatch costs 130,000 lire. A multicolored necklace with a "fruit salad" centerpiece is 50,000 lire.

BIJOUX CASCIO
Via dei Tornabuoni 32 (tel. 284-709)
Hours: *Monday through Saturday from 9:30 a.m. to 1:30 p.m. and 3:30 to 7:30 p.m. (closed Monday morning)*
Credit Cards: *AE, DC, MC, V*
English Spoken.

Cascio has cornered the market on top-grade imitation jewels and gold work. All the pieces come from the store's own workshops, and we must assume that the imitation Gucci, Cartier, Bulgari, and other famous labels must be made with Big Name approval—Bijoux Cascio is no fly-by-night operation. Prices are very reasonable. Diamond chokers which look as if they were plucked from a tray at Bulgari cost 85,000 lire. If you're looking for some jewelry to wow the folks back home—but don't want to spend a great deal on it—this is the best place in town.

PARFUMS-BIJOUX
Piazza Frescobaldi 11 (tel. 212-655)
Hours: *Monday through Saturday from 10 a.m. to 8 p.m. nonstop (closed Monday morning)*

FLORENCE SHOPS: JEWELRY/LACE

Credit Cards: *None*

There's a first-rate selection of fine costume and silver jewelry in this small shop. A thick silver ring with a large rhinestone is 103,000 lire. There is a huge choice of silver bangles and bracelets, ranging in price from 90,000 lire to 300,000 lire.

PRECIOUS

BURCHI
Ponte Vecchio 54 (tel. 287-361)
Hours: Monday through Saturday from 9:30 a.m. to 7:30 p.m. nonstop (closed Monday morning)
Credit Cards: AE, DC, MC, V
English Spoken.

This is your stop for excellent buys on modern gold and gemstones. All the work is done in Burchi's own workshops, and gold is a specialty.

MARIO BUCCELLATI
Via dei Tornabuoni 43 (tel. 296-579)
Hours: Monday through Saturday from 10 a.m. to 1:30 p.m. and 3:30 to 7:30 p.m. (closed Monday morning)
Credit Cards: *None*
English Spoken.

One of the worlds' great jewelers, Mario Buccellati's store in Florence is small, expensive, and luxurious. There are antique, modern, and modern copies of antique pieces here, as well as the famous Buccellati silver work, particularly figures of animals, flowers, fruit, and shells.

LACE

CIRRI
Via Por Santa Maria 38 (tel. 296-593)
Hours: Monday through Saturday from 9 a.m. to 1 p.m. and 3:30 to 7:30 p.m. (closed Monday morning)
Credit Cards: AE, DC, MC, V
English Spoken.

Cirri is a pretty little shop in the center of town which sells fine lace and embroidery. There are delicate clothes for babies and children, lingerie, and linens, as well as lots of small items like handkerchiefs and collars. All the work is done exclusively for Cirri, and all of it is handmade. Prices begin low: a lace handkerchief can cost as little as 9,000 lire, but can cost as much as 70,000 lire for a large and heavily decorated one. Lace tablecloths are 250,000 lire to

Punto Firenze, traditional Florentine art

650,000 lire, depending on size and complexity. A simple lace collar costs 29,000 lire.

TAF
Via Por Santa Maria 22 (tel. 213-190)
Hours: *Monday through Saturday from 9 a.m. to 1 p.m. and 3:30 to 7:30 p.m. (closed Monday morning)*
Credit Cards: *None*

Just down the street from Cirri (above), TAF is a similar shop offering more high-quality lace, embroidery, linens, and clothing. Items here are a shade cheaper, but the quality remains high. A lace handkerchief in a gift box is just 10,000 lire. A linen blouse with a little lace decoration on the collar is 32,000 lire.

LEATHER GOODS

BELTRAMI–BELTRAMI JUNIOR
Via dei Pecori 16 (tel. 213-290) Via dei Calzaiuoli 31 (tel. 214-030), Via dei Calzaiuoli 44, and Via Calimala 9 (tel. 212-288)
Hours: *Monday through Saturday from 9:30 a.m. to 7:30 p.m. nonstop (closed Monday morning)*
Credit Cards: *AE, DC, MC, V*
English Spoken.

FLORENCE SHOPS: LACE/LEATHER

The first two Beltramis listed are formal, beautifully decorated shops, selling the first-rate—and expensive—line of Beltrami leather goods, particularly boots and shoes. The main leather shop is at Via dei Calzaiuoli 31. A pair of black leather pumps is 325,000 lire and boots cost from 400,000 lire up.

Beltrami Junior is not, as the name suggests, a Beltrami outlet for children. Rather, it's a large shop on Via Calimala, near the straw market, which sells the more casual, less expensive Beltrami products. Here you'll find the classic black leather Beltrami boots for 240,000 lire—about 30% less than you'd pay in the United States.

BELTRAMI SPA
Via dei Panzani 1 (no phone)
Hours: *Monday through Saturday from 9:30 a.m. to 1 p.m. and 3:30 to 7:30 p.m. (closed Monday morning)*
Credit Cards: *AE, MC*

This is the Beltrami shop that sells last season's Beltrami goods. You buy spring items in the summer, summer items in the fall, etc.—but as a lot of Italian goods are introduced later in the States than in the home country, you might find yourself in advance of fashion, rather than playing catch-up. Prices here begin low and get lower. Once the merchandise is taken from the Beltrami shops around the city, it is sent to this location with the original price still on it. You have to ask the salespeople what the discount is—they speak Italian, but have been asked the question so many times they'll know exactly what you want to know. The basic discount is 20%, but can be as high as 50%. But there's more. If you have decided to buy several pairs of shoes or boots, a further 10% to 25% will be knocked off the discount price when you get to the cash register. Thus a pair of 350,000-lire boots could end up costing well under 200,000 lire—a savings of more than $100.

There is a single rack of Beltrami leather clothing, and while the same discount policy applies to it, the selection is so small that buying is very hit-or-miss.

Finally, Beltrami Spa has no sign on the street, and as mentioned in the stroll (Chapter VIII), the shop bears the number 1, but is in the middle of Via dei Panzani. All sales are final.

BOTTEGA VENETA
Piazza Ognissanti 3 (tel. 294-265)
Hours: *Monday through Saturday from 10 a.m. to 1:30 p.m. and 3:30 to 7 p.m. (closed Monday morning)*
Credit Cards: *AE*
English Spoken.

This small and exclusive shop facing the Hotel Excelsior sells nothing but Bottega Veneta goods. While the shop is not large, the selection is very good. A small leather handbag, made from the famous Bottega weave, is 325,000 lire.

The smaller pieces of luggage cost from 750,000 lire and run into several millions of lire.

CASADEI
Via dei Tornabuoni 33 (tel. 287-240)
Hours: *Monday through Saturday from 9:30 a.m. to 1 p.m. and 3:30 to 7:30 p.m. (closed Monday morning)*
Credit Cards: *AE, DC, V*
English Spoken.

This is one of just three Casadei stores in Italy, and the only one in the four cities covered in this book, but it is probably the finest. The shop itself is striking—stark white with pillars turning the whole showroom into a small colonnade—as are the women's boots and shoes for sale here. A pair of black boots with the Casadei nameplate costs 305,000 lire. Sporty silver lamé lace-up flats are 119,000 lire.

CASA DEL GUANTO
Borgo dei Greci 11 (tel. 341-6121)
Hours: *Monday through Saturday from 9:30 a.m. to 1:30 p.m. and 3:30 to 7:30 p.m. (closed Monday morning)*
Credit Cards: *AE, DC, MC, V*
English Spoken.

You'll find nothing but gloves in this small shop on the far side of the Palazzo Vecchio. There are lots of good buys to be had here, like a pair of men's cashmere-lined black leather gloves for 50,000 lire; the selection of gloves for women, in leather, kidskin, suede, and the like is enormous. A pair of red leather gloves, lined in silk, is 45,000 lire.

CASALINI
Via del Moro 44 (no phone)
Hours: *Monday through Saturday from 9:30 a.m. to 1:30 p.m. and 3:30 to 7:30 p.m. (closed Monday morning)*
Credit Cards: *None*

All the leather goods in this tiny shop on a side street near Via dei Tornabuoni are made on the premises. Casalini specializes in hand-tooled leather boxes—playing-card boxes, cigarette boxes, pillboxes, that sort of thing—and they are exquisitely built and very elegant. A jewelry box covered in blue leather, with a fine gold stripe, costs 145,000 lire. A small pillbox is 45,000

CELLERINI
Via del Sole 37 (tel. 282-533)
Hours: *Monday through Saturday from 9:30 a.m. to 1:30 p.m. and 3:30 to 7:30 p.m. (closed Monday morning)*

Credit Cards: *None*
English Spoken.

Cellerini makes leather goods for a number of well-known Italian designers, but you can buy the lavish handbags and suitcases directly from this shop without the fancy labels and the fancy markup. That is not to say that things are dirt cheap here—but they do cost less. A large, soft suitcase in fine leather, beautifully finished and lined, is 475,000 lire. An overnight bag is 325,000 lire. A shoulder bag in chocolate-brown leather is 200,000 lire.

CLEMENTE
Via dei Calzaiuoli 10 (tel. 298-749)
Hours: *Monday through Saturday from 9:30 a.m. to 1 p.m. and 3:30 to 7:30 p.m. (closed Monday morning)*
Credit Cards: AE, DC, MC, V
English Spoken.

Clemente has been selling leather goods, notably bags, belts, and luggage (no shoes), since 1839. The selection of luggage is particularly large, and prices are certainly competitive. A mid-size suitcase is 245,000 lire. Handbags range from 50,000 lire to 300,000 lire. There are some small items which cost very little, and the quality level of the inexpensive things is as good as the higher-ticket items. A sewing kit, for example, in a leather case is only 17,000 lire.

FENDI
Via dei Tornabuoni 27 (tel. 287-757)
Hours: *Monday through Saturday from 9:30 a.m. to 1 p.m. and 3:30 to 7:30 p.m. (closed Monday morning)*
Credit Cards: AE
English Spoken.

No Fendi selection could be as large as that in Rome—the sisters have virtually taken over a street there—but there is a lot of elegant leather to be had in Florence as well. A Fendi clutch handbag in black leather is 195,000 lire. The same item in shiny patent leather is 124,000 lire. The Fendi Fs (a trademark designed by Karl Lagerfeld, by the way) can also be found on luggage, shoulder bags, boots, and shoes.

GHERARDINI–GHERARDINI UOMO
Via della Vigna Nuova 57 (tel. 215-678) and Via Strozzi 25 (tel. 287-950)
Hours: *Monday through Saturday from 9:30 a.m. to 1 p.m. and 3 to 7:30 p.m. (closed Monday morning)*
Credit Cards: AE, MC
English Spoken.

In a few generations Gherardini has become one of the best-known names among Italian leather makers. The shop on Via della Vigna Nuova is the main one, and it has all the Gherardini luggage, clothing, and handbags; the other shop is devoted to menswear and accessories. A large black leather shoulder bag is 300,000 lire; a toilet case for a man in Gherardini vinyl with the Gherardini Gs all over it is 120,000 lire. Gherardini luggage is very expensive, but not as expensive here in Florence as it is at their shop on Via della Spiga in Milan. A crocodile-skin and vinyl cosmetic case is 950,000 lire in Florence, but well over 1 million lire farther to the north. There are also some small nonleather items which can be had relatively cheaply. A Gherardini key chain is 20,000 lire; a money clip, 21,500 lire.

GIACHI
Borgo San Jacopo 29A (tel. 213-604)
Hours: Monday through Saturday from 9:30 a.m. to 1:30 p.m. and 3:30 to 7:30 p.m. (closed Monday morning)
Credit Cards: AE
English Spoken.

This narrow little store has the Pitti line of leather goods, which are made just to the south of Florence in the little town of Arezzo. Sandals, informal flat shoes for day wear, handbags, and gloves can be found here. A soft, suede tote bag in taupe costs 275,000 lire. A pair of sling-back sandals in white leather costs 175,000 lire.

GUCCI
Via dei Tornabuoni 73 (tel. 264-011)
Hours: Monday through Saturday from 9:30 a.m. to 1:30 p.m. and 3:30 to 7:30 p.m. (closed Monday morning)
Credit Cards: AE, DC, MC, V
English Spoken.

You can spend $10 here, for a Gucci coffee mug, or you can spend thousands of dollars for a complete set of Gucci luggage. In between is everything in leather, or leather-covered, or just decorated with the stripe, the Gs, and the bridle. There are belts, bags, cocktail-bar sets, shoes, briefcases, portfolios, address books—even a holster for your .45. You can browse for hours and never get bored—and you'll find that prices here are much better than back home.

IL BISONTE
Via del Parione 35 (tel. 215-722)
Hours: Monday through Saturday from 10 a.m. to 1 p.m. and 3 to 7:30 p.m. (closed Monday morning)
Credit Cards: AE, DC, MC, V
English Spoken.

Another great Florentine name for suede and leather clothing, handbags, and luggage. A soft-leather briefcase, with a shoulder strap and room for everything, is 350,000 lire. A large gladstone bag with brass hardware and a zip is 650,000 lire. Suede jackets cost from 850,000 lire to 2.5 million lire.

MANNELLI
Borgo San Jacopo 3 (tel. 294-113)
Hours: *Monday through Saturday from 9:30 a.m. to 7:30 p.m. nonstop (closed Monday morning)*
Credit Cards: AE, DC, MC, V
English Spoken.

This shop is right in front of you as you come off the Ponte Vecchio on the Pitti side of the river. Mannelli has virtually nothing but handbags, and the prices are in the "have to be seen to be believed" category. A huge shoulder bag in mauve-colored soft leather is only 125,000 lire. If you buy a lot you might even get a small discount, but don't count on it.

MARIO VALENTINO
Via dei Tornabuoni 67 (tel. 261-338)
Hours: *Monday through Saturday from 10 a.m. to 1:30 p.m. and 3:30 to 7:30 p.m. (closed Monday morning)*
Credit Cards: AE
English spoken.

You can tell by looking at the shoes and boots here that Mario Valentino is not a somber, reserved Florentine. The wild gold, silver, and brightly colored leather goods immediately tip you off to the fact that this line originates farther to the south, in Naples. Apart from women's shoes, there is also Mario Valentino clothing which is designed by Gianni Versace.

RASPINI
Via dei Martelli 5 (tel. 298-336), Via Por Santa Maria 72 (tel. 215-796), and Via Roma 25 (tel. 213-077)
Hours: *Monday through Saturday from 9:30 a.m. to 7:30 p.m. nonstop (closed Monday morning)*
Credit Cards: AE, DC, V
English Spoken.

The three Raspini shops offer excellent value on shoes for men and women. The quality of the leather is first rate and the prices on their own brand of shoes are low. A pair of red leather high heels is 59,800 lire. A pair of men's oxfords is 95,000 lire. The Via Roma shop is the largest, but the other two have great selections as well.

ROBERTA DI CAMERINO
Via dei Tornabuoni 47 (tel. 241-317)
Hours: *Monday through Saturday from 10 a.m. to 1:30 p.m. and 3:30 to 7:30 p.m. (closed Monday morning*

Credit Cards: AE
English Spoken.

This is a Venetian company that began in the leather business and has since added everything else in women's wear to their range of products. The di Camerino handbags remain the most famous items in the inventory, however. A black leather clutch is 260,000 lire; more or less the same style in black crocodile is 300,000 lire. There is also very elegant luggage.

ROMANO
Piazza della Repubblica, at the corner of Via degli Speziali (tel. 296-890)
Hours: Monday through Saturday from 9:30 a.m. to 1 p.m. and 3:30 to 7:30 p.m. (closed Monday morning)
Credit Cards: AE
English Spoken.

Lots of leather shoes, boots, and skirts at this two-story shop right in the center of town. Romano has a number of Valentino leather goods as well as their own house brand. A pair of short black suede ankle boots is 125,000 lire.

SALVATORE FERRAGAMO
Via dei Tornabuoni 16 (tel. 292-123)
Hours: Monday through Saturday from 9:30 a.m. to 1:30 p.m. and 3:30 to 7:30 p.m. (closed Monday morning)
Credit Cards: AE, DC, MC, V
English Spoken.

The leather goods stretch through a warren of rooms in this beautiful shop, and while nothing is cheap, you'll spend less here than you would in the United States. Two-tone high heels in silver lamé and brown leather cost 275,000 lire. Tasseled ankle boots are 320,000 lire. The leather clothing is soft and luxurious, and begins at about 500,000 lire for a skirt.

SCARABEO
Via Por Santa Maria 23 (tel. 210-380)
Hours: Monday through Saturday from 10 a.m. to 7:30 p.m. nonstop (closed Monday morning)
Credit Cards: AE, MC, V
English Spoken.

A great leather shop with excellent prices on handbags, mostly braided. A squarish burgundy shoulder bag is 184,000 lire.

TRUSSARDI
Via del Parione 15 (tel. 214-402)

FLORENCE SHOPS: LEATHER/LINENS

Hours: *Monday through Saturday from 10 a.m. to 1:30 p.m. and 3:30 to 7:30 p.m. (closed Monday morning)*
Credit Cards: AE
English Spoken.

The classy greyhound-head trademark can be found gracing everything in this shop from a complete black leather three-piece suit (jacket, skirt, and hat) to a fully equipped Trussardi bicycle. The suit costs 1.75 million lire and the bike is 1.5 million lire. There are also bags in vinyl or leather, or a mixture of both, address books, and a hundred other high-quality leather accessories.

UMBERTO
Via dei Guicciardini 114 (tel. 293-091)
Hours: *Monday through Saturday from 9:30 a.m. to 1:30 p.m. and 3:30 to 7:30 p.m. (closed Monday morning)*
Credit Cards: AE, DC, MC, V
English Spoken.

A giant leather shop with everything from a lipstick case in tooled Florentine leather at 5,000 lire to an oversize leather suitcase for 330,000 lire.

LINENS

CESARI
Via dei Tornabuoni (tel.: not available)
Hours: *Monday through Saturday from 9:30 a.m. to 1:30 p.m. and 3:30 to 7:30 p.m. (closed Monday morning)*
Credit Cards: AE
English Spoken.

One of the preeminent names in Italian cloth and linens, Cesari in Florence is a luxurious shop which has a good selection of merchandise. Linen sheets are crisp and comfortable and can be had plain or with a little delicate embroidery. Prices begin at 125,000 lire. There are also plush blankets, quilts, and duvets.

FERRINI FIRENZE
Via Calimala 5 (tel. 287-595)
Hours: *Monday through Saturday from 9:30 a.m. to 1 p.m. and 3:30 to 7:30 p.m. (closed Monday morning)*
Credit Cards: AE, DC, MC, V

Directly across the street from the straw market, this is a fairly good-size shop which has good-quality linens at low prices. Thick, rich towels, for example, with some lacework are just 32,000 lire. Linen sheets and pillow cases in pale pastels are 80,000 lire to 220,000 lire.

PRATESI
Lungarno Amerigo Vespucci 8 (tel. 292-367)
Hours: Monday through Saturday from 9 a.m. to 1 p.m. and 3:30 to 7:30 p.m. (closed Monday morning)
Credit Cards: AE
English Spoken.

Tuscany is home base for this famous name, so this elegant shop on the Arno has all the Pratesi products, with prices a little lower here than elsewhere in the country. In addition to the usual Pratesi fabrics, sheets, towels, and tablecloths, this outlet has luxurious Pratesi nightwear as well. A long, lush Pratesi bathrobe in terrycloth is 223,000 lire. Slippers made from the same material are 69,000 lire.

LINGERIE

GENNI: see "Clothing, Women's Fashions"

LORETTA CAPONI: see "Clothing, Women's Fashions"

LUGGAGE (see "Leather Goods")

PAPER AND PAPER GOODS
(see "Stationery Supplies")

PORCELAIN AND POTTERY

GALLERIA MACHIAVELLI
Via dei Guicciardini 18–104 (tel. 298-400)
Hours: Monday through Saturday from 9:30 a.m. to 7:30 p.m. nonstop (closed Monday morning)
Credit Cards: AE, DC, MC, V
English Spoken.

This store is located in a little arcade just off Via dei Guicciardini, in what was once the house of Nicolo Machiavelli. The selection of typical Tuscan painted ceramic work is huge and comes in every shape, size, and price you can imagine. An exquisitely painted and glazed oval platter, large enough for a Thanksgiving turkey, costs 290,000 lire. A lamp base in the same style is 85,000 lire. A finely painted pillbox is only 10,000 lire. The store will ship all purchases.

MENEGATTI
Piazza del Pesce 2 (tel. 764-2106)
Hours: *Monday through Saturday from 9:30 a.m. to 1:30 p.m. and 3:30 to 7:30 p.m. (closed Monday morning)*
Credit Cards: AE, V
English Spoken.

Between the Ponte Vecchio and the Palazzo Vecchio is this nice old shop stuffed with pottery and majolica items. A hand-painted country-style wine pitcher costs 45,000 lire. Colorful coffee mugs are 18,000 lire.

TERRE DI TUSCIA
Via dei Bardi 63 (tel. 286-458)
Hours: *Monday through Saturday from 9:30 a.m. to 1:30 p.m. and 3:30 to 7:30 p.m. (closed Monday morning)*
Credit Cards: None

This tiny shop is crammed with all kinds of painted Tuscan pottery at great prices. A giant wine jug—it looks large enough to hold a jeraboam—is 195,000 lire; a smaller version is only 47,500 lire. In addition to the usual tablewares, there are also smaller items like a majolica shrine for 38,500 lire.

PRINTS AND ENGRAVINGS

BOTTEGA DELLE STAMPE
Borgo San Jacopo 54 (tel. 295-396)
Hours: *Monday through Saturday from 9:30 a.m. to 1:30 p.m. and 3:30 to 7:30 p.m. (closed Monday morning)*
Credit Cards: None

A profusion of prints, engravings, and drawings, some dating back to the 16th century. Particularly fine are the hand-colored botanical prints of the flora of Tuscany, for which you'll pay 45,000 lire and up, depending on size, condition, and the degree of color.

DUCCI
Lungarno Corsini 24 (tel. 214-550)
Hours: *Monday through Saturday from 9:30 a.m. to 1 p.m. and 3:30 to 7:30 p.m. (closed Monday morning)*

Credit Cards: *AE, DC, MC, V*
English Spoken.

Just to the left as you enter this shop is a large print room where you can spend hours looking through the bins of prints covering the long and turbulent history of the city, as well as views, maps, and engravings of paintings in the Pitti Palace and the Uffizi.

GIOVANNI BACCANI
Via della Vigna Nuova 75 (tel. 214-467)
Hours: Monday through Saturday from 9:30 a.m. to 1:30 p.m. and 3:30 to 7:30 p.m. (closed Monday morning)
Credit Cards: *AE, DC, MC, V*
English Spoken.

Baccani, or "The Blue Shop" as it's known, looks more like the library of a stately home than a store. The walls are paneled and painted and the place is filled with the smell of old ink and leather bindings. The prints and engravings are in a series of bins and you are free to browse for hours. Prices begin at just 10,000 lire, but Baccani sells more than just prints. There are also frames, boxes, paintings, and a lot of Florentine paper goods. Some things are very unusual, like the boxes and bookends decorated with trompe l'oeil designs. A set of bookends is 40,000 lire.

SHOES (see "Leather Goods")

STATIONERY SUPPLIES

&C
Via della Vigna Nuova 82 and 91 (tel. 287-839)
Hours: Monday through Saturday from 9 a.m. to 7:30 p.m. nonstop (closed Monday morning)
Credit Cards: *AE, DC, MC, V*
English Spoken.

&C ("Etc.") has some of the most beautiful and unusual Florentine paper products in the city. Featured in New York's Museum of Modern Art design collection—the only place in the United States where &C can be bought—&C has a way of taking old designs and updating them. The results are stunning: a leather-covered diary with a heavy brass clasp manages to evoke the 16th century and the 21st century at the same time. It costs 62,000 lire—a lot less than you'd pay in New York. &C aerograms on handmade paper—far too nice to consign to the mail—are only 2,000 lire.

&C, the most exclusive of the great Florentine papermakers

BOTTEGA ARTIGIANA DEL LIBRO
Lungarno Corsini 38–40 (tel. 263-488)
Hours: *Monday through Saturday from 9 a.m. to 7:30 p.m. nonstop (closed Monday morning)*
Credit Cards: AE, DC, MC, V
English Spoken.

Bottega Artigiana del Libro: For the finest marbled Florentine paper products

You can peek through a door in this shop and see the goods for sale being made in the back. Traditional marbled Florentine paper products are to be had here in quantity at excellent prices: a small marbled notebook is 8,000 lire; larger agendas are only 17,000 lire to 20,000 lire; a bridge pad is 9,000 lire; a large leatherbound notebook with marbled boards is 45,000 lire.

GIULIO GIANNINI E FIGLIO
Piazza Pitti 37 (tel. 212-621)
Hours: *Monday through Saturday from 9:30 a.m. to 1:30 p.m. and 3:30 to 7:30 p.m. (closed Monday morning)*
Credit Cards: AE, MC, V
English Spoken.

Giannini consists of two rooms of lavishly decorated Florentine paper goods. All the work is done by Giannini craftsmen and the work is, of course, first-rate. There are lovely marbled handmade papers, albums, boxes, and books. If you are here close to Christmastime, or are planning ahead, look at Giannini's lovely Christmas-card selection. The cards are on heavy paper and printed with beautiful reproductions of Renaissance nativity scenes. They cost 2,000 lire to 5,000 lire each and are available all year round. A small marbled blank book is only 15,000 lire.

PINEIDER
Piazza della Signoria (tel. 284-655) and Via dei Tornabuoni 76 (tel. 211-605)
Hours: *Monday through Saturday from 9 a.m. to 1 p.m. and 3:30 to 7:30 p.m. (closed Monday morning)*
Credit Cards: AE, DC, MC, V
English Spoken.

Paper doesn't come with a higher pedigree than this. Pineider has been making stationery for the crowned heads since the last century. The letter paper is thick and smooth, and the airmail bond so delicate that you might think it will melt in your hands. Pineider is not cheap, but compared to prices at their one shop in the Untied States (in Trump Tower in New York) prices here are a steal. A gift folder with 20 sheets of writing paper and 12 thick, creamy envelopes, each packet bound with white silk ribbons, costs 35,000 lire. The larger gift boxes with paper and envelopes in various sizes, as well as gift cards, cost 85,000 lire and up. Pineider will design a letterhead for you, but it will take a while and cost 250,000 lire and up.

VAINIO
Via Mazzetta 22 (no phone)
Hours: *Monday through Saturday from 9 a.m. to 1 p.m. and 3:30 to 7:30 p.m. (closed Saturday afternoon)*

Credit Cards: AE
English Spoken.

This store is the size of a small elevator, but that doesn't affect the quality, elegance, and taste of the fabulous handmade papers sold here. Designs are spare and modern—no bright colors or cute Florentine scrollwork here—but beautiful nonetheless. A folder containing 15 sheets of paper and 12 envelopes costs 7,500 lire.

WINES

Pegna, the grocery store which you'll find listed in the food section, has a good selection of wines from Tuscany as well as other parts of Italy. It does not, however, specialize in wines. The following shop does.

IL CANTINONE
Via Santo Spirito 6 (tel. 218-898)
Hours: Monday through Saturday from 1 to 9 p.m. nonstop (closed Sunday)
Credit Cards: *None*

In Tuscany wine means Chianti, and in Florence Chianti means Il Cantinone. It's a great old place, this, where you'll find that the food is a complement to the wine rather than the other way round. Il Cantinone is a restaurant that invites you to try a certain type of wine with your lunch or dinner—and should you like the wine you can buy a bottle out of their cellars and take it home with you. The food is good and not extortionately expensive and the wine is excellent.

Try (and then buy) a Chianti Classico like Monsanto, Capanelle, Riecine, or Villa Antinori. After your meal have a glass of Vin Santo, a Tuscan dessert wine which, taken with some *biscotti di mandorla* (almond cookies), will make you want to stay in Florence forever.

BOTTEGA VENETA

PART FOUR

SHOPPING VENICE

CHAPTER X

A VENICE OVERVIEW

For hundreds of years the Venetians were famous as merchants and traders. Venetian ships sailed to the most remote corners of the world, returning with their holds packed with rare and exotic wares which the Venetians turned around and sold to the rest of Europe at a healthy markup. In the course of doing this, they built the most beautiful city in the world, gave art some of its most gifted painters, and developed an architectural style all their own.

The Venetian trading spirit continues to this day. Millions of visitors flock to the city each year not only to see the sights but also to buy Venetian crafts and art objects, as well as goods from the rest of Italy. Venice is packed with shops, and given the number of visitors who throng the city each year one might expect to find an overwhelming number of unscrupulous merchants. Of course they do exist, but overall, shopping in Venice is no more expensive—and in some cases, cheaper—than in the rest of Italy.

BASIC ORIENTATION

Venice is divided by the Grand Canal, which winds like the letter "S" through the most famous and populous quarters of the city. The Grand Canal, along with the Piazza San Marco and the Rialto Bridge, are the three best-known landmarks and it is in relation to them that the shopping strolls in Chapter XI are oriented. The two main streets for shopping are the Frezzeria and the Merceria dell'Orologio. They run from the area around the Piazza San Marco (the Merceria actually joins the square) toward the Grand Canal.

The other side of the canal, the side which has the Accademia and Guggenheim Museum, is called the Dorsoduro.

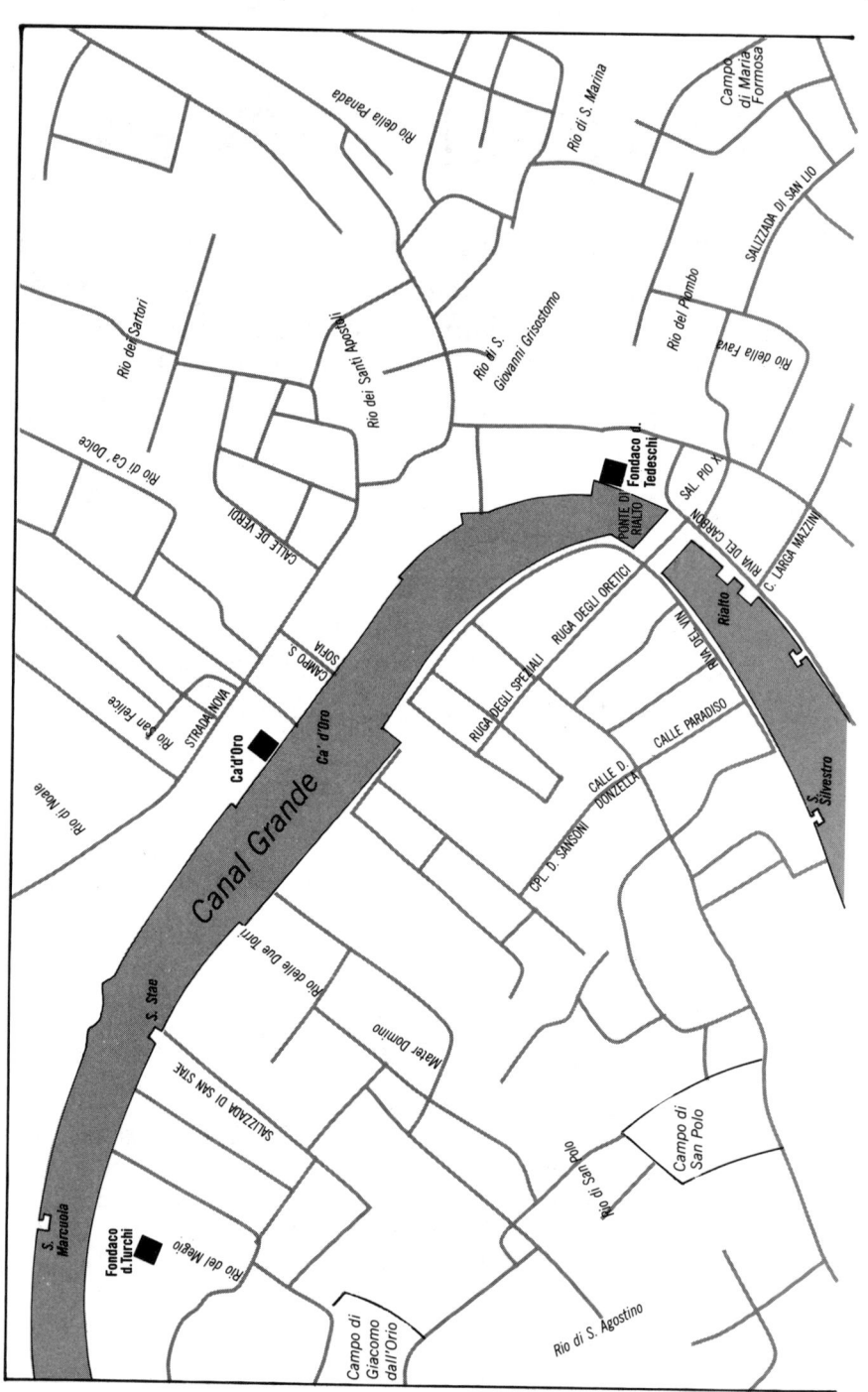

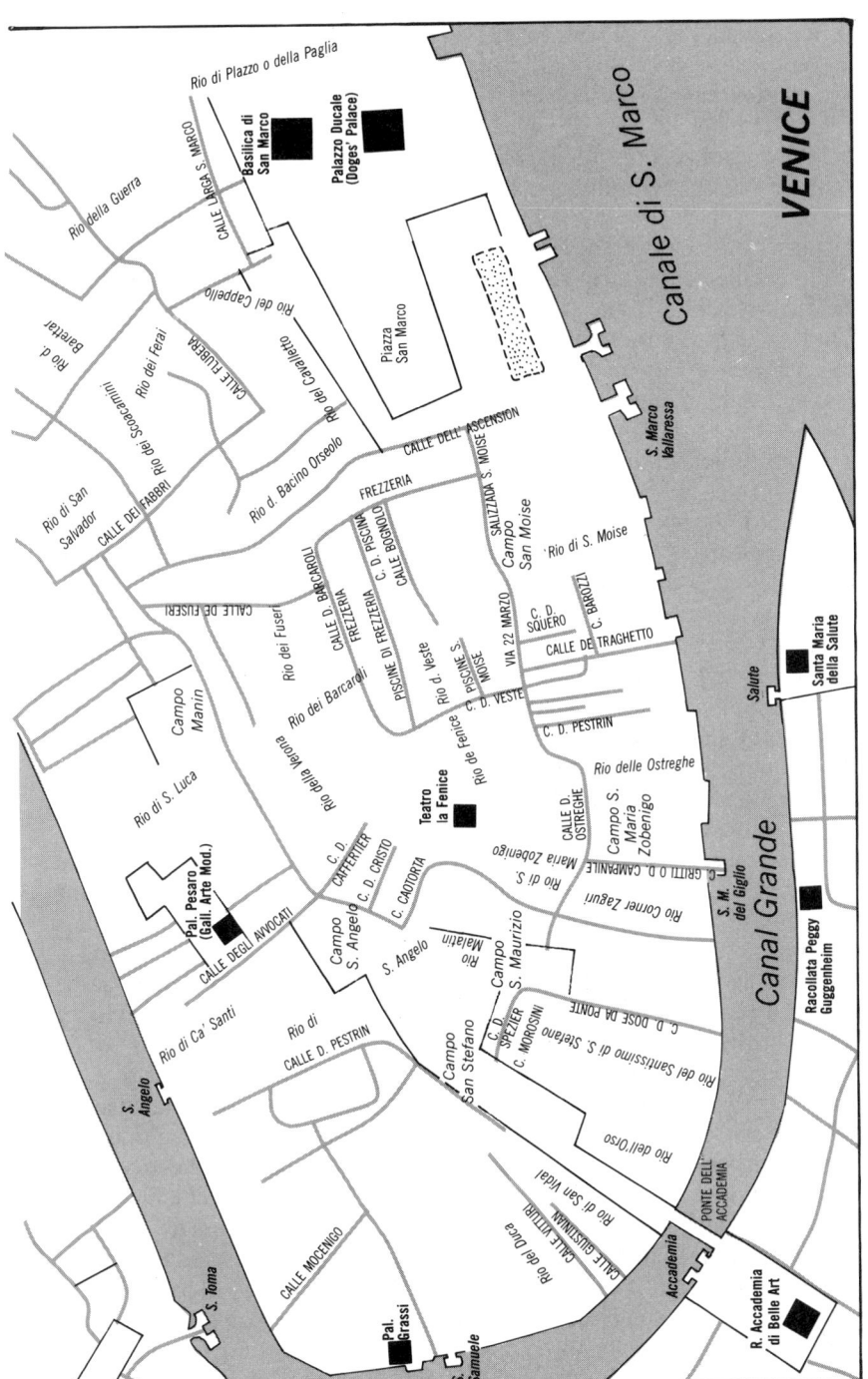

You should, I'm afraid, resign yourself to getting lost. People who have lived in Venice their entire lives still make mistakes, so the visitor must expect to wander the streets—sometimes for quite a while—before finding something vaguely familiar. The municipality of Venice has painted signs on walls directing you toward major points like the Piazza San Marco, the Piazzale Roma, and the train station (Stazione Santa Lucia). So you can always unravel the mystery of how to get back to your hotel, but you might find yourself wandering through sections of the city you never thought you'd visit. Best, though, to obtain a really detailed street map that shows all the tiny alleys, passageways, and dead-end streets (many maps don't) so that you can negotiate the city with ease. The Falk map in particular is excellent.

For a guidebook of this kind the problem of street numbers is a difficult one to resolve. Mailing addresses and street addresses in Venice are two different things—but shops, hotels, and restaurants usually go by the mailing address. The city is divided into six *sestiere* (sections) and addresses are given by the section name, followed by a number. Thus San Marco 1473 (the address of Valentino) does not mean 1473 St. Mark's Square, nor is there even a St. Mark's Street; it means 1473 St. Mark's Section. It might be near the Piazza or not, but both Valentino and Piazza San Marco are in the same district.

The Venetian system for numbering buildings is also a little difficult to master. A building marked "Number 1" is right next door to "Number 2." The building facing "Number 1" across the street might be "Number 2756." The reason for this is that numbers have an alarming habit of wandering off the streets themselves. "Number 3" might be on a corner. "Number 4," then, is the first building on the side street—and the numbers will continue down the side street, around a *campo* (square), and then head back up the side street until it rejoins the main street again.

Venetians speak an Italian all their own. Some learned philologists have said that their accent is Spanish, their pronunciation Slavic, and their spelling Germanic. When one realizes that there wasn't a country in Venice's glory days that was not a trading partner, that the Venetian empire ruled large parts of Greece, Yugoslavia, the Middle East, and parts of mainland Italy, and that the city itself was once under French and Austrian dominion, one can begin to see where the hybrid Venetian dialect just might be a little complicated.

In a sense, the Venetian Italian one hears and reads today is much like the English of the 16th century. There are no standard spellings or grammatical rules one can learn and be done with it. Added to that, the peculiar antiquarian bent of the Venice *commune* (city government) has decreed that the street signs you see painted, black lettering on a white field, on the sides of buildings be written in old Venetian rather than modern Italian. There isn't so much difference between them that you cannot get their general meaning, but there can be, on occasion, a certain amount of confusion. It's easy to recognize the Venetian "Ca'" in the place of the Italian "Casa," as in "Ca' D'Oro," but, as J. G. Link, an Englishman who has written one of the best guides to Venice (*Venice for Pleasure*; New York: Farrar, Straus, Giroux, 1984; $9.95) says: "The street names... generally tally with what you see written up [on the walls of the city], but they will rarely be the same as you will find on your map. Do not despair: what is meant is generally apparent." Mr. Link, who combines a deep knowledge and love of the city with a fine sense of humor, goes on to point out: "... do not worry if you see such words as 'dose,' 'ogio,' 'anzolo,' or 'Lunardo' instead of 'doge,' 'olio,' 'angelo,' or 'Leonardo,' or 'de la' or 'de le' when you expect 'della' or 'delle.' Consistency is not a virtue held very high by Venetians."

Finally, I cannot emphasize strongly enough that you *will* get lost. It's a fact of life in Venice—and half the fun of visiting the city in the first place.

Given this, it's no wonder that most shops hand out business cards with little maps on the back showing where they are located. But that doesn't solve the problem of finding a specific shop from a street address alone. All I can say is that even if you don't find some of the shops listed in this guide, you're sure to find ones that aren't—and you're in Venice to boot, so why complain?

GETTING FROM THE AIRPORT

The Venice airport, called **Marco Polo–Téssera**, is on the Italian mainland, 14 km (8½ miles) away from the city. There are three ways of getting from the airport to Venice: the typical way, the expensive exciting way, and the cheap exciting way. The typical way is to go by land, on an **airport bus**, which takes you through the industrial town of Mestre, across the causeway linking Venice to Italy proper, and drops you at the Piazzale Roma, a giant parking lot on the edge of the city from which you'll take the vaporetto into the center of the city. The bus leaves every half hour and costs 5,000 lire. The ride takes about an hour.

The expensive exciting way is to hire one of the sleek **water taxis**, called *motoscafi*, and sail in splendor across the northern part of the lagoon and deep into the city itself. The ride takes about 45 minutes. Water taxis are expensive: the trip from the airport to Piazzo San Marco will cost 100,000 lire or more.

You can also enter Venice by water for much less. There is a water-bus service, called **Cooperativa San Marco**, which travels to and from the airport every few minutes. The fare for the ride, which deposits you at the ferry terminal at Piazza San Marco, is 10,000 lire per person.

GETTING AROUND

The water-bus service within the city is excellent. The **vaporetti** of the ACTV, the Venetian Transit Authority, are marvelous craft, most of them running 24 hours a day, and are a wonderful inexpensive way of seeing the city. There are vaporetto stops all along the Grand Canal and tickets are purchased there, not in cigarette shops or at newsstands as in other Italian cities. Tickets cost 1,500 lire and are good for one ride.

The most frequently used vaporetto is the No. 1—in fact it's so standard, that the Venetians refer to it as "*il vaporetto,*" as if there weren't any others. The

No. 1 runs from the Lido, on the far side of the lagoon, to Venice, stopping at the Riva degli Schiavoni, San Marco, up the Grand Canal (on which it makes 14 stops), and finishes its journey at the train station. Departures are about every ten minutes.

As mentioned above, **water-taxi service** is very expensive, and despite the luxury in which you travel is really not worth the money. Furthermore, you don't jump in one and say "Take me to the Fendi shop," as most of the shopping areas in Venice are landlocked. Water taxis are best used when you have a lot of luggage and can't face lugging it on and off a crowded vaporetto. The fare from Piazza San Marco to the train station is approximately 60,000 lire—but get an estimate in advance. *Note:* The *ganzier,* the man who holds your boat, allowing you to get on and off at the quay, should be tipped for his service, usually 1,000 or so lire for each passenger.

In the old days, visitors to Venice used to hire **gondolas** for the length of their stay to ferry them wherever they might want to go. Unless money is no object, this is not done any more. As it is, the cost of a once-in-a-lifetime ride in a gondola is going to leave you feeling that you bought the boat, not rented it. A short cruise, taking about 30 minutes, costs approximately 50,000 lire. The gondolier decides the route, but he will return you to the place where you boarded. If you want to use a gondola as a taxi, with a specific destination in mind, then the price is open to negotiation. This doesn't mean it will be any cheaper—quite the opposite. A trip from the Rialto Bridge to the train station usually costs about 120,000 lire.

Gondolas on the Grand Canal

VENICE: GENERAL INFORMATION

There is an inexpensive and often overlooked water service that is a genuine piece of old Venice and is also very handy. If you're wandering down a side street and find yourself on the bank of the Grand Canal, looking at a rather shabby gondola operated by two men rather than one, you have stumbled upon one of the last **traghetti** in the city. There used to be hundreds of traghetti, or ferries, crossing the Grand Canal, but the work is not well paid and is back-breaking, so now there exist only seven crossing points on the length of the canal. The gondoliers shuttle back and forth between two fixed points, waiting on each side until they have a full load, usually three or four people. The fare for a crossing is usually 1,000 lire, which you pay as you board. Venetians always stand in a traghetto, but unless you have an extremely good sense of balance it's better to sit. Everyone knows you are a foreigner anyway. The traghetti are not cute, and offer no accordion music or gilt decorations. However, they do save miles of walking while you search for a bridge to cross the canal.

The seven traghetti still in operation cross between: San Barnaba and San Samuele, Sant'Angleo and San Tomà, San Marcuola and Fondeco dei Turchi, Riva del Carbon and Riva del Vin, Santa Sofia and Pescheria, the railway station and San Simeone Piccolo, and Santa Maria del Giglio and San Gregorio.

It's best to see the city **on foot**—and it's the only way you can shop. The streets do get crowded, however, and in the high tourist season you often feel as if you're waiting in some long, never-ending line rather than walking through the city. The plus side, though, is that unlike other large cities, you are not suffocated by exhaust fumes nor do you take your life in your hands when you cross the street; as siesta envelops the city, or midnight draws near, there is nothing but blissful quiet, no car horns or racing engines.

TOURIST INFORMATION

There are four EPT (*Ente Provinciale per il Turismo*) information offices in the city. Three are open year round, while the fourth is open only in the summer. The hours for all are Monday through Saturday from 9:30 a.m. to 1:30 p.m. and 3:30 to 7 p.m. They are closed Sunday, and English is spoken at each office. The addresses are: Stazione Santa Lucia (the main railway station; tel. 715-016), Calle del Rimedio 4421 (tel. 23-331), San Marco Ascension 71C (tel. 26-356), and at Piazzale Roma, Stazione Autolinee (open May through September; tel. 27-402). The handiest ones are at the rail station and Ascension. The Calle del Rimedio office is the administrative center.

WEATHER

The late spring and the early fall are the best times to visit Venice. The crowds have thinned a little and the cold and wet seasons have just ended or are yet to begin.

By late October the wind has come up and evenings are cold and damp. The real cold begins in December and lasts through February and into March. The winter season, however, has a lot to recommend it. The city is empty of visitors, so the shops, hotels, and restaurants are not crowded at all—*except* for one week before the onset of Lent, when the famous Venetian carnival erupts. Then the city is jammed for seven days, hotel rooms are unobtainable, and the main streets are so crowded that the police designate certain main drags as one way—for pedestrians! It's a wonderful time to see Venice at play, but not a good time for shopping or sightseeing. It's also usually cold and wet.

Acqua alta—flooding—usually occurs when there is a strong wind blowing off the sea. When the meteorologists decide that *acqua alta* is in the offing, a signal sort of like a foghorn is set off, moaning over the city every few minutes until the water actually arrives. Municipal workers immediately get busy laying down duckboards on main streets and in the Piazza San Marco, but occasionally they don't make it in time. Even then, water can rise higher than the boards—John Ruskin recalls seeing a gondola sail majestically into the lobby of the Danieli Hotel to pick up passengers. Flooding is most frequent in February and March.

High summer season is very hot and uncomfortable. Daytime temperatures regularly reach the 90° mark, and both days and nights are humid. It's also the time of year when the most visitors come to the city. But if it comes down to going to Venice in July or August or not going at all, brave the crowds and the heat and go! For the current temperature and weather forecast, you can call 1910.

THE ABCS OF SHOPPING VENICE

AMERICAN EXPRESS

The Venice branch of American Express is located at San Marco 1471. That's the official (mailing) address. If you are searching for it on foot you will find it on the Salizzada (also spelled Salizada) San Moisè, very close to the Campo San Moisè, near the Bauer Grünwald Hotel. In other words, if you are standing in the Piazza San Marco (with the Basilica di San Marco behind you) you walk through the arcade in the left-hand corner and across the Calle Ascensione, taking the through street directly in front of you. That is the Salizzada San Moisè. Follow it until you reach the American Express office, about 200 yards along on your left.

The office is open Monday through Friday from 9 a.m. to 6 p.m. (for travel arrangements), Monday through Friday from 9 a.m. to 5:30 p.m. (for financial transactions), and on Saturday from 9 a.m. to 1 p.m. (for all services).

The telephone number is 700-844.

VENICE: GENERAL INFORMATION

BANK HOURS

(See "The ABCs of Shopping Italy" in Chapter II.)

BUSINESS HOURS

As the business of Venice is, and always has been, business, hours are much less restrictive here than elsewhere in Italy. Many more shops stay open nonstop (that is, without a long break for lunch) and a great number of them are open on Sunday, if not year round, then certainly from late spring to the end of September.

Most shops open between 9 and 10 a.m., and if they close for a siesta, they do so around 1 or 1:30 p.m. They reopen from 3 until 7:30 p.m. Most are closed Monday morning. In August more business is carried on in Venice than in Rome, Milan, or Florence, but there are exceptions, so check ahead of time.

DINING

In the introduction to the city, I mentioned that prices are no higher in Venice than anywhere else in Italy. That's true—except when it comes to dining. For centuries, mainland Italians have derided the Venetians' lack of interest in dining well, claiming that they were more interested in the pursuits of commerce than in the delights of the table. Whatever the reason, meals are just not as good in Venice as elsewhere in Italy, and the giant tourist influx means that prices tend to be high even for mediocre food. Nonetheless, there are some excellent restaurants in Venice, and some fairly reasonable prices, but on the whole the meal that costs 100,000 lire in Rome will cost 150,000 lire in Venice. In the areas heavily trafficked by tourists, a cup of cappuccino, which might cost 1,000 lire in Florence, will fetch 2,000 lire in Venice. Obviously, the farther you wander off the beaten track the less you'll pay for your refreshments. Naturally, in the heart of things, at Quadri's or Florian's in the Piazza San Marco, you'll pay a premium price for everything. A cappuccino at Florian's costs 5,000 lire, and if it's summertime and the band is playing, there is a charge for the music as well!

HOLIDAYS

In addition to the general holidays listed in the "ABCs of Shopping Italy" in Chapter II, Venice celebrates two holidays peculiar to the city. Again, not everything closes on these days, but a large percentage of shops do have their shutters down. The holidays are February 2 (Festa della Purificazione della Vergine) and November 21 (Festa della Madonna della Salute). Both are holidays dedicated to the Virgin Mary. On the latter feast day a bridge of boats is built across the Grand Canal from San Marco to the Church of Santa Maria della Salute.

MARKETS

The major markets (*mercati*) in Venice are the Pescheria and the Erberia, which are side by side on the Dorsoduro side of the Rialto Bridge. They are predominantly food markets. The Ruga degli Orefici, the street that leads off the bridge to the markets, is lined with stalls selling local handcrafts, souvenirs, clothes, and a lot of gaudy, junky housewares. You might find a good buy here on a cheap purse or sweater, but on the whole the stands are not treasure troves for the bargain hunter.

POST OFFICE

The main post office is at the foot of the Rialto Bridge on the San Marco side of the canal. It is housed in the Fontego dei Tedeschi, occupying all of the street of the same name (tel. 86-212). Standard Italian hours are in effect here: Monday through Friday from 8:30 a.m. to 8 p.m. and on Saturday from 8 a.m. to noon.

SALES

(See "The ABCs of Shopping Italy" in Chapter II.)

TAXES

(See "The ABCs of Shopping Italy" in Chapter II.)

TELEPHONES

The general rules on how to use the phone, explained in "The ABCs of Shopping Italy" in Chapter II, apply in Venice. *Except* that SIP, the Italian phone company, is in the process of changing just about all the phone numbers in the city. Sometime within the next few years all numbers in the center of town will begin with the digits 52, followed by the number as it now stands. This applies to all numbers, except those beginning with the number 7. If you are dialing 765-320, for example, you drop the 7 and put 52 in its place, making the number 526-5320. If you dial a number and get a recording, hang up and substitute the new prefix.

CHAPTER XI

GREAT VENICE SHOPPING STROLLS

Except during the high tourist season and during Carnevale, there is no finer city to see on foot than Venice. As I have already mentioned, you don't have to flatten yourself against the sides of buildings to let a stream of noisy Fiats pass and you don't have to look both ways five times before crossing the street. Let the pace of the crowd carry you along, or if you are lucky enough to be here during the low season, set your own speed and enjoy the beauty of the city and the many fine shops you'll find on every *calle, riva,* and *ramo*. And don't worry about getting lost: it happens to everyone.

FROM SAN MARCO TO CAMPO MOROSINI

This walk begins at the far end of the Piazza San Marco and follows a straight—or as straight as one can manage in Venice—path toward the large square of Campo Morosini. (A *campo* is a square, by the way, but is never called a piazza—San Marco is the only piazza in Venice.) Except for one detour onto the Calle Vallaressa, you follow the same street all the way to the end—but it changes its name every few blocks. It begins as Salizzada San Moisè, becomes Via 22 Marzo, then Calle delle Ostreghe, widens into the Campo Santa Maria Zobenigo, narrows to become Calle Zaguri, breaks into the Campo San Maurizio, and becomes Calle Piovan, which leads into the Campo Morosini.

Starting in the **Piazza San Marco**, with your back to the basilica, walk through the portico, keeping the Correr Museum on your left. Once out of the piazza you'll be standing in a small street called **Calle dell'Ascension**. Here you'll find Vogini, an excellent shop for luggage and handbags. Also on this street is the Venetian branch of the Neapolitan shoemaker Mario Valentino.

Between them is the opening onto **Salizzada San Moisè**. Walk down that street and take your first left. This is **Calle Vallaressa** and it lies between San Moisè and the Grand Canal. On this short, narrow street you'll find some of the

The view from the campanile in Piazza San Marco

best-known names in Italian fashion. At no. 1337 is the flagship shop of Bottega Veneta. Just up the way, at no. 1318 is Miguel Cruz. Missoni is at no. 1312B, selling clothes for women and men, as well as Missoni fabrics. Basile and Yves Saint Laurent are the specialties of Nara Boutique, at Calle Vallaressa 1321. One of the great names of Venetian glass is Battiston, at Calle Vallaressa 1320.

The street is a dead-end, so you have to retrace your footsteps to **Salizzada San Moisè**. Turn left. On San Moisè is Fendi, at no. 1474. There is a print shop, Osvaldo Böhm, across the street at San Moisè 1349–1350. One of the two Bruno Magli shops in Venice is on San Moisè at no. 1583–1585 (we'll see the other on our shopping stroll along Calle Frezzeria). San Moisè is also the home of another fine shoe shop, Fratelli Rossetti, at no. 1477. L'Isola, a fine glass shop, is in the **Campo San Moisè**, in the square at the end of the street. Nearby, next to American Express, is Valentino.

On your left is the Bauer Grünwald Hotel, which stands next to the small canal, Rio di San Moisè. Cross this canal and you'll be standing in one of the few wide streets of Venice, **Via 22 Marzo**. As you walk along it, you'll find La Fenice, which sells Maud Frizon shoes. Then comes La Coupole, a shop offering many well-known names in men's and women's fashion.

Via 22 Marzo is also the main antiques street of Venice. There are antiquarian books, prints, and maps at Cassini (no. 2424), paintings at Frezzati (no. 2070), and fine art and objects at Casellati (no. 2404), Trois (no. 2251), and Scarpa (no. 2089).

Near the Hotel Saturnia e International is Enrica Massei, a high-quality shop specializing in cashmere, at Via 22 Marzo 2400. Next to it is a children's clothing shop, Maricla, at no. 2401. Also on 22 Marzo is Boni, which has its own brand of leather handbags, as well as a selection of Fendi products.

Toward the end of the street, at the corner of **Calle delle Ostreghe**, is Krizia.

Crossing the next bridge and continuing straight on, you come to the **Campo Santa Maria Zobenigo**, also known as Santa Maria del Giglio. In this square is F.G.B., specializing in Venetian carnival masks. Also in the square is Barbara, the Lancetti shop in Venice.

Continuing on, follow signs for the **Campo San Maurizio**. Here you'll find beautiful Venetian paper at Il Papiro. Also in the campo is BAC Art Studio, which has lovely prints of Venice as well as paper and blank books.

In the next square over, **Campo San Stefano**, is L'Ixa, a tiny but wonderful antiques shop. Campo San Stefano adjoins Campo Morosini, the end of this stroll.

At this point you can turn right and head for Campo Sant'Angelo, where the next stroll ends and do it in reverse; or turn to your left and head for the cultural highlight of the first stroll, the Accademia; or you can turn around and sit down in the nice outdoor café that takes up a chunk of the square.

A SIGHTSEEING SUGGESTION

The **Accademia** gallery, just across the Grand Canal from the Campo Morosini, is the most famous art museum in Venice. In the large, airy rooms you'll find works by the great Venetian masters of the 14th through the 17th centuries. It's not the kind of museum in which you'll feel compelled to study everything, but no matter where you look you're bound to see something of great beauty (and in some cases, fame).

The single most famous painting in the gallery is Giorgione's *The Tempest*, an enigmatic work, the meaning of which has never been wholly explained. People crowd around this small painting, staring at it in the hope that they will see something the august art historians have missed and thus unravel the mystery. In the picture, painted in 1505, we see a comely nude looking out of the canvas at the viewer. She is suckling a child. In the left of the painting is a soldier leaning on his staff, staring at the woman. In the background an evil-looking storm is brewing, hence the name of the painting. Interpretations are varied. Some say it's a stylized Renaissance view of the discovery of Moses in the bullrushes (peculiar to Venice, Moses is a saint; we walked this morning on "San Moisè"). Others are equally emphatic in saying that the story is an allegory: that the woman is suckling new and innocent life, while the soldier, a drunkard (although he looks perfectly sober), is a wastrel and killer and quite unaware of the doom, the storm, which is about to envelop him. Whatever the meaning, the female figure is possessed of the most captivating stare after the *Mona Lisa*.

There are some magnificent paintings in the Accademia that have well-known, well-documented anecdotes attached. Perhaps the best known is Paolo Veronese's giant *Feast at the House of Levi*. The painting takes up an entire wall, and when it was finished, Veronese was justly proud of it. It was then entitled

The Last Supper. But it was unlike any Last Supper that the church authorities of Venice had ever seen before. There were hundreds of figures, not the traditional 13, and there were also some figures considered quite unsuitable for the honor of partaking in this sacred moment—dogs, drunkards, dwarfs, and most offensive of all to an Italian ecclesiastical sensibility, Germans. Veronese was hauled into court and asked, rather sternly, if he thought having dwarfs and Germans in a Last Supper was appropriate. All he could say was that the picture was so very large that he needed to put in as many large figures as possible. The court of the Inquisition was not impressed with this line of defense and sent him away, giving him just three months to make the painting a little more sacred and a lot less profane. Apparently he stared at the giant masterpiece and when his time was up it was found that he had not changed a brushstroke. Instead he had changed the name. It was no longer *The Last Supper;* it was now *Feast at the House of Levi.* The church was satisfied, as it was more than likely, they felt, that Levi, a tax gatherer, would have such a bunch of ruffians at his table. Veronese himself is leaning against a pillar in the left foreground.

It would be hard to select the "top ten" in a gallery of this size and quality, but there are some masterpieces that should not be missed. These are Bellini's lovingly rendered views of Venetian pageantry (Room 20), the Carpaccio cycle of *The Legend of St. Ursula* (Room 21), Titian's *Presentation of the Virgin* (Room 24), and the Giovanni Bellini San Giobe altarpiece, known as *The Virgin with Saints* (Room 2).

The Accademia is at the Campo della Carità, Dorsoduro (Accademia vaporetto stop; tel. 22-247). It's open Tuesday through Saturday from 9 a.m. to 2 p.m. (on Thursday to 4 p.m.), and on Sunday and holidays from 9 a.m. to 1 p.m. (closed Monday). Admission is 3,000 lire (free on the first and fourth Saturdays and the first and third Sundays of each month).

REFRESHMENTS EN ROUTE

Dining in the area of the Accademia is a little difficult. But, needless to say, there are dozens of small bars where you can get a sandwich and a drink.

Snacks

If that's all you want, you can enjoy them with a view as well by following the streets away from the Grand Canal heading toward the Giudecca. Follow the Rio Terrà Antonio Foscarini, which is the main thoroughfare. Along this broad canal are a number of good outdoor cafés that will provide you with a drink, a sandwich, and a view—all at prices much lower than in the heart of town.

Restaurants

If you want a full meal and haven't found a place around the Accademia that looks *sympatico,* then you'll have to head back toward San Marco.

Harry's Bar, Calle Vallaressa 1323 (tel. 30-124), open from 1:30 to 3:30

p.m. and 7:30 to midnight; expensive. Credit Cards: DC, V. Frequented by Ernest Hemingway and Peggy Guggenheim in the "old days," Harry's is the most famous restaurant in Venice, and according to Michelin, it's the best. The little Red Book gave Harry's two stars its last time out. And while the food at Harry's is almost secondary to the history of the place, the food is very good too. Try one of the world-famous Harry cocktails and then the delicious risotto with asparagus. If you're in the mood for pasta you shouldn't miss the tagliolini verdi. Your second course should be fish, particularly the squid or grilled sea bass. A meal for two is about 200,000 lire and can cost more, depending on the wine. A 20% service charge is also added to all bills.

Antico Martini, Campo San Fantin 1983 (tel. 522-4121), open for dinner only; expensive. Credit Cards: AE, DC, MC, V. Antico Martini is one of the oldest *alta classe* restaurants in Venice. If it's summertime you'll dine on a lovely terrace facing the celebrated Teatro La Fenice. The food is top-notch, particularly the pastas and grilled fish. If you like liver, this is the place to have your fegato alla veneziana—its the best in town. Unless something on the à la carte menu really strikes your fancy, you can sample the best Antico Martini offers by dining from the prix-fixe menu, which will save you a good 35%.

PIAZZA SAN MARCO AND THE FREZZERIA

We begin this stroll by exploring shops in and around the Piazza San Marco itself. As might be expected, there are some shops under the porticoes that take full advantage of their position. They know that not all visitors are going to trek miles through narrow streets in search of the perfect piece of lace, for instance: it's much easier to buy it in the center of town where everyone speaks English and be done with it. You'll pay a large markup for the convenience—but you probably figured that out for yourself.

In addition to the square itself, we'll be traveling the length of the Frezzeria, a prime shopping street that begins at the far end of the piazza from the basilica, the way the first stroll did. But starting with the **Piazza San Marco** itself, the first big-name shop you should visit is Jesurum, which is just to the left of San Marco as you look at it from the Ponte Canonica. This is literally a temple of lace. This grand old shop is located in a 12th-century church, with mosaics and decorations intact.

Returning to the piazza, directly in front of the Doges' Palace, under the portico, is Tokatzian, another, more modern establishment specializing in handmade lace. Its address is Piazza San Marco 16. Now cross the piazza diagonally and past Quadri's café you'll come to a small bridge leading out of the square. On this bridge, the Ponte dei Dai, is Dario Ustino (at no. 171), hand-maker of traditional Venetian carnival masks.

Back on the piazza itself, but still moving away from the basilica, is Desiré, which has a vast selection of lace. It's located at Piazza San Marco 78.

The Piazza San Marco: "The drawing room of Europe," as Napoleon put it

Leaving the piazza, you're at the top of a small street called **Bocca di Piazza**. To your left is Roberta di Camerino (which is actually on a street called Ascension, at no 1255), one of the best-known Venetian names in fashion and leather goods. As you move onto Bocca di Piazza itself, you come to a small glass and mask shop, Sebastiana Perez, at Bocca di Piazza 1234A, with good prices for the neighborhood.

This brings you to the **Frezzeria** proper, where there are two fine shops, almost side by side and under the same management, featuring men's and women's wear: V&V Boutique at Frezzeria 1233 and Volpe at Frezzeria 1286.

There's elegant silk clothing for women at Pier, Frezzeria 1180, and more trendy clothes for women can be found just down the street at Controcorrente, Frezzeria 1232.

Beautiful and offbeat Venetian glass is available at Archimede Seguso, at Frezzeria 1236 (there's also a side entrance on Bocca di Piazza). Across the street is a lovely antiques and bric-a-brac shop, Arte Filatelia, at Frezzeria 1504.

At Frezzeria 1583 is the second of two Bruno Magli shops in Venice, with styles for both men and women. Then comes the second branch of La Coupole, at Frezzeria 1674, which carries lovely leather goods.

There are also two Élysée boutiques in Venice. Élysée 2 is on the Frezzeria at no. 1693. This is the Giorgio Armani outlet for Venice.

Gianni Versace is nearby at Frezzeria 1722, just down the street from Mozart's house. The boutique features men's and women's clothing as well as a wide range of leather accessories.

Metamauco, near the Teatro La Fenice, is a glass shop with a difference. Designs are more restrained than you might expect, and engraving is done on the premises.

Il Prato, at Frezzeria 1770, has a vast selection of handmade Venetian gifts, masks, costumes, and pictures.

At Frezzeria 1797 is Betta Scarpa, with stunning, rather flamboyant knitwear, all handmade.

As you cross the **Ponte dei Barcaroli**, near Teatro La Fenice and across the street from the house where Mozart lived, you'll come to the tiny shop of Bruno Rizzato, a Ponte dei Barcaroli 1831. He has been hand-making his masks here and decorating them to his own designs for so long that he's a Venice institution.

The Frezzeria now widens into a small square, the **Campo San Fantin**. In it you'll find a small but exquisite women's-wear shop, Araba Fenice.

IN THE NEIGHBORHOOD

Between the Frezzeria and the Merceria is **Calle Goldoni**, a wide street given over to all kinds of shops, most of them selling glass and crafts, but there are two clothing shops here that should not be missed. One is the head office of Élysée, Calle Goldoni 4485, which has men's and women's clothing, leather, and accessories from every important designer under the sun, from Giorgio Armani to Thierry Mugler. The other, nearby at Calle Goldoni 4512, is L'Équipe, featuring a gorgeous selection of menswear by Verri.

SIGHTSEEING SUGGESTIONS

Right at the beginning of this stroll are some of the most impressive sights to be seen in all of Venice. The Doges' Palace, Saint Mark's Basilica, and the Correr Museum are clustered, as you know, around the Piazza San Marco. It's possible to decide to just "look in" at each and then find that you've spent the entire day sightseeing instead of shopping.

The **Doges' Palace**, or Palazzo Ducale, was built to house not a duke but the leader of the Venetian Republic. There never was a single ruling family of Venice (although a lot of people tried to start one) — the city was a republic from its foundation in the 4th century until it was subjugated by Napoleon in the early 19th century. The doge was elected by the aristocracy of the city to rule over the Republic, but such was the Venetian fear of the development of a "cult of personality" that the doge spent his entire term of office within the confines of the palace, carefully watched by various administrators.

The building we see today has its foundations in the 8th century, but owing to fires over the years, in the main the palace dates from the 14th, 15th, and 16th centuries.

The sumptuous interior rooms recall a time when Venice claimed to be lord of "half and one-quarter of the Roman Empire," a claim that no one was in a position to dispute when the Republic was at its zenith in the 1500s. However, a series of fires in more modern times destroyed the very famous works of Fabriano, Bellini, Pisanello, and Titian that once graced these lavish rooms. The Doges' Palace is most valuable to us today not just for the splendor of its interior and exterior decoratin, but as a graphic illustration of just how mighty the few small, marshy Venetian islands became.

Doges' Palace: Splendid visions

At the end of the tour, the vast Sala del Maggior Consiglio leads to the sad "Bridge of Sighs," which crosses a small canal to the prisons behind the palace.

The Doges' Palace is open April to mid-October, Monday through Saturday from 8:30 a.m. to 6 p.m., on Sunday from 9 am. to 1 p.m.; and mid-October to March, Monday through Saturday from 9 a.m. to 4 p.m., on Sunday to 1 p.m.

The **Basilica di San Marco**, built as the doges' private chapel next door to the Doges' Palace, is the foremost church in the city and home to some of the great religious treasure that the Venetians brought back from their travels. Sadly, the four great bronze horses from the 4th century that stand over the central arched entry to the building have been overexposed to salt, wind, and pollutants in their 15 centuries of existence, and so they have been boarded up to undergo restoration. (There is talk of placing them in a museum and putting copies in their place, but that hasn't happened yet.)

The interior of this church seems as if it's encrusted with gold. The little light that manages to get in glitters on gilded mosaics. The mosaic of the Ascension in the nave dates from the 13th century, but the finest mosaics are those of the Holy Family in the side aisles.

Behind the main altar you can see the "Pala d'Oro," an altarpiece of solid gold and precious jewels. You can also visit the treasury of the basilica and see the golden images, icons, and the bejeweled statues that were stolen by the Venetians when they thoughtlessly looted Constantinople (now Istanbul) in the 14th century. It was one of the Republic's greatest victories, but easily one of her most shameful episodes.

The Basilica of San Marco is open Monday through Saturday from 9:30 a.m. to 5:30 p.m., and on Sunday from 2:30 to 5:30 p.m.

The **Correr Museum** has some of the finest works by the great Venetian painting family, the Bellinis. The museum, which takes up a portion of a gallery overlooking the Piazza San Marco, also provides a splendid bird's-eye view of the square. It's open Monday and Wednesday through Saturday from 10 a.m. to 4 p.m., and on Sunday from 9 a.m. to 12:30 p.m. (closed Tuesday).

The very end of this stroll leaves us close to the **Teatro La Fenice**. Built in 1791, La Fenice is one of the most important theaters in the country. It has been the site of the world premières of Verdi's *La Traviata*, Stravinsky's *The Rake's Progress*, and Britten's *Turn of the Screw*. If there is no rehearsal in progress, the management will be glad to give you a quick look around this gilded-and-velvet jewel-box theater.

THE MERCERIE AND THE RUGA RIALTO

The name "Mercerie" refers to the long street that meanders away from the Piazza San Marco all the way to the Rialto. It's really divided along the way into particular streets each named Merceria. For example, Merceria dell'Orologio near the clock tower on the Piazza San Marco, Merceria San Salvador farther down the street, and Merceria 2 Aprile closer to the Rialto Bridge. The stores generally list their address simply as a number on "Mercerie" (which I will do here as well). This can be a trifle confusing, so if you're interested in visiting a particular store, it's wise to telephone ahead and ask for a precise location.

The **Mercerie** begins at the Piazza San Marco, right under the arch that is topped by the huge clock where the two Moors strike the bell on the hour. Passing under the arch, you are standing at the head of the street.

You will see two famous names immediately: Gucci at no. 258 and Max Mara at no. 268. But don't forget La Bottega di Nino, featuring quality menswear—it has no number but it's right there nonetheless. La Buccia, at no. 218, has good prices on *moda giovane*, casual wear for young women. And there's more of the same at Donna, at Mercerie 705.

At Mercerie 729 there are beautiful leather goods—shoes and jackets—at La Bauta.

Then it's on to Luisa Spagnoli, at Mercerie 741. Cima, at Mercerie 4918, is the place to shop for wool and silk underwear, camisoles, and lingerie.

At Furla, leather is treated uniquely: bags, all made of leather, have been worked to look like far more exotic skins. They can be found at Mercerie 4954.

Casual but high-quality leather outerwear is the specialty at Rene, Mercerie 4893.

Al Duca D'Aosta, Mercerie 4922, is home to classic British-style clothing for men and women. Ai Tre Cedri is a fun store selling underwear and sleepwear for everyone from newborns to grownups. There's also some nice knitwear.

Near the **Rialto Bridge** is Marforio, a one-stop leather shop. They sell everything in leather—except shoes—at great prices.

After crossing the bridge and heading inland a little, off to your left you'll find a wide street called **Ruga Rialto**, which contains a number of good shops.

La Ruga, at Ruga Rialto 773, has excellent buys on sheepskin clothing for

Woven handbags, a specialty of Francis Model

men and women. Farther down this short street is Prima Donna, Ruga Rialto 1049, with low prices on good-quality women's wear. And there's value-for-money menswear on the same street at Brocca Rialto, Ruga Rialto 974.

Aliani, Ruga Rialto 654/655, is a quality food shop specializing in butter, cheese, and cold cuts. They make sandwiches to take away too. And finally there's Francis Model, Ruga Rialto 778, a top-notch source of first-rate leather handbags, some of which bear a curious resemblance to those made by famous designers.

IN THE NEIGHBORHOOD

Not far from the Ruga Rialto on **Campiello dei Meloni**, ZFW, Campiello dei Meloni 1478, specializes in modern prints of old photographs of Venice. It's also the best postcard shop in town.

Backtracking to the beginning of our stroll, you may have noticed a street to your right intersecting with the Mercerie called **Calle Largo San Marco**. This short street deserves a look too, because at no. 28 is Élite, a clothing boutique stocking Missoni and Gucci, and at no. 412 is Veneziartigiana, an artists' collective with some decidedly different glass and paper objects.

And nearby, off Calle Largo San Marco on **Calle Spadaria**, is Trussardi.

On the other side of the Mercerie, just past the clock tower, is another side street, **Calle Fiubera**, where, at no. 793, Valese Fonditore makes masks and Venetian carnival gear—but not to wear, as they are cast in heavy brass, bronze, and silver.

VENICE: GREAT SHOPPING STROLLS

Veneziartigiana, an artists' co-op in Venice, creates spectacular glass and paper objects

REFRESHMENTS EN ROUTE

Cafés

Now is the chance to visit the Doges' Palace or Piazza San Marco again. If you've done that already, splurge and have a drink at **Florian's** or **Quadri's**. Remember that when the hated Austrians ruled Venice in the 19th century, a Venetian sitting at a table at Quadri's, the Austrians' drinking spot, was considered a traitor. But fences have long since been mended, so take your pick.

Restaurants

Danieli Terrace, Riva degli Schiavoni 4196 (tel. 26-460), open from 1:30 to 3 p.m. and 7:30 to 11 p.m. daily. Credit Cards: AE, DC, MC, V. The food at this restaurant on the roof of the Danieli Hotel is first-rate, and the view couldn't be better. As you look out over San Giorgio and the lagoon you can feast on delicious fresh fish, perfectly cooked veal piccata, and tagliatelle alla buranella. A large selection of homemade desserts includes a particularly good Venetian specialty, tira mi su. Dinner for two with a good bottle of wine should cost about 200,000 lire. The view is included at no extra charge.

Corte Sconta, Calle del Pestrin 3886 (tel. 27-024), open from 12:30 to 3 p.m. daily for lunch and Wednesday through Sunday from 7 to 10 p.m. for dinner. No credit cards. It's already difficult to secure a table at this, Venice's finest restaurant, so I'm probably going to get in trouble for listing it here. Corte

Sconta absolutely disproves everything that has ever been said about bad dining in Venice. In these three casual rooms with their wood floors and simple wooden tables you'll receive superb food at quite reasonable prices. Meals tend to be four or five courses long, beginning with a single sautéed scallop, still in its shell, and proceeding from there. The management serves its own wines—two in the course of a meal—and the meals themselves are created from whatever happened to be freshest at the market that morning. A six-course dinner for two is about 150,000 lire. Reserve your table the moment the moment you arrive in Venice.

CHAPTER XII

THE ULTIMATE VENICE SHOPPING SPREE

There is a lovely historical continuity to shopping Venice. When you wander along the Mercerie or the Ruga Rialto remember you are treading—and buying—where shoppers have been trading *louis d'or, thalers* (the origin of the word "dollar"), *scudi,* and *libra* (English pounds) for seven centuries. The currency today might be traveler's checks and plastic credit cards, but the idea remains the same: Venetians sell, visitors buy—and both parties are *sure* they got the better half of the deal. The listings that follow include the best Venice has to offer—if you find something better, not included here, then you are lucky (and please let me know about it for future editions).

ANTIQUES

ARTE FILATELIA
San Marco, Frezzeria 1504 (tel. 523-6643)
Vaporetto Stop: *San Marco*
Hours: *Monday through Saturday from 10 a.m. to 1 p.m. and 3:30 to 7:30 p.m. (closed Monday morning)*
Credit Cards: AE, DC, MC V
English Spoken.

"Filatelia" might suggest that this wonderful, dark old shop sells nothing but rare stamps, but that's not the case. In a single cramped room there are fine pieces of predominantly 17th-century antique furniture, old objects like globes and scientific instruments, as well as prints, books, and coins. Prices can be reasonable. An 18-century engraved silver cigarette case costs 60,000 lire; more elaborate versions of the same go for 400,000 lire. A gold-and-crystal reliquary, used for a pendant, is 250,000 lire, and you'll receive documents authenticating its 18-century provenance.

CASELLATI
Calle Larga 22 Marzo 2404 (tel. 523-0966)
Vaporetto Stop: *San Marco*
Hours: *Monday through Saturday from 10 a.m. to 1 p.m. and 3:30 to 7:30 p.m. (closed Monday morning)*
Credit Cards: *None*
English Spoken.

An extremely elegant shop selling fine 17th- and 18-century furniture and objects. Casellati will interest serious collectors.

CASSINI
Calle Larga 22 Marzo 2424 (tel. 521-6107)
Vaporetto Stop: *San Marco*
Hours: *Monday through Saturday from 10 a.m. to 1 p.m. and 3 to 7:30 p.m. (closed Monday morning)*
Credit Cards: *None*

Cassini specializes in rare books and fine bindings from the last three centuries. There are also some prints and drawings.

FREZZATI
Calle Larga 22 Marzo 2070 (tel. 526-3802)
Vaporetto Stop: *San Marco*
Hours: *Monday through Saturday from 10 a.m. to 1:30 p.m. and 3:30 to 7:30 p.m. (closed Monday morning)*
Credit Cards: *None*

The accent here is on fine, rare oil paintings. Pictures in the inventory may date back to the 15th century, but the bulk of the collection dates from the 17th and 18th centuries. Naturally, Venetian schools are well represented.

L'IXA
Campo San Stefano 2958 (tel. 29-656)
Vaporetto Stop: *Santa Maria del Giglio*
Hours: *Monday through Saturday from 10 a.m. to 1 p.m. and 3 to 7 p.m.*
Credit Cards: *None*
English Spoken.

This is a tiny shop filled with oddments and antiques, just the place to look for something small to bring home as a gift or for a treat just for yourself. Prices are reasonable. Silver ex-voti (a Sacred Heart for example, or a Gesù Bambino) cost about 25,000 lire and date from the early 19th century.

SCARPA
Calle Larga 22 Marzo 2089 (tel. 522-1805)
Vaporetto Stop: *San Marco*

Hours: *Monday through Saturday from 9:30 a.m. to 1 p.m. and 3 to 7 p.m. (closed Monday morning)*
Credit Cards: *None*
English Spoken.

This is another of the quality antiques dealers which abound on Via 22 Marzo. The specialty here is rare objets, silver, and bric-a-brac, as well as some furniture and paintings of the 18th century.

TROIS
Calle Larga 22 Marzo 2251 (tel. 522-2905)
Vaporetto Stop: *San Marco*
Hours: *Monday through Saturday from 10 a.m. to 1 p.m. and 3 to 7 p.m. (closed Monday morning)*
Credit Cards: *None*
English Spoken.

Here you'll find Italian and French furniture and paintings of the 17th and 18th centuries of the highest imaginable quality. There is an excellent, knowledgeable staff.

CLOTHING

CHILDREN'S FASHIONS

There are dozens of clothing shops for children along the Mercerie and the Frezzeria, none of them truly outstanding, but all are dependable. Two shops, not on either street, are a cut above the rest.

MARICLA
Calle Larga 22 Marzo 2401 (tel. 769-075)
Vaporetto Stop: *San Marco*
Hours: *Monday through Saturday from 9:30 a.m. to 1 p.m. and 2 to 7:30 p.m. (closed Monday morning)*
Credit Cards: *AE, MC*
English Spoken.

This small shop is full of cute clothes for newborns, toddlers, and kids up to the age of 8 years old. Lots of rough-and-tumble wear—overalls, playsuits—and some more "formal" clothes for special occasions. A silk party dress with a Venetian lace collar, for a little girl age 6 or so, is 225,000 lire.

TOP TEN
San Marco, Calle Goldoni 4487 (tel. 523-0062)
Hours: *Monday through Saturday from 9:30 a.m. to 1:30 p.m. and 3 to 7:30 p.m. (closed Monday morning)*

Credit Cards: AE, MC, V
English Spoken.

This is a shop devoted almost exclusively to embroidered children's clothes. The work is all done by hand and is exquisitely rendered. Prices, as you might expect, are very high. An embroidered silk blouse for a girl of 10 is 145,000 lire. An embroidered dirndl is 450,000 lire.

MEN'S FASHIONS

BROCCA RIALTO
Ruga Rialto 974 (tel. 25-451)
Vaporetto Stop: San Silvestro
Hours: Monday through Saturday from 9:30 a.m. to 1:30 p.m. and 2:30 to 7:30 p.m. (closed Monday morning)
Credit Cards: AE, DC, MC, V
English Spoken.

Like most of the shops on the Ruga Rialto, Brocca is less expensive than shops on the Mercerie or the Frezzeria. Brocca specializes in shirts and sweaters. Their own beautifully finished cotton shirts are 89,000 lire.

DUCA D'AOSTA
San Marco, Mercerie 4922 (tel. 704-079)
Hours: Monday through Saturday from 9:30 a.m. to 7:30 p.m. nonstop, on Sunday in season from 10 a.m. to 6 p.m. (closed Monday morning year round)
Credit Cards: AE, DC, MC, V
English Spoken.

Very traditional menswear in the Brooks Brothers mode. A tweed suit is 750,000 lire.

GIANNI VERSACE
San Marco, Frezzeria 1722 (tel. 523-6369)
Vaporetto Stop: San Marco
Hours: Monday through Saturday from 9:30 a.m. to 7:30 p.m. nonstop
Credit Cards: AE, DC, MC, V
English Spoken.

(See Gianni Versace in "Clothing, Women's Fashions.")

LA BOTTEGA DI NINO
San Marco, Mercerie, near the clock tower (tel. 25-608)
Vaporetto Stop: San Marco

Hours: *Monday through Saturday from 10 a.m. to 1:30 p.m. and 3 to 7:30 p.m. (closed Monday morning)*
Credit Cards: *AE, DC, MC, V*
English Spoken.

La Bottega di Nino has menswear to satisfy every taste. For those who like an English cut, there is clothing by Daks, Ballantyne, and Dunhill. Italian names to be had here include Ermenegilda Zegna, Nino Cerruti, and Flying Cross. The British clothing is, not surprisingly, more expensive here than in London—a Daks suit costs 1.6 million lire. The Italian clothing is better priced. A beautiful Zegna tweed jacket is 420,000 lire—cheaper than at the flagship store in Milan. A Nino Cerruti suit is 1.25 million lire, about a third less than you'd pay in the United States. A Flying Cross blue blazer in silk and wool is 320,000 lire.

LA COUPOLE
San Marco, Frezzeria 1674 (tel. 706-063) and Via 22 Marzo 2366 (tel. 24-243)
Vaporetto Stop: *San Marco*
Hours: *Monday through Saturday from 9:30 a.m. to 7:30 p.m. nonstop, and also on Sunday March through October (closed Monday morning)*
Credit Cards: *AE, DC, MC, V*
English Spoken.

Menswear names at both La Coupole stores include Venturi and Enrico Coveri. A very elegant Venturi suit with a light pinstripe is 2 million lire. A casual Coveri sports jacket costs 475,000 lire.

L'EQUIPE
San Marco, Calle Goldoni 4512 (tel. 523-5463)
Hours: *Monday through Saturday from 10 a.m. to 1:30 p.m. and 3 to 7:30 p.m. (closed Monday morning)*
Credit Cards: *AE, MC, V*

A modern and slightly avant-garde shop which stocks the striking Milanese menswear Verri Uomo. A fashionable, loose-cut raw-silk jacket is 550,000 lire. A more formal two-button suit in linen is 1.2 million lire.

VOLPE
San Marco, Frezzeria 1286 (tel. 522-4426)
Vaporetto Stop: *San Marco*
Hours: *10 a.m. to 7:30 p.m. nonstop daily (closed Monday morning)*
Credit Cards: *AE, DC, MC, V*
English Spoken.

A large and reasonably priced selection of Nino Cerruti and Armani (primarily Mani) menswear can be found here. Pants by Cerruti begin at 225,000 lire. A Mani cotton jacket is 425,000 lire.

WOMEN'S FASHIONS

AI TRE CEDRI
San Marco Mercerie 5019 (tel. 24-005)
Hours: Monday through Saturday from 10 a.m. to 7:30 p.m. nonstop, and also on Sunday in season (closed Monday morning)
Credit Cards: MC

Ai Tre Cedri is in much the same category as Prima Donna above: good quality, low prices. There is a large selection of lingerie as well as "pulls"—sweaters in heavy wool. Outerwear is an inexpensive buy as well. A loose-cut, full-length gray wool overcoat is 129,000 lire. Sweaters are 35,000 lire to 100,000 lire.

ARABA FENICE
Campo San Fantin 1862 (tel. 522-9906)
Vaporetto Stop: San Marco
Hours: Monday through Saturday from 9 a.m. to 12:30 p.m. and 3 to 7:30 p.m. (closed Monday morning)
Credit Cards: AE, DC, MC, V
English Spoken.

A small, chic shop, Araba Fenice designs and markets its own slightly offbeat women's wear. Knits are the specialty, with a single-breasted pure-cashmere cranberry-colored overcoat costing 690,000 lire.

BARBARA
San Marco, Campo Santa Maria del Giglio 2463 (tel. 526-1831)
Vaporetto Stop: Santa Maria del Giglio
Hours: Monday through Saturday from 9 a.m. to 12:30 p.m. and 3 to 7:30 p.m. (closed Monday morning)
Credit Cards: AE, MC, V
English Spoken.

This small, beautiful, low-beamed shop stocks as much of the Roman Lancetti line as it can. The accent is on the famous Lancetti evening wear. A two-piece silk suit in oyster is 985,000 lire.

BETTA SCARPA
San Marco, Frezzeria 1797 (tel. 528-7051)
Vaporetto Stop: San Marco
Hours: Monday through Saturday from 10:30 a.m. to 12:30 p.m. and 3 to 7 p.m. (closed Monday morning)
Credit Cards: AE, DC, MC, V
English Spoken.

At Betta Scarpa you'll find reasonably priced evening wear, as well as lots of accessories: hats, combs, earrings, etc. Knitwear, particularly cashmere, is very good and prices, while not low, are at least not heart-stopping. A beautiful, lightweight wool knit cape gray on the outside and magenta on the inside, costs 700,000 lire.

CIMA
Mercerie del Capitello (Mercerie) 4918 (tel. 523-4988)
Hours: *Monday through Saturday from 9:30 a.m. to 7:30 p.m. nonstop, and also on Sunday from May to October (closed Monday mornings all year)*
Credit Cards: AE, DC, MC, V
English Spoken.

Cima sells nothing but high-quality wool and silk underwear, camisoles, teddies, and bras. Some are decorated with Venetian lace. The best buys here are silk wool-blend nightdresses, which cost 100,000 lire to 150,000 lire.

CONTROCORRENTE
San Marco, Frezzeria 1232–1233 (tel. 523-7093)
Vaporetto Stop: *San Marco*
Hours: *Monday through Saturday from 10 a.m. to 1 p.m. and 3 to 7:30 p.m. (closed Monday morning)*
Credit Cards: AE, DC, MC, V
English Spoken.

Out-of-the-ordinary Italian fashions for those who don't necessarily want to

Controcorrente: Modern fashions at unbeatable prices

lead the charge but would like to be in it nonetheless. Controcorrente has some unusual clothing for young women like short-waisted jackets with full-pleated backs in black denim. Prices are reasonable: the jacket described is 180,000 lire.

DONNA
San Marco, Frezzeria 705 (tel. 700-324)
Vaporetto Stop: *San Marco*
Hours: *Monday through Saturday from 9 a.m. to 7:30 p.m. nonstop (closed Monday morning)*
Credit Cards: AE, DC, MC, V
English Spoken.

Donna sells the Krizia line of denim clothing, notably Krizia jeans, which cost 89,000 lire to 140,000 lire. They also carry the full, lower-priced Titolo line by Basile, which, as everyone knows, is actually designed by Luciano Sopriani.

DUCA D'AOSTA
San Marco, Mercerie 4922 (tel. 704-079)
Hours: *Monday through Saturday from 9:30 a.m. to 7:30 p.m. nonstop, and on Sunday in season from 10 a.m. to 6 p.m. (closed Monday morning year round)*
Credit Cards: AE, DC, MC, V
English Spoken.

This traditional shop stocks clothing for men and women in the British/Brooks Brothers idiom. Everything is extremely tasteful if subdued, with earthy colors predominating. Prices are high. A forest-green wool sweater for a woman is 453,000 lire.

ELITE
Calle Larga San Marco 284 (tel. 521-6110)
Vaporetto Stop: *San Zaccaria*
Hours: *Monday through Saturday from 9 a.m. to 12:30 p.m. and 3 to 7 p.m. (closed Monday morning)*
Credit Cards: AE
English Spoken.

Elite is not unlike Duca d'Aosta in merchandise, clientele, and price, except that at Elite there are some formal clothes for women chosen from the Gucci and Missoni collections. Prices for these name-brand clothes are no more or less at Elite.

ÉLYSÉE–ÉLYSÉE 2
Calle Goldoni 4485 (tel. 523-6948) and San Marco, Frezzeria 1693 (tel. 522-3020)

Élysée: Home of Giorgio Armani in Venice

Hours: *Monday through Saturday from 10 a.m. to 1 p.m. and 3 to 7 p.m. (closed Monday morning)*
Credit Cards: AE, DC, MC, V
English Spoken.

These two stores have cornered the market on Giorgio Armani in Venice. At Élysée you'll find the upper end of the Armani line of leather and prêt-à-porter, as well as the more formal Armani clothes for men. In addition Élysée has Maud Frizon, Thierry Mugler, Tornabuoni, Santini e Dominici, and the cheaper Valentino lines. Élysée 2 is all Armani. There's Armani in every shape and form, making up the only Emporio Armani boutique between Milan and Rome.

ENRICA MASSEI
Calle Larga 22 Marzo 2400 (tel. 703-401)
Hours: *Monday through Saturday from 9:30 a.m. to 1:30 p.m. and 3:30 to 7:30 p.m. (closed Monday morning)*
Credit Cards: AE, DC, MC, V
English Spoken.

Cashmere is the thing to shop for here. A simple cashmere sweater with a crew neck is 325,000 lire. A sweater-dress is 745,000 lire.

FENDI
Salizzada San Moisè 1474 (tel. 705-733)
Vaporetto Stop: *San Marco*

THE SERIOUS SHOPPER'S GUIDE TO ITALY

Hours: *Monday through Saturday from 9:30 a.m. to 7:30 p.m. nonstop (closed Monday morning)*
Credit Cards: AE, DC, MC, V
English Spoken.

The three small rooms that make up the Fendi branch in Venice sell prêt-à-porter clothing, leather goods, and furs. Prices are lower here than anywhere else in Italy except Rome. A large Fendi suitcase in vinyl with leather trim is 750,000 lire. There are also inexpensive items like Fendi key chains for 45,000 lire, wallets for 65,000 lire, and scarves at 100,000 lire. This shop has a small discount area selling items from the season before. Savings can be 30% to 50%.

GIANNI VERSACE
San Marco, Frezzeria 1722 (tel. 523-6369)
Vaporetto Stop: *San Marco*
Hours: *Monday through Saturday from 9:30 a.m. to 7:30 nonstop*
Credit Cards: AE, DC, MC, V
English Spoken.

This is another dramatic-looking Versace shop, but on a smaller, more Venetian scale, staffed by people who haven't acquired the Milanese snootiness that tends to afflict the help at the greater names. This is the Versace outlet for men and women as well as for leather goods and accessories. Prices remain high. A cashmere sweater with a target pattern is 474,000 lire. A Versace sports jacket for a man is 775,000 lire. A leather agenda is 114,000 lire.

GUCCI
San Marco, Mercerie 258 (tel. 29-119)
Hours: *Monday through Saturday from 9:30 a.m. to 1 p.m. and 2 to 7:30 p.m. (closed Monday morning)*
Credit Cards: AE, DC, MC, V
English Spoken.

The Gucci in Venice is small and devoted mainly to leather goods. There is a small selection of women's clothing on the second level. The famous Gucci scarves cost between 120,000 lire and 175,000 lire, which is about standard.

KRIZIA
San Marco, Calle delle Ostreghe 2359 (tel. 32-162)
Vaporetto Stop: *Santa Maria del Giglio*
Hours: *Monday through Saturday from 9:30 a.m. to 1:30 p.m. and 3 to 7:30 p.m. (closed Monday morning)*
Credit Cards: AE, DC, MC, V
English Spoken.

The Krizia shop in Venice is small but well stocked. Prices are very good. A wool sweater-dress with a modified turtleneck and the Krizia bear logo is 290,000

VENICE SHOPS: CLOTHING

lire—less than you'd pay in Rome or Milan and about 50% of the Stateside price.

LA BUCCIA
San Marco, Mercerie 218 (tel. 37-678)
Hours: Monday through Saturday from 9:30 a.m. to 7:30 p.m. nonstop, and also on Sunday in season (closed Monday morning)
Credit Cards: AE, MC, V

La Buccia sells its own line of *moda giovane*, fashions for young women. The quality is high and the prices reasonable. A summer-weight suit is 220,000 lire.

LA COUPOLE
San Marco, Frezzeria 1674 (tel. 706-063) and Via 22 Marzo 2366 (tel. 24-243)
Hours: Monday through Saturday from 9:30 a.m. to 7:30 p.m. nonstop, and also on Sunday from March through October (closed Monday morning)
Credit Cards: AE, DC, MC, V
English Spoken.

At both stores you'll find big-name clothes for both men and women—Coveri, Kenzo, and Venturi, for example. Prices are reasonable, despite the august names. A woman's wool–silk-blend suit by Erreuno is only 300,000 lire. Coveri casual wear in the "Young You" line begins at about 100,000 lire for a sweater.

LUISA SPAGNOLI
San Marco, Mercerie 741–743 (tel. 706-131)
Hours: Monday through Saturday from 9:30 a.m. to 7:30 p.m. nonstop (closed Monday morning)
Credit Cards: AE, DC, MC, V
English Spoken.

Like the other Luisa Spagnoli shops in Italy, this one offers good-quality women's wear at relatively low prices. The knitwear is superb. A subtle but elegant, patterned waist-length sweater in violet wool costs 150,000 lire. A white cowl-neck sweater in the Spagnoli "Maserati" line is 215,000 lire.

MAX MARA
San Marco, Mercerie 268 (tel. 26-688)
Hours: Monday through Saturday from 9:30 a.m. to 1 p.m. and 2:30 to 7:30 p.m. (closed Monday morning)
Credit Cards: AE, DC, MC, V
English Spoken.

The elegant premises of Venice's Max Mara shop belie the reasonable prices, which seem lower here than elsewhere in Italy. The selection of women's wear is smaller than in Rome, though. A three-quarter-length corduroy skirt lined with silk is only 74,000 lire; a wool cable-knit sweater, perfect for a Venetian winter afternoon, is 85,000 lire.

MIGUEL CRUZ
San Marco, Calle Vallaressa 1318 (tel. 522-5525)
Vaporetto Stop: San Marco
Hours: Monday through Saturday from 9:30 a.m. to 1:30 p.m. and 3:30 to 7:30 p.m. (closed Monday morning)
Credit Cards: AE, DC, MC, V
English Spoken.

The very elegant Miguel Cruz line of clothing is sold in a tiny shop a few steps from Harry's Bar. Prices are high, but the designs are quite distinctive. A hooded jacket with a tie waist in gray wool costs 1.08 million lire, about what you'd pay in Milan.

MISSONI
San Marco, Calle Vallaressa 1312B (tel. 705-733)
Vaporetto Stop: San Marco.
Hours: Monday through Saturday from 10 a.m. to 1 p.m. and 3 to 7 p.m. (closed Monday morning)
Credit Cards: AE, DC, MC, V
English Spoken.

The tiny Missoni shop in Venice manages to stock women's clothing, men's clothing, accessories, and some fabrics—all of it in a store the size of a phone booth. The low overhead must account for the slightly lower-than-average prices. A multicolored knit two-piece suit, top and skirt, is 790,000 lire. A Missoni parasol (which I've never seen before anywhere) is 110,000 lire.

NARA BOUTIQUE
San Marco, Calle Vallaressa 1321 (tel. 522-3851)
Vaporetto Stop: San Marco
Hours: Monday through Saturday from 10 a.m. to 1 p.m. and 3:30 to 7:30 p.m. (closed Monday morning)
Credit Cards: AE, DC, MC, V
English Spoken.

Furnished with 1930s furniture, Nara is an elegant shop which sells Basile and Yves Saint Laurent exclusively. A Basile silk blouse is 220,000 lire. The YSL prices are as high as you'll find anywhere else in Italy.

PIER
San Marco, Frezzeria 1180 (tel. 523-1990)
Vaporetto Stop: San Marco

Hours: **Monday through Saturday from 10 a.m. to 1 p.m. and 2 to 7 p.m. (closed Monday morning)**
Credit Cards: **AE, DC, MC, V**
English Spoken.

Pier specializes in traditionally tailored clothing, English in origin but with an Italian accent. A classically cut silk blouse in a beautiful shade of pale yellow is 150,000 lire.

PRIMA DONNA
Ruga Rialto 1049 (no phone)
Vaporetto Stop: *San Silvestro*
Hours: **Monday through Saturday from 10 a.m. to 1:30 p.m. and 2:30 to 7:30 p.m., and also on Sunday in season (closed Monday morning)**
Credit Cards: **AE, DC, MC, V**
English Spoken.

An extensive selection of inexpensive, but good-quality women's clothing. Styles are modern, but not avant-garde. You'll find that your money goes far here—although you won't be buying anything by a famous name. A large, full-cut, lightweight but warm overcoat in red wool is only 180,000 lire.

VALENTINO
San Marco, San Moisè 1473 (tel. 705-733)
Vaporetto Stop: *San Marco*
Hours: **Monday through Saturday from 10 a.m. to 1:30 p.m. and 3:30 to 7:30 p.m. (closed Monday morning)**
Credit Cards: **AE**
English Spoken.

The small Valentino shop in Venice is, like Valentinos everywhere, expensive. As you might expect, the selection here is smaller than in Milan or Rome, so wait for those two towns if you can. If not, you'll find that the new Valentino above-the-knee evening wear begins at about 4.5 million lire. Summer-weight blouses begin at about 350,000 lire.

VOLPE
San Marco, Frezzeria 1286 (tel. 522-4426)
Vaporetto Stop: *San Marco*
Hours: **10 a.m. to 7:30 p.m. nonstop daily (closed Monday morning)**
Credit Cards: **AE, DC, MC, V**
English Spoken.

Volpe is part of the V&V Boutique chain in Venice. These shops stock the cheaper lines of Valentino, Enrico Coveri, Basile, and for men, Armani and Cerruti. This particular shop has clothes for men and women.

V&V BOUTIQUE
San Marco, Frezzeria 1233 (tel. 523-7093)
Vaporetto Stop: San Marco
Hours: 10 a.m. to 7:30 p.m. nonstop daily (closed Monday morning)
Credit Cards: AE, DC, MC, V
English Spoken.

See Volpe, above. This shop has women's clothes only and offers overnight alteration service.

FOOD

Notwithstanding the perennial jokes about the awfulness of Venetian food, there is one fine food shop of note in the city.

ALIANI
Ruga Rialto 654–655 (tel. 24-913)
Vaporetto Stop: San Silvestro
Hours: Monday through Saturday from 9:30 a.m. to 1:30 p.m. and 3:30 to 7:30 p.m. (closed Monday afternoon)
Credit Cards: None

Aliani is a marvelous, bustling *gastronomia* which has exceptional cold cuts, cheeses, oils, and wines. The best things to be had here are the prepared foods.

Aliani: Marvelous cheeses, oils, and wines plus the best take-out in Venice

Sformata alla parmigiana, the Italian version of a quiche, is 1,550 lire an *etto* (100 grams, or about 3½ ounces), fresh shrimp in oil and lemon are 3,750 lire an *etto*, delicious lasagne is 1,100 lire an *etto*, and a whole quail with a side order of polenta is just 2,000 lire a portion.

FURS

FENDI: see "Clothing, Women's Fashions

GLASS

You probably know, even before you visit Venice, that the city is crammed with glass shops—it's no exaggeration to say that there must be a thousand of them in the *sestiere* of San Marco alone. The stores turn up one after another on the major streets until, to be honest, you can't tell one from another. As I mentioned in Chapter III, a lot of Venetian glass is not Venetian at all. The selections that follow do not pretend to be a complete listing of glass shops in the city, but they all have one thing in common: they sell the real thing. That's not to say that shops *not* listed here sell fakes, but beware—a lot of them do!

ARCHIMEDE SEGUSO
San Marco, Bocca di Piazza 1236, or Frezzeria 1230 (tel. 34-898)
Vaporetto Stop: *San Marco*
Hours: *Monday through Saturday from 9:30 a.m. to 7:30 p.m. nonstop (closed Monday morning)*
Credit Cards: AE, DC, MC, V
English Spoken.

There are two addresses but only one shop. Archimede Seguso sells beautifully colored hand-blown glass that is modern and rather daring in design. This is not the kind of place where you'll find pieces decorated in a riot of enamels, goldwork, curliques, and filigree. Colors tend to be offbeat: deep ultramarine blue, pale lilac, violets, and turquoise predominate. A crystal-ball paperweight ranges in price from 58,000 lire to 110,000 lire, depending on color and size. Shipping and insurance can be arranged through the store.

INDUSTRIE VENEZIANE DI BATTISTON
San Marco, Calle Vallaressa 1320 (tel. 523-0509)
Vaporetto Stop: *San Marco*
Hours: *Monday through Saturday from 10 a.m. to 8 p.m. nonstop, and also on Sunday in season (closed Monday morning)*
Credit Cards: AE, DC, MC, V
English Spoken.

Fine Venetian glassware at Industrie Veneziane di Battiston

Battiston's selection of glass runs the gamut from the elaborate, overdecorated three-fire work in deep red with enamel accents, to spare and tasteful opaque pieces. There is a vast assortment of Venetian glass necklaces which are traditionally decorated with small glass fruits and flowers. Prices for these necklaces begin at 25,000 lire and go up to about 100,000 lire, depending on the complexity of the design and the colors used.

L'ISOLA
San Marco, Campo San Moisè 1468 (tel. 31-973)
Vaporetto Stop: San Marco
Hours: Monday through Saturday from 9:30 a.m. to 7:30 p.m. nonstop, and also on Sunday in season (closed Monday morning)
Credit Cards: AE, DC, MC, V
English Spoken.

The Murano-based studio of master glassmaker Carlo Moretti was founded in 1958, and in just 30 years his works have reached the forefront of the Venetian glass industry. Already the pieces produced in the early days have become much sought after by collectors, so a piece purchased today will probably appreciate in value. His works do not come cheap. Blown decanters in blue, pink, or green Murano crystal with a gold-leaf stopper begin at 300,000 lire. Clear crystal bottles, with vertical ribs and corn-tuft or flower stoppers, are 360,000 lire to 700,000 lire. A single low-ball glass is 40,000 lire. L'Isola will insure and ship all purchases, and accepts payment with an American check for all orders that are mailed.

Modern glass made in the age-old manner at L'Isola

METAMAUCO
San Marco, Frezzeria 1735, near La Fenice Theater (tel. 528-5885)
Vaporetto Stop: *San Marco*
Hours: *Monday through Saturday from 10 a.m. to 7 p.m. nonstop (closed Monday morning)*
Credit Cards: AE, DC, MC, V
English Spoken.

Metamauco specializes in blown glass, usually without color, but beautifully decorated with diamond-point engravings of Venetian arches and columns. The work is truly extraordinary and very tasteful. Furthermore, things are not terribly expensive. A set of six dessert cups is 180,000 lire. A tall vase with the Venetian arch engraving is 55,000 lire.

PAULY
San Marco, Piazzetta dei Leoni 316 (tel. 523-5575)
Vaporetto Stop: *San Zaccaria*
Hours: *Monday through Saturday from 10 a.m. to 1:30 p.m. and 3 to 7:30 p.m. (closed Monday morning)*
Credit Cards: AE, DC, MC, V
English Spoken.

Only two other names (Salvieti and Venini) are as well known for Venetian glass

Pauly: The most famous name in Venetian glass

as this venerable old firm. Pauly makes the ornate, baroque glass that made Murano famous. When electricity was installed in the Doges' Palace, Pauly provided the chandeliers. Prices are high, but along with high-quality glass you are buying a famous name and a little bit of history. Pauly will insure and ship all purchases.

SALVIATI
Piazza San Marco 78 (tel. 522-4257)
Vaporetto Stop: *San Zaccaria*
Hours: *Monday through Saturday from 10 a.m. to 1:30 p.m. and 3 to 7:30 p.m. (closed Monday morning)*
Credit Cards: AE, DC, MC, V
English Spoken.

Like Pauly, Salviati is one of the most celebrated names in glass, and again like Pauly, designs tend toward the elaborate and old-fashioned. Things can be had for a little money—for example, a ruby-red perfume bottle at 35,000 lire. Or things can be had for a lot of money—a giant 12-branch chandelier is 17 million lire.

SEBASTIANA PEREZ
San Marco, Bocca di Piazza 1234 (tel. 710-707)
Vaporetto Stop: *San Marco*

VENICE SHOPS: GLASS/LACE

Hours: *Monday through Saturday from 9:30 a.m. to 7:30 p.m., and also on Sunday in season (closed Monday morning)*
Credit Cards: AE, DC, MC, V

This is a more traditional glass shop, stocking the full range of brightly colored, highly decorated glass from the workshops of Murano. It's a good place to pick up some inexpensive examples of the art, made even more attractive by the fact that the staff does not hover over you urging you to buy—an unpleasant feature of many glass shops.

VENINI
San Marco, Piazza dei Leoncini (tel. 522-4045)
Vaporetto Stop: *San Zaccaria*
Hours: *Monday through Saturday from 9:30 a.m. to 7:30 p.m. nonstop (closed Monday morning)*
Credit Cards: AE, DC, MC, V
English Spoken.

This is the last of the "big three" Venetian glassmakers. Colors here tend to be more subdued than at Pauly and Salviati. The specialty here is the famous multicolored swirl pattern, known as *venature*. A decanter in this style will cost between 100,000 lire and 450,000 lire, depending on size and the colors employed.

LACE

DESIRÉ
Piazza San Marco 78 (tel. 27-011)
Vaporetto Stop: *San Zaccaria*
Hours: *Monday through Saturday from 9:30 a.m. to 7:30 p.m. nonstop, and also on Sunday in season*
Credit Cards: AE, DC, MC, V
English Spoken.

The lace sellers of Venice tend to be centered in or around the Piazza San Marco. Despite this *alta turistica* neighborhood, prices are quite reasonable on the smaller items. But, naturally, the higher the quality, the higher the price. Desiré has a large selection of lace and lace-trimmed linens. A small handkerchief with a floral border can cost as little as 2,500 lire. A large, hand-worked tablecloth is 550,000 lire.

JESURUM
Piazza San Marco 60 (tel. 522-9864) and San Marco, Ponte Canonica (behind St. Mark's Basilica)
Vaporetto Stop: *San Zaccaria*

Hours: Monday through Saturday from 9:30 a.m. to 7:30 p.m. nonstop (closed Monday morning)
Credit Cards: AE, DC, MC, V
English Spoken.

Jesurum is *the* name in Venetian lace, and it is the founders of this company (begun in the last century) to whom we owe the fact that a Venetian lace industry still exists. The art had all but died when Jesurum revived it. Of the two shops, the Ponte Canonica is the more impressive—it's housed in a deconsecrated church of the 12th century.

Jesurum has its own lace makers as well as a school to teach the art to future generations. With all this tradition behind it, you can expect a piece of Jesurum lace to be the finest—and probably the most expensive—to be had in Venice. Intricately worked table napkins, six to a set, are 125,000 lire. A tablecloth can cost anywhere from 500,000 lire to 1.5 million lire. Lace-decorated linens begin at 145,000 lire for a flat sheet. A lovely Jesurum handkerchief can be had for 45,000 lire.

There is a room devoted to antique lace for collectors. An 18th-century shawl in the intricate Venice stitch is 3 million lire. Antique fans, still in their original velvet-lined "Jesurum-Venise" boxes, cost 1.4 million lire.

TOKATZIAN
Piazza San Marco 16 (tel. 704-433)
Vaporetto Stop: San Zaccaria
Hours: 10 a.m. to 7:30 p.m. nonstop daily
Credit Cards: AE, DC, MC, V
English Spoken.

Facing the Doges' palace, Tokatzian is a nice little shop selling lace in all varieties. Despite the location, prices are good and just about all the lace is handmade. A beautiful lace handkerchief is 28,000 lire; a collar for a dress or blouse is 38,000 lire. A pair of lace booties for a newborn babe is 35,000 lire.

TREVISAN
Piazza San Marco 42 (tel. 523-2101)
Vaporetto Stop: San Zaccaria
Hours: 10 a.m. to 7:30 p.m. nonstop daily
Credit Cards: AE, DC, MC, V
English Spoken.

Another great lace shop on the Piazza San Marco. Items include delicate, handmade lace butterfly appliqués (10,000 lire) and a large selection of towels decorated with lace. The smallest of these costs just 6,000 lire, with prices going up to 75,000 lire.

Trevisan: Bib and bootie bonanza

LEATHER GOODS

BONI
San Marco, Via 22 Marzo (tel. 529-3103)
Vaporetto Stop: *San Marco*
Hours: *Monday through Saturday from 10 a.m. to 1 p.m. and 3:30 to 7:30 p.m. (closed Monday morning)*
Credit Cards: *AE, DC, MC, V*
English Spoken.

Boni is said to make handbags for Fendi, and while this has not been confirmed, a small number of Fendi leather items are available here. Big name or no, Boni makes a very fine line of their own handbags and furs. A large shoulder bag in soft leather is 345,000 lire. A small black leather clutch is 125,000 lire.

BOTTEGA VENETA
San Marco, Calle Vallaressa 1337 (tel. 28-489)
Vaporetto Stop: *San Marco*
Hours: *Monday through Saturday from 10 a.m. to 1:30 p.m. and 3:30 to 8 p.m. (closed Monday morning)*
Credit Cards: *AE, DC, MC, V*
English Spoken.

BOTTEGA VENETA

Temptations at Bottega Veneta's headquarters

This recently expanded store is the flagship of the famous Bottega Veneta line of leather goods, and prices are cheaper here than anywhere else in the world. The selection is huge, with lots of items not costing all that much. A beautiful gray leather wallet for a man is just 80,000 lire, a credit-card case is 70,000 lire, and a key case in dark red leather is 60,000 lire. The famous woven bags are good deals too: a small shoulder bag is 175,000 lire; a woven black satin evening bag is 410,000 lire. A pair of Bottega high heels is 230,000 lire in black satin, 300,000 lire in leather.

BRUNO MAGLI
San Marco, Frezzeria 1583–1585 (tel. 23-472) and Campo San Moisè 1302 (tel. 27-210)
Vaporetto Stop: *San Marco*
Hours: *Monday through Saturday from 10 a.m. to 7:30 p.m. nonstop (closed Monday morning)*
Credit Cards: AE, DC, MC, V
English Spoken.

The two Bruno Magli shops in Venice are slightly different in that the Calle Frezzeria store sells the famous Magli leather clothes and accessories as well as the equally famous Magli shoes. Prices are relatively inexpensive and much lower than you'd pay in the States. A soft suede three-quarter-length skirt in dark green is 439,000 lire. A Magli briefcase for a woman is 340,000 lire. A man's billfold is 45,000 lire. Prices on shoes are lower at the shoes-only shop near Piazza San Marco. A pair of burgundy-colored high heels with a suede bow costs 190,000 lire. A casual knee boot in soft brown leather is 160,000 lire. Men will find classic wingtips in black, burgundy, or brown for 160,000 lire. An oxblood tasseled loafer is 180,000 lire.

FENDI
San Marco, Salizzada San Moisè 1474 (tel. 705-733)
Vaporetto Stop: *San Marco*
Hours: *Monday through Saturday from 9:30 a.m. to 7:30 p.m. nonstop (closed Monday morning)*
Credit Cards:: AE, DC, MC, V
English Spoken.

(See Fendi in "Clothing, Women's Fashions.")

FRANCIS MODEL
Ruga Rialto 778 (tel. 522-3991)
Vaporetto Stop: *Rialto*
Hours: *Monday through Saturday from 9:30 a.m. to 1 p.m. and 3 to 7:30 p.m. (closed Monday morning)*
Credit Cards: AE, MC
English Spoken.

Fine leather goods at excellent prices at Francis Model

Francis Model is on the busy Ruga Rialto, just a few steps from the Rialto Bridge. Despite the fact that you're in one of the most touristy neighborhoods of the city, you'll find high-quality leather goods here at prices lower than you might expect. The shop sells purses and handbags exclusively. A blue leather shoulder bag with a brass clasp and buckle costs 135,000 lire. A Louis Vuitton-style vinyl duffle bag costs 225,000 lire. Woven bags begin at 85,000 lire for a clutch and go up to 400,000 lire for the largest size.

FRATELLI ROSSETTI
San Marco, San Moisè 1477 (tel. 522-0819)
Vaporetto Stop: *San Marco*
Hours: *Monday through Saturday from 10 a.m. to 1 p.m. and 2 to 7 p.m., and also on Sunday in season (closed Monday morning)*
Credit Cards: AE, DC, MC, V
English Spoken.

Fine footwear from Fratelli Rossetti

The Fratelli Rossetti shop in Venice is large and modern and has the full line of Rossetti shoes for men and women. Kidskin pumps for women are 188,000 lire. Black doeskin flats with rhinestone accents for evening wear are 215,000 lire. A pair of sturdy, but elegant suede walking shoes—just the thing you need in Venice—costs 195,000 lire. For men, there are shoes in a variety of leathers, like beautiful crocodile tasseled loafers for 690,000 lire. A pair of very elegant calfskin loafers is 142,000 lire.

VENICE SHOPS: LEATHER GOODS

FURLA
San Marco, Mercerie 4954 (tel. 523-0611)
Hours: *Monday through Saturday from 10 a.m. to 1 p.m. and 3 to 7:30 p.m. (closed Monday morning)*
Credit Cards: AE, DC, MC, V
English Spoken.

Furla is a narrow little shop which has an unusual selection of leather goods, mostly bags, belts, and gloves. Furla is best known for its leather bags that are stamped with molds to make the leather look far more exotic (and expensive). The bags look uncannily like crocodile, lizard, and ostrich, and come in a wide variety of colors, some of them quite unusual: violet, plum, ochre, kelly green. There are some pretty wild gloves and belts, as well as heavy chunky earrings. Prices are reasonable. A huge "crocodile" shoulder bag is 84,000 lire. A leather tote bag is 66,000 lire. A "crocodile" clutch evening bag is 77,000 lire.

GIANNI VERSACE: see "Clothing, Women's Fashions"

GUCCI
San Marco, Mercerie 258 (tel. 29-119)
Hours: *Monday through Saturday from 9:30 a.m. to 1 p.m. and 2 to 7:30 p.m., and also on Sunday in season (closed Monday morning)*
Credit Cards: AE, DC, MC, V
English Spoken.

The Gucci boutique in Venice is small but great

The small Gucci store in Venice is devoted mostly to leather goods, although the selection is limited. Prices seem a little lower than elsewhere in Italy, but not by much. A pair of black leather flats is 150,000 lire. A black leather key case costs 61,000 lire, and a matching wallet is 90,000 lire. A cloth wallet with the Gucci stripe is 82,000 lire.

LA BAUTA
San Marco, Mercerie 729 (tel. 522-3838)
Hours: Monday through Saturday from 9:30 a.m. to 7:30 p.m. nonstop (closed Monday morning)
Credit Cards: AE, DC, MC, V
English Spoken.

This huge store has a giant selection of footwear for men and women, as well as high-quality shearling and leather jackets. In addition to La Bauta's own brand of leather, the store is also the Venice source for Ferragamo, Pitti, and Diego Della Valle. The big names are a little more expensive here than in their own stores in Florence, Rome, and Milan. La Bauta's own brand of footwear is quite reasonable.

LA COUPOLE
San Marco, Frezzeria 1674 (tel. 706-063) and Calle 22 Marzo 2366 (tel. 24-243)
Vaporetto Stop: San Marco
Hours: Monday through Saturday from 9:30 a.m. to 7:30 p.m. nonstop, and also on Sunday from March through October (closed Monday morning)
Credit Cards: AE, DC, MC, V
English Spoken.

The suede and leather at both La Coupole shops is of outstanding quality, although the selection is limited. A suede dress in ruby red, beige, or gray costs 1.25 million lire. A pair of striking magenta leather gloves is 120,000 lire. (See also La Coupole in "Clothing, Women's Fashions.")

LA FENICE
San Marco, Via 22 Marzo (tel. 31-273)
Vaporetto Stop: San Marco
Hours: Monday through Saturday from 9:30 a.m. to 7:30 p.m. nonstop, and also on Sunday in season (closed Monday morning)
Credit Cards: AE, DC, MC, V
English Spoken.

La Fenice is a very elegant shop which features Maud Frizon shoes. A pair of silver-and-black suede high heels is 350,000 lire. However, La Fenice has some remarkable end-of-season sales when prices on Frizon are cut by as much as 50%. If you happen to be in Venice during February or July, you'll find some excellent bargains here.

LA RUGA
Ruga Rialto 773 (no phone)
Vaporetto Stop: San Silvestro
Hours: Monday through Saturday from 9:30 a.m. to 7:30 p.m. nonstop
Credit Cards: AE, DC, MC, V
English Spoken.

This cluttered shop on the Dorsoduro side of the Rialto Bridge has some wonderful buys on sheepskin jackets, coats, and gloves for men and women. A full-length shearling coat for a woman is 1.4 million lire. The same item for a man is 1.25 million lire.

MARFORIO
Mercerie 5033 (tel. 25-734)
Hours: Monday through Saturday from 9:30 a.m. to 7:30 p.m. nonstop, and also on Sunday in season
Credit Cards: AE, DC, MC, V
English Spoken.

Since 1875 Marforio has been the place for one-stop leather shopping in Venice. The shop is large, not heavily endowed in the character department, but the selection and prices on their own brands make Marforio well worth a look. All the leather goods, handbags, luggage, wallets, belts—everything except shoes—are made by Marforio's own workshops, so there are no famous names here. A leather tote bag in soft brown leather is 120,000 lire. A black evening bag is 79,000 lire. A shoulder bag (they come in a variety of colors) is 145,000 lire. Belts begin at 30,000 lire. In addition, Marforio will take dollars or dollar traveler's checks offering rates of exchange that are usually better than those quoted at banks.

MARIO VALENTINO
San Marco 1255–1257, near the Piazza San Marco (tel. 523-1333)
Vaporetto Stop: San Marco
Hours: Monday through Saturday from 9:30 a.m. to 7:30 p.m. nonstop, and also on Sunday in season
Credit Cards: AE, DC, MC, V
English Spoken.

The snappy, wild Mario Valentino line emanating from warm and sunny Naples is well represented in Venice. A pair of red polka-dotted high heels with gold lamé trim is 350,000 lire. A pair of green suede flats is 155,000 lire.

RENE
San Marco, Mercerie 4983 (tel. 523-7842)
Hours: *Monday through Satrurday from 9:30 a.m. to 8 p.m. nonstop, and also on Sunday in season*
Credit Cards: *AE, DC, MC, V*
English Spoken.

This is a good place to take on the *acqua alta* in elegance and style. Rene sells its own line of waterproof leather Wellington boots in red, blue, gray, yellow, and black. They cost 100,000 lire a pair. A clutch purse, made of the same material, is 89,000 lire. There is also a line of shearling coats for women, with prices beginning at about 1 million lire.

ROBERTA DI CAMERINO
San Marco, San Ascension 1255 (tel. 523-1333)
Vaporetto Stop: *San Marco*
Hours: *Monday through Saturday from 9:30 a.m. to 1 p.m. and 3 to 7:30 p.m. (closed Monday morning)*
Credit Cards: *AE, DC, MC, V*
English Spoken.

This huge, elegant shop is the flagship store for Roberta di Camerino, and with Bottega Veneta, represents the best in Venetian leather. The di Camerino handbags are best known, although you'll find the trademark "R" on leather clothing and shoes, as well as clothing made from cotton, linen, and wool. There are two floors of it to choose from. Evening bags in black leather with rhinestone accents are 345,000 lire. A crocodile bag is 440,000 lire. The velvet bags are less expensive: a small, elegant clutch is 235,000 lire. A brown leather shoulder bag costs 155,000 lire.

TRUSSARDI
San Marco, Calle Spadaria 695 (tel. 528-5757)
Hours: *Monday through Saturday from 9:30 a.m. to 7:30 p.m. nonstop, and also on Sunday in season*
Credit Cards: *AE, DC, MC, V*
English Spoken.

Exactly why this, the smallest Trussardi shop in Italy, should have the best prices on Trussardi leather is a mystery. However, if you like this name, this is the place to buy. A large wallet for a man is 79,000 lire and a smaller billfold is 45,000 lire (you'll pay about 35,000 lire more for either item in Rome). A large shoulder bag with brown leather trim is 211,000 lire. A large vinyl overnight bag is 290,000 lire.

VOGINI
San Marco, Calle Ascension 1291 (tel. 522-2573) and Calle Seconda de l'Ascension 1257 (tel. 522-2573)

VENICE SHOPS: LEATHER GOODS/MASKS

Vaporetto Stop: *San Marco*
Hours: *Monday through Saturday from 9:30 a.m. to 7:30 p.m. nonstop, and also on Sunday in season*
Credit Cards: *AE, DC, MC, V*
English Spoken.

Vogini seems to have cornered the luggage market in Venice. There are three shops: two main outlets, and a third facing the store on Seconda de l'Ascension. In the Calle Ascension shop (that's the one closest to the Piazza San Marco) you'll find a virtual warehouse of leather bags, mostly casual items, at extremely low prices. A huge, floppy triangular shoulder bag in high-quality burgundy leather costs 229,000 lire. A smaller version is 145,000 lire. There are also many woven leather bags—said to be made for Bottega Veneta—at very good prices. A small woven shoulder bag, available in about a dozen different colors, is 99,000 lire. At the posher Vogini on Seconda de l'Ascension, just around the corner, you'll find a huge selection of luggage, including the heavy-duty Mandarina Duck line. Small nylon and canvas bags with the heavy Mandarina Duck rubber begin at 28,000 lire and range to about 64,000 lire. The large carryalls are in the 100,000-lire to 200,000-lire range. Vogini also posts its own rate of dollar/lire exchange and it's consistently better than the bank and cambio rates.

LUGGAGE (see "Leather Goods")

MASKS

The famous Venetian masks have their origins in the riotous *carnevale* which takes place every year in the week before the beginning of Lent. Today the carnival is mostly a good excuse to get dressed up in peculiar costumes, dance in the street, and generally carry on as if you haven't a care in the world. In centuries past, however, carnival was a chance for unbridled indecency, when wives and husbands did their utmost to be unfaithful to one another and priests worked hard to break their vows of chastity. By the late 18th century things had gotten so out of hand that the carnival was banned. The prohibition was lifted not long after it was imposed and people immediately went back to wearing the masks which they had adopted so as not to be recognized as they cheated on their nearest and dearest. Gradually the different masks assumed different names. The heavy-chinned mask worn by men is Bauta, a symbol of swaggering masculinity. Neutra is a mask which mixes the facial characteristics of both sexes, worn by women very anxious to confuse their lovers. Moretta ("Little Moor") and the Orientale recall the Venetian commerce with the exotic and wonderful parts of the earth. The most popular mask is the long-nosed, almost bird-like visage known as Portafortuna ("luck bringer").

As with the makers of Venetian glass, there seems to be a mask shop on every corner in Venice. As one might expect, quality varies from shop to shop, although the best ones are those whose workshop is right out in the open where you can see the masks being handmade.

BRUNO RIZZATO
San Marco, Ponte dei Barcaroli 1831, near La Fenice Theater (tel. 28-111)
Vaporetto Stop: *San Marco*
Hours: *Monday through Saturday from 10 a.m. to 1 p.m. and 3 to 7:30 p.m. (closed Monday morning)*
Credit Cards: *None*

Right across the tiny Ponte dei Barcaroli from the house Mozart lived in when he was in Venice in the 18th century you'll find Bruno Rizzato's mask shop. It's something of an institution in Venice as he not only makes and designs masks, but he restores antique ones as well. His ancient shop is cluttered with the tools of his trade, molds, lacquers, and gilts, and you can't help feeling that Mozart might have dropped in here around carnival time to pick up a mask or two. If you buy a Portafortuna or a Bauta here, you can be sure that you're getting an excellent piece of craftsmanship as well as a bit of old Venice. Prices begin at 35,000 lire for an unadorned mask and go up to the hundreds of thousands of lire for the more elaborate creations.

DARIO USTINO
San Marco, Ponte dei Dai 171 (tel. 522-3474)
Vaporetto Stop: *San Zaccaria*
Hours: *Monday through Saturday from 10 a.m. to 1 p.m. and 3 to 7:30 p.m. (closed Monday morning)*
Credit Cards: *None*
English Spoken.

A small shop just off the Piazza San Marco where masks of all shapes, types, and materials are made right in front of you. Small decorative masks are just 7,000 lire. The masks meant to be worn are made from a variety of materials: papier-mâché, leather, brass, and ceramic. For 20,000 lire you can have a basic, plain white papier-mâché mask; 120,000 lire buys a colorful and wildly decorated mask. The ultimate status symbol is a mask covered in gold lealf costing 320,000 lire.

F.G.B.
San Marco, Santa Maria del Giglio 2459 (tel. 523-6556)
Vaporetto Stop: *Santa Maria del Giglio*
Hours: *Monday through Saturday from 10 a.m. to 1 p.m. and 3 to 7:30 p.m., and also on Sunday in season (closed Monday morning)*

VENICE SHOPS: MASKS

Credit Cards: *None*
English Spoken.

Excellent traditional Venetian masks, handmade in the shop. The hand-painting is of particularly high quality and prices are reasonable. A plain white Bauta is 25,000 lire. Painted masks begin at about 45,000 lire.

IL PRATO
San Marco, Frezzeria 1770 (tel. 703-375)
Vaporetto Stop: *San Marco*
Hours: *Monday through Saturday from 10 a.m. to 7:30 p.m. nonstop, and also on Sunday in season (closed Monday afternoon)*
Credit Cards: *AE, DC, MC, V*
English Spoken.

This is one-stop shopping for all your carnival needs. There are elaborate harlequin masks for 200,000 lire, a complete colombine costume for 750,000 lire, a silver carnival hood for 200,000 lire. Also examples of rare Venetian handcrafts, like elaborate marionettes costing 300,000 lire to 600,000 lire, and music boxes—one in the form of a carousel is 230,000 lire.

VALESE FONDITORE
San Marco, Calle Fiubera 793 (tel. 27-282)
Hours: *Monday through Saturday from 9:30 a.m. to 7:30 p.m. nonstop, and also on Sunday in season (closed Monday morning)*

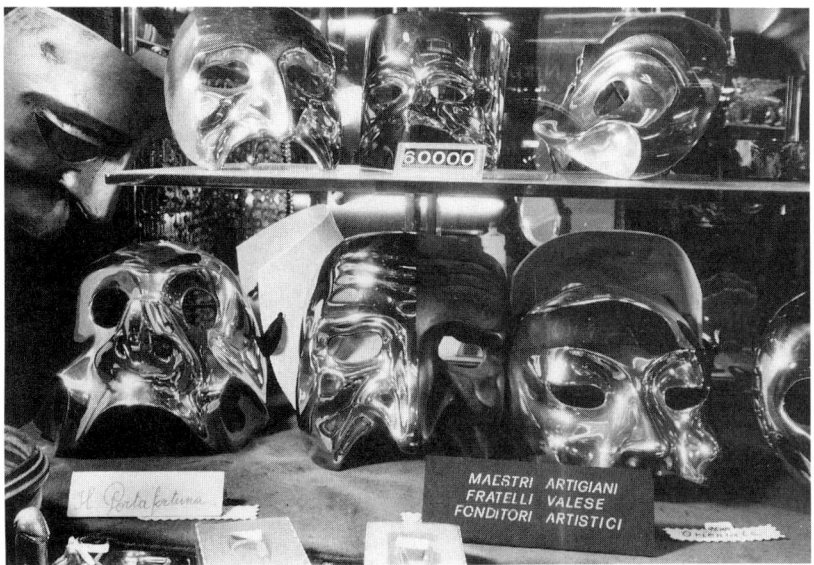

Traditional Venetian carnival masks built to last in brass and bronze by Valese Fonditore

Credit Cards: AE, DC, MC, V
English Spoken.

It tends to rain at carnival time, so a papier-mâché mask left out in the rain—unless it's properly varnished—tends to wilt. If you want something a little more durable, try Valese for masks made out of everything but papier-mâché. These are ornaments, meant to be hung on the wall or used as paperweights. They are made in brass, bronze, copper, pewter, and hammered iron. A Bauta mask on a stickpin is 10,000 lire. An Orientale in bronze is 95,000 lire. A Portafortuna, also in bronze, is 150,000 lire.

VENEZIARTIGIANA
San Marco, Calle Largo San Marco 412 (tel. 35-032)
Vaporetto Stop: *San Zaccaria*
Hours: *Monday through Saturday from 10 a.m. to 1 p.m. and 3 to 6 p.m. (closed Monday morning)*
Credit Cards: AE, DC, MC, V
English Spoken.

Housed in a 19th-century apothecary shop, Veneziartigiana is a collective of Venetian craftsmen producing traditional Venetian goods like masks, dolls, and costumes. Items here tend to be one-of-a-kind, and therefore rather expensive. The masks are perhaps the most elaborate I've seen in the city, and prices begin at 145,000 lire for a beautifully decorated Neutra. There are also handmade dolls costing 1.2 million lire.

Oh you beautiful dolls—find them at Veneziartigiana

PRINTS AND ENGRAVINGS

BAC ART STUDIO
San Marco, Campo San Maurizio 2663 (tel. 522-8171)
Vaporetto Stop: Santa Maria del Giglio
Hours: Monday through Saturday from 9:30 a.m. to 1 p.m. and 3 to 7:30 p.m. (closed Monday morning)
Credit Cards: None
English Spoken.

Bac Art Studio specializes in tasteful, not touristy, modern pictures and prints of Venice, as well as some fine paper goods. The collections of multiplate etchings of Venice are some of the finest to be found in the city—small, inexpensive, and signed by the artists. A set costs 250,000 lire. The framed etchings are the best deals, however. Views of Venice in various sizes range from 80,000 lire to 150,000 lire. The frames themselves qualify as minor works of art, as they are skillfully made and hand-painted. A blank book with an etched frontispiece is 70,000 lire. A small, beautifully made box for cigarettes or smaller pieces of jewelry, with an etching under the lacquer, is 50,000 lire.

LA FENICE
San Marco 1850, near La Fenice Theater (tel. 38-006)
Vaporetto Stop: San Marco
Hours: Monday through Saturday from 10 a.m. to 1:30 p.m. and 3 to 7:30 p.m. (closed Monday morning)
Credit Cards: AE, DC, MC, V
English Spoken.

A store for the more specialized collector of fine antique prints and illustrated books of the 16th, 17th, and 18th centuries. The quality and rarity of the prints is exceptional and the prices are high. A collection of views of the Palladian villas of the Brenta is 450,000 lire.

OSVALDO BÖHM
San Marco, Salizzada San Moisè 1349–1350 (tel. 522-2255)
Hours: Monday through Saturday from 9:30 a.m. to 7:30 p.m. nonstop (closed Monday morning)
Credit Cards: AE, DC, MC, V
English Spoken.

If you don't have time to wander through the back streets in search of old print shops, this excellent establishment just a few yards from the Piazza San Marco is sure to have exactly the antique view of Venice you want. A colored, 19th-century view of the Piazza San Marco, or of the Doge in his *Buncintoro* (ceremonial barge), costs between 140,000 lire and 200,000 lire, including the frame.

ZFW
San Polo, Campiello Meloni 1478 (tel. 522-4296)
Hours: Monday through Saturday from 10 a.m. to 1:30 p.m. and 3:30 to 7:30 p.m. (closed Monday morning)
Credit Cards: None
English Spoken.

ZFW has hundreds of postcards in color and black-and-white showing how Venice used to look, Venice in the snow—even the dramatic photograph of the campanile in Piazza San Marco thundering to the ground as it did at 9:52 a.m. on July 14, 1902. This is a good place for odd and inexpensive items—postcard collectors will be in heaven. Black-and-white cards begin at 200 lire. The most expensive item in the shop is a framed poster advertising art shows at the Accademia, at 75,000 lire.

SHOES (see "Leather Goods")

STATIONERY SUPPLIES

IL PAPIRO
San Marco, Campo San Maurizio 2764 (tel. 522-3055)
Vaporetto Stop: Santa Maria del Giglio
Hours: Monday through Saturday from 10 a.m. to 7:30 p.m. nonstop (closed Monday morning)
Credit Cards: AE, DC, MC, V
English Spoken.

There are five Papiro shops, four of them in Italy and one in New York. Smaller than both the Rome and New York stores, this one still has a representative selection of the lushly colored Papiro marbled blank books, cards, and objects. A small trompe l'oeil notebook in blue-and-red marbled paper with a leather binding is 75,000 lire. An obelisk covered in green marbled paper is 120,000 lire.

PART FIVE
SHOPPING ROME

CHAPTER XIII

A ROME OVERVIEW

Rome is widely thought to be a chaotic, *opera buffo* city filled with noisy, unruly people who don't work much and whose principal delight in life is to drive at break-neck speed the wrong way down one-way streets. While it's true that the Romans have an amazing tolerance for noise, that traffic *is* as mad as it looks, and that the art of lining up and waiting one's turn is unknown, Rome and the Romans are much more than these stereotypes. For every traffic-choked street there is a quiet side street; for every piazza which has been turned into a parking lot there is another which is tranquil, calm, and free of cars; for every rude Roman who cuts ahead of you in the bank there is another with courtly, old-world manners.

Of course, there is more. For some reason it has become fashionable to dismiss Rome as a city which has little to interest the shopper. This is just not so! Rome is crammed with shops selling such a wide variety of goods that it's hard to imagine that there isn't one which sells something to suit every taste and income. Just as a great Roman palazzo might be home to a prince living on the *piano nobile* and a poor art student housed in the garret, so the city itself is a jumble of grand shops and more modest ones existing side by side. You can spend millions of lire at the great names on the Via Condotti or considerably less on the Via Frattina, just two blocks away. You can buy a museum-quality antique on the Via Giulia or you can poke around in the secondhand shops on the Via Cappellari a few hundred yards away.

In addition to the shops, the weather in Rome is the best of the four cities covered in this book, and the food is the finest as well. How can you go wrong?

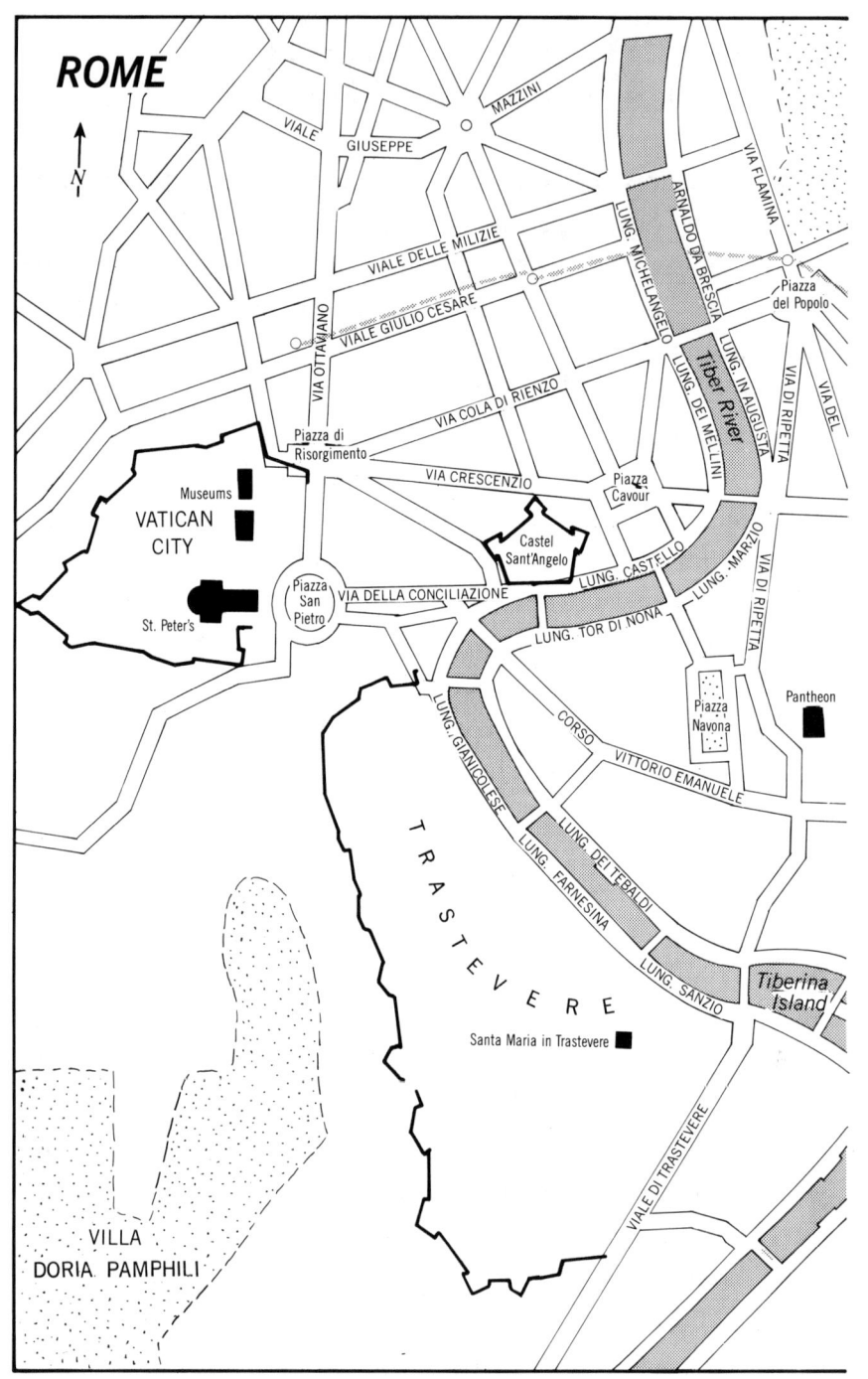

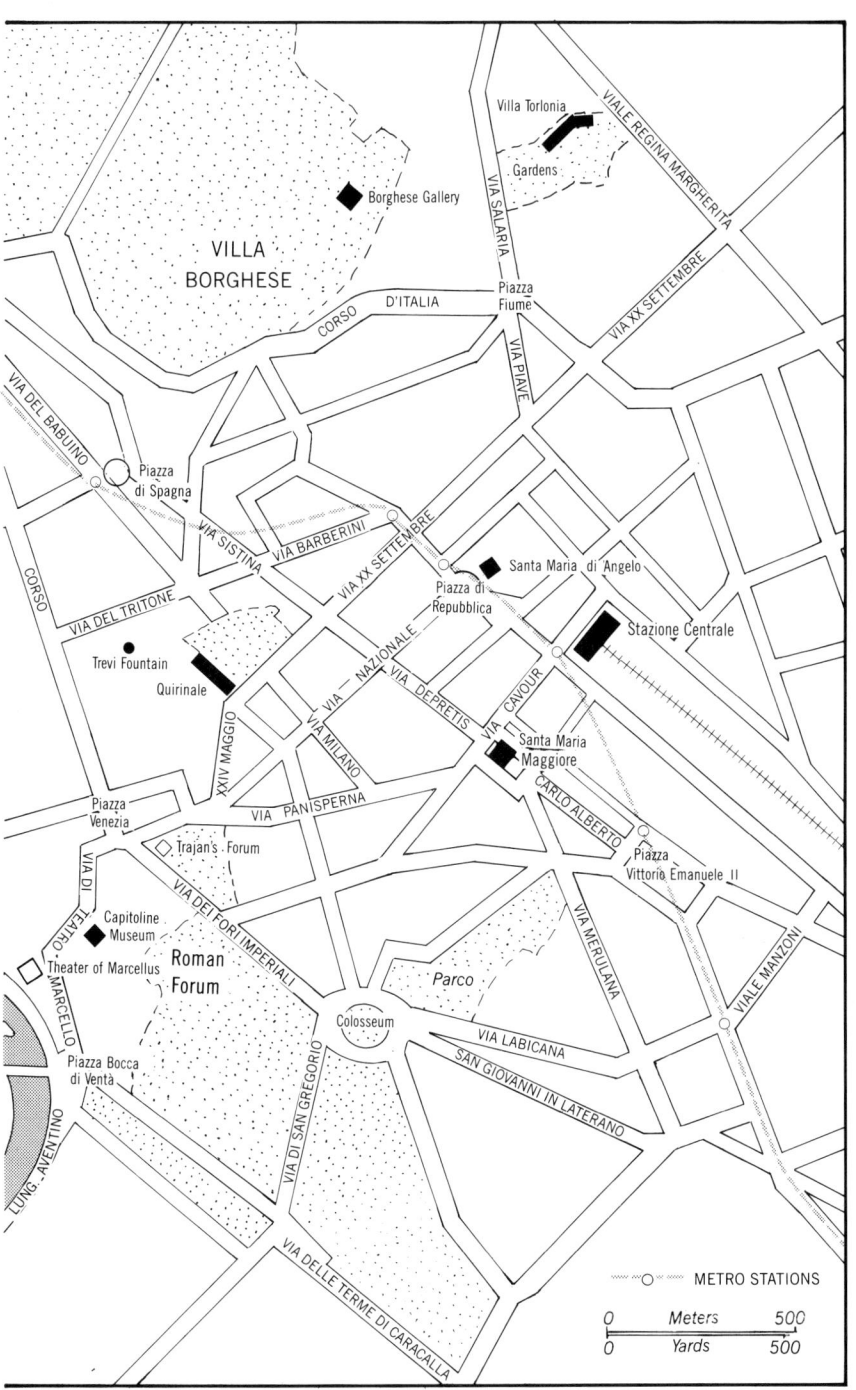

BASIC ORIENTATION

Rome is surrounded by large and modern suburbs which have little to interest the visitor. Rome within the old walls, the *centro storico* (historic center), is the part of the city with the major shops and sights. We'll go outside the walls once, to the suburb closest to downtown called Prati, in the stroll covering the important shopping street Cola di Rienzo.

The *centro storico* is the area stretching from the River Tiber to the Via Veneto and from the Piazza del Popolo to San Giovanni in Laterano. Within this area the major shopping districts are the Piazza di Spagna area, the Via Veneto, Via Nazionale, Campo dei Fiori, and the Piazza Navona.

The Piazza di Spagna is the largest and best-known shopping quarter. This area is trisected by three major streets, the Via del Corso, the Via Babuino, and the Via Ripetta. All three streets meet in the beautiful Piazza del Popolo, and within this triangle you'll find the most famous shopping streets in Rome, notably Via Condotti, Via Borgognona, Via della Croce, and Via Frattina. Other important streets are in the vicinity, like Via Sistina and Via Veneto, but not in the triangle itself.

Between the Piazza di Spagna and the main railway station, running from the Piazza della Repubblica to the Piazza Venezia, is the Via Nazionale, a very long and very busy shopping street where prices are generally lower than in the Piazza di Spagna neighborhood.

A spur of land which juts out into the River Tiber, to the west of the Via del Corso, is the most picturesque section of the city. This area is divided by the busy Corso Vittorio Emanuele. On one side of the street, the area between the Corso Vittorio Emanuele and the river, is the Campo dei Fiori, a colorful piazza which is the central point for the important shopping streets of Via Giubbonari, Via Giulia, and Via Cappellari.

The Corso Vittorio Emanuele is also the boundary for the neighborhood incorporating the Piazza Navona and Via Coronari, the most important street for antiques in the city.

GETTING FROM THE AIRPORT

Work has begun to connect the small but excellent Rome Metro system to the main airport, known as **Leonardo da Vinci–Fiumicino**. The projected finishing date for this link is sometime in the 1990s, so at present there are just two ways of traveling from the airport: bus and taxi.

The **bus** service runs from the arrival area of the airport every 15 minutes from 7 a.m. to 12:45 a.m. From 1:30 to 6:30 a.m. the bus leaves every hour. The buses are city owned and go by the acronym ACOTRAL. Tickets, which cost 5,000 lire, must be purchased at the ACOTRAL desk in the terminal. Once on board the bus you must cancel your ticket in the box mounted on a bracket near the rear door. The bus goes directly to the main train station, Stazione Termini, in

ROME: GENERAL INFORMATION

the center of town. The trip takes between 30 and 60 minutes, depending on traffic.

Taxis are plentiful at the airport. A taxi ride from the airport costs approximately 50,000 lire. Don't think you are being cheated if you're charged more than the figure on the meter: there's a 10,000-lire supplement levied on all trips from the airport, between 10 p.m. and 7 a.m. there's an additional 3,000-lire supplement, and all day Sunday there's a further 1,000 lire to be paid. If you think you've been overcharged, ask to see the driver's *Cartello delle Tariffe Supplementari* which is written in four languages.

If you are arriving on a charter flight you will probably land at Rome's second airport, **Ciampino**. There is a bus which meets charters; however, it takes you not to the center of town but to an outlying Metro stop called Subaugusta. From there it's a 15-minute subway ride into the center of town. Taxis charge 35,000 lire to 40,000 lire, but it's wise to ask for an estimate in advance.

Needless to say, those guys who stand in the arrivals building of both airports whispering "Taxi? Taxi?" are touts who will overcharge you unmercifully. Ignore them.

GETTING AROUND

Subway

Rome's subway, known as **La Metropolitana**, is clean, fast, quiet, and efficient, and there are four subway stops in the central shopping district, the Piazza di Spagna. However, as that area is so concentrated and the four stops so close together, it's unlikely that you would take the Metro from one stop to another. None of the other shopping districts is served by the Metro except Via Cola di Rienzo.

The four stations in the Piazza di Spagna area are Spagna, Barberini, Repubblica, and Flaminio. The subway stop closest to Cola di Rienzo is called Lepanto.

Overall, the Metro is made up of two lines, Linea A, and Linea B. The newer **Linea A** runs roughly north-south from Ottaviano, near the Vatican, to Cinecitta, 22 stops away. All the shopping stops mentioned above are on this line. **Linea B** runs from Stazione Termini to the suburb called EUR.

The subway fare is 700 lire. Tickets may be bought at tobacconists and newsstands displaying the "Vendita Biglietti/ATAC" sign. They can also be bought from vending machines in the stations themselves—you must have exact change.

Buses

Except at rush hour when the Rome buses are unbearably crowded, the ATAC bus service is good. Again, there would be little point in taking buses in the Piazza di Spagna area, but you might want to take a no. 56 or a no. 60 bus from the Via del Tritone (one of the major streets in the triangle) to the Campo dei Fiori / Piazza Navona boundary, Corso Vittorio Emanuele.

There is a strict protocol for bus riding. If you have purchased a bus pass (good for a month at a cost of 23,000 lire), you are accorded the privilege of getting on the bus through the front door. You don't have to show the pass—all bus riding is on the honor system, although there are spot-checks by inspectors. If you have bought a good-for-one-ride 700-lire bus ticket, you get on through the rear door and cancel the ticket in the machine provided. Everyone exits through the center door.

A new type of ticket is the *biglietto orario*. For 1,000 lire, you buy one ticket which is good from 5 a.m. to 2 p.m. or from 2 to 9 p.m. With that in hand, you can get on and off as many buses as you please during those hours. You enter through the rear door and cancel it only the first time you get on a bus. These tickets can only be purchased at the small green ATAC booths at major bus stops. The bus passes and the ordinary 700-lire tickets can be bought at the vendors with the "Vendita biglietti/ATAC" sign.

Taxis

Taxis are inexpensive, plentiful, and because of special lanes reserved for buses and taxis alone, quite a fast means of getting around town. They cost 2,500 lire on the drop and 300 lire for every 90 seconds thereafter. There are supplements: 2,500 lire after 8:30 p.m., 1,000 lire on Sunday from 7 a.m. to 10 p.m., and 2,000 lire all day on Sunday. Tips should be about 10% but are not really mandatory.

You can phone for a taxi at 3570 or 4994, but you'll have to speak Italian. At the end of a meal you can ask your waiter to call a cab for you, but you pay for the driver's time from the moment he takes the job. He'll arrive at the restaurant with something like 3,000 lire or 4,000 lire showing on the meter already.

On Foot

This is by far the best way to see and shop Rome. Rome has thousands of narrow streets that must be explored on foot. Furthermore, in the main shopping district around the Spanish Steps most of the streets are restricted to pedestrian traffic only.

Even if you're not on a pedestrian street, you might find yourself walking in the middle of the street—the sidewalks are often occupied by parked cars.

Crossing a busy traffic street is something of a sport here, something akin to running with the bulls in Pamplona. To cross a busy street where there is no crosswalk, you have to wait for a slight lull in the traffic and then step boldly off the curb, staring fixedly at the drivers approaching you. They will either slow down and let you cross or speed up and try to get by before you step in front of them. They are not consciously trying to run you down—it just seems that way.

ROME: GENERAL INFORMATION

TOURIST INFORMATION

There's a Visitors Information Office in the Stazione Termini at the end of platform 3, and the main regional tourist office, EPT (Ente Provinciale per il Turismo), is at Via Parigi 11 (tel. 461-851), about a five-minute walk from the station. English is spoken. They're open Monday through Saturday (closed Sundays and holidays) from 8:30 a.m. to 1:30 p.m. and from 2:30 to 7 p.m.

WEATHER

Spring and autumn are the most pleasant seasons in Rome, with temperatures ranging from the middle 60s to the high 70s. Evenings are cool and pleasant, and colder (obviously) in the fall months. Summers are hot and humid, particularly in August when the entire city wilts under the sun.

Romans seem to be under the impression that they don't have a winter. They do, and while it's never as cold as, say, Helsinki, it has snowed considerable amounts twice in the last three years. If it doesn't snow it rains, sometimes for weeks on end, particularly in January and February. But there are days when the sun comes out, the temperatures rise, and suddenly everyone is taking their cappuccino al fresco.

THE ABCs OF SHOPPING ROME

AMERICAN EXPRESS

The American Express office in Rome is conveniently located in the Piazza di Spagna, a few yards from the Spanish Steps. The address is Piazza di Spagna 38 (tel. 67-641). It's open Monday through Friday from 9 a.m. to 6 p.m. for travel arrangements, Monday through Friday from 9 a.m. to 5:30 p.m. for financial transactions, and on Saturday from 9 a.m. to 1 p.m. for all services.

BUSINESS HOURS

Unless a shop is "Orario No-Stop," shopping hours are from 9 or 10 a.m. to 1:30 p.m. Shops reopen between 4 and 5 p.m. and close again between 7 and 8:30 p.m. It's up to the individual shopkeeper what hours he wishes to keep. Count on finding just about everything closed on Monday morning and all day on Sunday.

HOLIDAYS   (See "The ABCs of Shopping Italy" in Chapter II).

MARKETS

The principal flea market in Rome is **Porta Portese,** located on the Trastevere side of the river at the Ponte Aventino (that's a bridge). It's held every Sunday morning from dawn until midday, and you'd be well advised to get there early as the crowds are thick and the pickings—for the out-of-towner—are slim. Although the market is vast, antique and bric-a-brac hunters will be disappointed. Porta Portese has long since ceased to be a good place to pick up some antique oddment at a reasonable price. There are some good buys, but you have to hunt for them. Bargaining is the name of the game, of course, but the rather fierce stallkeepers do not suffer fools gladly. Guard your purse and wallet closely as pickpockets do work the crowd.

The **San Giovanni market,** next to the enormous Basilica of San Giovanni in Laterano, is open mornings, every day except Sunday. This is primarily a clothing market and good buys are to be had on out-of-season items—heavy overcoats in July, swimwear in January. A lot of clothes are secondhand, so those who like to dress in '40s, '50s, or '60s style just might find the right piece of hep, cool, fab clothing here.

The largest market in the city is in **Piazza Vittorio Emanuele,** near the important church of Santa Maria Maggiore. It's open daily (except Sunday) in the morning. The market completely covers the huge square and is mostly given over to food, fruit, and vegetables, although a large section of the market sells household goods: mops, buckets, cutlery, and clothing. There is even some cheap new furniture. The Piazza Vittorio Emanuele market is a piece of real

The Piazza Vittorio Emanuele: Browsing Roman-style

Rome, off the tourist trail. Market connoisseurs—people who love any kind of market—should see this, as should those interested in experiencing a genuine slice of Roman living. For the serious shopper, however, the market has little of interest. There are no stalls selling imperfect or discontinued name-brand merchandise, nor are there any good fakes and knockoffs as in Florence. The clothing stalls sell low-priced items, but nothing out of the ordinary.

POST OFFICE

The rules for Italian government post offices mentioned in "The ABCs of Shopping Italy" in Chapter II apply in Rome. The main post office is in the Piazza San Silvestro, open Monday through Friday from 8 a.m. to 8 p.m., and on Saturday from 8:30 a.m. to noon. Next door is the international telephone center where calls can be placed to any country on earth from 8 a.m. to 9:45 p.m. nonstop.

The best way to mail things home from Rome is to mail them from a separate country—the Vatican. The Holy See, being a sovereign state, maintains its own mail service. It's a hundred times faster and more efficient than the Italian service, and the clerks are multilingual. Their package service is limited—they will not accept packages weighing more than a kilogram. If there is a letter inside, your parcel is sent at the letter rate, which can be quite expensive. However, if you mail through the Vatican you can be sure that your package will arrive at its destination in good time and in good condition.

SALES   (See "The ABCs of Shopping Italy," in Chapter II.)

TAXES   (See "The ABCs of Shopping Italy," in Chapter II.)

CHAPTER XIV

GREAT ROME SHOPPING STROLLS

Eleanor Clark, who wrote one of the most lyrical books about Rome, *Rome and a Villa,* says (and she was right), "the streets of the city constitute a great rich withinness... [even a visitor] can tell that he is *in* something and not outside something as he would be in most cities.... in Rome to go out is to go home." Since the days of the Empire, Roman life has been lived in the streets. Whole families gather in the street to eat, play cards, even to watch TV—and also to watch their neighbors and complete strangers go about the business of living. As you meander through the streets of Rome you might think yourself inconspicuous, searching for the right pair of shoes or new suit, but you are not as anonymous as you may feel. To the old *portiera,* vigilantly guarding the gates of her apartment building, or the kids kicking a soccer ball in the middle of a traffic-clogged street you are simply a bit player, a walk-on, in the never-ending drama that enlivens the streets of Rome.

THE SHOPPING TRIANGLE AROUND THE PIAZZA DI SPAGNA

The area around the Piazza di Spagna is crowded with shops, most of them on streets that parallel one another. Because of this, I've found it wise to split our itinerary in the Triangle itself into three parts, plus another for the nearby area above the Piazza di Spagna.

The first part covers Via Condotti, the most famous shopping street in Rome, and the area south from the Piazza di Spagna. The second leads us through the area from the Piazza di Spagna north to the Piazza del Popolo. The third takes us

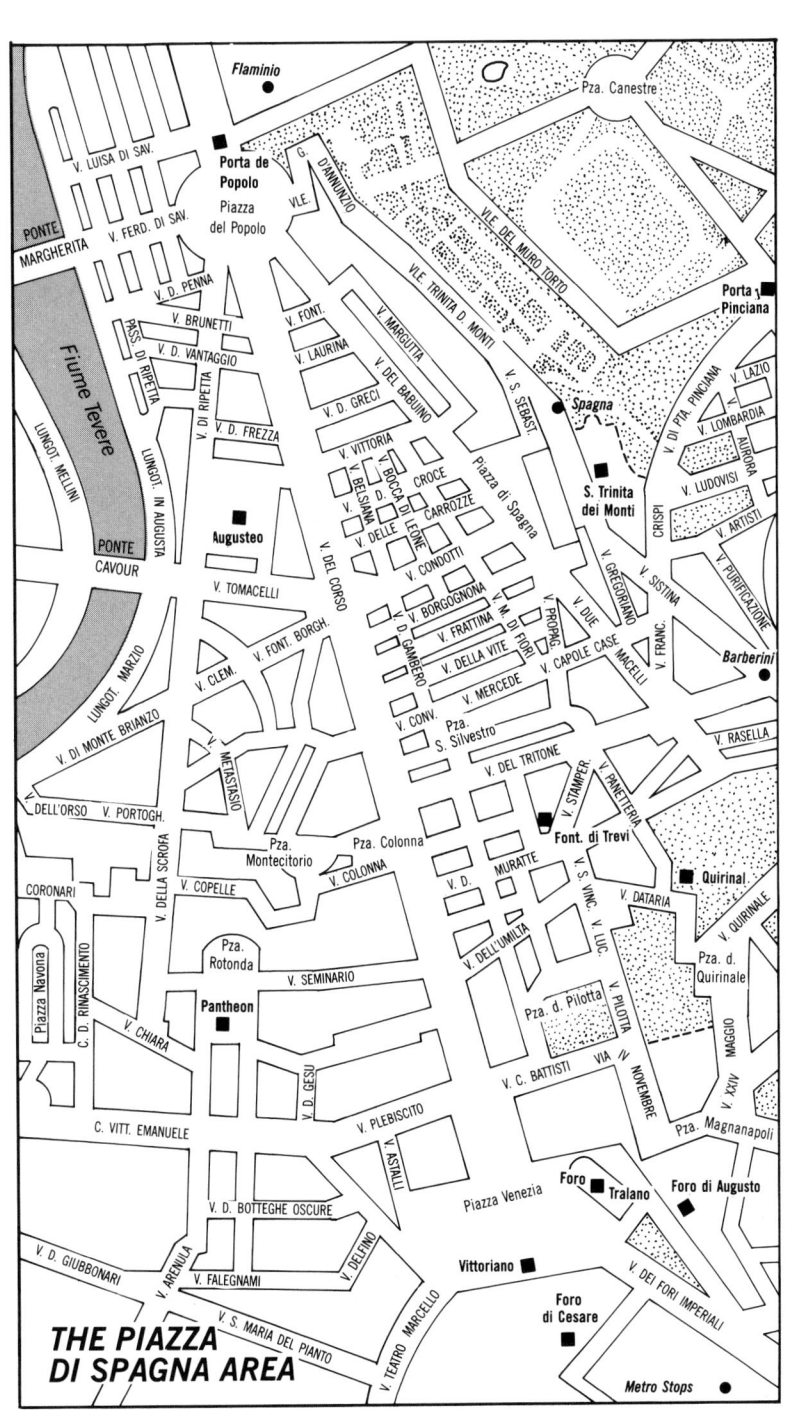

down Via del Corso from the Piazza del Popolo to the Piazza Venezia. Last, we move out of the Triangle above the Piazza di Spagna to the Via Vittorio Veneto and the surrounding area.

VIA CONDOTTI AND SOUTH

Standing in front of the Spanish Steps, with your back to them, you are facing Via Condotti. In this first part of our stroll we'll cover Via Condotti and the streets to your left: Via Borgognona, Via Frattina, Via Belsiana, and Via Mario di Fiori.

The first store of note on **Via Condotti** is the men's- and women's-wear shop Runci, at no. 94. Next to it is the main Richard-Ginori in Rome, at Via Condotti 88. Across the street at no. 8 is the primary branch of Gucci in the city. Next to that famous name is another, the world-famous jewelers Bulgari, at Via Condotti 10.

On the corner of Via Condotti and Via Mario dei Fiore is Valentino Uomo, and the same building houses Valentino Piu. Across Via Condotti at no. 22 is the second of three Gucci shops on this route, this one specializing in clothing for women. Next to that, at Via Condotti 73, is Salvatore Ferragamo.

Facing that is the stunning Beltrami, Via Condotti 18. On the same side of the street, at no. 19, is Benetton. Across the street is the old established Roman clothier Cucci, at Via Condotti 67. Its neighbor is another Ferragamo, this one exclusively for menswear. Mila Schön is next door at Via Condotti 64. Then comes Hermès, Via Condotti 60.

Campanile is a beautiful leather-goods shop at Via Condotti 58. The street finishes at Via Condotti 46 where there is a new, large Max Mara.

You have to backtrack a bit here, going back up Via Condotti to the side street **Via Belsiana**. On this short, narrow street is Gherardini, the famous Florentine leather house, at Via Belsiana 48.

Walk up Via Condotti to another side street, **Via Bocca di Leone,** where at no. 16 you'll find the flagship Valentino.

Returning toward the Piazza di Spagna, turn right on Via Mario dei Fiori and one block along you'll come to **Via Borgognona**. This quiet street is considered the home of Italian fashion in Rome. At the end closest to the Piazza di Spagna is Alicia Rosas, the prima dona of daring silk evening wear, at Via Borgognona 9–10. Heading down the street, the shops on the left-hand side all have double-digit numbers but on the right-hand side they're all single digits—and, most confusingly, they all seem to be no. four.

Fendi seems to have taken over the street. There are six branches of the name, two of them at no. 4. At no. 4L you'll find Fendi purses; at no. 4E, Fendi shoes. Across the street, on the two-digit side, there is Fendi everything at the Fendi flagship store, no. 36. At no. 40 is Fendi clothes; at no. 38, Fendi luggage; and at no. 39, Fendi furs.

Also on the left-hand side is Missoni at no. 38. Gianni Versace has two shops on Via Borgognona: Versace Uomo is at no. 29, and a few doors away is Versace Donna at no. 41.

Gianfranco Ferré has two shops as well. The shop for women, Gianfranco Ferré Boutique, is at no. 42. The Ferré Uomo shop, at no. 6, faces the Versace Uomo.

The third Gucci of this tour is at Via Borgognona 25. Next door at no. 24 is Eddy Monetti for women.

Number 4 is home to Céline. At no. 4A you'll find fabrics by Polidori and at no. 4C there's Polidori Uomo. Number 4D houses the beautiful but tiny FMR bookshop. Next comes the Fendi shoe store already mentioned (at no. 4E), followed by handmade hats at Mara, at no. 4G, followed closely by another Fendi bags at no. 4L. Boots and shoes for men and women by Tanino Crisci can be found at no. 4M. Finally we leave no. 4 behind and at no. 5A are more leather goods, this time by Fratelli Rossetti.

Facing the Polidori shops mentioned above is Laura Biagiotti's fabulous new store at Via Borgognona 43. Next door is the high-fashion footwear of Diego della Valle, at no. 46.

Working your way back up the street, you'll find nine high-fashion names stocked at Lionello Ajô, Via Borgognona 35.

Turn right on Via Belsiana. This leads one block to **Via Frattina,** where you'll find shopping a little less pricey than on Via Borgognona. The street is as long as Via Borgognona, but wider and usually much more crowded.

At Via Frattina 2 is Simone Donna, which specializes in knitwear for ladies. Then comes the lingerie and swimwear of Brighenti, Via Frattina 7. There's more beachwear and lingerie at Tusseda, Via Frattina 25.

There are two Mario Valentino stores on the street: at no. 58 you'll find shoes, leather clothing, and luggage; at no. 84 there are more shoes. Testa, Via Frattina 104, has fine clothes for men, as does Valentini Uomo at no. 111. Giofer, at no. 118, is the place to buy ties—they stock nothing but.

Luciano Lozzi, Via Frattina 102, has a giant selection of handbags, luggage, and other leather goods. La Cicogna is at Via Frattina 138 and has two floors of clothes for children. Next door is Emanuel Zoo, Via Frattina 141, which specializes in their own fashions for young women.

This leads you back to the Piazza di Spagna and the next part of our stroll.

NORTH FROM THE PIAZZA DI SPAGNA

This route covers the streets north of the Spanish Steps between the Piazza di Spagna and the Piazza del Popolo. It begins where the first part of our stroll began, at the head of Via Condotti, with your back to the Spanish Steps.

Heading down Via Condotti again, turn right onto **Via Bocca di Leone.** You won't have traveled far before you hit three big-name designers, one right next to the other. The first is Ungaro, at Via Bocca di Leone 24. Next door is the women's-wear branch of Gianni Versace, at Via Bocca di Leone 26. Then comes

The Piazza del Popolo, the most splendid entrance to the city

the Rome branch of the clothing and leather house Trussardi, at Via Bocca di Leone 27.

Via Bocca di Leone intersects with **Via delle Carozze.** Turn right on that street and you'll come to the amusing shop called Impianti Elettrici, Via delle Carozze 17A, which sells old radios, record players, and other antique gadgets.

One block over is **Via della Croce,** the principal fine-food street in Rome — except that the delicatessens on this street are most famous for stocking hard-to-get foreign items like Aunt Jemima Pancake Mix and Skippy Peanut Butter. Of course, Italian delicacies are available as well.

You should take a look at Ercoli, at Via della Croce 32, for delicious cured meats and cold cuts; Foccaci, at no. 43C, for cured sausages made from game (venison and wild boar are the specialties); and Guerra, at Via della Croce 8, where you'll find magnificent ready-made pasta dishes like ravioli, tortellini, and tortellone.

But there's more than food on Via della Croce. You'll find exclusive shoes for women at Mada, Via della Croce 57, and the bustling stationers, Vertecchi, at no. 70, which has lots of Italian-designed pens and notebooks.

Leave Via della Croce by Via Mario dei Fiori and walk one block to **Via Vittoria.** Starting where Via Vittorio intersects with the Via del Corso, you'll find excellent knitwear for women at Gregg, Via Vittoria 70.

Continuing up the street toward Via del Babuino, stop in at Maurizio Righini, at Via Vittoria 63, for leather goods. Across the street at MC, no. 18, you'll find casual wear for women. There are very expensive clothes for children at Children's Club, across the street at nos. 27 and 52. There are two Nia boutiques on the street, one at no. 48 and another at no. 30. Next door to one of them is the small antique shop specializing in art nouveau and art deco pieces,

1900, at no. 37. The street ends at Marcella Neroni, home of high-quality knits, at Via Vittoria 37.

On **Via del Babuino** itself are a number of good shops to see, but the best-known name brands on the street are undoubtedly Giorgio Armani and Missoni. Armani's store for men and women is at Via del Babuino 102A, to your right. To your left, at no. 140, also on Via del Babuino, is the Emporio Armani, the outlet for Armani sportswear and casual clothing. Missoni is the other giant of the street. The shop for women's wear is at Via del Babuino 96–97.

There are more famous names at L'Atelier Saletti, Via del Babuino 179, which stocks women's wear by Valentino and Lancetti.

There is menswear at Ravasi, at no. 178, as well as at Bernabei, no. 117.

Romani, Via del Babuino 94, is known for its stylish clothes for younger women, as is Touche at no. 91. Gente, Via del Babuino 82, stocks hip clothing for men and women. Eli Colaj, at no. 65, has unusual casual clothes as well as some very lush wedding dresses.

There are a number of good antique shops on Via del Babuino as well. Aldo di Castro, at no. 71, has some of the finest antique Roman prints in the city. Armando Perera has an old, cluttered gallery stuffed with frames, books, prints, and drawings. Collectors of militaria should definitely stop at A. Soligo, Via del Babuino 161.

It's time to visit the **Piazza di Spagna** itself. Heading back up Via del Babuino, you reenter the square where Via del Babuino and Via della Croce intersect. To your left, fronting the square are a number of nice shops, notably Étienne Aigner, Piazza di Spagna 7, and Pratesi, at Piazza di Spagna 10. Just where the Via Condotti meets the piazza is Missoni Uomo, Piazza di Spagna 78, with Krizia right next door at no. 77.

On the left-hand side of the square, facing the American Express office, is a cluster of smaller shops, notably Sermoneta at no. 61, which has an extraordinary selection of gloves.

Two streets enter the Piazza di Spagna on the American Express side of the square. One is called Via di Propaganda, and the other, running parallel to it, is **Via Due Macelli.** On the latter, at no. 68, is one of two Pineider stationers in Rome. On **Via di Propaganda** is Herzel, an offbeat leather-goods shop. At the corner of Via di Propaganda and Via della Mercede is the fine Italian furniture maker Poltrona Frau. At the end of Via Propaganda (the street has changed its name to Via di Sant'Andrea delle Fratte) is Nazareno Gabrielli, at no. 3, which has the full line of their exceptional leather goods.

DOWN VIA DEL CORSO

Via del Corso is the spine of this neighborhood and has hundreds of shops on it. The street runs from the Piazza del Popolo to the Piazza Venezia. Most of the stores on the roughly three-mile-long thoroughfare seem to be copies of one another: small, crammed with merchandise, and catering mostly to the teenage market—hence the blaring rock music coming from each storefront and the large crowds of kids that pack the street when school is out. They wander up and down the Corso, looking at the teen fashions and at each other. Naturally, not all the shops cater to the younger set, but so many do that the stores all seem to blend together after a while. Nonetheless, the Corso is definitely worth a stroll (avoid Saturday afternoon if you can, when the street is most crowded) if you are in the market for inexpensive casual wear.

Starting at the Piazza del Popolo end, you'll find inexpensive leather clothing for men and women at Alfieri, Via del Corso 2. There are lots of colorful, cheap shoes at Dominici, at no. 14. There are some good buys to be had on name-brand casual wear—mostly by Trussardi and Enrico Coveri—at Visconti, Via del Corso 25. Gazelle, at no. 30, has very inexpensive leather clothing.

There is a vast selection of shoes at I Cervone, Via del Corso 38. Lineasport, Via del Corso 49, has sportswear by Fila, Ellesse, Kappa, and Cerruti. Linealui, next door, has more big-name casuals—Fendi, Valentino, Ferré, Missoni—at very good prices.

The exception to the teen-type shops on Via del Corso is Schostal, Via del Corso 158. This old-fashioned haberdasher was founded before the nation of Italy was born, and has become the Brooks Brothers of Rome.

The other shop you should look at is the Rome branch of the single major department store chain in Italy, La Rinascente, at the corner of Via del Corso and Piazza Colonna.

These are just a few of the stores of Via del Corso—enough, I hope, to steer you toward or away from it, depending on your taste for cheap chic and your tolerance for crowds.

In the Neighborhood

There are three small side streets in the Triangle that should be explored. These are Via dei Greci and Via di San Giacomo, which run from Via del Babuino to Via del Corso; and Via dell'Oca, which is near Piazza del Popolo, off Via Ripetta.

On **Via dei Greci** is the adult department of the Naj Oleari line, at Via dei Greci 32. At no. 27 is A piu A, a new source of beautiful clothing for women. Off Via dei Greci in a little courtyard (the entrance is at no. 43) is Picone, which has casual clothes for women.

One block away on **Via di San Giacomo** you'll find an excellent furniture and design shop, Pitti, no. 39, and a fine men's shoe shop, Brugnoli, at no. 25. Also at no. 25 is the other Naj Oleari shop, this one featuring housewares and children's clothes. At no. 29 is Chiwawa, a store crammed to the rafters with Kappa sportswear for the whole family.

On **Via dell'Oca** is Soleiado, which has bags, fabrics, and objects from Provence, and Bomba de Clercq, which has lovely handmade Italian sweaters. Soleiado is at no. 38 and Bomba de Clercq at no. 39.

ABOVE THE SPANISH STEPS

This route takes in the last neighborhood in the area of the Piazza di Spagna. It's not actually inside the Triangle but is very close. The streets covered are Via Sistina, Via Vittorio Veneto, and Via Barberini.

The open-air book market in the Piazza Borghese

The walk begins at the very top of **Via Veneto,** at the Porta Pinciana. Via Veneto was once the most fashionable street in Rome, the center of *La Dolce Vita* of the 1950s where the rich, the famous, and the beautiful came to promenade and preen for the paparazzi. Today the street remains the home of some very high-ticket shopping, but the beautiful people have largely deserted the area.

With the old Roman wall to your back, head down Via Veneto on the left side of the street. The first shop of note is the tiny women's clothier Eliza, Via Veneto 157, which has some good buys on Valentino. Next, at Via Veneto 151 is a first-rate menswear shop, Lello Calia, followed closely by the first of three Raphael Salato leather-goods shops on Via Veneto. This is the largest and it's at no. 149.

Cross the street here and see the next Raphael Salato at no. 104. There is a Raphael Junior at no. 98. The largest Bruno Magli shoe store in the city is at Via Veneto 70, across the street from the American Embassy.

Cross the street again and walk past the embassy, heading along Via Bissolati. This street is a little on the uninteresting side—most of its length is given over to airline offices—but it does lead to the top of **Via Barberini,** and our next stop.

There is another Bruno Magli at Via Barberini 94. Continuing down the street toward the Piazza Barberini, you'll find a CIR lace shop at no. 88 and a Luisa Spagnoli right next door at no. 84.

Across the street, at Via Barberini 79, is the headquarters of the stylish men's tailor Brioni. Facing that is another fine menswear shop, Maurizio, at no. 72. Children with a taste for fashion can be accommodated at Leri, Via Barberini 48. At the end of the street is Cesari, Via Barberini 1, home of beautiful linens, lingerie, and beachwear.

You are now in Piazza Barberini. On the right side of the piazza is the beginning of **Via Sistina** which leads back to the Spanish Steps. The first address of note on that street is Herzel, Via Sistina 5, the sister store to the Herzel we saw on Via di Propaganda. There is more leather at Capodarte, Via Sistina 14A. Across the street at no. 119 is beautiful lingerie by Luisa Romagnoli at Tomassini. Near the intersection of Via Sistina and Via Capo le Case is another leatherworks, this one for boxes and bags, Ginocchi, at Via Sistina 35. On the corner is yet another high-quality leather-goods shop, Grispini.

Gattinoni, Via Sistina 44, is a good choice for women's fashions, as is Mario Fossi at no. 46. Fossi faces Piccadilly, a charming shop for children's clothes at Via Sistina 92. Next to it is Harper, Via Sistina 88, which has more clothes for women. A larger Harper faces it at no. 52. Still on that side of the street is an excellent menswear shop, Sistina Uomo, Via Sistina 58.

You have to cross the street again, this time to see beautiful leather goods at Roeckl, Via Sistina 83, and more clothes at Femme Sistina, at no. 75.

This brings you to the Hassler Hotel which stands at the top of the Spanish Steps. To your left is the beginning of Via Gregoriana, which is almost exclusively residential although true devotees might want to peek in at the very elegant headquarters of Valentino which stand a few doors down. It's not a shop, but for some people it might be the object of a pilgrimage.

A SIGHTSEEING SUGGESTION

In a sense the entire neighborhood is a cultural sight, given the age and beauty of the buildings and the grace of the Piazza di Spagna and the Spanish Steps. However, the greatest cultural center in the vicinity is the **National Gallery of Art** in the Palazzo Barberini.

The palace was built by Bernini and Borromini for the powerful Barberini family in the 17th century. The princes Barberini lived in the building until this century, when the Italian government bought it for use as a gallery.

The collection is large and varied, and includes a number of works by well-known artists. The most famous piece in the collection is undoubtedly Raphael's *La Fornarina,* the so-called "Baker's daughter," said to be a portrait of Raphael's mistress. Other prominent paintings include a horrifying *Judith and*

Holofernes by Caravaggio, Filippo Lippi's *Tarquinia Madonna*, and his *Annunciation*.

The Palazzo Barberini is open Tuesday through Saturday from 9 a.m. to 2 p.m., and on Sunday from 9 a.m. to 1 p.m. The collection is closed all day Monday. The palace is on Via della Quattro Fontane, a few steps from the Piazza Barberini.

REFRESHMENTS EN ROUTE
Bars

The neighborhood abounds in bars and cafés, but three are so famous they should be mentioned by name.

Caffè Greco, Via Condotti 86; open Monday through Saturday from 8 a.m. to 7:30 p.m. nonstop. This is said to be the oldest café in Rome, dating from the middle of the 17th century. Since it opened its doors the clientele in this elegant old establishment have included Goethe, Tennyson, Elizabeth Barrett Browning, Hans Christian Andersen, and, they say—but can't prove—Casanova. In the large backroom, with marble tables and plush banquettes, you'll be served excellent coffee, pastry, and homemade ice cream by waiters in wing collars and swallow-tail coats.

Babington's Tea Rooms, Piazza di Spagna 23; open Tuesday through Sunday for lunch only. Stepping out of the Piazza di Spagna and into Babington's is something of a shock. You leave Rome and enter a corner of England. Babington's was founded in the last century by the Misses Babington, who thought that English visitors to the city deserved to be served a good cup of tea after a long day of sightseeing. The tea rooms have hardly changed since then, though the clientele has. The English still come, but so do Italians who like the typically British atmosphere, the tea, and the huge selection of pastries and sweets.

Gran Caffè Doney, Via Veneto 141; closed Monday. When *La Dolce Vita* was at its height, Doney and its arch-rival across the street, Café de Paris, fought it out to see which watering hole could attract the most celebrities. It ended in a tie, but somehow Doney is the name people remember. You can take a rather expensive cappuccino at one of the comfortable sidewalk tables and watch the crowds go by on the Via Veneto—for people-watching, Doney is hard to beat.

Restaurants

Caffè Vittoria, Via Vittoria 3 (no phone); closed Sunday; credit cards not accepted. This intimate little restaurant is the perfect place for those who want a single-course lunch but don't want to eat standing up in a bar or hurried along in a fast-food place. Caffè Vittoria is a pretty restaurant with a lot of dark wood, quilted banquettes, and brass hardware. The food is good too, particularly the baked pastas and the filling sandwiches. Lunch for two with wine will cost about 25,000 lire.

Nino, Via Borgognona 11 (tel. 679-5676); closed Monday; no credit cards. This is one of the famous, perennially crowded restaurants in the area of the Spanish Steps. The food tends to be Tuscan, but there are some Roman dishes on the menu as well. The best first course is a hearty zuppa di fagioli, bean soup, but pasta lovers will appreciate the bucatini and penne. The best of the second courses are the lamb cutlets and deliciously light, fried artichokes. Dinner for two with house wine will cost about 80,000 lire.

Mario, Via della Vite 56 (tel. 678-3818); closed Sundays. Credit Cards: AE, DC, MC. Sometimes it seems as if Mario and Nino are in competition with one another. They are a few blocks apart, attract huge crowds, and both go in for predominantly Tuscan food. Each restaurant has its supporters and detractors. You should try the famous pappardelle alla Mario, wide, flat pasta in a meat sauce. The best of the second courses are the juicy steaks and the fine game, particularly the wild boar. As at Nino, dinner for two will cost around 80,000 lire.

Trattoria Scanderbeg al Piccolo Arancio, Vicolo Scanderbeg 112 (tel. 678-6139); closed Monday; reservations suggested. Credit Cards: AE, MC, V. Very close to the main shopping district, but not actually in it (but a three-minute walk from the Trevi Fountain) is Piccolo Arancio. You'll find this small, simple restaurant on a dark, quiet side street, and it's definitely worth hunting for. Piccolo Arancio is a relative newcomer to the Rome restaurant scene, but certainly a welcome one. It's hard to believe that so close to the Trevi Fountain there exists a restaurant as good and as inexpensive as this one—so many other places in the neighborhood have succumbed to the temptation to feed as many tourists as they can, with food as bad as they can get away with, with prices as high as the law allows. Piccolo Arancio has two small rooms simply decorated with whitewashed walls. There are a number of appealing pasta first courses, notably fuselli con melanzane, with chunks of eggplant lightly garlicked but very tasty; and spaghetti alla rughetta, spaghetti with rughetta, tomatoes mixed with a little hot red pepper. The second courses are equally well prepared. There is polpettone (a sort of Roman meatloaf) in a cream-and-basil sauce, an excellent steak bordelaise, and involtini di pollo, rolled chicken stuffed with prosciutto and cheese in a mushroom and white wine sauce. Desserts are all made on the premises and are ravishing, particularly the mousses: lemon, strawberry, and chocolate. Dinner for two with a good house wine is an inexpensive 45,000 lire to 50,000 lire.

VIA COLA DI RIENZO

Via Cola di Rienzo is a long, straight street which runs from the river to the Piazza Risorgimento, bordering the Vatican. The street begins at the river end, but as there is little in the first few blocks, it's wise to begin the walk at the Vatican end of the street. Furthermore, as Cola di Rienzo is a wide street that

ROME: GREAT SHOPPING STROLLS

carries a great deal of traffic so that it's inconvenient to cross back and forth along its length as we've done elsewhere, it's best to walk down one side and then back up the other to return to your starting point.

With your back to the Piazza Risorgimento and the looming bulk of the Vatican museums, take the right-hand side of the street first. The first shop of note is Dickinson at Via Cola di Rienzo 292, a large, good-value shoe store for men and women. Next comes Baci e Gioe ("Kisses and Jewels"), a tiny handmade-jewelry store, at no. 278.

At the corner of Via Varrone is a large children's clothier La Cicogna, Via Cola di Rienzo 264. At no. 250 is Jaqueline, which has a good selection of fashionable women's clothing. There is good name-brand menswear a few doors away at To You Uomo, Via Cola di Rienzo 242. You can shop for incredibly inexpensive footwear at Remi, Via Cola di Rienzo 230.

The selection of luggage and bags is nothing short of astonishing at no. 206, where you'll find Casagrande.

For a Roman, the best-known names on Via Cola di Rienzo are side by side. These are Franchi at no. 204 and Castroni at no. 196. Franchi is a tempting shop of prepared food and Castroni is the most elaborate coffee and specialty-food store in the city.

There are more inexpensive shoes at Gattegna Junior, Via Cola di Rienzo 178. La Calza, at no. 172, is packed with every kind of stocking imaginable. There are more shoes at Match, at no. 166. Prices go up a bit for footwear at Ferdin, Via Cola di Rienzo 154, but they come down again when you cross the street to no. 75 where you'll find Donèl.

Working your way back up the street, you pass Baby House, Via Cola di Rienzo 117, which has inexpensive clothing for kids. There are good prices on name-brand bags at Masliz, Via Cola di Rienzo 129. Menswear by Valentino and Trussardi is available at the elegant Manager store, and name-brand sportswear for the entire family at Iraci Sport, Via Cola di Rienzo 147.

It's back to shoes for not much money at Ramirez, Via Cola di Rienzo 151.

Men should make a short detour off Via Cola di Rienzo to inspect Uomo In. This is a huge store with lots of designer clothing. It's on **Via Attilio Regolo** at no. 15. The street intersects with Via Cola di Rienzo.

Returning to Via Cola di Rienzo, there's a nice Stefanel at no. 191, followed by a giant Richard-Ginori china store at Via Cola di Rienzo 221. Bruno Magli is at no. 237.

The last shop of note on the street is Celleno. It appears to be on Via Cola di Rienzo, but its address is actually Piazza dell'Unità 49. This is a menswear shop with great prices on great names like Armani and Missoni, to mention just two.

A SIGHTSEEING SUGGESTION

This listing is not so much a cultural attraction as a cultural overdose. A few blocks away from Piazza Risorgimento is the entrance to the **Vatican museums**.

There are miles of galleries in the museum, and as the finest cultural guide to the city, Georgina Masson's *The Companion Guide to Rome*, suggests, it's unwise to try and tackle all of it in a single visit. The result of such folly, says Miss Masson, is "mental indigestion and physical exhaustion."

It's almost impossible to catalog the splendors of this amazing collection, but a highlight (if not *the* highlight) is the Sistine Chapel. This is slowly undergoing restoration—about half has been completed—and the effects are amazing. Detractors of the project say that it's the greatest act of vandalism in the history of art. Supporters of the cleaning maintain that the finest piece of Renaissance painting we have is at last being seen as it should be.

As the hundreds of years' accumulation of dirt and candle soot come off the ceiling, Michelangelo scholars are having to revise their theories on the master. It was thought that Michelangelo's genius lay in his use and development of form to the relative exclusion of color. As his fresco is cleaned, it reveals that he was a master colorist as well. This is all very learned debate; for the layman, the point is that now you can see the ceiling clearly and in detail. Even if you visited the chapel the last time you were in Rome, you should see it again. You'll be surprised!

The Vatican museums are open weekdays from 9 a.m. to 2 p.m. During Easter week and from July 1 to September 30 they are open weekdays from 9 a.m. to 5 p.m. and on Saturday to 2 p.m. The entrance fee is 7,000 lire.

REFRESHMENTS EN ROUTE

Bars

Both **Franchi** and **Castroni,** mentioned in the strolls, have standup bars where you can get something to drink and eat. Castroni is famous for its coffee, so that's the place to have a cappuccino. Franchi does not serve coffee, but it has delicious snacks and pizza by the slice, which go well with a soft drink or something stronger. Both establishments are open from 9 a.m. to 7:30 p.m. nonstop. Both are closed on Thursday afternoon.

Restaurants

Dining is a little tough in this neighborhood as many of the restaurateurs are used to dealing with the tourists who visit the Vatican. The proprietors figure they'll never see the visitors again, so what's the point of exerting oneself? Sad, but true. There are exceptions, of course.

Il Matriciano, Via dei Gracchi 55 (tel. 359-5247); closed Wednesday. Credit Cards: AE. This is a good trattoria situated on a street which runs parallel to Via Cola di Rienzo. Given the name, one would expect the bucatini alla matriciana to be good and it is, as is the spaghetti carbonara. A well-recommended second course is stufatino, a hearty beef stew, as well as straccetti ("little rags"), paper-thin slices of beef that have been sautéed in a white wine sauce. A meal for two should cost about 60,000 lire.

THE HEART OF OLD ROME

This long stroll takes us through the core of the picturesque part of the city, the areas around the Campo dei Fiori and the Piazza Navona. As two of the major streets covered here, Via dei Coronari and Via Giulia, deal exclusively with antiques, those not intersted in antiques should skip to the end of the trip where you'll find a section on the bargain-basement clothes-shopping street, Via dei Giubbonari.

The stroll begins at the end of **Via dei Coronari,** at the corner of Via dei Coronari and Via Zanardelli. This is at the far end of the Piazza Navona. This very old street was once the home to the makers of rosaries, but now it is the preeminent street for antiques in the city. A lot of the shops situated here sell exclusively English antiques—at prices much higher than in England—so they have been excluded.

At Metastasio Casa D'Arte, Via dei Coronari 33, 18th-century Italian furniture and paintings abound. There are more antiques, these a little newer, at Studio Interni, Via dei Coronari 40.

There's a brief time out from antiques at no. 55. Here you'll find modern china and porcelain in every shape and variety at La Porcellana Bianca. Every piece has something in common—every item in the shop is white.

Il Cenacolo, Via dei Coronari 187, is on your right set in the ground floor of the Palazzo Lancellotti. Here you'll find Italian pictures, furniture, and ceramics of the 16th and 17th centuries. Also at no. 187 is Studio C&T, which has Italian objects and paintings from the 16th century to the neoclassical period. La Chiocciola, Via dei Coronari 185, has 18th- and 19th-century furniture of great quality.

Galleria Coronari, at no. 59, has lovely furniture and paintings. Lo Scrittoio, Via dei Coronari 103, specializes in desks from the 17th to the 19th centuries. Antique lace, with special pieces from Burano, Fagagna, and Cantu, is found at Quel Quelcosa, Via dei Coronari 110. The street closes with beautiful prints at Chiambrelli, Via dei Coronari 144.

You must now cross the busy Corso Vittorio Emanuele, a couple of blocks from Via dei Coronari, and make your way to the Piazza D'Oro, a small square dominated by the giant church of San Giovanni dei Fiorentini. This places you at the head of the long, wide, rather grand street, **Via Giulia.** The street itself was laid out and named for Pope Julius II, the great patron of Michelangelo. Along its length are some fine antique shops, but very little else.

Proceeding down the street toward the giant Palazzo Farnese at the far end, the first of many galleries you encounter is Galleria Romana, Via Giulia 81. Neoclassic objects and paintings are the specialties here.

There are good 17th- and 18th-century paintings at Piccirilli Antichita, Via Giulia 103. Then comes the elegant little shop Liberty Deco, Via Giulia 107, which, as its name suggests, specializes in objects of this century, right up to the 1950s. A very beautiful antique shop, La Chimera, is at no. 122.

Galleria Giulia, at no. 148, is another elegant source of 17th-century and

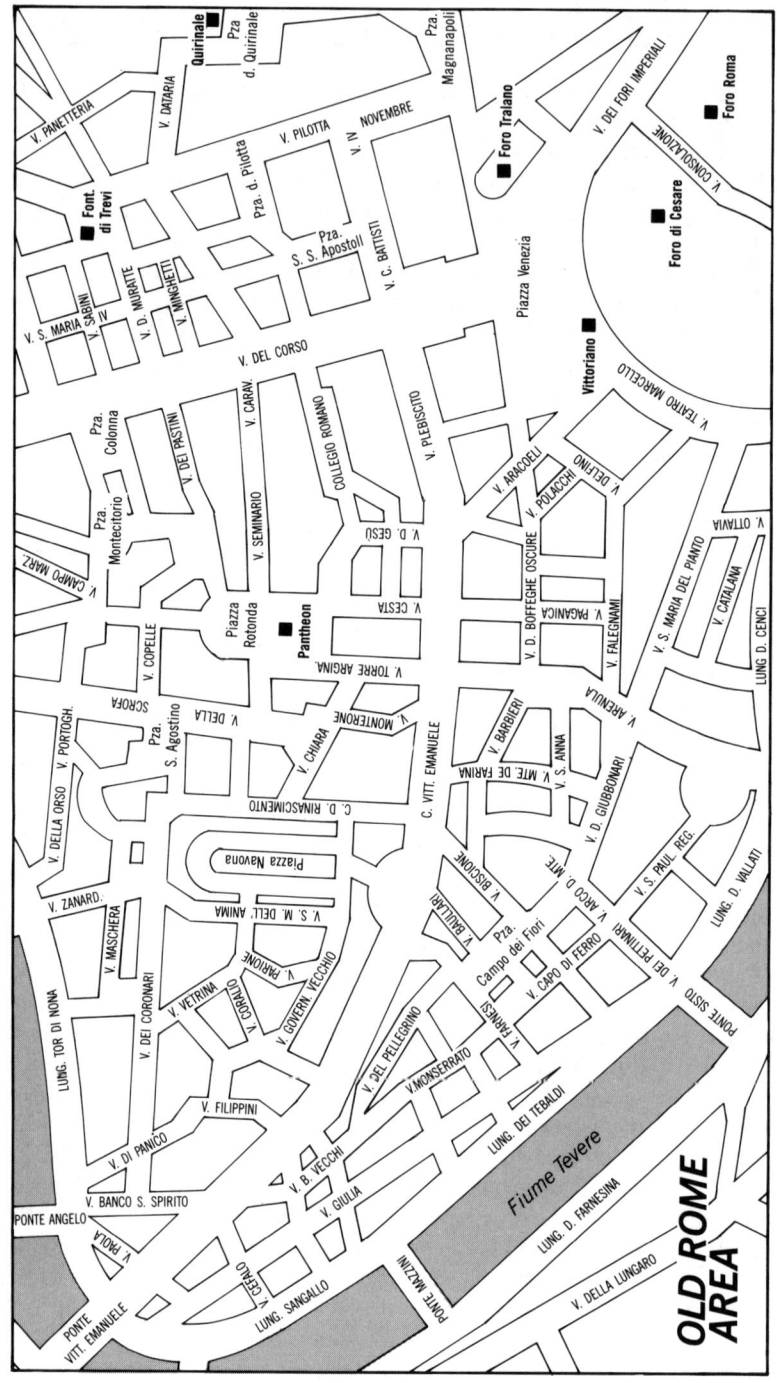

ROME: GREAT SHOPPING STROLLS

neoclassical works of art. Also on the left side of the street is Davoli Antichita, where there are paintings, watercolors, bronzes, and furniture from the 17th to 20th centuries. It's at no. 168, at the corner of Via in Caterina.

At Monetti, Via Giulia 169, you'll find Empire and Biedermeier furniture, as well as paintings and objects exclusively from the 19th century.

At the arch of the Palazzo Farnese is Galleria Antiquaria dell'Arco, which has furniture of the last three centuries. Finally comes La Pinacoteca di Via Giulia, no. 188, which has nothing but Italian paintings of the 19th century.

Crossing the Piazza Farnese, in the far left-hand corner of the square (with the palazzo behind you), you'll come to a narrow street called Vicolo del Gallo. Follow this street until you reach the Campo dei Fiori. Here make a sharp left into **Via Cappellari,** a small, dark street which seems to have nothing of interest on it. Walk down a block or so and you'll come to the first of many secondhand furniture and odds-and-ends shops. They line the street, dark, furniture-filled caves with the carpenters working out in the narrow street itself refinishing or "restoring" pieces which range from gems to junk. None of the shops appears to have a name and you probably won't be given a receipt for any purchases.

In the main these shops sell furniture—there are giant oak refectory tables or small side tables—and items can be as new as the 1950s or as old as the 1500s. Bargaining is the name of the game, and for an extra fee the seller will deliver your purchase—but only within Rome. After that, it's your problem.

The shops themselves stretch far back into the workshops, and while the workmen are not the most inviting folk in the world, they know that if you can't see the merchandise, you aren't going to buy anything. So burrow far back into the shops—they don't mind—and see what you can find. Prices are so low that even including the cost of transportation it just might be worth buying a big piece of Italian country furniture here and shipping it home.

There is one thing to note: Italians are not as fond of blond wood with a light layer of varnish or linseed oil as Americans are. It's not uncommon for the workers on the Via Cappellari to slop a heavy covering of dark-brown varnish on unfinished pieces. If you don't want that, insist that the piece be left *"senza vernice."*

Returning to the Campo dei Fiori, we come to one of Rome's most colorful squares, home to a wonderful food market every morning except Sunday. Behind the statue of Giordano Bruno (a heretic burnt on that spot in the 16th century) is a movie theater. To the right of that, as you face the theater, is the beginning of the last street in this stroll, **Via dei Giubbonari.**

You'll see immediately that you've left the *alta classe* world of the Via Condotti far behind. Rock music blares from almost every doorway and the clientele is young.

The first shop of note you come to is Robin, Via dei Giubbonari 48, a fanciful and original shoe shop for young men. Facing it is Pin Up, at no. 78, which has trendy casual wear for young women. Next comes an inexpensive shop for menswear, Momento, at no. 92. Innsport, Via dei Giubbonari 99, has every name in every kind of sportswear for every member of the family.

Across the street is Xavier, Via dei Giubbonari 26, which has inexpensive casual wear for women. On the left-hand side of the street is a similar shop for men, James, at no. 107.

At this point on the street, at no. 30, is Books on Italy, selling works on Italian history and art, in English. The incredibly knowledgeable management will search for specific rare or out-of-print titles. It's open by appointment only.

The last shop of note is at the end of Via dei Giubbonari where it widens into the Piazza Benedetto Cairoli. There, at no. 7, is Tagliacozzo, a giant and quite old-fashioned haberdasher catering to the entire family at wholesale (almost) prices.

IN THE NEIGHBORHOOD

In every part of this walk we have passed near shops that should be seen.

In the neighborhood of the beginning of the stroll is **Via Pianellari,** where at no. 17 you'll find Mondo Antico, a fascinating shop filled with old paper puppets and dolls, as well as scenes of old Rome, carefully painted and mounted in boxes like stage sets. Nearby, on **Via Ripetta** at no. 148 is Forma e Memoria, perhaps the most interesting of the modern Italian design shops in Rome. Not far away on **Via della Scrofa,** at no. 7A, is the other Pineider stationery in the city.

Closer to the Piazza Navona, on **Via Santa Maria dell'Anima,** a street running parallel to the square, is L'Oriuolo, no. 40, an antique shop which specializes in late-19th- and early-20th-century gadgets and the like.

Near Via Giulia is **Via dei Banchi Vecchi,** where at no. 29 is La Gazza Ladra, a tiny antiques shop specializing in walking sticks.

Very close to the end of Via dei Giubbonari, on **Via dei Barberi,** a narrow side street, is Spazio Sette, at no. 7, one of the most exquisite sources of Italian furniture and Italian-designed objects in the city.

On the far side of the Largo Argentina (the nearest major landmark to Spazio Sette) you'll find **Via del Gesù.** On Via del Gesù is Carlo Bises & Figli, Rome's finest fabric shop, located amid the splendor of the Palazzo Altieri. It's at Via del Gesù 93.

REFRESHMENTS EN ROUTE
Bars

Bar La Pace, Piazza della Pace 2 (no phone); closed Monday. This is a lovely old bar set in a small piazza near the Piazza Navona. The dark interior with its single classical pillar, old dark-wood bar, and a dozen marble-top tables is a cozy place to sit on a winter day and have a cappuccino. In the summertime the shaded outdoor tables are a perfect place to sip a cold drink and rest from your shopping rounds. Bar la Pace does not serve any kind of food, but their fruit drinks and coffees are excellent. Beer, mixed drinks, and wine are available as well.

ROME: GREAT SHOPPING STROLLS

Gelateria Da Quinto, Via Tor Millina 15 (no phone); closed Monday. A stone's throw from the Piazza Navona and the famous, overpriced gelaterias you'll find there, Da Quinto is a single whitewashed room serving some of the finest ice cream in the city. Romans know Quintos' product to be superior to the places in the Piazza Navona and they patronize it so regularly that Quinto makes enough money in the summer months to allow him to close in the winter—the gelateria is only open from Easter to October. The ice cream, needless to say, is superb, and of course, homemade. All the flavors are good, but the standouts are pistacchio, melone, and plain old vanilla (which is called "crema" in Italian). There are no tables—all business is strictly take-away. But you can get a cone and sit in the Piazza Navona and watch the tourists at the elegant cafés being overcharged.

Restaurants

Pino e Dino, Piazza di Montevecchio 22 (tel. 656-1319); closed Monday; credit cards not accepted. Dining al fresco on a warm summer night at Pino e Dino is perhaps the most romantic experience you can have meal-wise in Rome. The resetaurant is set in a tiny, quiet square where the buildings enclosing it are draped with ivy—the noise and traffic of Rome seem miles away. Then there's the food. The pheasant savoiarda is delectable, as is the pasta in a black truffle sauce Veronese. Once in a while Pino e Dino serve peacock, but if it's not on the menu the night you happen to be there you'll still manage to eat well. The elegance and variety of the menu do not come cheap. Dinner for two with a good wine will cost 200,000 lire.

Osteria Ar Galletto, Vicolo del Gallo 1, on a corner of the Piazza Farnese (tel. 656-1714); closed Sunday; credit cards not accepted. If you're lucky enough to get a table outside in the summer, you can dine well and look at the façade of the Palazzo Farnese at the same time. Galletto is a family-run restaurant—mama cooks, papa oversees, and the boys wait tables—and a very happy family they seem to be too. Begin your meal with some of the finest prosciutto crudo in the city, or have a hearty bucatini alla matriciana. If you're in luck the cook has prepared a limited number of crêpes for a first course. These are deliciously light, stuffed with prosciutto and mushrooms and covered in a béchamel sauce. The best of the second courses are a fine steak, fileto di bue, saltimbocca, and ossobuco. In season the best dessert is tiny wild strawberries, fragole di bosco, with homemade ice cream. Dinner for two with a house wine runs about 75,000 lire to 85,000 lire.

VIA NAZIONALE

No one can say that the Via Nazionale is a street of any appreciable charm—it strongly resembles Via del Corso and Via Cola di Rienzo—but it does have some good shops selling clothes at good prices.

The stroll begins at the large, circular piazza called Piazza della Repubblica (which real Romans call "Piazza della Esedra") and continues straight down the street to about its midpoint where you'll find the Bank of Italy. Beyond that the stores thin out.

The first name of note is Fiorucci, Via Nazionale 236A. Across the street from that is a large, well-stocked Benetton, at Via Nazionale 17. Back on the Fiorucci side of the street is a great bag and leather-goods shop, Regal, at no. 234. Next door, at no. 233, is Box, a hip shop for modern fashions. Puer, Via Nazionale 231, is more upscale in its clothing. Stefanel, at no. 227, is the stop for more Benetton-ish casuals and knits.

Crossing the street, you come to Prada, at Via Nazionale 30, which has beautiful clothes and leather goods for women for less than you'd pay at their Milan shops, although the selection is smaller. On the same side of the street there's Ellesse for everybody at Tamar, Via Nazionale 33. Firenze Riclama, Via Nazionale 36, is a tiny shop selling beautiful lingerie and lace.

Prada: Milan fashions at lower prices

Recrossing the street you come to Odette, Via Nazionale 224, which has a ton of leather clothing for men and women. Pon Pon, next door at no. 222, has an immense collection of costume jewelry.

Crossing the street for the last time, we come to two shops that sell designer names at less than designer prices. Osé, Via Nazionale 68, has clothes by Byblos and Fendi, and Sabry, right next door at no. 70, has Krizia Poi, the Titolo line by Basile, and Laura Biagiotti.

The last stop on the street is Frette, home of beautiful linens and lingerie. It's at Via Nazionale 84.

IN THE NEIGHBORHOOD

This is a scoop. After careful research and a great deal of wandering the streets, the only Loehmann's-style discount house in Rome has been found. A few hundred yards off Via Nazionale on **Via Napoli,** you'll find Discount System. This barn of a place has clothing and accessories, by every major designer, marked down to at least 50% of their normal price.

The shop is on Via Napoli, but the entrance is on Via Viminale 1 at no. 35.

A SIGHTSEEING SUGGESTION

The **Baths of Diocletian / Museo Nazionale Romano.** This vast museum, housed in the ruins of the Roman Baths of Diocletian, has some of the most famous works of antique sculpture in the world. The gem of the collection is the Ludovisi Throne, with the famous birth of Aphrodite depicted on the front. The museum also possesses the delightful frescoes that once decorated the House of Livia (Augustus's scheming wife, if "Masterpiece Theater" is to be believed) on the Palatine Hill. The soaring, majestic **Santa Maria degli Angeli** church, a masterpiece by Michelangelo, adjoins the museum.

The quiet of the church and the graceful poses of the ancient statuary make this a very peaceful place to wind down after the hurly-burly of the Via Nazionale.

The museum and the church are open Tuesday through Saturday from 9 a.m. to 1:45 p.m., on Sunday from 9 a.m. to 12:45 p.m. (closed Monday). You'll find the main entrance to both in the Piazza della Repubblica.

REFRESHMENTS EN ROUTE

On a little side street off the Via Nazionale you'll find two restaurants which represent both ends of the economic scale: one is extremely cheap, the other is extremely expensive. Both are good.

Frascati, Via del Boschetto 28 (no phone); closed Sunday. Credit Cards: None. No reservations required. Once upon a time, you could find restaurants like this on every corner in Rome: cheap and unpretentious, serving good food to the neighborhood regulars. Alas, this type of place becomes more and more rare with the passing of every year. However, Frascati is thriving. The first courses are the traditional Roman pastas: *penne all'arrabiata, fettuccine con buro e sugo, spaghetti carbonara,* and *bucatini all'amatriciana.* All are good, with the exception of the carbonara, which can be a bit dry. The best of the second courses are a delicious, moist roast veal with roast potatoes, *trippa alla Romana* (Saturday nights only), and baby lamb chops roasted with rosemary. Have fresh fruit as a dessert and drink the good house white wine. Dinner for two should cost no more than 25,000 to 30,000 lire.

Ristorante Bonne Nouvelle, Via del Boschetto 73 (tel. 486-781); closed Sunday. Credit Cards: AE, DC. Bonne Nouvelle (I'm sure you don't have to be reminded) is French for "good news," and this beautiful new restaurant is certainly good news for Rome's beautiful people. They leave their Ferraris and Bentleys in the narrow street outside and then dine well and in great luxury at this chic new place. Fish is the specialty here, either as a first or as a second course. Two prime selections are bavette con scampi, flat spaghetti in a shrimp-and-cream sauce, and risotto alla pescatora, rice in a fish sauce. The best second course is the perfectly grilled "catch of the day," notably the spigola, a sea bass.

CHAPTER XV

The Ultimate Rome Shopping Spree

Whether Rome is your first, last, or only stop in Italy, you are bound to find something in the Eternal City you'll want to buy. Emperors, kings, queens, cardinals, princes, English milords, movie stars, and oil sheiks have not yet managed to strip the city of its treasures. There's plenty for everyone — you only have to know where to look.

ANTIQUES

ARMANDO PERERA
Via del Babuino 118 (tel. 679-2069)
Metro Stop: *Spagna*
Hours: *Monday through Saturday from 10 a.m. to 1 p.m. and 4 to 7:30 p.m. (closed Monday morning)*
Credit Cards: *None*

This cluttered, dusty old shop in the heart of the major shopping district is a marvelous place to browse for smaller, offbeat Italian antiques, objets d'art, prints, drawings, and books. Since 1911 the Perera family has been dealing in bric-a-brac, and the present *professore*, who watches over his shop from a desk at the back of the store, is a storehouse of information on every item. Prices are reasonable. Good 18th- and 19th-century prints can cost as little as 15,000 lire; more unusual items, like a reliquary devoted to San Vitale, all gilded baroque filligree and scrollwork, is 250,000 lire.

DAVOLI
Via Giulia 168 (tel. 655-0097)
Hours: *Monday through Saturday from 10 a.m. to 1 p.m. and 4:30 to 7:30 p.m. (closed Monday morning)*
Credit Cards: *None*
English Spoken.

Davoli is a small, elegant shop where, unlike other, grander antiques houses on Via Giulia, you are encouraged to take your time and browse. Specialties here range from the 17th to the 20th century, with an accent on objets d'art, particularly 18th-century bronzes, and paintings (especially watercolors); there is some Italian furniture of the 18th and 19th centuries.

GALLERIA ANTIQUARIO DELL'ARCO
Via Giulia 178 (tel. 654-1520)
Hours: Monday through Saturday from 10 a.m. to 1 p.m. and 4 to 7 p.m. (closed Monday morning)
Credit Cards: None
English Spoken.

This is another of the smaller galleries on Via Giulia. There is some 18th-century Italian furniture, but the real standouts are the small jewelry pieces of the 18th and 19th centuries. A brooch from the middle 1700s in garnets and amethyst is 2.4 million lire.

GALLERIA CORONARI
Via dei Coronari 59 (tel. 656-9917)
Hours: Monday through Saturday from 10 a.m. to 1:30 p.m. and 4:30 to 7:30 p.m. (closed Monday morning)
Credit Cards: AE, DC, V
English Spoken.

This is one of the most delightful antique shops on the entire Via dei Coronari. It's a single small room packed with bric-a-brac, mechanical toys, antique dolls, porcelain, and jewelry, as well as some 19th-century furniture and clocks. Galleria Coronari is the perfect place to pick up an antique trinket small enough to fit into your carry-on luggage. Prices vary. A tiny, but elegantly worked silver-and-enamel picture frame, dating from the 1810s or early 1820s, is 45,000 lire. Silver ex-voti of Italian soldiers (purchased by mothers who wanted to keep their boys safe in the Ethiopian war of the 1880s) are rare but a good price at 75,000 lire. Porcelain dolls of the 19th century that look like figures from *Little Women* are 450,000 lire and up, depending on size and condition. A complete dollhouse from the turn of the century is 300,000 lire.

GALLERIA ROMANA
Via Giulia 81 (tel. 654-1447)
Hours: Monday through Saturday from 10 a.m. to 1 p.m. and 4 to 7:30 p.m. (closed Monday morning)
Credit Cards: None
English Spoken.

Galleria Romana consists of two very plush rooms—lush red walls, deep-scarlet carpeting—containing some exceptional pieces of neoclassical furniture, objects, and paintings. There are enormous burled-walnut credenzas and plinths supporting marble busts of Imperial Roman notables dating from the 18th century. There are some particularly fine clocks of the same period, including an exquisite Grecian clock in ebony with a porcelain face at 1.4 million lire, and small pieces of furniture—a tapestry-covered chair, for example, is 1.8 million lire. A full set of tapestry-covered furniture, including side chairs, armchairs, and settee, would cost in the 25-million-lire range.

IL CENACOLO
Via dei Coronari 187 (tel. 654-2260)
Hours: Monday through Saturday from 9:30 a.m. to 1:30 p.m. and
   4 to 7 p.m. (closed Monday morning)
Credit Cards: AE
English Spoken.

Housed on the ground floor of the late-16th century Palazzo Lancellotti, Il Cenacolo sells antiques that match its architecture. Most of the pictures, furniture, sculpture, and ceramics are 16th-century Italian and are of very good quality. A set of gilded wooden candelabra from the middle 1500s is 1.3 million lire. Ceramics from the same era in good condition are expensive: a delicately painted ewer is 5.25 million lire.

IMPIANTI ELETTRICCI
Via della Carozze 17A (no phone)
Hours: Monday through Saturday from 10 a.m. to 1:30 p.m. and
   4:30 to 8 p.m. (closed Monday morning)
Credit Cards: None

This is more a museum devoted to 20th-century technology than an antique shop. Here, in a single crowded room, you'll find early-20th-century gadgets like "Vitaphones" (the wax-cylinder-playing forerunner of the record player), typewriters manufactured before the invention of the standard keyboard, and of course, the big horn-type record player the RCA dog (whose name was Nipper, by the way) was always staring into while trying to find his master's voice. While you might not have planned on taking a 1930s Bakelite radio (875,000 lire) or a giant gun-metal-gray dictaphone (1.2 million lire) home as a souvenir of Italy, it's fun to browse here.

LA CHIOCCIOLA
Via dei Coronari 185 (tel. 654-1954)
Hours: Monday through Saturday from 10 a.m. to 1 p.m. and
   4 to 7:30 p.m. (closed Monday morning)
Credit Cards: None

If inlaid furniture and marquetry are to your particular taste, you'll find an abundance of it here—some of it new, most of it antique. There are inlaid pieces running from the small—an end table, for example—to an eight-foot-tall secretary desk with room for half a library of books on its upper shelves.

LA CHIMERA
Via Giulia 122 (tel. 654-8354)
Hours: Monday through Saturday from 10 a.m. to 1:30 p.m. and 4:30 to 8 p.m. (closed Monday morning)
Credit Cards: AE
English Spoken.

This is one of the most elegant antique shops on Via Giulia. In two small rooms you'll find fine Empire and neoclassical furniture and objects, particularly marble portrait busts and desks. Furniture prices begin at about 2 million lire for a small side table and rocket up from there.

LA PINACOTECA DI VIA GIULIA
Via Giulia 188 (tel. 656-4291)
Hours: Monday through Saturday from 10 a.m. to 1:30 p.m. and 4 to 8 p.m. (closed Monday morning)
Credit Cards: None
English Spoken.

La Pinacoteca deals exclusively in 19th-century Italian paintings, ranging from small pastoral landscapes to portraits of Roman grandees long dead. You'd have to have a fairly specialized knowledge of 19th-century Italian painting to know what you're doing here as the best-known Italian school of the 19th century, the Macchiaioli, are not exactly household names. The proprietor of the shop, however, has a genuine love for the subject and a profound knowledge of the era, and is sure to steer you toward a good Giovanni Fantoni (the leader of the Macchiaioli), or fellow travelers like Tranquillo Cremona and Guiseppe de Nittis. Prices begin in the low millions for the lesser names and rise quickly to great heights for the better works by the masters.

LIBERTY DECÒ
Via Giulia 107 (tel. 654-2204)
Hours: Monday through Saturday from 10 a.m. to 1:30 p.m. and 4:30 to 8 p.m. (closed Monday morning)
Credit Cards: AE
English Spoken.

Although the accent here is on art deco styles, you'll also find lamps and glassware dating from the turn of the century to as recently as the 1950s. The furniture is almost exclusively from the '20s, the bulk of it Italian, but some

French as well. A beautiful art deco eight-drawer desk in walnut is 3 million lire; the perfect deco lamp to go with it is 950,000 lire.

L'ORIUOLO
Via di Santa Maria dell'Anima 40 (tel. 687-7105)
Hours: *Monday through Saturday from 10:30 a.m. to 1 p.m. and 4 to 8 p.m. (closed Monday morning)*
Credit Cards: AE, DC
English Spoken.

This is a great little shop just one block from the Piazza Navona. The tiny store is jammed with old cameras, musical instruments, telescopes, and radios, as well as heaps of antique costume jewelry. A strand of fake pearls, long enough to make a flapper happy, is just 35,000 lire. A bellows camera from around the time of World War I is 1.4 million lire. A pair of cufflinks with little pictures of ocean liners on them costs 20,000 lire.

L'Oriuolo always has delightful surprises in store

LO SCRITOIO
Via dei Coronari 103 (tel. 687-5536)
Hours: *Monday through Saturday from 10 a.m. to 1 p.m. and 4 to 7:30 p.m. (closed Monday morning)*

Credit Cards: *None*
English Spoken.

Lo Scritoio specializes in desks of all shapes, sizes, and ages, up to the early part of this century. Some are huge, and office type; others are small, delicate knee-hole escritoires. All are in perfect condition. Prices range from 4.5 million lire for a 19th-century partners desk to many millions more for an 18th-century Empire secretary.

METASTASIO CASA D'ARTE
Via dei Coronari 33 (tel. 657-667)
Hours: Monday through Saturday from 10 a.m. to 1 p.m. and
  4:30 to 7:30 p.m. (closed Monday morning)
Credit Cards: *None*
English Spoken.

This beautiful store, with arches and a beamed ceiling, sells some of the finest 18th-century Italian and French furniture on Via dei Coronari. All pieces are in perfect condition, some unrestored, others skillfully worked. There is a nautical accent to the items for sale here—marine paintings and prints are the major art objects—so sea chests and brass-edged galley tables are items of particular interest.

MONETTI
Via Giulia 169 (tel. 687-7436)

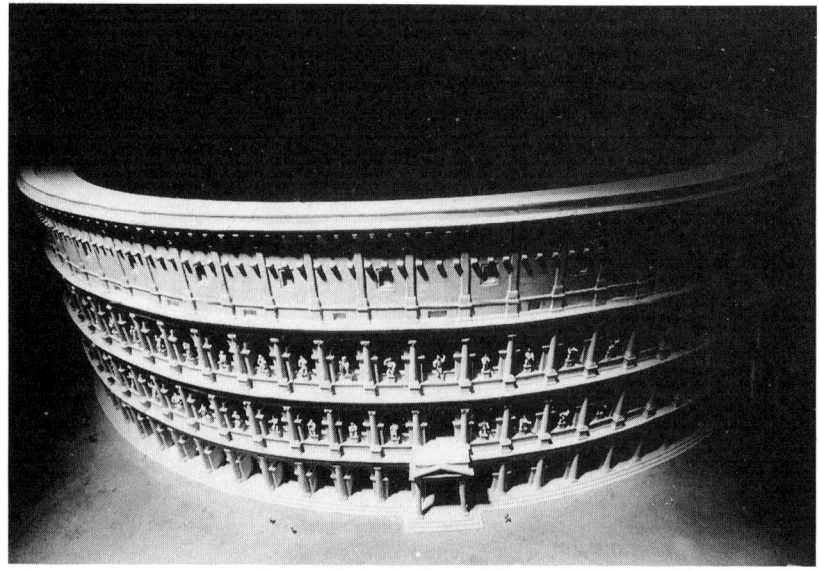

Monetti's architectural models make classic buildings look new

Hours: *Monday through Saturday from 10 a.m. to 1:30 p.m. and 4:30 to 8 p.m. (closed Monday morning)*
Credit Cards: *None*
English Spoken.

Monetti is a small, elegant shop which stocks 18th- and 19th-century Italian paintings as well as prime examples of Empire and Biedermeier furniture and objects. A Biedermeier chest in walnut is 7.5 million lire.

1900
Via Vittoria 37 (tel. 678-9465)
Hours: *Monday through Saturday from 9:30 a.m. to 1:30 p.m. and 4:30 to 7:30 p.m. (closed Monday morning)*
Credit Cards: *AE, DC*
English Spoken.

In the heart of "fashion" Rome, 1900 specializes in art nouveau and art deco furniture and objects. They are crammed into one small room, but each piece is in mint condition and prices are high. A very simple art nouveau hatstand is 1 million lire and more elaborate pieces, like a wild art deco dressing table with inlays, is 4.5 million lire. The staff is accommodating, however, and certainly know their subject.

PICCINILLI ANTICHITA
Via Giulia 103 (tel. 656-4088)
Hours: *Monday through Saturday from 10 a.m. to 1:30 p.m. and 4 to 8 p.m. (closed Monday morning)*
Credit Cards: *None*
English Spoken.

Piccinilli is a tiny, elegant gallery dedicated mostly to antique silver, the bulk of it Italian and French dating from the 18th and 19th centuries.

QUEL QUELCOSA
Via dei Coronari 110 (tel. 687-5358)
Hours: *Monday through Saturday from 10 a.m. to 1:30 p.m. and 4 to 8 p.m. (closed Monday morning)*
Credit Cards: *AE, DC*
English Spoken.

Quel Quelcosa is a tiny, ornate shop, stuffed with all manner of curiosities, including a good deal of antique lace, notably Burano, Cantu, and Fagagna: tablecloths, sheets, curtains, and veils. Some of the items, like the sheets, are new lace, not antique. Prices on antique lace are about the same here as they are in Venice. In addition, there are things like complete dinner services from the '20s (800,000 lire) and some mechanical toys.

Quel Quelcosa sells lovely lace, toys, and bric-a-brac

SOLIGO
Via del Babuino 161 (tel. 361-4158)
Hours: Monday through Saturday from 10 a.m. to 1:30 p.m. and 4 to 8 p.m. (closed Monday morning)
Credit Cards: AE, DC, MC, V
English Spoken.

Soligo is packed to the rafters with all kinds of military antiques from every era and country. Here you can buy a small five-pounder fieldpiece from the Franco-Prussian War (it would be interesting to see how Customs reacts), sabers, and dueling pistols of the last 200 years, as well as hundreds of uniforms, prints, and portraits of military men. The management is a bit standoffish with unknowledgeable amateurs, but those who know their weapons and history will be at home here. A simple print from the Boer War of the Battle of Spion Kop is 285,000 lire. The weapons cost many millions, depending on degree of ornament, historical significance, and condition.

STUDIO C&T
Via dei Coronari 187 (tel. 654-2260)
Hours: Monday through Saturday from 10 a.m. to 1:30 p.m. and 4 to 8 p.m. (closed Monday morning)
Credit Cards: None
English Spoken.

ROME SHOPS: ANTIQUES/ART GALLERIES

This is another large shop on the Via dei Coronari devoted to Italian paintings and objects from the 16th through the 19th centuries. Of particular interest are the religious pieces. A polychrome figure of a saint, about half life-size and in very good condition, costs 6 million lire. An early-19th-century silver crucifix is 450,000 lire.

STUDIO INTERNI
Via dei Coronari 40 (tel. 689-7858)
Hours: Monday through Saturday from 10 a.m. to 1:30 p.m. and 4 to 8 p.m. (closed Monday morning)
Credit Cards: AE, DC
English Spoken.

In four carpeted rooms you'll find large, overpolished pieces of Empire and late-19th-century furniture, much of it English. There is also some Italian silver and glass from the 18th century.

ART GALLERIES

Rome has largely conceded its position as modern art capital of Italy to Milan. However, there are a number of galleries here that merit a look for those interested in the contemporary Italian art scene.

GALLERIA GIULIA
Via Giulia 148 (tel. 654-2061)
Hours: Monday through Saturday from 10 a.m. to 1:30 p.m. and 4 to 8 p.m.
Credit Cards: None
English Spoken.

This is perhaps the most prestigious gallery in the city, and shows the top names in Italian art as well as artists of great stature from the United States and Europe.

IL GABBIANO
Via Frezza 18 (tel. 679-5720)
Hours: Monday through Saturday from 10 a.m. to 1:30 p.m. and 4 to 8 p.m. (closed Monday morning)
Credit Cards: None
English Spoken.

A lovely gallery showing Italian and foreign artists. Works on display are almost exclusively figurative, and among the great names that exhibit here regularly are Balthus, Botero, and Giorgio Morandi. Il Gabbiano is also the Rome gallery to the American painter William Bailey and the brilliant Italian representational painter Tommasi Ferroni.

IL NARCISO
Via Alibert 25 *(tel. 679-7317)*
Hours: *Tuesday through Saturday from 10:15 a.m. to 12:45 p.m. and 5 to 8 p.m.*
Credit Cards: *None*
English Spoken.

A small gallery just off the Via del Babuino, Il Narciso has a slightly offbeat reputation, showing such artists as Gustavo Foppiani and Renato Guttuso.

IL PONTE
Via di San Ignazio 6 *(tel. 679-6114)*
Hours: *Tuesday through Saturday from 11 a.m. to 7 p.m. nonstop*
Credit Cards: *None*
English Spoken.

One of Rome's newer galleries, where you are likely to catch the first glimpse of an up-and-coming artist rather than the established names. Il Ponte has launched the work of newcomers like Nino Longobardi and Giancarlo Iacomucci. Il Ponte is also the home gallery of American-born Roman printmaker Nona Hershey, who makes marvelously evocative prints of her adopted city.

BOOKS

ANGLO AMERICAN BOOKSHOP
Via della Vite 57 *(tel. 679-5222)*
Metro Stop: *Spagna*
Hours: *Daily from 9:30 a.m. to 1 p.m. and 4 to 7 p.m. (closed Monday morning)*
Credit Cards: *AE*
English Spoken.

This is a tiny book shop crammed with everything you might need: every guidebook under the sun, learned works on Italian art history, architecture and archeology, as well as the latest who-cares-if-its-trash-its-fun-and-I'm-on-vacation paperbacks. The knowledgeable proprietor makes a special effort to stay current, stocking up to the minute hardcovers from the United States and England. Unfortunately, these tend to be rather expensive, costing a good 50 to 60 percent over the list price you would pay in the United States. However, this shop, located in the very heart of Rome, is easy to get to, so it is your best bet for vacation reading matter.

BOOKS ON ITALY
Via dei Giubbonari 30 *(tel. 654-5285)*
Hours: *Thursday from 5 to 7 p.m., or by appointment*

Credit Cards: *None*
English Spoken.

On the third floor of an apartment building on the Via dei Giubbonari is this exceptional collection of books in English dealing with Italy. There are approximately 1,000 volumes in the collection, covering Italy from every angle: art, history, sociology, and topography. There's even a selection of novels set in Italy. Prices range from a modest 4,000 lire for an out-of-date *Frommer's Dollarwise Guide to Italy* to a magnificent 1787 first edition of Henry Swinburne's *A Traveller in Southern Italy* at 1.2 million lire.

FMR
Via Borgognona 4D (tel. 679-3466)
Hours: Monday through Saturday from 10 a.m. to 1:30 p.m. and 4:30 to 7:30 p.m. (closed Monday morning)
Credit Cards: AE
English Spoken.

Franco Maria Ricci produces the most beautiful art magazine in Italy, much along the lines of the American *Connoisseur*, and at this small jewel-box of a shop, you can buy the magazine and the full line of lavishly produced art books as well. You can pay 5.4 million lire for an 18-volume set of Diderot's *Encyclopédie* bound in full leather or a beautifully illustrated Huysman's *La Bas* in black silk for 50,000 lire. There are also exquisite diaries, address books, and calendars ranging in price from 30,000 lire to 100,000 lire.

THE ECONOMY BOOK CENTER
Via Torino 136 (tel. 474-6877)
Metro Stop: Repubblica
Hours: Monday through Saturday from 9:30 a.m. to 7:30 p.m.
Credit Cards: AE, DC (25,000-lire minimum purchase)
English Spoken.

The Economy is large, spacious, and well stocked. It keeps a wide range of guides to Rome and Italy on hand, as well as a giant selection of paperbacks. They will also buy your old paperbacks—you won't get much for them, but at least you don't have to lug them around.

CLOTHING

CHILDREN'S FASHIONS

For additional children's clothing listings, see "Lace."

BABY HOUSE
Via Cola di Rienzo 117 (tel. 351-933)

Metro Stop: *Lepanto*
Hours: *Monday through Saturday from 9:30 a.m. to 1:30 p.m. and 4 to 8 p.m. (closed Monday morning)*
Credit Cards: AE, DC, MC, V

In a country where children's clothing seems to cost as much as clothes for adults, there is a need for more shops like this. It's a good-sized store and the people, while they don't speak English, are very helpful and affable. Prices are low. A cable-knit double-breasted sweater for a girl aged 4 to 6 years of age is 36,000 lire. A little print dress with a Peter Pan collar, in 100% cotton, for ages 2 to 3 is 36,500 lire. There is also some Valentino for kids, and as you might expect, prices on these items are much higher. A Valentino sweatshirt, with the big "V," for ages 10 to 12, is 66,000 lire. A Valentino denim shirt is 67,000 lire. A cotton shirt in bright red for a child of 8 or 9 is 66,000 lire.

BENETTON
Via Condotti 19 (tel. 679-0042)
Metro Stop: *Spagna*
Hours: *Monday through Saturday from 9:30 a.m. to 7:30 p.m. nonstop (closed Monday morning)*
Credit Cards: AE, DC, MC, V
English Spoken.

The 0–12 division of Benetton, the kids' line, is incorporated in this single elegant store on Rome's classiest street. Prices remain low, though. Tennis shorts are 39,500 lire. Nice rugby shirts for boys and girls are 65,000 lire. Benetton jeans are 40,000 lire. A pair of corduroys in black, brown, or navy is 45,000 lire.

CHILDREN'S CLUB
Via Vittoria 27 and 52 (tel. 678-3115 or 678-4073)
Metro Stop: *Spagna*
Hours: *Monday through Saturday from 9:30 a.m. to 1:30 p.m. and 4 to 8 p.m. (closed Monday morning)*
Credit Cards: AE, DC, V
English Spoken.

These two shops face one another across the Via Vittoria. The one at no. 27 is for younger children, and at no. 52 you'll find clothes in the 10- to 14-year-old bracket. In the younger department are beautifully made dresses for little girls in linen, with puffed sleeves, for 140,000 lire. A bright-yellow cable-knit sweater is 70,000 lire. A daisy-pattern blouse for a 10-year-old girl is 76,000 lire. If you're in the market for a wing collar for a 6-year-old boy, you can find one here for 52,000 lire. A boy's denim blazer is 110,000 lire.

At the shop for older kids, the clothes are of the same quality, but carry higher prices. A silk party frock with a lace collar for a 12-year-old girl is 245,000 lire. A pair of boy's cords is 125,000 lire. A blue blazer for a boy is 185,000 lire.

EMPORIO ARMANI
Via del Babuino 140 (tel. 678-8454)
Metro Stop: *Spagna*
Hours: *Monday through Saturday from 9:30 a.m. to 1 p.m. and 3:30 to 7:30 p.m. (closed Monday morning)*
Credit Cards: AE, DC, MC, V
English Spoken.

The kids' department here is as deadly serious as the adults' (see "Men's Fashions" and "Women's Fashions," below) and prices are pretty high. A baggy blue blazer for a boy costs 215,000 lire. A yellow cotton short-sleeve shirt, also for a boy, is 55,000 lire. A rough cotton jacket for a boy or a girl is 192,000 lire. A pair of checkered shorts for a girl in her early teens is 54,000 lire. An Emporio Armani sweatshirt—and they have them in every size—will cost between 35,000 lire and 65,000 lire.

IRACI SPORT
Via Cola di Rienzo 147 (tel. 359-5423)
Metro Stop: *Lepanto*
Hours: *Monday through Saturday from 9:30 a.m. to 1:30 p.m. and 4 to 7:30 p.m. (closed Monday morning)*
Credit Cards: AE, DC, MC, V

Kids with an interest in sports will be in heaven here. There is Ellesse and Fila, to cite just two big names, in all shapes and varieties. A pair of Fila shorts is 25,900 lire, a tennis dress is 35,000 lire, and tennis shoes are 45,000 lire for girls and 50,000 lire for boys. Genuine Italian soccer shorts, also by Fila, are 35,000 lire, and a pair of soccer boots is 65,000 lire. Polo shirts for boys and girls, by Ellesse, Fila, and Tacchino, range from 35,000 lire to 60,000 lire.

IRENE PERINI
Via del Babuino 31 (tel. 678-9044)
Metro Stop: *Spagna*
Hours: *Monday through Saturday from 9:30 a.m. to 1 p.m. and 4 to 8 p.m. (closed Monday morning)*
Credit Cards: AE, DC, MC, V
English Spoken.

This is perhaps the most exclusive outfitter of extremely small people in Rome. With exposed beams in the ceiling and kilim carpets on the floor, Perini makes her young clients comfortable. She also outfits them in designer wear like

Burberry, Daniel Hechter, Christian Dior, Les Copains, and Gianfranco Ferré. This does not come cheap. A Gianfranco Ferré shirt for a 1-year-old is 88,000 lire. A red Les Copains blazer for a girl 10 to 12 years old is 275,000 lire.

LA CICOGNA
Via Frattina 138 (tel. 679-1912)
Metro Stop: *Spagna*
   and
Via Cola di Rienzo 264 (tel. 653-0557)
Metro Stop: *Lepanto*
Hours: *Monday through Saturday from 9:30 a.m. to 1:30 p.m. and 4 to 8 p.m. (closed Monday morning)*
Credit Cards: **AE, DC, MC, V**

There are nine La Cicogna stores in Rome, but these two are the most centrally located. The one on Via Frattina is larger and more expensive than the one on Via Cola di Rienzo. At both, you'll find good-quality medium-priced clothes for newborns up to 12 years, and everything from a playsuit to a tuxedo. A sailor suit for a little girl on Via Frattina is 201,000 lire. A full, pleated skirt is 68,500 lire. On the Via Cola di Rienzo side of town, there's a sprinkling of designer names, notably Valentino. A boy's top (for ages 6 to 8) is 33,900 lire. Valentino overalls for a baby are 23,800 lire, and a minute red wool Valentino cardigan is 47,500 lire.

LERI
Via Barberini 48 (tel 474-0834)
Metro Stop: *Barberini*
Hours: *Monday through Saturday from 9:30 a.m. to 1:30 p.m. and 3:30 to 7:30 p.m. (closed Monday morning)*
Credit Cards: **AE, DC, MC, V**

Leri has a number of shops in Rome, but this one is the easiest to get to. It's small—they all are—but has a good selection of clothes for babies and toddlers. A blue cotton summer dress for a little girl of 7 to 9 is 48,000 lire. A boy's denim jacket by the ubiquitous Valentino is 161,000 lire. A cotton shirt by Leri is 22,000 lire.

NAJ OLEARI
Via di San Giacomo 25 (tel. 678-0045)
Metro Stop: *Spagna*
Hours: *Monday through Saturday from 10 a.m. to 1:30 p.m. and 4 to 8 p.m. (closed Monday morning)*
Credit Cards: **AE, DC, MC, V**
English Spoken.

The cute, cute, cute clothes at Naj Oleari are supposed to be for little boys and little girls, but they're better suited to girls as sugar and spice are definitely two of the ingredients that go into the making of the stuff. There are Naj Olearis all over Italy but this is the largest, and the selection of sundresses and overalls in colorful and busy Naj Oleari fabrics is most extensive here. A dress for a 2-year-old with baby whales (or are they dolphins?) in pink, pale blue, or pale green is 89,000 lire. A skirt for a girl a little older (5 years, perhaps) is 95,000 lire.

PICCADILLY
Via Sistina 92 (tel. 679-3697)
Metro Stop: *Barberini*
Hours: *Monday through Saturday from 9:30 a.m. to 1:30 p.m. and 4 to 8 p.m. (closed Monday morning)*
Credit Cards: *AE*
English Spoken.

A small, cheery shop catering more to little girls than to little boys, Piccadilly has very traditional kids' clothes at fairly reasonable prices. A plaid dress with a Peter Pan collar (for age 5 to 7) is 74,000 lire. A pale-pink sweater for a newborn is 24,000 lire. A cotton dress with a scalloped collar, puffed sleeves, and gathered at the waist is 70,000 lire.

MEN'S FASHIONS

BENETTON
Via Condotti 19 (tel. 679-0042)
Metro Stop: *Spagna*
Hours: *Monday through Saturday from 9:30 a.m. to 7:30 p.m. nonstop (closed Monday morning)*
Credit Cards: *AE, DC, MC, V*
English Spoken.

The Benetton line for men is less extensive than that for women and children, but it's growing. Furthermore, it relies less on the knitwear that made Benetton famous to attract male shoppers. At the beautiful Via Condotti store—brand new and quite a place to see—the men's department is dedicated completely to casual wear and, as I've said before, prestige addresses don't seem to make any difference in price. A lovely linen-and-cotton tennis sweater with a deep V neck is 99,000 lire. A candy-striped shirt with white and red, green, purple, orange, or yellow stripes—an item which, it seems no Italian male under the age of 25 can live without—is 45,000 lire. A pair of Benetton blue jeans to wear with it is 52,900 lire.

BERNABEI
Via del Babuino 117 (tel. 679-2049)
Metro Stop: *Spagna*

Hours: *Monday through Saturday from 9:30 a.m. to 1:30 p.m. and 4 to 8 p.m. (closed Monday morning)*
Credit Cards: AE, DC, MC, V
English Spoken.

Bernabei is an elegant shop paneled in blond wood and furnished with leather banquettes. The clothes are as traditional as the decor. The classically tailored Italian menswear includes some beautifully crafted summer-weight suits in a discreet check. They are two-piece and two-button, and cost 770,000 lire. There are also made-to-measure suits—the fabrics tend to be English, but there are some Italian materials as well—beginning at 1.5 million lire. Allow four weeks for fittings and manufacture. The store will send them on at an extra charge. There is some excellent knitwear as well, notably spring-weight pullovers in white, brown, or magenta at 120,000 lire. Bernabei makes its own shirts. A striped button-down is 110,000 lire.

BRIONI
Via Barberini 79 (tel. 485-855)
Metro Stop: *Barberini*
Hours: *Monday through Saturday from 10 a.m. to 1:30 p.m. and 3:30 to 7:30 p.m. (closed Monday morning)*
Credit Cards: AE, DC, MC, V
English Spoken.

Brioni: Luxury menswear for oil barons and TV tycoons...and others

ROME SHOPS: CLOTHING

The producers of the TV series "Dynasty" claim that Blake Carrington wears nothing but made-to-measure Brioni suits. If you see yourself as an oil-baron type, then seek out this rather unassuming tailor shop which has a reputation totally out of proportion to the modesty of the premises. A made-to-measure two-piece suit costs about 2.5 million lire, depending on the material chosen. Brioni will keep your pattern on file and you can order up new suits as needed (don't gain any weight). An off-the-rack suit is 1.6 million lire. Brioni is famous for suits, but also makes some extremely luxurious shirts and sweaters. A silk shirt, off the rack, is 240,000 lire. A cashmere sweater with a crew neck is 600,000 lire.

CELLENO
Via Cola di Rienzo/Piazza dell'Unità 49 (tel. 353-115)
Metro Stop: *Lepanto or Ottaviano*
Hours: *Monday through Saturday from 9 a.m. to 1 p.m. and 3:30 to 7:30 p.m. (closed Monday morning)*
Credit Cards: AE, DC, MC, V
English Spoken.

Celleno is definitely a find. If you want to get decked out in the finest Italian designers and not take out a mortgage on your house, then you won't do better price-wise than here. The selection is not huge, but you won't find Armani, Missoni, Versace, Zileri, or Valentino for less anywhere else. An Armani two-piece double-breasted suit in dove-gray cotton is 655,000 lire. A Missoni red cable-knit sweater is 220,000 lire. A Versace pinstripe suit in wool is 685,000 lire. A Zileri two-button suit is 658,000 lire. The big finish: a Valentino dark-blue summer-weight suit is 700,000 lire.

CUCCI
Via Condotti 67 (tel. 629-1882)
Metro Stop: *Spagna*
Hours: *Monday through Saturday from 9:30 a.m. to 1:30 p.m. and 4 to 8 p.m. (closed Monday morning)*
Credit Cards: AE, DC
English Spoken.

Cucci doesn't care about fashion. If you don't either, but still want to make sure that you're always correctly dressed for any occasion, then Cucci is just the shop for you. A pair of cavalry twill trousers is 320,000 lire. A tweed suit is 1 million lire.

DATTI
Via del Babuino 55 (tel. 678-1483)
Metro Stop: *Spagna*

Hours: *Monday through Saturday from 9:30 a.m. to 1:30 p.m. and 4 to 8 p.m. (closed Monday morning)*
Credit Cards: *AE, DC, MC, V*
English Spoken.

Datti is another of the Via del Babuino shops catering to the man who wants traditional clothing but with a little Italian flair. A lightweight two-piece suit in a mild check is 880,000 lire. One of their lovely house-brand sports shirts is 120,000 lire.

EMPORIO ARMANI
Via del Babuino 140 (tel. 678-8454)
Metro Stop: *Spagna*
Hours: *Monday through Saturday from 9:30 a.m. to 1 p.m. and 3:30 to 7:30 p.m. (closed Monday morning)*
Credit Cards: *AE, DC, MC, V*
English Spoken.

A young man looking for the best in the "fun" Armani line will find everything in this large, somber shop. A houndstooth jacket, something casual for day or evening, is 400,000 lire. A short-sleeve shirt decorated with concentric circles is 150,000 lire. A pair of black polished cotton trousers is 120,000 lire. A red tie with the Armani eagle logo is 48,000 lire, and a blue button-down shirt is 100,000 lire. There is also some rather eccentric footwear: brown denim oxford shoes with a heavy rubber sole are 150,000 lire. A pair of clear plastic lace-up shoes for the beach (one assumes) costs 65,000 lire.

FIORUCCI
Via Nazionale 236A (tel. 463-175)
Metro Stop: *Repubblica*
Hours: *Monday through Saturday from 9:30 a.m. to 8 p.m. nonstop (closed Monday morning)*
Credit Cards: *AE, DC, MC, V*
English Spoken.

There's not a great deal to interest a man at the new Fiorucci on Via Nazionale. The brightly colored shirts and the blue jeans are old hat by now, and the famous Fiorucci putti don't appear on any of the menswear. A pair of jeans is 80,000 lire. The Hawaiian-type shirts are 45,000 lire to 65,000 lire.

GIANFRANCO FERRÉ
Via Borgognona 6 (tel. 679-7445)
Metro Stop: *Spagna*
Hours: *Monday through Saturday from 9:30 a.m. to 7:30 p.m. nonstop (closed Monday morning)*
Credit Cards: *AE, DC, MC, V*
English Spoken.

Given the size of the Gianfranco Ferré shop for women just down the street, it's a little suprising that the Ferré menswear shop should be so small. It is tiny, but very luxurious, and the young men who work there—dressed from head to toe in Ferré—are the ultimate advertisements for the product. Ferré's slightly eccentric clothing looks great on them, but it's up to you to decide how it will look on you—and if you can afford it. Considering that a T-shirt with the GFF logo costs 90,000 lire, you might want to tread lightly in this particular shop. A T-shirt made from suede is exactly ten times the price of the cotton one, 900,000 lire. A Ferré polo shirt in dark-blue cotton is 90,000 lire. Gianfranco Ferré has brought the price of his suits in line with the other Gs, Giorgio Armani and Gianni Versace. A rough-silk two-piece, two-button suit, with a longer-than-average jacket and full-cut trousers, is 980,000 lire, as is a dressier cotton pinstripe. A pair of casual pleated pants in linen are cheap (considering) at 220,000 lire.

GIANNI VERSACE
Via Borgognona 29 (tel. 679-5292)
Metro Stop: *Spagna*
Hours: *Monday through Saturday from 10 a.m. to 1:30 p.m. and 3:30 to 8 p.m. (closed Monday morning)*
Credit Cards: AE, DC, MC, V
English Spoken.

Versace's store for men is an awkwardly shaped mirrored complex of rooms where most of the clothing is shown on mannequins or kept out of sight in drawers. It's not that they discourage casual browsing—on the contrary, the salespeople are most accommodating—it's just that the place is not very well set up for it. It helps to know what you're interested in before you go. Gianni Versace's clothes seem to be losing a little of their *épater le bourgoisie* quality. Recent additions to the collection include a blue blazer with lapels that remind me of Savile Row and a white-on-white sports jacket that would be at home at Palm Beach. The blazer costs 790,000 lire; the sports jacket, 880,000 lire. A conservatively cut two-piece double-breasted suit in gray linen costs 1.17 million lire, and a silk shirt to wear under it is 245,000 lire.

GIORGIO ARMANI
Via del Babuino 102 (tel. 679-3777)
Metro Stop: *Spagna*
Hours: *Monday through Saturday from 9:30 a.m. to 1:30 p.m. and 4 to 8 p.m. (closed Monday morning)*
Credit Cards: AE, DC, MC, V
English Spoken.

In keeping with Versace and Ferré, Armani also has a small shop. Armani has softened his look as well. A double-breasted two-piece suit which, while unmistakably Armani, would not look out of place in the boardroom is 1.2

million lire. It's gray with the finest of pinstripes. A lovely silver-gray striped shirt is 135,000 lire and a pair of casual roughwear cotton pants is 275,000 lire. There is a small selection of shoes. A pair of very nice gray suede wingtips is 305,000 lire.

GUCCI
Via Condotti 22 (tel. 679-8343)
Metro Stop: *Spagna*
Hours: *Monday through Saturday from 10 a.m. to 7:30 p.m. nonstop (closed Monday morning)*
Credit Cards: *AE, DC, MC, V*
English Spoken.

Gucci's clothing for men shares quarters with his women's wear, and like the women's clothes, the casual wear is of most interest here. Prices are not all that bad. 190,000 lire for a faultlessly cut pair of linen pants, and a good Sea Island cotton sport shirt can be had for 130,000 lire. The suits are conservative and well made, but nothing really exceptional at 1.2 million lire and up.

INNSPORT
Via dei Giubbonari 99 (tel. 691-771)
Hours: *Monday through Saturday from 10 a.m. to 1:30 p.m. and 4 to 7:30 p.m. (closed Monday morning)*
Credit Cards: *None*

A good-value, but not very charming, shop for Italian-made skiwear. A Fila parka is 275,000 lire. A full-blown Fila skisuit is 350,000 lire. There is also skiwear by Ellesse and Tacchino.

IRACI SPORT
Via Cola di Rienzo 145 (tel. 359-5423)
Metro Stop: *Lepanto*
Hours: *Monday through Saturday from 9:30 a.m. to 1:30 p.m. and 4 to 7:30 p.m. (closed Monday morning)*
Credit Cards: *AE, DC, MC, V*

Iraci Sport is the best shop for sportswear in town and everyone knows it—that's why it's always crowded. The prices on men's Fila, Ellesse, and Tacchino are hard to beat. A Fila tennis sweater is 110,000 lire; polo shirts by the same maker range from 55,000 lire to 70,000 lire. The same item from Ellesse will cost 45,000 lire to 70,000 lire. Fila tennis shorts are 45,000 lire; those by Tacchino are 35,000 lire.

JAMES
Via dei Giubbonari 107 (tel. 654-7729)

Hours: *Monday through Saturday from 9:30 a.m. to 1:30 p.m. and 4 to 8 p.m. (closed Monday morning)*
Credit Cards: *None*

James is another of the inexpensive youth-oriented shops on the Via dei Giubbonari. Here you'll find a good selection of inexpensive preppie-style clothing. Cotton pants are 75,000 lire to 100,000 lire. Crew-neck sweaters are 50,000 lire. The Italian versions of Topsiders are 45,000 lire to 65,000 lire. Cotton button-down shirts are 45,000 lire to 50,000 lire.

LAURA BIAGIOTTI
Via Borgognona 43 (tel. 679-1205)
Metro Stop: *Spagna*
Hours: *Monday through Saturday from 10 a.m. to 8 p.m. nonstop (closed Monday morning)*
Credit Cards: *AE, DC, MC, V*
English Spoken.

The Biagiotti line for men, housed in the same shop as the women's wear (the "iceberg"; see "Women's Fashions" for a store description), is relatively new. The clothing is also clean lined, well cut, and dashing without being flamboyant. The prices aren't bad either, considering Biagiotti's reputation and the quality of the merchandise. A herringbone two-piece suit in cotton is 550,000 lire. Men's pleated slacks in black linen are 185,000 lire.

LELLO CALIA
Via Veneto 151 (tel. 493-505)
Metro Stop: *Barberini*
Hours: *Monday through Saturday from 9 a.m. to 1 p.m. and 3:30 to 8 p.m. (closed Monday morning)*
Credit Cards: *AE, DC, MC, V*
English Spoken.

The movie stars of the *La Dolce Vita* era may have forsaken the cafés of the Via Veneto, but I suspect they still return to shop there—the male ones at any rate. One of the best sources of Italian casual wear is Lello Calia. Shirts and sweaters are the particular standouts, both those bearing Calia's own label or the names of the more famous, like Valentino and Cerrutti. A Valentino polo shirt is 85,000 lire, which is pretty low (I've seen them as high as 290,000) and a striped green-and-white casual long-sleeve is 180,000 lire. The shirts bearing Lello Calia's own label are very inexpensive. A pure-cotton, summer-weight short-sleeve shirt is 24,900 lire, and they come in stripes and in checks. A dressier long-sleeve shirt is 39,000 lire.

LINEALUI
Via del Corso 50 (tel. 678-3058)

Hours: *Monday through Saturday from 9:30 a.m. to 1:30 p.m. and 4 to 8 p.m. (closed Monday morning)*
Credit Cards: *AE, DC, MC, V*

This is your stop for big-name casual wear at good prices. There's a lot of Valentino here, items you won't find at the Valentino Uomo on Via Condotti. A nice sports coat in cotton with a check is 1,995,000 lire. A gorgeous white Valentino tennis sweater with a red V-neck is just 78,000 lire. Valentino jeans are 79,000 lire. Missoni Uomo is well represented too: a denim duster is 272,000 lire, and a Missoni sweater is 112,000 lire. Enrico Coveri is well covered, with jeans, denim jackets, sweaters, and sweatshirts in the 65,000-lire (for jeans and sweatshirts) to 85,000-lire (for jean jackets and sweaters) range. There is also a vast selection of the Gianfranco Ferré "Oaks by Ferré" casual line. It's exclusively denim and very much in the Levi's mode. A jean jacket is 145,000 lire; one cut below the waist is 155,000 lire. A pair of Ferré jeans is 74,000 lire.

LINEASPORT
Via del Corso 49 (tel. 678-3058)
Hours: *Monday through Saturday from 9:30 a.m. to 1:30 p.m. and 4 to 8 p.m. (closed Monday morning)*
Credit Cards: *AE, DC, MC, V*

This is a branch of Lineasport, but it sells more activewear than its sister shop. Here you'll find average prices on Ellesse and Fila—not as good as those at Iraci Sport, but better than at a lot of other places.

MANAGER
Via Cola di Rienzo 139 (tel. 383-917)
Metro Stop: *Lepanto*
Hours: *Monday through Saturday from 9:30 to 1:30 p.m. and 3:30 to 8 p.m. (closed Monday morning)*
Credit Cards: *AE, DC, V*

"Il look manager" is what Italians call young professional fashions (also known as "yuppie," pronounced "yoopie"), and this rather elegant shop is the kind of place that "Il manager" of tomorrow shops for the right clothes to impress "il boss." (After doing "lo stretching" at "Il health club," of course.) The shop stocks two big names—Valentino Uomo and Trussardi Uomo—and it's interesting to see these two names side by side (prices and styles are very similar). A well-cut Valentino blue blazer is 490,000 lire; the same item by Trussardi is 500,000 lire. A two-piece winter-weight double-breasted wool suit by Valentino is 1.78 million lire; a Trussardi winter-weight suit, though not double breasted, is 1.44 million lire. There is also a wide selection of beautiful silk ties bearing the Manager label. A rep tie, in silk, is 35,000 lire.

MAURIZIO
Via Barberini 72 (tel. 474-4798)
Metro Stop: *Barberini*
Hours: *Monday through Saturday from 10 a.m. to 1:30 p.m. and 3:30 to 7:30 p.m. (closed Monday morning)*
Credit Cards: *AE, DC, MC, V*

Maurizio is a good place to shop for formal and casual wear. It's a smallish place, but still manages to offer a good selection of its own brands of clothing. A summer-weight jacket in linen is 420,000 lire. Polo shirts in a half a dozen colors are 85,000 lire. A silk two-piece, two-button suit is 675,000 lire. A vast variety of ties begins at 40,000 lire for silk.

MILA SCHÖN
Via Condotti 65 (tel. 678-4805)
Metro Stop: *Spagna*
Hours: *Monday through Saturday from 9:30 a.m. to 1:30 p.m. and 4 to 8 p.m. (closed Monday morning)*
Credit Cards: *AE, DC*
English Spoken.

The Mila Schön clothing for men is perfectly tailored, always in fashion, but somehow it's just a bit dull when compared to the other men's fashions that great Italian designers have produced. The plush little store on the Via Condoti has a full selection of the men's clothing line at prices that match their larger flagship store in Milan. The reversible Mila Schön tie is 80,000 lire, and there are hundreds to choose from. A blue double-breasted blazer is 650,000 lire.

MISSONI UOMO
Piazza di Spagna 78 (tel. 679-2555)
Metro Stop: *Spagna*
Hours: *Monday through Saturday from 9:30 a.m. to 1:30 p.m. and 3:30 to 7:30 p.m. (closed Monday morning)*
Credit Cards: *AE, DC, MC, V*
English Spoken.

The Missoni shop for men is right next door to Krizia and about the same size—that is, tiny. The prices are not! In fact they are the highest Missoni prices I've seen in Italy. One of the famous colorful zigzag knit sweaters is 440,000 lire. A cardigan in the same style is 620,000 lire. A pair of Missoni socks is 38,000 lire. Jeans are 78,000 lire. There are no bargains here.

MOMENTO
Via dei Giubbonari 92 (tel. 339-765)

Hours: *Monday through Saturday from 9:30 a.m. to 1:30 p.m. and 4 to 8 p.m. (closed Monday morning)*
Credit Cards: *AE, DC, V*

Cheap, young, hip clothes for men is the stock in trade of Momento. The blaring rock music, the casual service, and the lowish prices are the trademarks of shops like this, but if you're looking for something casual and cheap to take back to the States, then this is a good place to shop. Prices are low. Bright "go to hell" patterned shirts are 29,000 lire to 39,000 lire. A new silk jacket, roomy enough for two, with a '50s retro design is 105,000 lire.

POLIDORI UOMO
Via Borgognona 4C (tel. 678-4843)
Hours: *Monday through Saturday from 9:30 a.m. to 1:30 p.m. and 4 to 8 p.m. (closed Monday morning)*
Credit Cards: *AE*
English Spoken.

Polidori began life as a maker of fine Italian fabrics, particularly silks. Now they have branched out into men's clothing and the results are first-class. While Polidori is not as traditional as Cucci, nor is it in the vanguard of fashion as is, say, Gianfranco Ferré, the clothes are classic but fashionable. Prices are high. A simple crew-neck knit sweater is 340,000 lire, and a cotton shirt is 220,000 lire. Suits in cotton or wool are 1 million lire and up; silk suits begin at 1.56 million lire. All the materials used are Polidori's own, of course, and are beautiful.

RAVASI
Via del Babuino 178 (tel. 361-3256)
Metro Stop: *Spagna*
Hours: *Monday through Saturday from 9:30 a.m. to 1:30 p.m. and 4 to 8 p.m. (closed Monday morning)*
Credit Cards: *AE, DC*
English Spoken.

Preppie clothing is a big deal in Italy these days, and the best of the shops seem to be centered on Via del Babuino. Ravasi is an intimate, beautifully appointed shop catering to the Italian taste for American fashion—although all the clothes are made in Italy. A formal two-piece suit in navy-blue wool is 850,000 lire. A lighter, more casual suit in a cotton-and-linen blend is 490,000 lire.

SALVATORE FERRAGAMO
Via Condotti 66 (tel. 678-1130)
Metro Stop: *Spagna*
Hours: *Monday through Saturday from 10 a.m. to 7:30 p.m. nonstop (closed Monday morning)*
Credit Cards: *AE, DC, MC, V*
English Spoken.

Ferragamo has its own menswear shop on the Via Condotti, a few doors away from the main store. The men's department is small but very elegant, with a prime selection of clothing considering the size of the shop. A beautifully made two-piece suit in gray cotton with a faint mauve check is 655,000 lire. A silk two-piece suit is 995,000 lire (I know of one that was offered for sale in New York for the equivalent of 1.7 million lire—almost twice the price). A Ferragamo polo shirt is 112,000 lire. A heavy maroon sweater is 250,000 lire. Lovely cotton shirts are a bit on the high side at 185,000 lire for a button-down. A Ferragamo tie will cost you 50,000 lire.

SCHOSTAL
Via del Corso 158 (tel. 679-1240)
Hours: *Monday through Saturday from 9 a.m. to 1 p.m. and 4 to 8 p.m. (closed Monday morning)*
Credit Cards: *None*

Schostal is a Roman institution. Although the store is cramped, always crowded, and devoid of any plush touches, everyone from princes of the House of Savoy to Italian presidents have bought socks, ties, underwear, pajamas, and sweaters here. Schostal's old-fashioned counters have been jammed for over 100 years. The salespeople, all of them women dressed in the same kilts and white blouses, are like waitresses in a restaurant that caters mostly to regulars: they know what size cardigan "il commandatore" wears, and what kind of socks will most please "il principe." Not that you'll see the commander or the prince actually shopping there. The clientele of this exclusively male shop is made up almost entirely of women who know their husbands' tastes better than the husbands themselves. Prices are ridiculously low when one considers the old-fashioned quality of the merchandise. A pair of all-cotton pajamas, striped of course, is 65,000 lire. Socks in pure cotton or pure wool are 6,500 lire to 10,000 lire a pair. Sweaters are inexpensive also: a wool cardigan is 50,000 lire; a sleeveless sweater, 35,000 lire. A man dressed from head to toe in Schostal will certainly turn no heads, but he'll know that the clothes he's wearing will last for years and never go out of fashion—mainly because they were never *in* fashion.

SISTINA UOMO
Via Sistina 58 (tel. 678-6451)
Metro Stop: *Barberini*
Hours: *Monday through Saturday from 10 a.m. to 1:30 p.m. and 4 to 8 p.m. (closed Monday morning)*
Credit Cards: *AE, DC, MC, V*
English Spoken.

A small shop for menswear right on Via Sistina that caters primarily to the casual end of the market. The store is not all that much to look at, but the salespeople are unfailingly polite and helpful. It's a good place to pick up some summer wear, especially seersucker. A seersucker jacket with a white or dark-purple stripe is 380,000 lire. A lightweight seersucker shirt is 90,000 lire. There are also some fine knits, like a nice soft pullover in 100% wool for 75,000 lire or a royal-blue cable-knit with a V-neck and a white stripe around the waist for 90,000 lire.

TESTA
Via Borgognona 13 (tel. 679-6174)
   and
Via Frattina 104 (tel. 679-1296)
Metro Stop: *Spagna*
Hours: *Monday through Saturday from 9:30 a.m. to 1 p.m. and 4 to 8 p.m. (closed Monday morning)*
Credit Cards: AE, DC, MC, V
English Spoken.

The larger of the two Osvaldo Testa shops for men is on Via Borgognona, but both carry much the same merchandise—although the one on Via Frattina, being a bit smaller, has less of a selection. Testa specializes in clothes which, while traditional in cut, tend to be a little flashier in color than those sold at the other big names in the neighborhood. A sports jacket at either shop, in a plaid or check, will cost between 320,000 lire and 450,000 lire. A rough-weave cotton suit is 750,000 lire, while a flashy pinstripe with wide lapels in wool is 980,000 lire. Testa also has some nice outdoor wear, like a short suede jacket for 420,000 lire or a three-quarter-length softened-canvas sou'wester in green or red at 240,000 lire.

TO YOU UOMO
Via Cola di Rienzo 242 (tel. 653-0605)
Metro Stop: *Lepanto*
Hours: *Monday through Saturday from 10 a.m. to 1:30 p.m. and 3:30 to 8 p.m. (closed Monday morning)*
Credit Cards: AE, DC, MC, V

You'll find lots of trendy clothing for men at To You, mainly the Byblos and Sopriani lines with prices lower on this side of the river than on the other (as usual). A Byblos shirt with a colorful print is 100,000 lire; a dark Byblos jacket with an even darker stripe is 330,000 lire. A pair of Byblos pants to wear with it is 198,000 lire. The very hip Cesare Paciotti line of shoes is available here as well. A pair of suede loafers is 170,000 lire. The Luciano Sopriani line of clothing for men is hard to find, but they have it here. A Sopriani polo shirt is 116,000 lire. Sopriani casual pleated linen pants in light brown are 230,000 lire.

UOMO IN
Via Attilio Regolo 15 (tel. 311-177)
Metro Stop: *Lepanto*

ROME SHOPS: CLOTHING

Hours: Monday through Saturday from 10 a.m. to 1 p.m. and 3:30 to 8 p.m. (closed Monday morning)
Credit Cards: AE, DC, V

This store seems to be about a block long, and also appears to stock virtually every Italian designer you can name (they don't have Versace, but that seems to be the biggest name missing). Prices are pretty good too, particularly on Cerruti. A pair of pleated charcoal-gray pants is just 150,000 lire; a cable-knit sweater, also by Cerruti, is 110,000. A pair of Cerruti jeans—which I had never seen before—costs 69,000 lire. Prices for Valentino designs are surprisingly low here too. A sports jacket in a faint gray check costs 490,000 lire, while a rough-wear Valentino answer to an L. L. Bean jacket is just 260,000 lire. Missoni is not much of a bargain here (though still cheaper than at Missoni Uomo in the Piazza di Spagna), with sweaters in the 200,000-lire to 300,000-lire range. A pair of Missoni jeans costs 85,000 lire. The Oaks line by Gianfranco Ferré is well represented, with prices about the same as those at Linealui on Via del Corso: a Ferré denim shirt is 29,000 lire and jeans are 79,000 lire.

VALENTINO UOMO
Via Condotti at the corner of Via Mario dei Fiori (tel. 678-3656)
Metro Stop: *Spagna*
Hours: Monday through Saturday from 10 a.m. to 1:30 p.m. and 4 to 8 p.m. (closed Monday morning)
Credit Cards: AE, DC, MC, V
English Spoken.

The two stories of clothing in this luxurious shop will delight Valentino fans. Unfortunately, no matter how you slice it, you can't escape without spending a lot of money, and in some cases, having very little to show for it. However, the fun of shopping the head office, as well as the courtly sales help, take the sting out of some of the prices. Still, 290,000 lire for an ordinary polo shirt does seem astronomical, no matter whose name is on it. Actually, the larger items are better buys: you can have a lovely casual, two-piece dark-brown summer-weight cotton suit for just over 1 million lire (1.05 million lire to be exact), while a pair of black linen pants costs 550,000 lire and a simple striped cardigan is 460,000 lire. A cream-colored three-quarter-length suede jacket is a "steal" at 1.35 million lire. A similar jacket in the United States would be a good $400 more. One of the classic gray Valentino suits costs 2.3 million lire, which is cheaper than you'd find it in both the United States and the big Valentino in Milan.

VISCONTI
Via del Corso 25 (tel. 361-3308)
Hours: Monday through Saturday from 10 a.m. to 7:30 p.m. nonstop (closed Monday morning)
Credit Cards: AE, DC, MC
English Spoken.

Visconti is one of the few reasons to shop the Via del Corso. It's a large, pleasant shop which features its own house brand of clothing as well as some items by major designers. The accent here is on casual wear, like a pair of classic Bermuda shorts by Henry Cotton at 89,000 lire, Trussardi jeans at 89,000 lire, and Enrico Coveri sportswear. The Coveri epaulette shirt in 100% cotton is 105,000 lire.

WOMEN'S FASHIONS

ALICIA ROSAS
Via Borgognona 9–10 (tel. 679-2334)
Metro Stop: *Spagna*
Hours: *Monday through Saturday from 10 a.m. to 1:30 p.m. and 4 to 8 p.m. (closed Monday morning)*
Credit Cards: AE, DC, MC, V
English Spoken.

If you don't want to be noticed on the beach or at a ball, Alicia Rosas is probably not the shop for you. This high-fashion designer specializes in evening wear and beachwear, and it's eye-catching to say the least. The best-known creations— and they are swooned over by Rome's debutante set—are silk dresses gathered at the waist with yard upon yard of silk going into making up the sleeves and shoulders. An evening gown in white silk spills over the body as if it had been liberally coated with whipped cream. The same style is available in vibrant orange, magenta, or yellow. An Alicia Rosas creation costs 2.2 million lire. The swimwear is a little more restrained, but it too shows a degree of flamboyance, not to mention a lot of skin. A skimpy black one-piece suit covered with orange bow ties is 150,000 lire.

A PIU A
Via dei Greci 27 (tel. 679-4370)
Metro Stop: *Spagna*
Hours: *Monday through Saturday from 9:30 a.m. to 1:30 p.m. and 4 to 7:30 p.m. (closed Monday morning)*
Credit Cards: AE, V

A new addition to Rome's fashion scene, A Piu A (that's what the sign says, although it's almost impossible to read) has interesting, inexpensive clothes for day and evening wear. A beautiful silk crêpe evening gown with rhinestone points, cut very tight in the hips, is 250,000 lire. A one-piece silk dress, very elegant but a bit severe—perfect for the Big Business Meeting—is 200,000 lire.

BENETTON
Via Condotti 19 (tel. 679-0042)
Metro Stop: *Spagna*
Hours: *Monday through Saturday from 9:30 a.m. to 7:30 p.m. nonstop (closed Monday morning)*

ROME SHOPS: CLOTHING

Credit Cards: AE, DC, MC, V
English Spoken.

Benetton has arrived. The mass clothier now has shops not only on Via Monte Napoleone in Milan, but has recently opened a lovely vaulted-ceilinged shop on Via Condotti itself. The store is beautiful but, in keeping with the Benetton philosophy, prices at this *alta classe* location seem no higher than at a Benetton way out in the suburbs. Here you'll find clothes for the entire family. Women will appreciate beautiful, heavyweight cable-knit sweaters in white 100% wool at 74,900 lire. A pair of Benetton jeans is 52,900 lire. A nicely tailored blue blazer for summer wear is just 109,000 lire.

BOMBA DE CLERCQ
Via dell'Oca 39 (tel. 361-2881)
Metro Stop: *Flaminio*
Hours: *Monday through Saturday from 10 a.m. to 1:30 p.m. and 4 to 8 p.m. (closed Monday morning)*
Credit Cards: AE
English Spoken.

Bomba de Clercq sells nothing but its own handmade sweaters, knitting here being more an art than a craft. There is a large, but not overabundant, selection of sweaters and they come in all styles: bulky heavy knits, sporty crew-necks, and elegant knit creations for evening wear. Bomba de Clercq has attracted a small but influential band of devotées, so much so that this name has already

Bomba de Clercq: The sweater as art form

established a small shop in New York's Soho (100 Thompson St.). Prices are reasonable, considering the quality. A simple sleeveless wool sweater is 60,000 lire, but prices can rise to 350,000 lire for a mohair- and silk-blend cocktail sweater.

BOX
Via Nazionale 233 (tel. 475-4518)
Metro Stop: Repubblica
Hours: Monday through Saturday from 9:30 a.m. to 7:30 p.m. nonstop (closed Monday morning)
Credit Cards: MC, V

This is a fun, trendy, crowded store that sells clothes for teenagers and those who want to dress like them. There are a couple of name brands available here, notably Emporio Armani and the cheaper Enrico Coveri lines, but mostly the names are creations of Box itself. A linen miniskirt with front pockets is 98,000 lire. The big, baggy sweater that no Italian teen seems to be without costs in the 150,000-lire to 250,000-lire range.

BRIGHENTI
Via Frattina 7 (tel. 679-1484)
Metro Stop: Spagna
Hours: Monday through Saturday from 9:30 a.m. to 1:30 p.m. and 4 to 8 p.m. (closed Monday morning)
Credit Cards: AE, MC

Brighenti has a giant selection of lingerie and swimwear, most of it their own make. Nightdresses in linen with a lace trim cost between 100,000 lire and 200,000 lire. The cheapest bathing suit is 60,000 lire, though it's possible to pay 180,000 for a simple bikini.

CHIWAWA
Via di San Giacomo 29 (no phone)
Metro Stop: Spagna
Hours: Monday through Saturday from 9:30 a.m. to 1:30 p.m. and 4 to 7:30 p.m. (closed Monday morning)
Credit Cards: AE
English Spoken.

Chiwawa has all the charm and ambience of a subway station, but if you like Kappa sportswear that won't bother you a bit. It's all they sell and it's piled high in this little store just off Via del Corso. There's every kind of Kappa clothing available, and the prices are the lowest in the city: a complete red Kappa warmup suit is 49,900 lire, a pair of Kappa tennis shorts is 24,900 lire, and a tennis dress costs 36,000 lire.

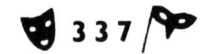

ROME SHOPS: CLOTHING

CUCCI
Via Condotti 67 *(tel. 679-1882)*
Metro Stop: *Spagna*
Hours: *Monday through Saturday from 9:30 a.m. to 1:30 p.m. and 4 to 8 p.m. (closed Monday morning)*
Credit Cards: AE, DC
English Spoken.

Fashions come and fashions go, hemlines rise and fall, but Cucci goes on doing business as it always has, oblivious—perhaps disdainful—of the vagaries of fashion. Here you'll find very traditional clothes for the kind of woman who still wouldn't be caught dead in a pair of white shoes after Labor Day. If you happen to attend the Show Jumping at the Piazza Siena in May or are invited to a country house in Tuscany (and *not* a converted peasant cottage), you'll be sure to be surrounded by women wearing Cucci. Prices are not high compared to the flashier fashion houses on the street: a severely tailored blue wool suit is 875,000 lire; a silk blouse with a bow collar is 190,000 lire.

EDDY MONETTI
Via Borgognona 24 *(tel. 679-6996)*
Metro Stop: *Spagna*
Hours: *Monday through Saturday from 9:30 a.m. to 1:30 p.m. and 4 to 8 p.m. (closed Monday morning)*
Credit Cards: AE, DC, MC, V

Until recently, Eddy Monetti was best known as a men's clothier catering to Italian anglophiles. Now, however, there is a Monetti shop for women that's as Italian as Rome itself. Two narrow rooms on the Via Borgognona house the women's wear, selling such non-British items as delicate silk chiffon pleated evening dresses in peach and other colors for 574,000 lire to 800,000 lire. There are also beautiful silk and linen cowl-neck sweaters at 200,000 lire.

ELI COLAJ
Via del Babuino 65 *(tel. 678-8983)*
Metro Stop: *Spagna*
Hours: *Monday through Saturday from 10 a.m. to 1:30 p.m. and 4 to 8 p.m. (closed Monday morning)*
Credit Cards: AE
English Spoken.

Eli Colaj is where the Roman nobility go to have their daughter's wedding dresses made—and while they're there, they might order a mother-of-the-bride gown to wear to the function. Silks here are of absolutely the finest quality and any lace a dress might need is likely to be antique. A Colaj creation for a wedding or ambassadorial reception (or if the pretender to the Italian throne is having a do in his city of exile, Geneva) is always made to measure. Prices in this category begin at about 5 million lire, and with fittings and what have you, can take up to three months to make. There are off-the-rack casual clothes too. A green-and-black striped one-piece dress with a wide belt and hat to match is 525,000 lire.

ELIZA
Via Veneto 157 (tel. 493-546)
Metro Stop: *Barberini* or *Spagna*
Hours: *Monday through Saturday from 9:30 a.m. to 1:30 p.m. and 4 to 8 p.m. (closed Monday morning)*
Credit Cards: AE, DC, MC, V
English Spoken.

This tiny shop on the Via Veneto is notable for good prices on Miss V and Krizia Poi—prices are very low, considering the location. A Miss V cotton blouse is 65,000 lire. Krizia Poi sweaters with the animal head are 100,000 lire.

EMANUEL ZOO
Via Frattina 141 (tel. 679-0891)
Metro Stop: *Spagna*
Hours: *Monday through Saturday from 9:30 a.m. to 1:30 p.m. and 4 to 8 p.m. (closed Monday morning)*
Credit Cards: AE, MC
English Spoken.

Colorful, glittering, and up-to-the-minute inexpensive fashion can be found at Emanuel Zoo. The clothes are by no means traditional, but they stop well short of avant-garde. Prices are reasonable: a silk skirt with a swash of glittering sequins is 175,000 lire; a brightly patterned cotton blouse is 79,000 lire.

EMPORIO ARMANI
Via del Babuino 140 (tel. 678-8454)
Metro Stop: *Spagna*
Hours: *Monday through Saturday from 9:30 a.m. to 1 p.m. and 3:30 to 7:30 p.m.*
Credit Cards: AE, DC, MC, V
English Spoken.

If the various Emporio Armani stores around the country are supposed to sell Armani's "fun" sportswear, why are all the stores so *serious?* You enter the low-lit, gray-on-gray store, extremely aware of the hush and the disdainful looks of the salespeople, who are very beautiful and leave one in no doubt as to their knowing it. As not one of them appears to be over 20, I can only assume that this is the arrogance of youth. Never mind, refuse to be intimidated—they work here, but *you* have the money. The full line of Armani casuals is to be found here, everything from shoes to luggage. A short-short speckled skirt in linen is 62,000 lire. A matching, loose-cut cotton jacket is 210,000 lire. A nautical-style blue-and-white cotton sweater is 82,000 lire and a blue cotton top emblazoned with the EA eagle logo costs 42,000 lire. A pair of suede and clear-plastic flats is 110,000 lire. An Armani denim shoulder bag, again with the eagle logo, is 110,000 lire. Armani jeans are 74,000 lire. These are reasonable prices and the merchandise is interesting, but, hey gang, lighten up!

FEMME SISTINA
Via Sistina 75 (tel. 678-0260)
Metro Stop: *Spagna*
Hours: *Monday through Saturday from 9:30 a.m. to 7:30 p.m. nonstop (closed Monday morning)*
Credit Cards: AE, DC, MC, V
English Spoken.

Femme Sistina is right at the top of the Spanish Steps a few yards from the elegant Hassler Hotel. The clothing tends to be casual, the kind of thing one wears midafternoon in Palm Springs or Beverly Hills. A two-tone off-the-shoulder linen dress for summer day wear is 439,000 lire. More formal chiffony evening wear begins at about 650,000 lire.

FENDI
Via Borgognona 40 (tel. 679-7641, 679-7642, 679-7643, or 679-7644)
Metro Stop: *Spagna*
Hours: *Monday through Saturday from 9:30 a.m. to 7:30 p.m. nonstop (closed Monday morning)*
Credit Cards: AE, DC, MC, V
English Spoken.

There are five Fendi shops within a few yards of one another on Via Borgognona, each dealing with a particular specialty, except for the flagship which sells everything. The one listed here is the clothes Fendi. It's a simple, square room lined on two sides with racks. You are encouraged to browse without having the salesgirl breathing down your neck—so often the case at the great names. Prices here run from the reasonable (a beautiful denim mini for 105,000 lire) to the moderate (a silver raincoat for 390,000 lire) to the expensive but worth it (a butter-smooth brown leather skirt for 590,000 lire). You would pay twice as much for a similar item at a far less illustrious house in Rome, and three times as much in Milan.

FIORUCCI
Via Nazionale 236A (tel. 463-175)
Metro Stop: *Repubblica*
Hours: *Monday through Saturday from 9:30 a.m. to 8 p.m. nonstop (closed Monday morning)*
Credit Cards: AE, DC, MC, V
English Spoken.

The Fiorucci mania that hit the United States in the latter part of the 1970s has abated somewhat, and Fiorucci is no longer quite the name it once was in Italy either. However, the new shop on Via Nazionale is still doing a sell-out business to devotées of the playful, sexy styles. Prices are low. A two-piece bathing suit with the famous Fiorucci putti wearing sunglasses is sure to turn heads at the beach and costs 57,600 lire. A pair of Fiorucci espadrilles, again with the little angels—no shades this time—costs 20,000 lire. The famous Fioruccio jeans are 65,000 lire. Fiorucci's answer to the Swatch (the putti are back) is 39,000 lire.

FIRENZE RICAMA
Via Nazionale 36 (tel. 464-695)
Metro Stop: *Repubblica*
Hours: *Monday through Saturday from 9:30 a.m. to 1:30 p.m. and 4 to 8 p.m. (closed Monday morning)*
Credit Cards: AE, V
English Spoken.

Firenza Ricama sells lace and lingerie from Florence. There's a ton of it here, all crammed into a tiny shop, but it's worth fighting your way in to take a look at pure-silk camisoles for 124,000 lire, with matching bottoms for 84,000 lire. A complete set of Valentino underwear—peach-colored bra, garter belt, and panties—is 165,000 lire.

GATTINORI
Via Sistina 44 (tel. 679-6704)
Metro Stop: *Barberini*
Hours: *Monday through Saturday from 9:30 a.m. to 1:30 p.m. and 4 to 7:30 p.m. (closed Monday morning)*
Credit Cards: None

Gattinori is a good stop for those who want to be in fashion but don't want to spend a fortune. Gattinori is by no means a bargain basement—far from it!—but it's not as expensive as it looks. A "little black dress" with a scoop neck is 350,000 lire. A linen pants suit in off-white is 295,000 lire.

GENTE
Via del Babuino 82 (tel. 460-269)
Metro Stop: *Spagna*
Hours: *Monday through Saturday from 9:30 a.m. to 1:30 p.m. and 4 to 7:30 p.m. (closed Monday morning)*
Credit Cards: AE
English Spoken.

A small, dark hi-tech store in décor, Gente sells hip, casual clothing for the Italian equivalent of Sloane Rangers. A rough-wear jacket in waterproof flax is

ROME SHOPS: CLOTHING

438,000 lire. Gray cotton pleated pants, suitable for a game of croquet or strong enough for a ramble in the woods, are 120,000 lire.

GIANFRANCO FERRÉ
Via Borgognona 42 (tel. 679-744)
Metro Stop: *Spagna*
Hours: *Monday through Saturday from 9:30 a.m. to 7:30 p.m. nonstop (closed Monday morning)*
Credit Cards: AE, DC, MC, V
English Spoken.

Gianfranco Ferré's new shop on Via Borgognona looks like a very clean factory: rising through the center of the three-story shop is what looks like a stainless-steel smokestack. Stainless steel glints everywhere, contrasting with the gray marble floors. While not exactly homey, it's a magnificent setting for the clothes of the "architect" of fashion. As you might expect, prices are high. A white linen classic-lined, broad-shouldered three-quarter-length sleeved dress costs 1,135,000 lire. A black-and-white checked suit, with a jacket falling to mid-thigh, in a cotton-and-linen blend is 1.74 million lire. There are some Ferré shoes as well: brown leather flats overlaid with designer stitching are 350,000 lire.

GIANNI VERSACE
Via Bocca di Leone 26 (tel. 678-0521)
Metro Stop: *Spagna*
Hours: *Monday through Saturday from 10 a.m. to 7:30 p.m. nonstop (closed Monday morning)*
Credit Cards: AE, DC, MC, V
English Spoken.

Versace also has a dramatic-looking new shop, though rather a small one. The store is decorated completely in black and glass and is a little intimidating. The prices are intimidating too: a black evening dress with a ruff collar is 1.9 million lire.

GIORGIO ARMANI
Via del Babuino 102 (tel. 679-3777)
Metro Stop: *Spagna*
Hours: *Monday through Saturday from 10 a.m. to 7:30 p.m. nonstop (closed Monday morning)*
Credit Cards: AE, DC, MC, V
English Spoken.

Unlike their brethren down the street at Emporio Armani, the folks at the main Giorgio Armani shop are very nice and bend over backward to please you. The store is surprisingly small, but there is a good range of women's merchandise available. Prices seem a little lower than in Milan, but not by much. A square-shouldered two-piece summer-weight suit is 1.45 million lire. An Armani skirt in beige cotton is 530,000 lire, and a three-quarter-length silk top is 890,000 lire. A white cotton top with a Peter Pan collar is 620,000 lire. A square-shouldered houndstooth-pattern silk dress for evening wear is 1.38 million lire. There are also some Armani leather goods: a black leather ankle-length skirt is 1.8 million lire; a pair of white suede day shoes, 380,000 lire.

GREGG
Via Vittoria 70 (tel. 678-4131)
Metro Stop: *Spagna*
Hours: *Monday through Saturday from 10 a.m. to 1:30 p.m. and 4 to 7:30 p.m. (closed Monday morning)*
Credit Cards: AE
English Spoken.

Gregg sells knitwear of its own creation in lush cottons and cashmeres. A fawn-colored cashmere sweater is 230,000 lire. A long cashmere sweater, ribbed and belted at the waist, is 480,000 lire. Less exotic knits are inexpensive. Good cotton and cotton-and-linen blends can be had in the 75,000-lire to 150,000-lire range.

GUCCI
Via Condotti 22 (tel. 679-8343)
Metro Stop: *Spagna*
Hours: *Monday through Saturday from 10 a.m. to 7:30 p.m. nonstop (closed Monday morning)*
Credit Cards: AE, DC, MC, V
English Spoken.

In keeping with a number of other designers, Gucci has "boutiqued" itself: leather and jewelry at one location, accessories at another, and clothes at yet another. Via Condotti 22 is the "clothes" Gucci. The shop is airy and bright and not crammed with stuff as at the other two Guccis in town. The clothes themselves are quite conservative and not dotted all over with Gs and bridles. The casual wear is most interesting, but you'll still pay a hefty price for the name. A safari-type suit with a jacket and skirt in khaki linen is 805,000 lire. A black suit with a pair of full-cut pleated pants is 950,000 lire. A simple pair of linen pants is 190,000 lire.

HARPER
Vis Sistina 52 and 88 (tel. 678-5563)
Metro Stop: *Barberini*
Hours: *Monday through Saturday from 10 a.m. to 1:30 p.m. and 4 to 8 p.m. (closed Monday morning)*
Credit Cards. AE, DC, MC
English Spoken.

ROME SHOPS: CLOTHING

Harper is a good supplier of the franchised lines of a number of great Italian names. Here you'll find Krizia Poi, Coveri, Oaks by Ferré, and Miss V. The store itself is quite lavish, with marble floors and dark-wood fittings (don't walk through the floor-to-ceiling mirror at the back thinking it's another room), and the salespeople are quite helpful. Prices are good, considering you're on Via Sistina. A pair of Krizia Poi jeans in beige is 79,000 lire, and a short, tough-looking Krizia Poi black jacket is 134,000 lire. As you might expect, even the Miss V line from Valentino is head and shoulders price-wise above everyone else. A yellow silk day dress with tiny black polka dots is 768,000 lire. A Miss V blue blazer costs 395,000 lire, and a navy-blue linen skirt to go with it is 188,000 lire.

HERMÈS
Via Condotti 60 (tel. 679-7687)
Metro Stop: *Spagna*
Hours: Monday through Saturday from 10 a.m. to 1:30 p.m. and 4 to 7:30 p.m. (closed Monday morning)
Credit Cards: AE, DC, MC, V
English Spoken.

See Hermès in "Leather Goods."

IL BACO DA SETA
Via Vittoria 55 (tel. 679-3907)
Metro Stop: *Spagna*
Hours: Monday through Saturday from 9:30 a.m. to 1:30 p.m. and 4 to 8 p.m. (closed Monday morning)
Credit Cards: AE, DC, V
English Spoken.

Il Baco da Seta is a tiny shop on a narrow street selling high-quality silk clothes at remarkably low prices. A pink two-piece silk suit, with an ankle-length skirt and a blouse with full sleeves is just 220,000 lire.

INNSPORT
Via dei Giubbonari 99 (tel. 691-771)
Hours: Monday through Saturday from 10 a.m. to 1:30 p.m. and 4 to 7:30 p.m. (closed Monday morning)
Credit Cards: None

A good no-nonsense shop for Fila, Ellesse, and Tacchino sportswear, particularly for those who ski. An Ellesse ski parka is 240,000 lire; a pair of ski gloves, also by Ellesse, is 85,000 lire. A full Fila ski suit costs between 235,000 lire and 400,000 lire.

IRACI SPORT
Via Cola di Rienzo 147 (tel. 359-5423)

THE SERIOUS SHOPPER'S GUIDE TO ITALY

Metro Stop: *Lepanto*
Hours: *Monday through Saturday from 9:30 a.m. to 1:30 p.m. and 4 to 7:30 p.m. (closed Monday morning)*
Credit Cards: *AE, DC, MC, V*

This is absolutely *the* sport shop in town, stocking the widest variety of Fila, Ellesse, and Tacchino sportswear. The place is always jammed because Romans know that for selection and price, Iraci can't be beat. A Fila tennis dress is 50,000 lire, which is cheap by anyone's standards. Fila tennis shoes are 89,000 lire; an Ellesse warmup suit is 175,000 lire.

JAQUELINE
Via Cola di Rienzo 250 (tel. 344-2122)
Metro Stop: *Lepanto*
Hours: *Monday through Saturday from 9:30 a.m. to 1:30 p.m. and 4 to 7:30 p.m. (closed Monday morning)*
Credit Cards: *AE, MC*

This is a good source of Max Mara clothing at less than Max would charge on the Via Condotti. A very dressy pleated gold-colored skirt is just 190,000 lire here—as opposed to 300,000 lire across the river. A pair of pleated linen pants is 140,000 lire, about 35,000 lire less than at the main shop.

KRIZIA
Piazza di Spagna 77 (tel. 679-3419)
Metro Stop: *Spagna*
Hours: *Monday through Saturday from 9:30 a.m. to 7:30 p.m. nonstop (closed Monday morning)*
Credit Cards: *AE, DC, MC, V*
English Spoken.

It's a bit odd that Rome, which must draw more Krizia-hungry shoppers than any other city in Italy, should have such a tiny Krizia store to serve them—but it does! In the selling space of a good-size station wagon you'll find a fair selection of the Krizia line—no Krizia Poi, though—including some of the Krizia costume jewelry. Prices are breathtakingly high. A pink silk skirt is 610,000 lire. A matching square-neck knit top with some of the black Krizia jewelry is 500,000 lire. If you aren't going to the several-story Krizia shop in Milan or to the small, but very inexpensive, Krizia shop in Venice, this is it as far as Rome goes. Try to hold out for the other two cities, but remember that Krizia in Rome is still cheaper than Krizia in the United States (unless you get the Krizia-designed but Hong Kong–made stuff available at some stores Stateside—there's none of that in Italy).

LA CALZA
Via Cola di Rienzo 172 (tel. 233-6123)

Metro Stop: *Lepanto*
Hours: *Monday through Saturday from 9:30 a.m. to 1:30 p.m. and 4 to 8 p.m. (closed Monday morning)*
Credit Cards: *None*

In another minute store, La Calza sells nothing but stockings—thousands of them. Prices are low. Basic ivory, taupe, gray, or black are 5,000 lire. Seamed stockings are a little more, at 7,500 lire to 10,000 lire. Patterned stockings begin at 18,000 lire.

L'ATELIER SALETTI
Via del Babuino 179 (tel. 360-8872)
Metro Stop: *Spagna*
Hours: *Monday through Saturday from 10 a.m. to 1:30 p.m. and 4 to 7:30 p.m. (closed Monday morning)*
Credit Cards: *AE*
English Spoken.

L'Atelier Saletti is rather a peculiar shop. Extremely elegant, all marble and dark wood, it's on a very swank street and stocks some of the greatest names in Italian fashion, notably Valentino and Lancetti—but the prices aren't that bad. Consider this: a red wool, full-length double-breasted Valentino overcoat with a silk lining and deep side pockets at 890,000 lire. It's not bargain basement, but much cheaper than I've seen before. A Valentino sweater is a more pricey 490,000 lire; a Valentino linen suit is 870,000 lire, and a one-piece summer dress, 680,000 lire.

LAURA BIAGIOTTI
Via Borgognona 43 (tel. 679-1205)
Metro Stop: *Spagna*
Hours: *Monday through Saturday from 10 a.m. to 8 p.m. nonstop (closed Monday morning)*
Credit Cards: *AE, DC, MC, V*
English Spoken.

Entering Laura Biagiotti's brand-new store on Via Borgognona feels like what it must be like to walk inside an iceberg. Not that it's cold—it's just so white! The walls are white; the floors are white; the ceiling, which seems to be about 300 feet above you, is white—even the salespeople wear white. But I have to admit that, once your eyes become used to the glare, the shop is quite amazing to look at! The clothes are not white, and neither are the hundreds of other things sold there. Things like the Biagiotti line of glasses, shoes, and leather goods. The clothes are interesting and fresh. A tight, pleated-silk crêpe skirt in bright red is 610,000 lire. An evening dress with a V-neck, dolman sleeves, and gathered tightly at the waist, in dark-blue silk is 870,000 lire. A pair of Biagiotti sunglasses is 95,000 lire. A pair of high heels in smooth red leather with a black patent-leather toe cap costs 235,000 lire.

LINEALUI
Via del Corso 50 (tel. 678-3058)
**Hours: Monday through Saturday from 9:30 a.m. to 1:30 p.m. and
     4 to 8 p.m. (closed Monday morning)**
Credit Cards: AE, DC, MC, V

This store is nothing to look at, but it's your stop for really big-name casual wear—names like Fendi, Oaks by Ferré, Enrico Coveri, and Valentino. A Ferré jean jacket is 138,000 lire, and a pair of jeans is 74,000 lire. A Missoni set of overalls is 230,000 lire and a denim duster is 272,000 lire. A Valentino T-shirt is 49,000 lire; a Valentino plaid shirt, 95,000 lire.

LINEASPORT
Via del Corso 49 (tel. 678-3058)
**Hours: Monday through Saturday from 9:30 a.m. to 1:30 p.m. and
     4 to 8 p.m. (closed Monday morning)**
Credit Cards: AE, DC, MC, V

This place is connected to Lineasport (see above) and stocks the sportier line of sportsclothes—clothes you might actually play a sport in. The names here are standard, as are the prices: Ellesse, Fila, and Kappa. If you aren't going to make it across the river to Iraci Sport, Lineasport should suit any sportswear needs. Tennis clothes by Fila are a little more than elsewhere: a V-neck top, for example, costs 57,000 lire; warmup pants, 95,000 lire. A Rome T-shirt by Kappa is just 13,000 lire.

LIONELLO AJÔ
Via Borgognona 35 (tel. 678-2660)
Metro Stop: *Spagna*
**Hours: Monday through Saturday from 10 a.m. to 1:30 p.m. and
     4 to 7:30 p.m. (closed Monday morning)**
Credit Cards: AE, DC, MC, V
English Spoken.

Lionelle Ajô is a small, paneled shop—so small, in fact, that it's hard to believe that this is the one-stop-shopping source of nine well-known designers. On the Ajô racks you'll find clothing by Sonia Rykiel, Angelo Tarlazzi, Jean-Paul Gaultier, Alma-Spazio, Anne-Marie Baretta, Moschino, Vicky Tiel, Koshino, and Callaghan. Sonia Rykiel knitwear is made in Italy so a sweater at Lionello Ajô is likely to cost you less here than in Paris or London. An angora sweater is 320,000 lire. Jean-Paul Gaultier is cheaper in Milan and Paris, as is Koshino. Of course, Junko Koshino is a designer for the Alma-Spazio line (as is, by the way, Gianni Versace), so you might be getting Koshino with an Alma label. A knit skirt from the Alma line here is 325,000 lire. Moschino denim dresses are very big at Lionello Ajô, and you can have a nice casual just-below-the-knee shift with a big brass-and-leather Moschino belt for 250,000 lire. Overall, Ajô is a good place to get an idea of what's what in the fashion field these days—it's a good place to start.

LUISA SPAGNOLI
Via Barberini 84 (tel. 465-881)
Metro Stop: Barberini
Hours: Monday through Saturday from 9:30 a.m. to 1:30 p.m. and
   4 to 8 p.m. (closed Monday morning)
Credit Cards: AE

You'll find Luisa Spagnoli shops all over Italy and their stock in trade is good-quality, fashionable clothing that doesn't cost a fortune. A two-piece cotton suit here costs 250,000 lire. Silk blouses, plain or patterned, range from 85,000 lire to 150,000 lire.

MARCELLA NERONI
Via Vittoria 37 (tel. 679-7505)
Metro Stop: Spagna
Hours: Monday through Saturday from 9:30 a.m. to 1 p.m. and
   3:30 to 7:30 p.m. (closed Monday morning)
Credit Cards: AE, DC, V
English Spoken.

Via Vittoria, as you discovered on our stroll, is a little side street near the Piazza di Spagna which seems to have an interesting shop on every corner. Marcella Neroni led the movement away from the Via Condotti and is now perhaps the best-known name on the street. The clothing, which comes from the Neroni atelier, is beautifully made and designed in a slightly modern vein. The knitwear is exceptional. Prices are on the high side, but worth it. Scalloped, ribbed sweaters in jet black or shimmering white for evening wear are 330,000 lire. Filmy pleated black silk pants are 190,000 lire.

MARIO FOSSI
Via Sistina 46 (tel. 679-1707)
Metro Stop: Spagna
Hours: Monday through Saturday from 9 a.m. to 1 p.m. and 4 to 8 p.m.
   (closed Monday morning)
Credit Cards: AE, DC, MC, V
English Spoken.

Mario Fossi is a relative newcomer to Via Sistina, but he has weighed in with some big names, notably the "Segno" line by Luciano Sopriani and the casual Oaks by Ferré. A white cotton Ferré suit is 450,000 lire. A brown-and-white striped silk blouse by Sopriani is 139,000 lire.

MAX MARA
Via Condotti 46 (tel. 679-3638)
Metro Stop: *Spagna*
Hours: *Monday through Saturday from 10 a.m. to 7:30 p.m. nonstop (closed Monday morning)*
Credit Cards: *AE, DC, MC, V*
English Spoken.

The beautiful new Max Mara store on the Via Condotti appears to be MM's attempt at the big time. It seems to be succeeding, bringing fashionable clothes to the august Via Condotti without hoisting prices above the average person's pocketbook. A long linen duster, known as a *spolverino* in Italian, in black, is 355,000 lire. A lovely matching pleated silk skirt costs 599,000 lire. A very smart double-breasted beige jacket cut wide in the sleeves is 299,000 lire. A silk blouse—they come in a number of soft, pastel colors—runs 190,000 lire. For inclement weather there is a beautiful full-length raincoat at 395,000 lire.

MC
Via Vittoria 18 (tel. 679-6350)
Metro Stop: *Spagna*
Hours: *Monday through Saturday from 10 a.m. to 1:30 p.m. and 4 to 8 p.m. (closed Monday morning)*
Credit Cards: *AE, DC, MC, V*
English Spoken.

MC is another of the great Via Vittoria stores that are often overlooked by the casual shopper. This narrow little shop sells everything from casual clothes to evening wear to swimwear, most of it with the MC label. However, there is some Erreuno clothing from Graziella Ronchi's design house. There's a certain amount of confusion over which designer actually creates the clothes. In Milan I was told that Erreuno comes from the studio of Gianfranco Ferré; in Rome, at MC they say that Giorgio Armani is responsible. Either way, the clothes are extremely attractive and inexpensive. An Erreuno day dress for summer wear is 295,000 lire. Evening wear is more expensive, but not heart-stopping. It begins in the 700,000-lire range. There is more to MC than just Erreuno, however: some lovely blouses in silk and polished cotton. A filmy pink blouse, in silk, with a V neck and short sleeves is 180,000 lire. The swimwear is different and a little on the expensive side. A two-piece suit that looks like the marbled paper you see at fine bookbinders is 122,000 lire. A simple, wide-brimmed straw hat in red, black, or white, for the beach or a garden party, is just 40,000 lire.

MILA SCHÖN
Via Condotti 64 (tel. 678-4805)
Metro Stop: *Spagna*
Hours: *Monday through Saturday from 9:30 a.m. to 1:30 p.m. and 4 to 8 p.m. (closed Monday morning)*

Credit Cards: AE, DC
English Spoken.

The small, plush Mila Schön shop on Via Condotti is far less impressive than the flagship store in Milan, but prices at the two shops are about the same. The severely tailored clothing doesn't appeal to everyone, but the trademark cashmere shawls are hard to resist, even at 400,000 lire. Other clothes in the line are just as expensive—two-piece suit is 850,000 lire; evening wear begins in the millions of lire.

MISSONI
Via del Babuino 96–97 (tel. 679-0050)
Metro Stop: *Spagna*
Hours: *Monday through Saturday from 10 a.m. to 1:30 p.m. and 3:30 to 7:30 p.m. (closed Monday morning)*
Credit Cards: AE, DC, MC, V
English Spoken.

Despite the fact that Missoni is Milan based, the Rome shop is larger, more lavishly designed, and better stocked. The sales help are nicer too. If Missoni is for you—and if you can afford it—it's better to buy here than in Milan. Let's start small. A pair of patterned Missoni stockings is 15,000 lire. Moving up a bit, you'll find that 575,000 lire will buy you a multicolored one-piece print dress—expensive, perhaps, but about 30% less than you'd spend in the States. A full-length skirt in bright-red linen with a tucked waist is 396,000 lire—again, a lot less than elsewhere. The Missoni knits are still expensive. A black-and-white knit pleated skirt with flecks of color is 880,000 lire. A short knit skirt in an eccentric multicolored design—but not the zigzag—is 675,000 lire. A knit suit in blue and white is 2 million lire.

NAJ OLEARI
Via dei Greci 32 (tel. 679-4803)
Metro Stop: *Spagna*
Hours: *Monday through Saturday from 10 a.m. to 1:30 p.m. and 4 to 8 p.m. (closed Monday morning)*
Credit Cards: AE, DC, MC, V
English Spoken.

Naj Oleari, long the cute outfitters of kids who could afford their prices, have introduced a line of clothing for their parents. The best way to characterize it is to call it "cute new wave," if you can imagine such a thing. A pink suit with a long top and a long matching skirt decorated with cups and saucers costs 170,000 lire. A blouse with Vespa motor scooters all over it costs 112,000 lire.

NIA
Via Vittoria 30 and 48 (tel. 679-8109)

Metro Stop: *Spagna*
Hours: *Monday through Saturday from 9:30 a.m. to 1:30 p.m. and 4 to 8 p.m. (closed Monday morning)*
Credit Cards: *AE, DC, V*
English Spoken.

Yet another of Via Vittoria's good buys. Nia at no. 30 is a fanciful, cute store stocking casual clothes for women, a touch more sophisticated than Laura Ashley. A patterned summer-weight skirt with a draw-string waist is 100,000 lire. A layered peasant dress with a lace-up bodice runs 280,000 lire. A simple dark-blue silk blouse with a Peter Pan collar is 50,000 lire. The other branch of the shop is across the street at no. 48. The clothes here are a little more formal, but still good value and high quality. A three-quarter-length peach-colored mohair sweater with a straight collar is 138,000 lire. A blue wool blazer with pointed lapels costs 640,000 lire.

OSÉ
Via Nazionale 68 (tel. 463-452)
Metro Stop: *Repubblica*
Hours: *Monday through Saturday from 9:30 a.m. to 1:30 p.m. and 4 to 8 p.m. (closed Monday morning)*
Credit Cards: *AE, DC, MC, V*

Osé features Byblos clothes for women at good prices. A Byblos silk top is 120,000 lire and a Byblos mini is 190,000 lire. There are some Fendi products too, at a few thousand lire less than you'll pay on Via Borgognona—but it's a lot more fun to go to the real store. If you can't make it there, Osé will sell you a Fendi knee-length skirt in denim for 185,000 lire or a mini for 106,000 lire—which is a whole 1,000 lire *more* than at Fendi in the high-rent district.

PICONE
In the courtyard at Via dei Greci 43 (tel. 679-0064)
Metro Stop: *Spagna*
Hours: *Monday through Saturday from 9:30 a.m. to 1 p.m. and 3:30 to 7:30 p.m. (closed Monday morning)*
Credit Cards: *AE, MC, V*
English Spoken.

Picone is situated in a light airy courtyard which, although in the heart of town, is shielded from traffic sounds and amazingly quiet. The shop, too, is light and airy, as are the clothes: loose, casual, and extremely simple—perfect for summer wear. A linen dress decorated with the Picone sun symbol is 145,000 lire.

PIN UP
Via dei Giubbonari 78 (tel. 654-7804)

ROME SHOPS: CLOTHING

Hours: *Monday through Saturday from 9:30 a.m. to 1:30 p.m. and 4 to 8 p.m. (closed Monday morning)*
Credit Cards: *None*

If you want to buy a teenager a piece of teen clothing from Italy, then Pin Up is the best place to go. Here, for a modest sum you can outfit yourself so *a la giovane* you'd fool a truant officer into thinking you were an Italian kid. The baggy sweaters and overlong, baggy-sleeved blazers that are the cornerstones of every *ragazza*'s wardrobe are easy to find here at prices beginning at about 60,000 lire.

PRADA
Via Nazionale 30 (tel. 462-463)
Metro Stop: *Repubblica*
Hours: *Monday through Saturday from 9:30 a.m. to 1:30 p.m. and 4 to 8 p.m. (closed Monday morning)*
Credit Cards: *AE, MC*

In Milan, Prada has a couple of extremely elegant shops selling the famous Prada leather goods. Here in Rome you find the same name, owned by the same people, but there's hardly a piece of Prada leather in sight. This large shop on Via Nazionale sells shoes (by Fratelli Rossetti) and wedding dresses and fabrics, but no Prada. It does sell clothes by Carla Raedelli. A sequined top is 340,000 lire. A matching skirt runs 276,000 lire.

PUER
Via Nazionale 231 (tel. 475-4407)
Metro Stop: *Repubblica*
Hours: *Monday through Saturday from 9:30 a.m. to 1:30 p.m. and 4 to 8 p.m. (closed Monday morning)*
Credit Cards: *AE, DC, MC, V*

Puer is the most elegant shop on Via Nazionale and it sells some elegant names, as well as some elegant knockoffs of well-known designers. Max Mara and Sport Max are the big draws, with an MM green silk suit costing 490,000 lire. A drop-waisted yellow cotton jacket by Sport Max, with a matching skirt, is 226,000 lire. A simple, classically cut linen dress by Puer itself is just 159,000 lire.

ROMANI
Via del Babuino 94 (tel. 679-2323)
Metro Stop: *Spagna*
Hours: *Monday through Saturday from 10 a.m. to 1:30 p.m. and 4 to 7:30 p.m. (closed Monday morning)*
Credit Cards: *AE, DC, V*
English Spoken.

This is perhaps the trendiest of the stores on the otherwise rather staid Via del

Babuino, a favorite stop among younger Roman women shopping for casual and evening wear that's different but not outrageous. Prices are pretty good. A complete knit suit, cut wide in the shoulders but with a hip-hugging matching skirt, in peach cotton with white trim, is 300,000 lire. A white silk skirt, which also shows every curve, is 290,000 lire. You'll also find a small selection of bags and costume jewelry here, as well as shoes. Leather prices are reasonable. A pair of red leather pumps is 95,000 lire.

RUNCI
Via Condotti 94 (tel. 679-5819)
Metro Stop: *Spagna*
Hours: *Monday through Saturday from 9:30 a.m. to 1:30 p.m. and 4 to 8 p.m. (closed Monday morning)*
Credit Cards: AE
English Spoken.

Runci falls very much into the Cucci mode: elegant, well-made clothes that have little to do with today's fashion scene. If you're looking for tweeds for the country, a traditional blue blazer, or something unflashy to wear to a society wedding, then Runci is the shop for you. A silk blouse is 220,000 lire. A three-quarter-length pleated tweed skirt is 450,000 lire.

SABRY
Via Nazionale 70 (tel. 670-661)
Metro Stop: *Repubblica*
Hours: *Monday through Saturday from 9:30 a.m. to 1:30 p.m. and 4 to 8 p.m. (closed Monday morning)*
Credit Cards: AE, DC, MC, V

Sabry is a bustling store on the busy Via Nazionale which sells Krizia Poi, Krizia Jeans, Titolo by Basile (which is the discount version of the discount Luciano Sopriani), and Laura Biagiotti. The Krizia prices are average—the usual 79,000 lire for jeans—as are the prices on Basile, but the Biagiotti pricetags are the lowest I've seen. A Laura Biagiotti denim skirt is 99,500 lire. A denim jacket by the same designer runs 98,000 lire.

SALVATORE FERRAGAMO
Via Condotti 73 (tel. 679-8402)
Metro Stop: *Spagna*
Hours: *Monday through Saturday from 10 a.m. to 7 p.m. nonstop (closed Monday morning)*
Credit Cards: AE, DC, MC, V
English Spoken.

The large new Ferragamo shop on Via Condotti is devoted to women's wear and leather goods (I'll deal with the leather under that category). The clothes you'll find here are well cut and correct—a lot like (dare one say it?) the clothing of

Ferragamo's arch-competitor Gucci. Plaids, both busy and staid, are to be had in abundance. The knitwear is beautifully made and a touch expensive: a cotton cardigan is 370,000 lire. Evening wear costs abut what you'd expect: a black evening dress with a touch of brocade at the collar is 880,000 lire. The best buy in the shop, it seemed, was a silk pink-and-gold scarf—the equal of Gucci in quality if not size—for just 49,000 lire.

SIMONE DONNA
Via Frattina 2 (tel. 678-6568)
Metro Stop: *Spagna*
Hours: *Monday through Saturday from 10 a.m. to 1:30 p.m. and 4 to 8 p.m. (closed Monday morning)*
Credit Cards: *None*

If you can't afford the grander names for Italian knit goods, then Simone Donna is a good place to look for reasonably priced knitwear. The merchanise is inexpensive, but not cheaply made—and it's fashionable. Prices begin at about 45,000 lire for a nice V-neck sweater in cotton. Cashmere is a lot more, in the 200,000-lire to 300,000-lire range.

STEFANEL
Via Cola di Rienzo 191 (tel. 352-954)
Metro Stop: *Lepanto*
   and
Via Nazionale 227 (tel. 266-767)
Metro Stop: *Repubblica*
Hours: *Monday through Saturday from 9:30 a.m. to 1:30 p.m. and 4 to 8 p.m. (closed Monday morning)*
Credit Cards: *AE, DC, MC, V*

There are a number of Stefanels in the city, but these two are the nicest I've seen—particularly the one on Via Cola di Rienzo. At that location you'll find a vast collection of Stefanel products at reasonable prices. A baggy double-breasted blazer in linen is 119,000 lire. A bulky diamond-patterned sweater costs 72,500 lire. On Via Nazionale you'll find a lot of duplication of merchandise, and the prices are identical—but this one is closer to the center of town, so you might want to shop here instead of trekking across the river. A pair of cotton slacks is 72,500 lire and a plain gray baggy pullover is 49,500 lire.

TAMAR
Via Nazionale 33 (tel. 786-8811)
Metro Stop: *Repubblica*
Hours: *Monday through Saturday from 9 a.m. to 1 p.m. and 4 to 8 p.m. (closed Monday morning)*
Credit Cards: *AE, DC, MC, V*

If your thirst for Ellesse sportswear has still not been slaked, then head to Tamar. An Ellesse running suit is 126,000 lire and Ellesse shorts are 43,200 lire. A heavy warmup suit runs 194,000 lire, and a tennis top, 60,500 lire.

TOUCHE
Via del Babuino 91 (tel. 679-2487)
Metro Stop: *Spagna*
Hours: *Monday through Saturday from 9:30 a.m. to 1:30 p.m. and 3:30 to 7:30 p.m. (closed Monday morning)*
Credit Cards: AE
English Spoken.

This is where Roman women shop when they're looking for something casual. Earth tones predominate, and the clothes themselves are extremely fresh and rather simple. A rough-cotton full-length rust-colored skirt is 204,000 lire. A striped cotton suit is 590,000 lire.

UNGARO
Via Bocca di Leone 24 (tel. 679-9931)
Metro Stop: *Spagna*
Hours: *Monday through Saturday from 10 a.m. to 1:30 p.m. and 4 to 8 p.m. (closed Monday morning)*
Credit Cards: AE, DC, MC, V
English Spoken.

Most Ungaro products are made in Italy so it's safe to assume that, while the prices are stratospheric, they are cheaper here than in the United States. Ungaro has a new store in Rome (the old Via Borgognona location is long gone) and most of the line is represented in the new place. A tailored two-piece silk-and-linen suit with a long jacket and slightly flared three-quarter-length skirt is 1.09 million lire. Something for daytime but dressy nonetheless, an A-line dress with flap pockets and short cuff sleeves in linen costs 890,000 lire.

VALENTINO
Via Bocca di Leone 16 (tel. 679-5862)
Metro Stop: *Spagna*
Hours: *Monday through Saturday from 10 a.m. to 1:30 p.m. and 4 to 8 p.m. (closed Monday morning)*
Credit Cards: AE, DC, MC, V
English Spoken.

Valentino's flagship store is as hushed as a chapel at vespers. The discreet and very beautiful sales help whisper to shoppers in Italian, French, English, and Japanese. Making a purchase is something of a religious experience. Despite the *gravitas* of all this, the salespeople are very gracious and leave you alone until you've found something you want to try on—or until you flee from the store completely overcome by the prices. Couture, made to measure that is, costs 10 million lire and up. Prêt-à-porter is less, but not by much. A drop-waist silk evening gown costs 5.5 million lire. A simple pleated white cotton skirt is 850,000 lire. A waist-length silk jacket costs 1.75 million lire.

You'll also find some lovely leatherwear as well. A pair of bronze leather high heels (which look as if they were made of rattan) is 290,000 lire. A pair of stunning leather gloves with a gold filigree is a whopping 450,000 lire.

XAVIER
Via dei Giubbonari 26 (tel. 356-3456)
Hours: *Monday through Saturday from 9:30 a.m. to 1:30 p.m. and 4 to 8 p.m. (closed Monday morning)*
Credit Cards: *None*

Geographically and price-wise rather a long way from Valentino, Xavier, a small shop on the narrow Via dei Giubbonari, is a good source of cheap-chic clothing for the younger crowd, particularly colorful sweaters and blouses in the 50,000-lire to 100,000-lire range.

DEPARTMENT STORE

LA RINASCENTE
Via del Corso at the corner of Piazza Colonna (tel. 679-7691),
and
Piazza Fiume 2 (tel. 841-231)
Hours: *Monday through Saturday from 9:30 a.m. to 7:30 p.m. nonstop (closed Monday morning)*
Credit Cards: *AE, DC, MC, V*
English Spoken: *Via del Corso only*

La Rinascente is the largest of the Italian department store chains, and while they simply haven't caught up with the department store revolution of the United States, they still do what department stores do best: offer a lot of good-value-for-money merchandise under one roof. The main Rinascente, on the Via del Corso, has two floors of its own brand, Ellerre, clothes for men, women, and children. Unusual and larger sizes, particularly in women's wear, are well represented. In addition, both branches of the store (and, to be honest, you're unlikely to visit the one in off-the-beaten-track Piazza Fiume) have good hosiery counters, costume jewelry departments, and perfume sections. The best thing about La Rinascente is the exceptional exchange rates it offers for those wishing to pay with dollars or dollar traveler's checks—their rates are always higher than the banks.

THE SERIOUS SHOPPER'S GUIDE TO ITALY

DISCOUNT SHOPPING

DISCOUNT SYSTEM
Via Viminale 35 (tel. 474-6545)
Metro Stop: *Repubblica*
Hours: *Monday through Saturday from 9 a.m. to 1 p.m. and 3:30 to 7:30 p.m. (closed Monday morning)*
Credit Cards: *AE*
English Spoken.

One block off Via Nazionale you'll find the brand-new premises of Discount System, Rome's first genuine discount store. While not exactly luxurious, this discount shop is a lot nicer than the cavernous *blocchisti* in Milan (see "Discount Shopping" in Chapter VI). There are some great bargains to be had here, but you'll have to dig for them as there's a great deal of chaff mixed in with the wheat. All the clothing and leather goods come from Italy's best-known names, though judging by the items on the racks you can tell that some of the stuff didn't exactly fly out of the chic shops in Rome and Milan when the garments were selling at full price.

Basically, at Discount System you are looking at a lot of orphaned styles—all of them in good shape and with the labels—but you get the feeling that Valentino, Krizia, or Armani wished they had designed something else that day. But that's not to say that there aren't some gems. A Valentino tote bag which normally sells for 150,000 lire is 75,000 lire here. A beautiful red leather semicircular Trussardi evening bag is 165,000 lire, not the 330,000 lire you'd have paid for it at Trussardi on Via Bocca di Leone. There is a lot of women's clothing by Krizia, Fendi, Max Mara, Trussardi, and Erreuno, as well as jeans by just about every Italian designer you can think of.

The menswear is by Armani, Enrico Coveri, Valentino, Gianfranco Ferré, Nino Cerruti, and Missoni.

Discount System is only going to get better as time goes on, so it should be put on your "must visit" list. As every item in the store is discounted 50% or better, it's worth a look whenever you're in town.

TAGLIACOZZO
Piazza Benedetto Cairoli 7 (tel. 654-2255)
Hours: *Monday through Saturday from 9:30 a.m. to 1:30 p.m. and 4 to 8 p.m. (closed Monday morning)*
Credit Cards: *None*

If Tagliacozzo did TV ads, they'd be on late at night and would have some guy bellowing: "My wife thinks I'm crazy, she tells me I'm givin' the stuff away..." etc., etc. Tagliacozzo occupies a couple of small rooms stuffed with everything from sweatshirts to wedding gowns, and they're priced to move. You have to do a lot of fishing before you come up with something you might want to buy—and, to be fair, you might just see a pile of junk where others see bargains—and there are lots of "any item on this table for 10,000 lire" stalls. But as the cheapest shop on the cheapest street in this book (it's right at the end of Via dei Giubbonari), you might want to brave the crowds and take a look. You could find a perfect bathing suit for 9,900 lire, or you might find nothing at all!

FABRICS AND TEXTILES

BISES
Via del Gesù 93 (tel. 678-0941)
Hours: *Monday through Saturday from 9:30 a.m. to 1:30 p.m. and 4 to 8 p.m. (closed Monday morning)*
Credit Cards: AE, DC, MC, V

Bises is absolutely *the* shop for fabrics in Rome. It's housed in the magnificent Palazzo Altieri, and most of the rooms have fading frescoes on the ceilings. Room upon room of farbics unfold here—each room stacked floor to ceiling with every imaginable Italian cloth, from simple cottons to elaborate brocades. The salespeople are aware that their supply is a little daunting and if you give them some idea of what you're looking for (or better still, a swatch), then they'll scurry up a ladder and return with a bolt of just the right thing. If you'd rather browse, you are welcome to do that too, but you could be at it until closing. Most of the fabrics are made for Bises, but there are some designers represented,

Bises: *The* shop for fabrics in Rome

notably Valentino. Prices range from low (pure cotton in dozens of colors for about 30,000 lire a meter) to high (150,000 lire for a meter of moire silk of the highest quality).

NAJ OLEARI
Via di San Giacomo 25 (tel. 678-0045)
Metro Stop: *Spagna*
Hours: *Monday through Saturday from 10 a.m. to 1:30 p.m. and 4 to 8 p.m. (closed Monday morning)*
Credit Cards: AE, DC, MC, V
English Spoken.

The cute Naj Oleari fabrics are available by the meter. They are all cotton and of course feature all the busy little prints in a variety of pastel colors. A meter of material costs between 59,000 lire and 100,000 lire.

POLIDORI
Via Borgognona 4A (tel. 678-4842)
Metro Stop: *Spagna*
Hours: *Monday through Saturday from 9:30 a.m. to 1 p.m. and 4 to 8 p.m. (closed Monday morning)*
Credit Cards: AE, DC, MC, V
English Spoken.

Polidori caters to women who would rather buy expensive Italian fabrics, take them home and have their personal dressmaker fashion a piece of couture for them. The plain and patterned linens and cottons are of the highest quality, but Polidori's reputation is built on silk. Polidori sells the finest bolt silk in Rome—plain or patterned, raw or finished. Less exotic fabrics cost between 75,000 lire and 100,000 lire a meter; silks begin at 150,000 lire a meter.

SOLEIADO
Via dell'Oca 38 (tel. 361-0402)
Metro Stop: *Flaminio*
Hours: *Monday through Saturday from 10 a.m. to 1:30 p.m. and 4 to 7:30 p.m. (closed Monday morning)*
Credit Cards: AE
English Spoken

This is the European name for the Pierre Deux line of Provençal fabrics so popular in the United States. Prices are much lower on the Soleiado you can buy in Paris, but Italian prices are lower than American. Here you'll find a meter of the dark-blue and yellow pattern material for 65,000 lire. It would be 30% cheaper in Paris but 20% more in the United States. There are also some ready-made clothes—sundresses and smocks mostly—at 175,000 lire to 250,000 lire, as well as soft pocketbooks, wallets, and bags at 35,000 lire to 100,000 lire.

FOOD

CHOCOLATES

MORIONDO AND GARIGLIO
Via della Pilotta 2 (tel. 678-6662)
Hours: Monday through Saturday from 9:30 a.m. to 1:30 p.m. and 4 to 7:30 p.m. (closed Monday morning)
Credit Cards: *None*

There are more lavish *chocolatiers* in Rome than Moriondo and Gariglio but there's none finer. Tucked into the corner of the vast Piazza Pilotta, near the Trevi Fountain, Moriondo and Gariglio is almost literally a hole in the wall. There is no sign—just a doorway, and beyond that a tiny, tiny shop. If you're not looking for it, you won't find it. As you face the giant Pontifical Gregorian University which dominates the square, Moriondo and Gariglio is the little red doorway to your right. The selection of their homemade chocolate (it *is* homemade—the kitchen is in the back) is not large, but the quality is second to none in the city. All the chocolates are delicious, particularly the dark chocolate filled with mint cream, the hazelnut-and-chocolate clusters, and the chocolate-covered cherries. The large, solid-chocolate hearts, which can be purchased around Valentine's Day, come in dark or milk chocolate and are delicious. Despite the modest surroundings, this world-class chocolate does not come cheap: 100 grams (one *etto*, about 3 ½ ounces) of mixed chocolates is 5,000 lire. The hearts, depending on size, range from 10,000 lire to 50,000 lire.

ICE CREAM

DA QUINTA
Via Tor Millina 15 (no phone)
Hours: Monday through Saturday from 10 a.m. to 10 p.m., Easter to October only (closed the rest of the year)

Tourists, and those Romans who don't know any better, always buy their ice cream in the places around the Piazza Navona. They shouldn't! The view is nice, but the service is surly and the prices are ridiculously inflated. Those in the know go to Da Quinta, a block or two away, and get the best ice cream in the city and then go sit in the Piazza Navona, securing the same view at a third the price. Da Quinta doesn't have a great selection of flavors—he prefers to stick with the old favorites and do them right. The Vanilla (called "crema") is excellent, as are the chocolate, pistachio, banana, and strawberry. There are also some fruit sherbets that are not too sweet but are deliciously cooling on a hot day—the lemon is the best. Cones, with a mixture of all the ice creams and a big dollop of fresh whipped cream, begin at 2,000 lire and go up to 5,000 lire—but be warned: a large cone is a *lot* of ice cream.

GIOLITTI
Via degli Uffici del Vicario 40 (tel. 679-4206)
Hours: *Monday through Sunday from 11 a.m. to 12:30 a.m. nonstop (closed Monday morning)*
Credit Cards: *None*

Giolitti is the best-known ice-cream parlor in the city. It's so well known, in fact, that it's beginning to suffer from its own notoriety. Not the quality of the product, you understand—that remains wonderfully high—it's just that the place is so popular that it's getting harder and harder to buy an ice cream cone there. After dinner on a summer night Italians and foreigners alike are lined up six deep at the counter, and try as they might, the employees just can't keep up with demand. If you do manage to get through the crowd, you'll find that the struggle was well worth it. The pistachio, melone, and gianduia (nut-encrusted dark chocolate) are excellent. Cones start at 2,000 lire and go up to 10,000 lire for a chocolate-covered cone the size of a top hat.

PASTRIES

BERNASCONI
Largo Argentina 1 (tel. 654-8141)
Hours: *Monday through Saturday from 8:30 a.m. to 7:30 p.m. nonstop*
Credit Cards: *None*

Bernasconi is one of the best-known pastry shops in the city. Set right in the busy Largo Argentina, this huge shop is always thronged with people buying pastries to go—beautifully parceled and beribboned—or selecting a pastry to eat while they have a cup of coffee at the bar at the far end of the room. There are dozens of different types of pastries and cookies to choose from, but the pastry that put Bernasconi on the map is a "bombe," a doughnut without the hole, served hot and rolled in confectioner's sugar. They cost 2,000 lire each and are sweet beyond belief!

IL FORNO DEL GHETTO
Via Portico D'Ottavia (no number) (no phone)
Hours: *Monday through Saturday from 8 a.m. to 7 p.m. nonstop*
Credit Cards: *None*

Il Forno del Ghetto is always crowded with locals, who can't seem to get enough of the pastries which have been made on these premises for centuries. The most famous sweets are the cherry tarts, the almond cakes, and the Italian version of cheese cake. Nothing seems to cost very much: a cherry tart, large enough for six, is 12,000 lire.

LA BELLA NAPOLI
Corso Vittorio Emanuele 246 (tel. 657-048)
Hours: Tuesday through Sunday from 9 a.m. to 7:30 p.m. nonstop
Credit Cards: None

The best Neapolitan pastries in the city have been served in this unassuming little bar for decades now. Transplanted Neapolitans flock there on Sunday morning to buy sfogliatelle (puff pastry filled with cream or chocolate), pastareale (almond-paste cookies), or perhaps a baba (a sponge cake glazed with an orange liqueur). La Bella Napoli is one of the few *pasticcerias* which has booths and waiters, so you don't have to drink your cappuccino and eat your pastry standing at the bar.

SPECIALTY FOODS

CASTRONI
Via Cola di Rienzo 196 (tel. 687-4383)
Hours: Monday through Wednesday, Friday, and Saturday from 8:30 a.m. to 8 p.m. nonstop
Credit Cards: None

Castroni is *the* specialty-food shop in the city. Remember of course, that specialty foods in Italy mean hard-to-find items like crunchy peanut butter, taco shells, and water chestnuts—in fact, there sometimes seem to be more foreigners shopping at Castroni than Italians. Of course, Italian delicacies can be had here too. Castroni is one of the few places where porcini mushrooms can be found year round—although when they're out of season they are packed in a light oil. A single small mushroom will cost 12,000 lire. Castroni is also the home of various exotic oils. There are rare Tuscan vintage olive oils, as well as even more exotic oils like pepperoncino oil (8,500 lire for a 100 milliliters, (about half a cup), garlic oil at the same price, and oil flavored with white truffles at 13,000 lire for 50 milliliters (about two tablespoons). Sun-ripened tomatoes, which are so expensive in the United States, are exceedingly cheap here: just 4,800 lire a kilo. Fresh truffles, which are expensive everywhere, are expensive here too: you can pay as much as 16 million lire for a one-kilo truffle—that's 160,000 an *etto* (3 ½ ounces).

ERCOLI
Via della Croce 32 (tel. 679-1645)
Metro Stop: Spagna
Hours: Monday through Saturday from 9 a.m. to 1:30 p.m. and 5 to 8 p.m. (closed Thursday afternoon)
Credit Cards: None

If you're planning a picnic in the *campagna*, Ercoli is one of two shops you should consider when buying cold cuts. Here you'll find fabulous Parma and San

Daniele hams, delicioun salamis, mortadella, and a host of other Italian cold cuts.

FOCACCI
Via della Croce 43C (tel. 679-1228)
Metro Stop: Spagna
Hours: Monday through Saturday from 9 a.m. to 1:30 p.m. and 5 to 8 p.m. (closed Thursday afternoon)
Credit Cards: None

Focacci is the other place. Sausages and hams are the specialties here: as well as the Parmesan versions, you get hams from Hungary, Milan, and Poland. There are sausages made from game, like venison and wild boar, as well as a vast selection of cheeses and olives.

FRANCHI
Via Cola di Rienzo 204 (tel. 687-4151)
Metro Stop: Lepanto
Hours: Monday through Saturday from 9 a.m. to 7:30 p.m. nonstop (closed Thursday afternoon)
Credit Cards: None

Franchi: You'll never go hungry in Rome

The food at Franchi is, frankly, beautiful. At a long L-shaped counter you'll find everything from salamis and hams to perfectly boiled and buttered lobster tails. There are hundreds of cheeses: mozzarellas, smoked provalones, infornata con tartuffi (baked cheese with truffles), strong cacciottas from Apulia, and a hundred more. There are also prepared salads, roasted peppers, shrimp cocktails, and ready-made pastas. This is one of the finest places in the city to buy truffles. As everywhere else, they are expensive: expect to pay 175,000 lire to 200,000 lire an *etto* (3½ ounces). Castroni has a small bar in one corner where freshly fried suppli (rice and cheese balls) and croquette (flash-fried potatoes) are sold. Stand up at the bar and have one with a cold drink.

GUERRA
Via della Croce 8 (tel. 679-3102)
Metro Stop: *Spagna*
Hours: *Monday through Saturday from 9 a.m. to 1:30 p.m. and 4:30 to 7:30 p.m. (closed Thursday afternoon)*
Credit Cards: *None*

Guerra is the downtown home of ready-prepared foods. There are fabulous pastas—tortellini, ravioli, tortellone—as well as delicious salamis, sausages, quiches, and salmon en croûte.

FURNITURE

FORMA E MEMORIA
Via di Ripetta 148 (tel. 654-7622)

Forma e Memoria: For simple but elegant housewares and furnishings

Hours: *Monday through Saturday from 10 a.m. to 1 p.m. and 3:30 to 7:30 p.m. (closed Monday morning)*
Credit Cards: AE
English Spoken.

Forma e Memoria is a spare, elegant shop selling extremely simple but very tasteful furniture. Those of you who go for the minimal, "less is better" look will be delighted with Forma e Memoria's use of plain woods, black lacquers, and simple black marble. There are some quirky standouts, like the Memphis-designed Alessio tea and coffee pots, and an entire kitchen packed in a steamer trunk (refirgerator, stove, sink, coffee maker, the works). If the portable kitchen at 17 million lire is a little pricey, or the black marble table at 6.85 million lire is a little bulky for your carry-on, Forma e Memoria also has some beautiful house items, like glassware and ashtrays, as well as decorated file boxes for recipes, postcards, tax receipts, whatever.

PITTI
Via di San Giacomo 19 (tel. 679-5930)
Metro Stop: *Spagna*
Hours: *Monday through Saturday from 10 a.m. to 1:30 p.m. and 4 to 7:30 p.m. (closed Monday morning)*
Credit Cards: AE

Pitti is a very smart, two-level shop which sells all manner of furniture, particularly modern brass and glass coffee tables and deep, multicolored couches. However, the furniture is not necessarily the thing to shop for here. It's the housewares. For more details on the shop, see "Housewares."

POLTRONA FRAU
Via di Propaganda 8 (tel. 679-2271)
Metro Stop: *Spagna*
Hours: *Monday through Saturday from 10 a.m. to 1:30 p.m. and 4 to 8 p.m. (closed Monday morning)*
Credit Cards: AE
English Spoken.

The Frau company has been hand-making furniture in the northern part of Italy for eight decades now, and they've been doing it so well it's no wonder that some of their designs, now 50 years old, are still being snapped up as if they were new on the market. The famous, bulbous Frau "poltrona" (armchair) in red leather has been around since the 30s and is still selling like crazy—even at 5 million lire each. There is modern Frau furniture, like their suede-covered couches and austere flat-back armchairs (also covered in suede), but it's the more traditional designs people like best. The modern couch is 9.5 million lire and the armchair runs 2.4 million lire.

SPAZIO SETTE
Via dei Barbieri 7 (tel. 654-7139)

Hours: *Monday through Saturday from 10 a.m. to 1:30 p.m. and 4 to 8 p.m. (closed Monday morning)*
Credit Cards: AE, DC, MC, V
English Spoken.

There are few furniture and housewares shops that are housed in 17th-century palazzi, but Spazio Sette is. Even if you aren't in the market for a piece of furniture, it's worth going to have a look at this beautiful store. You'll find the furniture on the top floor (the floor nearest the frescoed ceiling), and it's all modern, high-tech, and different. There are some beautiful wooden pieces, notably a desk big enough for the biggest Mister Big, as well as fabulous glass-fronted bookshelves (the desk is 7.5 million lire; the bookshelves run 1.2 million lire per unit). A lot of the upholstered furniture belongs to the "anything to be different" school of design, and it's not, in truth, very comfortable or nice to look at. However, there are some comfy black cotton upholstered armchairs at just 400,000 lire each, as well as a magnificent 12-foot sofa that's soft but supporting at the same time. The price on the sofa depends on the fabric you want it covered in—it ranges from 8 million lire in plain cotton to 15 million lire or so in suede. The other two floors of this magnificent store are devoted to housewares. For more information, see "Housewares."

HANDCRAFTS

MONDO ANTICO
Via dei Pianellari 17 (tel. 656-1261)
Hours: *Monday through Saturday from 10 a.m. to 12:30 p.m. and 3 to about 6 p.m. (closed Monday morning)*
Credit Cards: *None*

The hours listed for Mondo Antico are a little iffy only because the owner—a very nice man, by the way—keeps the hours that suit him. You might see him in his cluttered shop at midnight or you might see the place shuttered for days. But if you find it open, and have a taste for curiosities, then you're in luck. Mondo Antico sells what are best described as Roman versions of Joseph Cornell boxes. The owner of the shop finds prints of Rome or interiors of Roman churches and palaces; then he carefully cuts them into their component parts, hand-colors each, and then reassembles them three-dimensionally within a glass-fronted box he has covered with his own handmade paper. The results are enchanting, and a lot better than a Colosseum ashtray as a memento of your trip to Rome. Supplies, like the hours, are uncertain. Sometimes he'll have as many as three or four boxes on hand; other times none at all. In October or so, he retools and makes nothing but nativity scenes, the Holy Family with a 17th-century Roman background. Two years ago you could have bought a view of the Piazza Navona for 25,000 lire. The boxes are now going for 100,000 lire and up. Buy one while you can.

HATS

MARA
Via Borgognona 4G (tel. 679-5448)
Metro Stop: *Spagna*
Hours: Monday through Saturday from 9:30 a.m. to 1:30 p.m. and 4 to 8 p.m. (closed Monday morning)
Credit Cards: None

It's hard to believe that shops like this still exist. In a tiny parlor, furnished with Louis XV furniture, you discuss the hat you'd like with Signora Mara. Once you have decided what you want, Mara and her assistant sit in the back of the shop and work for weeks until your creation is ready. The hats tend to be dainty, classic, and a touch old-fashioned. Mara, however, has business enough to see her through the next few years, as she is the preeminent milliner in the city. She does a roaring trade in bridal veils—if you consider one handmade silk veil every eight weeks for 1.4 million lire "roaring"—and they are passed from mother to daughter like the works of art they are. Mara hints that she has provided hats and veils for heads that normally wear crowns, but she is far too discreet to mention any names. A simple, off-the-rack cloche or turban is 100,000 lire. Specially made hats range upward from 500,000 lire.

HOUSEWARES

FORMA E MEMORIA
Via di Ripetta 148 (tel. 654-7622)
Hours: Monday through Saturday from 10 a.m. to 1 p.m. and 3:30 to 7:30 p.m. (closed Monday morning)
Credit Cards: AE
English Spoken.

For more details on this store, see "Furniture." There isn't that much in the way of housewares at Forma e Memoria, but what there is should be seen. The furniture is expensive, but the glass and cardboard items are not. There are lovely long-stemmed martini-type glasses here with a colored shaft at just 6,000 lire each. The decorated file boxes are 12,000 lire to 20,000 lire; a beautiful black marble pepper mill is 30,000 lire.

NAJ OLEARI
Via di San Giacomo 25 (tel. 678-0045)
Metro Stop: *Spagna*
Hours: Monday through Saturday from 10 a.m. to 1:30 p.m. and 4 to 8 p.m. (closed Monday morning)
Credit Cards: AE, DC, MC, V
English Spoken.

Naj Oleari makes a number of items for the home in its trademark ultra-cute style. You'll find things like big, bright umbrellas covered in the Naj Oleari cloth patterns for 45,000 lire, a gardening set in a Naj Oleari carrying case for 75,000 lire, as well as things for the bath: soaps, potpourris, and bath scents.

PITTI
Via di San Giacomo 19 (Tel. 679-5930)
Metro Stop: Spagna
**Hours: Monday through Saturday from 10 a.m. to 1:30 p.m. and
   4 to 7:30 p.m. (closed Monday morning)**
Credit Cards: AE

Pitti has some of the most interesting housewares in the city. For example, an exceptional Colosseum tea service designed by the eccentric Milanese designer Piero Fornesetti. Each cup is the Colosseum in miniature, as are the creamer, sugar bowl, and teapot. It's an expensive bit of trompe l'oeil. Each cup is 45,000 lire, the teapot is 175,000 lire, and the creamer and sugar bowl are 80,000 lire each. Also interesting is a set of trompe l'oeil arched bookends at 70,000 lire a set.

SPAZIO SETTE
Via dei Barbieri 7 (tel. 654-7139)
**Hours: Monday through Saturday from 10 a.m. to 1:30 p.m. and
   4 to 8 p.m. (closed Monday morning)**

Spazio Sette: Probably the only furniture and kitchenware store in the world housed in a Renaissance palazzo

Spazio Sette was listed previously in the "Furniture" section, but there's far more than furniture to be had here. On the first and second floors of this stunning store are perfectly designed pieces of cookware, lamps, and objects for everyday use. There are even some toys. Robust ashtrays in heavy, clear glass are 35,000 lire to 50,000 lire, depending on size. A set of perfectly designed kitchen knives, running from a tiny paring knife up to a cleaver, cost 175,000 lire. On the mezzanine are magnificent pasta pots and collanders that would be the delight of any avid pasta cook.

VALENTINO PIU
Via Condotti 13 (tel. 679-5207)
Metro Stop: *Spagna*
Hours: *Monday through Saturday from 10 a.m. to 1:30 p.m. and 4 to 8 p.m. (closed Monday morning)*
Credit Cards: *AE, DC, MC, V*
English Spoken.

Valentino Piu is next to, but upstairs from, Valentino Uomo. On the first floor above street level you'll find a series of small rooms which have every Valentino product you can't wear. There are Valentino pens and lighters, as well as Valentino linens, towels, and fabrics. The Valentino porcelain is a good way to buy the name but not mortgage your house to do it. A lovely Valentino china creamer and sugar bowl is 85,000 lire. A simple tea cup and saucer is 75,000 lire. Everything comes beautifully giftwrapped and securely packed, so an item from Valentino Piu makes a great wedding gift.

JEWELRY

ANTIQUE

L'ORIUOLO
Via di Santa Maria dell'Anima 40 (tel. 687-7105)
Hours: *Monday through Saturday from 10 a.m. to 1 p.m. and 4 to 8 p.m. (closed Monday morning)*
Credit Cards: *AE, DC*
English Spoken.

Masses of offbeat antique jewelry are found at this fascinating little shop near the Piazza Navona (see also Antiques"). Most of the jewelry is for women, though there are some great cufflinks and tie bars for men as well. Most of the designs (for men and women) are costume pieces, but there are some gemstone items as well—not Harry Winston quality, but not bad either. Most of the jewelry dates from the 1920s through the 1950s. Prices are reasonable: '20s-style bangles in Bakelite which would have looked great on Nancy Cunard are 25,000 lire apiece. Rope upon rope of different textured and multicolored beads from the 1930s are 50,000 lire to 90,000 lire. There's a ton of '50s-style clip-on earrings with eccentric Jean Arp–type designs priced as low as 15,000 lire and as high as 50,000 lire.

COSTUME

BACI E GIOIE
Via Cola di Rienzo 278 (tel. 653-0555)
Metro Stop: Lepanto
Hours: Monday through Saturday from 9:30 a.m. to 1:30 p.m. and 4 to 8 p.m. (closed Monday morning)
Credit Cards: AE, DC, MC, V

There's a mixture of costume jewelry and what Italians call *gioielli poveri* (literally "poor jewels," jewelry made with inexpensive materials like silver and semiprecious stones) at this small, cheerful shop on Via Cola di Rienzo. The costume pieces are very much in the clunky-funky mode—large necklaces in black and red plastic decorated with "diamonds." The "real" jewelry ranges from the very delicate—a necklace of freshwater pearls and gold, at 125,000 lire—to silver and turquoise necklaces and bracelets which, although made in Italy, clearly owe something to the American West.

PON PON
Via Nazionale 222 (tel. 461-466)
Metro Stop: Repubblica
Hours: Monday through Saturday from 9:30 a.m. to 1:30 p.m. and 3:30 p.m. to 7:30 p.m. (closed Monday morning)
Credit Cards: AE, V

As you come through the door of Pon Pon you may think you're in a shop the size of a refrigerator—no matter, the tiny space is jammed with beads and bangles, decorated belts, shoes, combs, and barets. Then you realize there's a second floor where you'll find thousands of items in the funky-but-fun department. Prices are low, low, low—and some things are, in a word, tacky beyond belief. But a lot of the stuff is quite attractive. An imitation gold or silver beaded choker is 30,000 lire. There is an amazing array of clip-on earrings, some with "rubies" the size of croquet balls (12,000 lire); yet there are others, like a pair of "pearl and diamond" clip-ons, which you could wear to an opening night at the opera and unless someone was gauche enough to peer at them with a jeweler's loupe they'd pass for the real thing. You'll also find a vast selection of hair ornaments: velvet bows (with or without rhinestones ranging from 6,000 lire to 15,000 lire), combs, clips, and hairbands, some of which are tasteful enough for a member of the DAR and others that most people wouldn't be caught dead in.

The leather items tend to be on the wild side. A wide spangled belt with a giant clasp is 45,000 lire. The leather and clear-plastic flats (not unlike the ones we saw at Emporio Armani) are 49,000 lire.

PRECIOUS

BULGARI
Via Condotti 10 (tel. 679-3876)
Metro Stop: *Spagna*
Hours: *Monday through Saturday from 10 a.m. to 1:30 p.m. and 4 to 8 p.m. (closed Monday morning)*
Credit Cards: AE
English Spoken.

At the height of the tourist season people line up to look in the *windows* of Bulgari, though few dare to enter the hallowed portals. Window-shopping might be all you can manage at Bulgari, as prices for just about anything begin in the many millions of lire and quickly shoot up to the many millions of dollars, Swiss francs, yen, and Deutschmarks. Of course, if you buy a piece of jewelry from Bulgari, you are buying the best.

LACE

CIR
Via Barberini 88 (tel. 483-470)
Metro Stop: *Barberini*
Hours: *Monday through Saturday from 9:30 a.m. to 1:30 p.m. and 4 to 8 p.m. (closed Monday morning)*
Credit Cards: DC

Cir has beautiful, genuine Florentine lace at prices that are competitive with Florence itself. A simple but elegant top with a lace collar is just 32,000 lire. A set of four embroidered placemats covered in little yellow flowers with matching napkins is 72,000 lire for all eight pieces. There are also some lovely clothes for little girls. A yellow dotted Swiss dress with a white yoke, embroidered with white flowers suitable for a girl 3 to 5 years old, is 56,000 lire. For an older girl, in the 8- to 9-year-old range, you can get a beautiful pure-silk dress with puff sleeves, a full skirt, and a delicately embroidered collar for 186,000 lire.

LEATHER GOODS

There are hundreds of leather good shops in Rome and I doubt that a comprehensive list of all of them would be compiled in a single, manageable volume. To further complicate matters, there are leather shops that sell all kinds of goods, from shoes to luggage, some that sell women's shoes and men's accessories (but no men's shoes), and those that sell no shoes at all. Instead of breaking this category down into dozens of smaller listings, I have mentioned what items are available at which stores.

ALFIERI
Via del Corso 2 (tel. 361-1976)
Metro Stop: *Flaminio*
Hours: *Monday through Saturday from 9:30 a.m. to 1:30 p.m. and 4 to 8 p.m. (closed Monday morning)*
Credit Cards: DC

Alfieri is your stop for rock-bottom prices on leather clothing for men and women. The quality is not the highest, but the prices are as low as anyone could ask for—and the selection is huge. A leather miniskirt available in a dozen different colors will cost 79,000 lire. A double-breasted heavy leather jacket in black or brown for a woman is 379,000 lire; the same item for a man is 400,000 lire. A black leather three-quarter-length skirt, cut very tight in the hips, is 165,000 lire. Men will find that 345,000 lire buys them a lined bomber jacket, and 50,000 lire will buy a man's black leather waist-length jacket in a softer, better-quality hide.

BELTRAMI
Via Condotti 18 (tel. 679-1330)
Metro Stop: *Spagna*
Hours: *Monday through Saturday from 10 a.m. to 7:30 p.m. nonstop (closed Monday morning)*
Credit Cards: AE, DC, MC, V
English Spoken.

Of all the Beltramis covered in this book, this one is the most beautiful. Occupying a huge section along the most prime stretch of Via Condotti, this gorgeous shop is graced with white marble floors and fountains, and salesgirls who themselves appear to have been carved from white marble. Prices here are much less than you'd expect—less than Milan, and a lot less than the United States (but not less than Beltrami Spa in Florence; see "Leather Goods" in Chapter IX). A pair of white leather half-heel day shoes costs 185,000 lire. A modern update of the old '60s chelsea boot, in white, red, or black, is 220,000 lire. A silver lamé sandal is 160,000 lire. Men's shoes are "inexpensive" also: a conservative but distinctive man's black oxford is 290,000 lire; a perfectly made loafer in black or brown runs 260,000 lire.

BRUGNOLI
Via di San Giacomo 25 (tel. 679-5280)
Metro Stop: *Spagna*
Hours: *Monday through Saturday from 10 a.m. to 1:30 p.m. and 4 to 8 p.m. (closed Monday morning)*
Credit Cards: AE, DC, V
English Spoken.

A wood-framed doorway crowned with a circular beveled-glass window marks the entrance to Brugnoli, certainly Rome's most beautiful men's shoe shop. Inside you'll find quilted couches, polished wood and brass, and extremely polite sales staff. Brugnoli sells men's shoes only, and they tend to be either of English make or English style. A pair of suede wingtips, made in Italy, but looking as if they come from the West End, costs 145,000 lire. A pair of oxblood loafers, with a dash of Italian style, is 125,000 lire. Once a year, in the spring, Brugnoli sells off-the-rack riding boots in butter-smooth leather for as little as 300,000 lire.

BRUNO MAGLI
Via Veneto 70 (tel. 464-355)
    and
Via Barberini 94 (tel. 486-850)
Metro Stop: *Barberini*
    and
Via Cola di Rienzo 237 (tel. 351-972)
Metro Stop: *Lepanto*
Hours: *Monday through Saturday from 9:30 a.m. to 1 p.m. and 3 to 7:30 p.m. (closed Monday morning)*
Credit Cards: AE, DC, MC, V
English Spoken: Via Veneto store only

The largest of these three Bruno Magli stores is the one on Via Veneto, and the smallest is on Via Barberini. All three are excellent shops, but with a large degree of merchandise cross-over. The Magli name on shoes for men and women is one of the best in Italy and their prices are not yet as high as other big names. They're also a lot cheaper here than they are in the United States.

A pair of suede slippers for women costs 50,000 lire at all three stores. Black patent-leather sling-back high heels are 175,000 lire, while lower-heeled slings are 150,000 lire. The classic Magli high heel in beautiful, smooth leather is 155,000 lire. Flats in red, sky or midnight blue, black, or white are 110,000 lire.

Men's shoes are traditional and extremely well made. A loafer in dark brown is 110,000 lire, wingtips are 280,000 lire, and a nice cordovan loafer is 195,000 lire.

CAMPANILE
Via Condotti 58 (tel. 678-3041)

Metro Stop: *Spagna*
Hours: *Monday through Saturday from 9:30 a.m. to 1:30 p.m. and 4 to 8 p.m. (closed Monday morning)*
Credit Cards: *AE, DC, MC, V*
English Spoken.

Campanile is a striking, modern store which stocks very elegant shoes and leather goods for men and women. A pair of black high heels is 170,000 lire. A pair of knee-high boots in soft light leather, black or brown, is 450,000 lire. Men's shoes are in the 150,000-lire to 200,000-lire range. Campanile also has a large selection of Gianfranco Ferré leather goods. A briefcase with the GFF logo is 400,000 lire.

CAPODARTE
Via Sistina 14A (tel. 475-968)
Metro Stop: *Barberini*
Hours: *Monday through Saturday from 9:30 a.m. to 1:30 p.m. and 4 to 8 p.m. (closed Monday morning)*
Credit Cards: *AE, DC, MC, V*
English Spoken.

The selection of shoes for men and women at Capodarte is enormous, ranging from hiking boots to dress shoes. The selection is so vast and the price range so broad that you're sure to find something here to interest you. Most of the shoes are sold under the Capodarte name, but there are some Fratelli Rossetti shoes, for men only, at standard prices.

CASAGRANDE
Via Cola di Rienzo 206 (tel. 687-4610)
Metro Stop: *Lepanto*
Hours: *Monday through Saturday from 9:30 a.m. to 1:30 p.m. and 3:30 to 7:30 p.m. (closed Monday morning)*
Credit Cards: *AE, DC, MC*
English Spoken.

Casagrande is a great source of name-brand bags and luggage, particularly Emilio Pucci. A tie-top tote bag in brown leather is 125,000 lire, and a mid-size white leather shoulder bag runs 125,000 lire. A perfectly made Pucci brown leather lady's briefcase is 350,000 lire. Valentino leather goods are also excellent buys here. A red leather wallet with lots of room for change and credit cards costs 85,000 lire. A Valentino wallet, also in red leather but with a brass-clasp change purse, goes for 103,400; a larger version of the same is 132,000 lire. A Valentino key case in midnight blue is 33,600 lire.

CÉLINE
Via Borgognona 4 (tel. 679-1063)

Metro Stop: *Spagna*
Hours: *Monday through Saturday from 9:30 a.m. to 7:30 p.m. nonstop (closed Monday morning)*
Credit Cards: AE, V
English Spoken.

Housed in a lovely palazzo facing the grand old Hotel Inghilterra, Céline is a beautiful shop and one you should see, even if you aren't buying. The sales help can be a little standoff-ish, but if you can summon up the courage to stare them down, take your time here and take a look. Although famous for women's shoes, Céline also has a large women's-wear section. Leather, though, is the thing to shop for—and it's hard to believe that these prices are any lower in Céline's main Paris store: for example, a blue leather, three-quarter-heel day shoe in lovely kidskin is 190,000 lire, and a red leather shoulder bag runs 355,000 lire. A shoulder bag in vinyl with the logo is 140,000 lire. The same amount will buy you a black leather Céline clutch, a smaller version of the same is 110,000 lire. A black patent-leather shoulder bag with an artfully worked gold-chain strap is 345,000 lire.

The clothing is quite costly, although a Céline polo shirt in white or red cotton doesn't seem excessive at 75,000 lire. A white suit in a military style—brass buttons, patch pockets—with a three-quarter-length skirt is 650,000 lire. A yellow linen suit—the jacket has a beautiful lace collar—costs 690,000 lire.

DICKINSON
Via Cola di Rienzo 292 (tel. 653-0443)
Metro Stop: *Lepanto*
Hours: *Monday through Saturday from 9:30 a.m. to 1:30 p.m. and 4 to 8 p.m. (closed Monday morning)*
Credit Cards: DC, MC
English Spoken.

Here you'll find good-value Italian shoes for men and woman. A well-made pair of men's wingtips in black or brown is 110,000 lire; tasseled loafers are 98,000 lire. The shoes for women are a little on the trendy side, and Dickinson's big seller seems to be raw silk high heels, which come in midnight blue, beige, black, bright red, and sky blue at just 35,000 lire. Sling-back half heels in white, green, or mauve are 32,000 lire. A pair of basic brown leather open-toe sling-back high heels costs 39,000 lire.

DIEGO DELLA VALLE
Via Borgognona 46 (tel. 659-2124)
Metro Stop: *Spagna*
Hours: *Monday through Saturday from 10 a.m. to 2 p.m. and 3:30 to 7:30 p.m. (closed Monday morning)*

Credit Cards: AE, MC
English Spoken.

Diego della Valle's new shop on Via Borgognona perfectly reflects the kind of merchandise sold there. The shoes are for women of taste and refinement, largely unconcerned with this years' "in" look—they are always well dressed. This sort of elegance comes at a pretty steep price. A pair of flats in black leather or black velvet is 185,000 lire. A stacked-heel day shoe with a simple cameo adornment runs 245,000 lire.

DOMINICI
Via del Corso 14 (tel. 361-0591)
Hours: *Monday through Saturday from 9:30 a.m. to 7:30 p.m. nonstop (closed Monday morning)*
Credit Cards: AE, DC, MC, V
English Spoken.

This chain of inexpensive, trendy shoe stores used to be called Santini and Dominici—the Santini has been dropped now, but the styles remain the same. Sometimes it's a little hard to tell if a shoe is for a man or a woman, as all the shoes are colorful, offbeat, and lots of fun. A pair of green patent-leather lace-ups for a man costs 139,000 lire. The famous Dominici woven-leather flats—incorporating five or six different colors of leather—for women are 79,000 lire. A pair in just black-and-white leather is 79,000 lire also. Tasseled moccasins for a woman (I think) in white, red, or blue are 89,000 lire. Suede flats come in eight different colors for a mere 19,000 lire.

On the far side of town, at the corner of Via Cavour and Via Panisperna—a part of the city you'd be unlikely to visit unless you were going to see the great Basilica of Santa Maria Maggiore—is the Dominici discount outlet. This small, drab store has all the shoes that just couldn't cut it in the main shopping district—some of them are pretty strange, but they can be had here for peanuts. A pair of red vinyl flats is 8,000 lire. A pair of black and sky-blue loafers for a man runs 19,000 lire. If you're in the neighborhood, it's worth a look.

DONÈL
Via Cola di Rienzo 75 (tel. 457-908)
Metro Stop: *Lepanto*
Hours: *Monday through Saturday from 9:30 a.m. to 1:30 p.m. and 4 to 8 p.m. (closed Monday morning)*
Credit Cards: None

Inside Donèl you'll find a very elegant store, all white columns and white leather banquettes, but you might never enter the place. This is one of those shoe stores typical of Via Cola di Rienzo where the display windows are bigger than the shops themselves. You can see virtually every item they stock without speaking to a salesperson—all the shoes for men and women, as well as their line of handbags are in the window. Prices are low. A blue suede moccasin is 34,900 lire. A white leather half heel is 27,900 lire and a yellow leather sling-back with an open toe runs 29,900 lire. Men's brown lace-ups are 59,900, and a wingtip in black or brown will cost 70,000 lire.

The small selection of Donèl's own leather bags and purses begin at 79,000 lire for a good-size shoulder bag and don't go much beyond 150,000 lire.

ETIENNE AIGNER
Piazza di Spagna 7 (tel. 678-6995)
Metro Stop: *Spagna*
Hours: *Monday through Saturday from 9:30 a.m. to 1:30 p.m. and 3:30 to 7:30 p.m. (closed Monday morning)*
Credit Cards: *AE*
English Spoken.

With a French first name and a German surname, Etienne Aigner is of course Italian—Tuscan to be exact. This shop in the Piazza di Spagna is one of the most beautiful shops in the city. Aigner has eschewed the hi-tech chrome-and-glass look that so many designers have gone in for recently. This shop, from its massive wood portals to its dark-wood and leather interior, looks more like an old hunting lodge than a store. There are leather goods available here for men and women as well as a selection of clothing. An Etienne Aigner shoulder bag in rich, soft leather is 318,000 lire. A classic low-heeled loafer for a woman costs 179,000 lire. A suede skirt reaching to just below the knee is 1,164,00 lire.

The shoes for men are very traditional and quite expensive: a pair of loafers is 225,000 lire; a pair of black lace-ups, 290,000 lire.

FENDI
Via Borgognona 4E, 4L, 36, and 38 (tel. 679-7641, 679-7642, 679-7643, or 679-7644)
Metro Stop: *Spagna*
Hours: *Monday through Saturday from 9:30 a.m. to 7:30 p.m. nonstop (closed Monday morning)*
Credit Cards: *AE, DC, MC, V*
English Spoken.

It it's got a Fendi "F" on it, you'll find it on this street. The Fendi sisters have taken over Via Borgognona and dotted it with shops selling their entire range of merchandise. The shop at no. 36 is the flagship and it has everything: clothes, luggage, and menswear, but leather is the mainstay. Prices are the lowest in Italy. A big woven shoulder bag, Fendi's answer to the Bottega Veneta bag, is 118,000 lire. A small shoulder bag in white crocodile costs 150,000 lire. There's even a discount tray at this location where you can pick up some inexpensive Fendi gifts to wow the folks back home. A cotton wallet with the Fs all over it is just 9,500 lire. A leather key case (only one F) runs 12,500.

ROME SHOPS: LEATHER GOODS

At no. 38 you'll find Fendi luggage. In 1987 they featured the vinyl-and-cotton green-and-brown-striped style, and again you can secure some excellent buys. A change purse, with the stripes, the "Fs," and leather trim, is 34,000 lire, a foldover clutch handbag runs 80,000 lire, and a toilet kit is 38,000 lire. The larger, hard-sided suitcases in black with leather trim are 235,000 lire for a small overnight case, 400,000 lire and up for the larger sizes.

There are more bags at no. 4L. A ribbed canvas bag is 72,000 lire, and a leather shoulder bag or a giant leather-trimmed tote bag runs 93,500 lire.

Fendi shoes are at no. 4E. A very elegant striped half heel in leather is 187,000 lire. A pair of gold-flecked leather high heels for evening wear costs 198,000 lire. A sling-back high heel in brown or black is 189,000 lire.

FERDIN
Via Cola di Rienzo 154 (tel. 678-5641)
Metro Stop: *Lepanto*
Hours: *Monday through Saturday from 9:30 a.m. to 1:30 p.m. and 3:30 to 7:30 p.m. (closed Monday morning)*
Credit Cards: AE, DC, MC, V

Ferdin is one of the few shops in Rome that stocks the Florentine brand Casadei shoes for women. These ultra-elegant shoes will cost a fortune anywhere, but here at Ferdin the prices are a little lower. Colorful two-tone sling-backs with a half heel, in blue and white, red and black, or white and black, are 165,000 lire a pair. Beautiful leather high heels with a little lamé trim are 178,000 lire. An open-toed high heel in deep blue runs 165,000 lire.

FRATELLI ROSSETTI
Via Borgognona 5a (tel. 678-2676)
Metro Stop: *Spagna*
Hours: *Monday through Saturday from 10 a.m. to 7:30 p.m. nonstop (closed Monday morning)*
Credit Cards: AE, DC, MC, V
English Spoken.

The Fratelli Rossetti shop on Via Borgognona is a single whitewashed room selling the full line of Rossetti shoes for men and women. A stunning lady's half boot in suede and kidskin, stamped to resemble crocodile, is 175,000 lire. Kidskin high heels in soft blue, black, plum, jade, bronze, or patent leather are 142,000 lire. A pair of moiré silk flats with rhinestone accents are 210,000 lire.

The men's line is equally distinguished. A pair of fantastic crocodile loafers runs 690,000 lire. A pair of kidskin desert boots is 270,000 lire. A magnificent pair of wingtips in dark brown costs 260,000 lire.

GATTEGNA JUNIOR
Via Cola di Rienzo 178 (tel. 687-4660)

Metro Stop: *Lepanto*
Hours: *Monday through Saturday from 9:30 a.m. to 1:30 p.m. and 3:30 to 7:30 p.m. (closed Monday morning)*
Credit Cards: *AE, DC, V*

A good source of no-name inexpensive shoes. A three-quarter-length brown boot for a woman in good leather is just 75,000 lire. There's a good selection of high heels in the 40,000-lire to 50,000-lire range.

GAZELLE
Via del Corso 30 (tel. 361-4194)
Hours: *Monday through Saturday from 9:30 a.m. to 1:30 p.m. and 4 to 7:30 p.m. (closed Monday morning)*
Credit Cards: *DC, V*

Gazelle has inexpensive leather clothing for men and women. It won't last forever, but you won't pay much for it either. A pair of lined black leather pants for a woman costs 195,000 lire, while the same item for a man costs 225,000 lire. A knee-length leather skirt is just 139,000 lire, and a mini runs 115,000 lire. An aviator jacket for a man is 380,000 lire, and a waist-length suede jacket with a zip costs 295,000 lire.

GHERARDINI
Via Belsiana 48 (tel. 679-5501)
Metro Stop: *Spagna*
Hours: *Monday through Saturday from 10 a.m. to 1:30 p.m. and 4 to 8 p.m. (closed Monday morning)*
Credit Cards: *AE, DC, MC, V*
English Spoken.

The Florentine leather house of Gherardini is an old established name which has only recently opened a branch in Rome. Not content with an ordinary store, the Gherardini family took over a deconsecrated church in the heart of the downtown shopping district. Gherardini specializes in tasteful, refined luggage and handbags. Prices are very high. A very beautiful cosmetic case in vinyl with leather trim is 1.23 million lire, much more than you'd pay in Florence, but about the same as in Milan. There are some inexpensive Gherardini items, like leather change purses at 56,000 lire, key cases at 45,000 lire, and lipstick cases at 30,000 lire.

GIANNI VERSACE
Via Borgognona 41 (tel. 678-1732)
Metro Stop: *Spagna*
Hours: *Monday through Saturday from 10 a.m. to 7 p.m. nonstop (closed Monday morning)*
Credit Cards: *AE, DC, MC, V*
English Spoken.

Versace has a second shop for ladies' leather goods a few blocks away from his clothing shop for women, near his men's store. The store, as you would expect, is a stunner, in the now-familiar Versace minimalist style. The prices are not minimalist at all: a simple pair of low black flats with a rounded heel is 305,000 lire; a large blue leather shoulder bag is 380,000 lire, and a red shoulder bag runs 295,000 lire.

GINOCCHI
Via Sistina 35 (tel. 463-925)
Metro Stop: *Barberini*
Hours: *Monday through Saturday from 9:30 a.m. to 1:30 p.m. and 4 to 8 p.m. (closed Monday morning)*
Credit Cards: AE, DC, MC, V
English Spoken.

Ginocchi sells everything in leather except clothes and shoes, but the most interesting objects for sale here are beautifully handmade, hand-tooled leather boxes for jewelry, cufflinks, and the like. They range in size from pillbox to the size of a lunch pail, tend to be dark blue or green, and always sport a fine gold trim. They range in price from 29,000 lire for a small one up to 100,000 lire for a large jewel box. In addition to these items, you'll also find a large selection of butter-soft wallets for men and women, in all sizes and shades of leather beginning at 37,000 lire. There are some very traditional ladies' handbags beginning around 89,000 lire for a white leather clutch.

GRISPINI
Via Sistina, at the corner of Via Francesco Crispi 59 (tel. 679-0290)
Metro Stop: *Barberini*
Hours: *Monday through Saturday from 9:30 a.m. to 1:30 p.m. and 3:30 to 7:30 p.m. (closed Monday morning)*
Credit Cards: AE, DC, MC, V
English Spoken.

Grispini is just up the street from Ginocchi, but there is little in the way of merchandise overlap. Grispini has a large selection of beautiful wallets for men and women, starting at 35,000 lire. The real finds here, though, are handbags and purses. A Bottega Veneta look-alike is 250,000 lire, and they have Krizia shoulder bags for as little as 200,000 lire—they also have a giant Krizia shoulder bag with the Krizia "Ks" cut out at 400,000 lire. (You can get the same item at Discount System for 60% less; see "Discount Shopping.")

GUCCI
Via Condotti 8 (tel. 678-9340) and Via Borgognona 25 (tel. 678-3232)
Metro Stop: *Spagna*
Hours: *Monday through Saturday from 10 a.m. to 7:30 p.m. nonstop (closed Monday morning)*

Credit Cards: AE, DC, MC, V
English Spoken.

The main difference between these two Guccis is that the one on Via Condotti is bigger and carries Gucci everything. As in all the main Gucci stores in Italy, it's possible to spend a lot or a little, depending on what you're in the market for. At the Via Condotti shop a man's loafer with the double-G bridle is 240,000 lire; a Gucci ashtray with the same logo goes for 24,000 lire. A red leather lady's loafer is 165,000 lire and a pair of sandals runs 105,000 lire. Although the store is large, it's always jammed with people—the salesperson-to-shopper ratio must be one to one, and they hover—they'll also drag out every bag, shoe, and purse in the place to make sure you get exactly what you want. There's no armtwisting to buy, but there's always a salesperson at your elbow. It's wise, therefore to check out the windows before you go in. Gucci clearly marks the prices of everything on display, so you can browse outside without having to play "guess the price."

Prices don't differ all that much from the other Guccis in Italy. A red vinyl-and-leather overnight bag is 360,000 lire; a leather tote is 275,000 lire. A leather shoulder bag costs 175,000 lire.

Over on Via Borgognona prices seem a little lower but the merchandise is largely the same. The salepeople act in much the same way (there must be a Gucci school somewhere). They can be beaten at their own game, however. I witnessed a marathon bargaining session between a Japanese tourist and a salesperson—she wanted a discount, and after much negotiation she got it. Of course, she had bought ten handbags, seven briefcases, and half a dozen other items, but she got them at 15% off. (Gucci would deny this happened, but I was there and saw the whole thing.)

Bargaining—unless you're buying in bulk—is not the name of the game, though. The rest of us must pay 98,000 lire for a sling-back brown leather flat or 330,000 lire for a big black leather shoulder bag. A smaller shoulder bag in taupe kidskin is 180,000 lire. A Gucci beach towel will cost 65,000 lire. The least expensive item at this particular Gucci is a pair of very nice espadrilles for 44,000 lire—with the Gucci "Gs" all over the sole!

HERMÈS
Via Condotti 60 (tel. 679-7687)
Metro Stop: Spagna
Hours: Monday through Saturday from 10 a.m. to 7:30 p.m. nonstop (closed Monday morning)
Credit Cards: AE, DC, MC, V
English Spoken.

There are those who say that Hermès in Rome is less expensive than the one in Paris. That might be, but a small black leather handbag at 1.8 million lire is not my idea of a bargain. A larger version of the same is 2.3 million lire. The shop is very impressive and looks a lot like the head office in Paris, but there is one item that's actually cheaper here than there: the famous Hermès scarf at 160,000 lire—about 20% cheaper than in Paris. It's purely speculation, but could it be that they're actually made in Italy?

HERZEL
Via di Propaganda 14 (tel. 679-5114)
Metro Stop: *Spagna*
and
Via Sistina 5 (tel. 462-232)
Metro Stop: *Barberini*
Hours: Monday through Saturday from 10 a.m. to 1:30 p.m. and 3:30 to 7:30 p.m. (closed Monday morning)
Credit Cards: AE, DC, MC, V
English Spoken.

If you're in the market for some decidedly different Italian shoes, then the two small Herzel shops are for you. They have a wild selection of women's boots, shoes, and sandals, all of them spangled, glittery, shiny, or decorated with bits of fur, silver studs, or fake jewels. Silver lamé sandals that lace up the ankle and are decorated with "rubies" are 75,000 lire. A pair of multicolored high heels in gold leather is 125,000 lire. Flats with fur and silver trim are 165,000 lire.

I CERVONE
Via del Corso 38 (tel. 679-3850)
Hours: Monday through Saturday from 9:30 a.m. to 1:30 p.m. and 4 to 8 p.m. (closed Monday morning)
Credit Cards: AE, DC, MC, V

I Cervone has a vast selection of fashionable, inexpensive shoes for men and women. The shop itself isn't much to look at—it's crammed with shoes—but the quality and the prices make up for the lack of ambience. A pair of dark-blue half-heel pumps costs 79,000 lire and the leather is great. A sling-back high heel in silver, gold, or bronze lamé is 69,000 lire. A delicate suede moccasin is only 49,000 lire. Men will find good-quality slip-ons at 79,000 lire to 99,000 lire, wingtips for 160,000 lire, leather desert boots for 65,000 lire, and oxfords for 175,000 lire.

LUCIANO LOZZI
Via Frattina 102 (tel. 678-2678)
Metro Stop: *Spagna*
Hours: Monday through Saturday from 9:30 a.m. to 1:30 p.m. and 4 to 8 p.m. (closed Monday morning)
Credit Cards: AE, DC, MC, V
English Spoken.

Handbags and luggage are the things to shop for at this good-size shop on Via Frattina. Most of the merchandise comes with the Lozzi name on it, but there's a selection of Mandarina Duck as well. A leather tote in black is 79,000 lire. A patent-leather clutch runs 45,000 lire, and a brown leather shoulder bag, 175,000 lire. The Mandarina Duck prices are about standard for Rome: the smaller change purses and wallets are 25,000 lire to 40,000 lire; the large luggage pieces are 150,000 lire to 350,000 lire.

MADA
Via della Croce 57 (tel. 679-8660)
Metro Stop: *Spagna*
Hours: *Monday through Saturday from 10 a.m. to 1:30 p.m. and 4 to 8 p.m. (closed Monday morning)*
Credit Cards: AE, DC, MC, V
English Spoken.

Mada is a small, fashionable shop with good buys on ladies' shoes, boots, and handbags. A giant shoulder bag in smooth black leather with brass hardware is 126,000 lire, a pair of silver lamé sandals runs 100,000 lire, and a lovely pair of red boots with tassels is 280,000 lire.

MARIO VALENTINO
Via Frattina 58 and 84 (tel. 679-1242 or 679-1246)
Metro Stop: *Spagna*
Hours: *Monday through Saturday from 10 a.m. to 7:30 p.m. nonstop (closed Monday morning)*
Credit Cards: AE, DC, MC, V
English Spoken

There are men's and women's shoes only at no. 84 and shoes, leather clothing, and luggage at no. 58. Mario Valentino is an acquired taste, but if you like the flamboyant shoes and clothes, then these two shops are for you. A pair of bright-red loafers with a stacked heel for a man is 230,000 lire. A pair of gold loafers for a woman—with an even higher heel—is 220,000 lire.

MASLIZ
Via Cola di Rienzo 129 (tel. 556-889)
Metro Stop: *Lepanto*
Hours: *Monday through Saturday from 9:30 a.m. to 1:30 p.m. and 4 to 8 p.m. (closed Monday morning)*
Credit Cards: AE

This is a tiny shop on Cola di Rienzo which has some fine buys on women's wallets and bags. A large Valentino wallet in a cool shade of blue is 70,000 lire; a Versace wallet in gray leather is 130,000 lire, and a matching credit-card case is 35,000 lire. There's Mandarina Duck too, a mid-size overnight bag costing 155,000 lire. An Enrico Coveri shoulder bag in beautiful dark-brown leather is 275,000 lire for a large one, 265,000 lire for a slightly smaller one.

MATCH
Cola di Rienzo 166 (tel. 675-7895)
Metro Stop: Lepanto
Hours: Monday through Saturday from 9:30 a.m. to 1:30 p.m. and 4 to 8 p.m. (closed Monday morning)
Credit Cards: AE, MC

This is another of the "it's all in the window" shoe stores on Via Cola di Rienzo—and it's proof positive that the inexpensive shoe is alive and well in Italy. It would be hard to pay more than 50,000 lire for a basic black high heel or 35,000 lire for a flat. Men will find loafers and oxfords in the 50,000-lire to 85,000-lire range.

MAURIZIO RIGHINI
Via Vittoria 63 (tel. 678-4655)
Metro Stop: Spagna
Hours: Monday through Saturday from 10 a.m. to 1:30 p.m. and 3:30 to 7:30 p.m. (closed Monday morning)
Credit Cards: AE, DC, MC, V

Righini has been making very upmarket luggage and bags since the 1930s, but like other great Italian leather houses, has added a lot of nonleather items to its range of merchandise. The store on Via Vittoria is a series of small, paneled rooms with a staff who would quite willingly jump through hoops if you asked them to. Someone has to pay for all this, of course, and Righini is not cheap. A pair of black slip-on crocodile loafers for a man is 690,000 lire. A large suitcase in a paisley print runs 600,000 lire, and a Righini bathrobe, made out of terrycloth, costs 450,000 lire. An extremely nice leather tote bag is 420,000 lire, and a small evening bag in jet-black leather is 225,000 lire.

NAZARENO GABRIELLI
Via Sant'Andrea delle Fratte 3 (tel. 679-1461)
Metro Stop: Spagna
Hours: Monday through Saturday from 10 a.m. to 2 p.m. and 3 to 7 p.m. (closed Monday morning)
Credit Cards: AE, DC, MC, V
English Spoken.

Nazareno Gabrielli is one of the most exclusive names in Italian leather goods for women. The small, hushed Rome shop, tucked away next to a church just off the Piazza di Spagna, has all the Gabrielli products, including the famous tweed-and-leather traveling bags that made the name famous. A large one costs 680,000 lire. A white leather clutch runs 275,000 lire, and a white shoulder bag, 325,000 lire. A small overnight bag in canvas and leather is 250,000 lire. It's possible to own a piece of Nazareno Gabrielli without spending a fortune: a herringbone tweed keycase costs 30,000 lire.

ODETTE
Via Nazionale 224 (tel. 454-767)
Metro Stop: *Repubblica*
Hours: *Monday through Saturday from 10 a.m. to 7:30 p.m. nonstop (closed Monday morning)*
Credit Cards: AE, DC, MC, V

Odette is another of those stores that sells leather clothing for men and women, all at decent prices and of reasonable quality. There are racks and racks of leather skirts, pants, and jackets—some pretty ghastly, but most quite appealing. And prices are low: a suede skirt is 248,000 lire, a smooth-leather dress runs 590,000 lire, and a pair of black leather silk-lined pants, 198,000 lire. Men will find three-quarter-length black leather jackets for 565,000 lire, a similar item, only shorter, is 478,000 lire.

RAMIREZ
Via Cola di Rienzo 151 (tel. 679-2467)
Metro Stop: *Lepanto*
Hours: *Monday through Saturday from 9:30 a.m. to 1:30 p.m. and 4 to 8 p.m. (closed Monday morning)*
Credit Cards: AE, MC, V

This is another inexpensive "all in the window" store with shoes for men and women. Men's shoes tend toward the conservative and cheap—you can get a pair of loafers here for as little as 29,900 lire. The shoes for women tend to be a little on the flashy side: spangly silver sling-backs cost 65,000 lire. If you want leather made to look like silver leopardskin, you'll have to pay 69,000 lire. But it's not all glitz at Ramirez. A very elegant black half heel, which looks as if it could have come out of the window of Diego Della Valle, is just 89,900 lire.

RAMPONE
Via del Babuino 98 (tel. 678-4231)
Metro Stop: *Spagna*
Hours: *Monday through Saturday from 10 a.m. to 1:30 p.m. and 4 to 8 p.m. (closed Monday morning)*
Credit Cards: AE, DC, MC, V
English Spoken.

Rampone is a fine shoe and leather-goods shop for women which sells a number of top names. Here you'll find Prada lace-up flats for 89,000 lire (cheaper than Milan), or black high heels at 188,000 lire. A Jacque St. Juste shoulder bag in smooth, soft black leather is 385,000 lire.

RAPHAEL JUNIOR
Via Veneto 98 (tel. 456-692)
Metro Stop: *Barberini*

ROME SHOPS: LEATHER GOODS

Hours: *Monday through Saturday from 10 a.m. to 7:30 p.m. nonstop (closed Monday morning)*
Credit Cards: AE
English Spoken.

As you might expect, this is the children's shoe division of the Raphael Salato chain. All the shoes for boys and girls bear the Salato name and cost quite a bit. A pair of Mary Janes à la Italiana—they come in blue patent leather and have gold accents on the strap—is 75,000 lire. A pair of boys' brown desert boots costs 85,000 lire.

RAPHAEL SALATO
Via Veneto 104 and 149 (tel. 493-507)
Metro Stop: *Barberini*
Hours: *Monday through Saturday from 10 a.m. to 7:30 p.m. nonstop (closed Monday morning)*
Credit Cards: AE
English Spoken.

The leather goods at Raphael Salato prove that the Via Veneto has lost none of its fashion allure

The two Raphael Salato shops on Via Veneto are elegant and extensive, and sell shoes for men and women. Apart from the Salato label, they also carry Andrea Pfister and Fratelli Rossetti. Salato's own shoes for women are different without being trendy. White sling-back high heels with a very sharply pointed toe are

230,000 lire. The same shoe in silver lamé runs 245,000 lire. Black satin Andrea Pfister high heels are 345,000 lire, and a pair of Andrea Pfister boots costs 600,000 lire.

Men's shoes are less exciting. The Fratelli Rossetti shoes are the same style and prices found at the flagship shop down on Via Borgognona. A Raphael Salato man's black lace-up with a rounded toe is 220,000 lire.

REGAL
Via Nazionale 234 (tel. 233-0929)
Metro Stop: *Repubblica*
Hours: *Monday through Saturday from 9:30 a.m. to 1:30 p.m. and 3:30 p.m. to 7:30 p.m. (closed Monday morning)*
Credit Cards: AE, DC, MC, V

Regal is a typical Via Nazionale shop: crowded with people and goods, and bursting with bargains. This is a great place to shop for some fine names in ladies' bags and wallets. The two main names here are Valentino and Mandarina Duck. A wide, woven Valentino belt in brown leather is 60,000 lire. A change purse in chocolate-colored leather is 85,000 lire, and a matching change purse costs 75,000 lire. A Mandarina Duck shoulder bag runs 69,000 lire, and an overnight bag in black, gray, or yellow nylon, 145,000 lire.

REMI
Via Cola di Rienzo 130 (tel. 687-4406)
Metro Stop: *Lepanto*
Hours: *Monday through Saturday from 9:30 a.m. to 1:30 p.m. and 3:30 p.m. to 7:30 p.m. (closed Monday morning)*
Credit Cards: AE, DC, MC, V

Remi is by no means the most glamorous men's and women's shoe shop in Italy, but with the prices they charge it doesn't really matter. There's something for everybody at this cluttered store—with prices beginning as low as 18,000 lire for your basic black leather high heel. No, it won't last forever, but you don't expect it to. Men's shoes begin at around 30,000 lire.

ROBIN
Via dei Giubbonari 48 (tel. 656-4479)
Hours: *Monday through Saturday from 9 a.m. to 1 p.m. and 4 to 8 p.m. (closed Monday morning)*
Credit Cards: None

Robin is another good, inexpensive shoe shop for younger men and women. Prices are moderate to downright cheap. It's an excellent source of sandals for women. Well-made, dressy leather sandals in black, brown, or blue sell for between 35,000 lire and 50,000 lire. A blue denim sling-back with a silver toe is 49,500 lire. Men's shoes tend to be casual: Italian boat and deck shoes are in the 40,000-lire to 60,000-lire range, and good-quality loafers cost 65,000 lire.

ROME SHOPS: LEATHER GOODS

ROECKL
Via Sistina 83 (tel. 679-0376)
Metro Stop: *Barberini*
Hours: *Monday through Saturday from 9:30 a.m. to 7:30 p.m. nonstop (closed Monday morning)*
Credit Cards: AE, DC, MC, V
English Spoken.

All of Roeckl's handbags, belts, luggage, and wallets are handmade, but that doesn't mean they cost a fortune. High-quality handbags in natural grain or dyed leather begin at about 80,000 lire and range up to 250,000 lire for a perfect black evening bag. There is a variety of leather belts for men and women, some finely tooled, others rather plain. They range in price from 40,000 lire to 100,000 lire.

SALVATORE FERRAGAMO
Via Condotti 73 (tel. 679-8402)
Metro Stop: *Spagna*
Hours: *Monday through Saturday from 10 a.m. to 7 p.m. nonstop (closed Monday morning)*
Credit Cards: AE, DC, MC, V
English Spoken.

Ferragamo's large new store on Via Condotti has a marvelous selection of their wonderful footwear for women at prices much lower than in the United States. A simple pair of perfect brown slip-ons is 165,000 lire. Summery two-tone crocodile and white patent-leather flats are 375,000 lire. Simple black leather flats run 140,000 lire. Satin high heels go for 225,000 lire and come in black or midnight blue. There are some lovely bags as well: an oval shoulder bag in soft brown leather is 320,000 lire, a big brown leather tote with brass trim runs 160,000 lire, and a black leather clutch, 135,000 lire.

SERMONETA
Piazza di Spagna 61 (tel. 679-1960)
Metro Stop: *Spagna*
Hours: *Monday through Saturday from 9:30 a.m. to 7:30 p.m. nonstop (closed Monday morning)*
Credit Cards: AE, DC, MC, V
English Spoken.

Right in the Piazza di Spagna, across the street from American Express, Sermoneta has been the place to buy gloves for decades. Crammed into two tiny floors are thousands of gloves for men and women in every imaginable size, design, lining, and hide. Prices are unbelievably low. A pair of smooth green leather three-button gloves is 40,000 lire (5,000 lire more if lined with silk). A pair of women's rust-colored suede gloves with a ruffled wrist is 50,000 lire. A pair of women's silk-lined, black kidskin gloves runs 30,000 lire (the same pair with a cashmere lining is only 45,000 lire). For men, there are fine leather

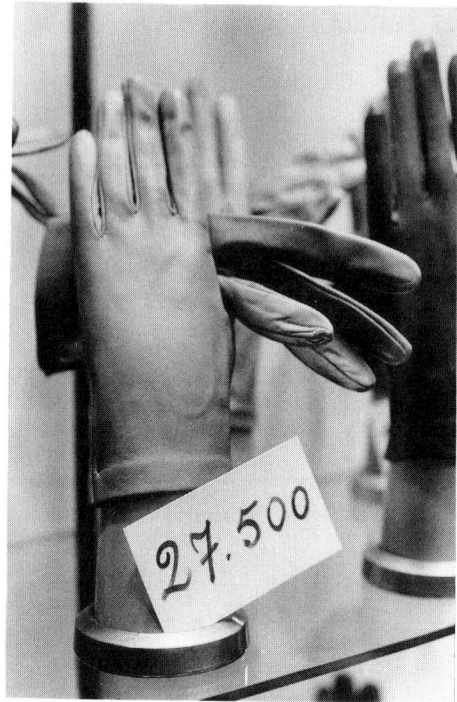

Sermoneta: Specializing in expensive-looking gloves at bargain prices

gloves lined with wool, in brown or black, for as little as 20,000 lire. A pair of "expensive" men's gloves—black leather with a warm cashmere lining—go for 35,000 lire.

TANINO CRISCI
Via Borgognona 4M (tel. 679-5461)
Metro Stop: *Spagna*
Hours: *Monday through Saturday from 9:30 a.m. to 1:30 p.m. and 4 to 8 p.m. (closed Monday morning)*
Credit Cards: AE, DC, MC, V
English Spoken.

Tanino Crisci has been making high-quality boots and shoes for men and women for decades, and this elegant store on the Borgognona has them all. A pair of perfect knee-high black boots for a woman runs 325,000 lire. They are virtually handmade, and finer leather would be hard to come by. A pair of red leather walking shoes is 229,000 lire, and a pair of white high heels, 200,000. Men with an eye toward traditional clothes will appreciate the fine oxfords, wingtips, and loafers, as well as the beautiful black evening lace-ups. The oxfords are 200,000 lire; the wingtips, in black or dark brown, cost 265,000 lire; and loafers range from 145,000 lire to 275,000 lire. The evening shoes are 285,000 lire.

TRUSSARDI

Via Bocca di Leone 27 (tel. 678-0280)
Metro Stop: *Spagna*
Hours: *Monday through Saturday from 10 a.m. to 7 p.m. nonstop (closed Monday morning)*
Credit Cards: AE, DC, MC, V
English Spoken.

Trussardi is the great new name in Italian leather goods, following in the tradition started by Gucci and Ferragamo. At the very chic Trussardi shop next to Versace on Via Bocca di Leone you'll find items like a Trussardi bicycle, with a leather saddle, saddle bags, and handlebar grips for 1.3 million lire, as well as leather bags with the distinctive Trussardi greyhound-head motif for 120,000 lire. There are also vinyl and canvas products, like a Trussardi tote bag, again with the greyhound head, at 66,000 lire, and a lovely, lined overnight bag for 245,000 lire. There are desk sets in leather, including a blotter, address book, and diary, for 325,000 lire, as well as masculine items like a tobacco pouch in green suede at 125,000 lire.

LINENS

CESARI

Via Barberini 1 (tel. 460-048)
Metro Stop: *Barberini*
Hours: *Monday through Saturday from 9:30 a.m. to 1:30 p.m. and 4 to 8 p.m. (closed Monday morning)*
Credit Cards: AE, DC, MC, V
English Spoken.

Cesari is a vast linen and lingerie shop right on the Piazza Barberini. As at other shops in this chain, the quality is very good, the selection wide, and the prices usually prohibitive. This is not the case at the Rome branch. I was struck by the difference in price between this store and the sister shop in Florence: prices are a good 25% to 30% cheaper here. Crisp linen sheets are 100,000 lire as opposed to 125,000 lire in Florence. Embroidered towel sets, from small guest towels to large bath towels, range from 49,000 lire to 79,000 lire. A beautifully embroidered terrycloth bath towel—far too nice, in fact, for the purpose—is 39,800 lire (it would cost at least 50,000 lire in Florence).

FRETTE

Via Nazionale 84 (tel. 462-641)
Metro Stop: *Repubblica*
Hours: *Monday through Saturday from 9 a.m. to 1:30 p.m. and 4 to 8 p.m. (closed Monday morning)*
Credit Cards: AE, DC, MC, V

The Frette shop on Via Nazionale feels as if it should be somewhere else, in a pricier part of town, to be exact. It's a very large, plush, expensive linen shop, selling high-priced sheets, tablecloths, blankets, and towels, as well as a huge selection of sleepwear and beachwear. One of the famous bright-red all-wool Frette blankets, for a double or a queen-size bed, costs 400,000 lire. Beautiful 100% cotton sheets with embroidered borders are 120,000 lire for a twin, 189,000 lire for a double, 325,000 lire for a king-size. Frette makes some of the nicest beach towels I've ever seen: a giant, thick colorful cotton towel is 65,000 lire (same as Gucci, but much nicer).

PRATESI
Piazza di Spagna 10 (tel: 679-0673)
Metro Stop: *Spagna*
Hours: *Monday through Saturday from 9:30 a.m. to 1:30 p.m. and 4 to 8 p.m. (closed Monday morning)*
Credit Cards: AE, DC, MC, V
English Spoken.

Pratesi, of course, is the preeminent name in Italian linens. This particular store, on the far side of the Piazza di Spagna, is one of the finest I've seen, with an extremely accommodating staff. The prices are lower here than in Milan, but the Milanese shop is nicer to look at. Pratesi is not cheap, no matter where you buy it, though it's a lot cheaper in Italy than in the United States. A full set of yellow embroidered double-size cotton sheets is a steep 810,000 lire. A beautifully worked satin quilt for a double bed runs 712,000 lire. Pratesi also makes luxurious lingerie. A white silk negligée trimmed in gold lace is 293,000 lire; a blue terrycloth bathrobe goes for 225,000 lire.

LINGERIE

TOMASSINI
Via Sistina 119 (tel. 461-009)
Metro Stop: *Barberini*
Hours: *Monday through Saturday from 9:30 a.m. to 1:30 p.m. and 4 to 8 p.m. (closed Monday morning)*
Credit Cards: AE, DC, MC, V
English Spoken.

Given the extraordinary degree of elegance and hand-work involved in a piece of Luisa Romagnoli lingerie (Tomassini is the only shop in Rome that sells the name), the prices are reasonable. The shop is small and consequently the selection is not that extensive, but for a relatively reasonable sum of money you're sure to find the perfect piece of lingerie here. A sleeveless, embroidered, cotton summer nightdress costs 140,000 lire. A shorter nightdress in white cotton with a scoop neck and ribboned sleeves and neck is just 78,000 lire. The most expensive item I saw was a long, flowing negligée in a pale-pink, dotted Swiss cotton with a lacy collar and sleeves, at 240,000 lire.

TUSSEDA
Via Frattina 25 (tel. 679-3576)
Metro Stop: Spagna
Hours: Monday through Saturday from 9:30 a.m. to 1:30 p.m. and 3:30 to 7:30 p.m. (closed Monday morning)
Credit Cards: AE, MC, V

Tusseda is a little less reserved than Tomassini, but it has fine lingerie nonetheless—and at much lower prices. A silk nightdress in pale blue with a lacey bodice is 175,000 lire. A pale-peach satin bed jacket with three-quarter-length sleeves runs 299,000 lire. There's also an extensive selection of beachwear.

LUGGAGE (see "Leather Goods")

MOSAICS

SAVELLI: IL MOSAICO ARTE E TRADIZIONE
Via Sant' Ufficio 27 (tel. 654-7017)
Hours: Monday through Saturday from 9:30 a.m. to 1 p.m. and 4 to 7 p.m. (closed Monday morning)
Credit Cards: AE, MC, V
English Spoken.

Standing in St. Peter's Square, facing the basilica, you'll find Savelli to your left, through the colonnade. This large shop has the biggest selection of mosaics in the city—probably in Italy, outside of the mosaic capital of the country, Ravenna. The works available include reproductions of the most famous mosaics of ancient Rome, like those found at Ostia, Pompei, Herculaneum, the Baths of Caracalla, and the Imperial Palace on the Palatine Hill.

Early Christian Rome is also well represented, with modern copies of the mosaics from the catacombs and other ancient places of worship.

The same craftsmen who produce the copies also make modern works, usually of a devotional nature. At Savelli you'll find Madonnas, popes, saints, and angels.

Prices range from about 50,000 lire for a small modern work to many millions for a large, colorful, intricate copy of an Imperial Roman scene. Mosaics are heavy, so Savelli will ship your purchase at an extra cost. However, their service is efficient and careful and well worth the money.

PAPER AND PAPER GOODS
(see "Stationery Supplies")

PORCELAIN

LA PORCELLANA BIANCA
Via dei Coronari 55 (tel: 656-2323)
Hours: Monday through Saturday from 9:30 a.m. to 1:30 p.m. and 3:30 to 7:30 p.m. (closed Monday morning)
Credit Cards: None

As the name says, white porcelain—that's all there is, white porcelain—but white porcelain in every possible shape, size, and variety. There are beautiful dinner plates at 35,000 lire each, cruets at 18,000 lire, casseroles from 40,000 lire to 100,000 lire (depending on size), salt and pepper shakers from 12,000 lire to 25,000 lire, and my particular favorite, a creamer shaped like a cow for 18,500 lire.

PITTI
Via di San Giacomo 19 (tel. 679-5930)
Metro Stop: *Spagna*
Hours: Monday through Saturday from 10 a.m. to 1:30 p.m. and 4 to 7:30 p.m. (closed Monday morning)
Credit Cards: AE

See "Furniture" or "Housewares."

RICHARD-GINORI
Via Condotti 88 (tel. 678-4151)
Metro Stop: *Spagna*
   and
Via Cola di Rienzo 221 (tel. 352-138)
Metro Stop: *Lepanto*
Hours: Monday through Saturday from 9:30 a.m. to 1:30 p.m. and 3:30 to 7:30 p.m. (closed Monday morning)
Credit Cards: AE, DC, MC, V
English Spoken: Via Condotti only

The shop on Via Condotti is the class operation—small, quiet, extremely expensive, while the shop on Via Cola di Rienzo is larger and cheaper. Look on Via Condotti (the people are very nice), but shop on Via Cola di Rienzo. At Via Cola di Rienzo you'll find a Richard-Ginori china service for 12 in fine porcelain with a wildflower pattern for 1,631,950 lire. The set is 41 pieces, including a casserole and platter. A plain black-and-white-patterned service for 12 is

468,000 lire. Another 41-piece service for 12 in an art deco orange-and-silver line-and-lozenge pattern costs 1.55 million lire. A simple stoneware service for 12 in pale blue is 378,000 lire. One of Richard-Ginori's famous ovenproof casseroles with the Italian fruit pattern is 125,000 lire—roughly 40% less than you'd spend in the United States.

VALENTINO PIU
Via Condotti 13 (tel. 679-5207)
Metro Stop: *Spagna*
Hours: *Monday through Saturday from 10 a.m. to 1:30 p.m. and 4 to 8 p.m. (closed Monday morning)*
Credit Cards: AE, DC, MC, V
English Spoken.

See "Housewares."

PRINTS AND ENGRAVINGS

ALDO DI CASTRO
Via del Babuino 71 (tel. 679-4900)
Metro Stop: *Spagna*
Hours: *Monday through Saturday from 9:30 a.m. to 1 p.m. and 3:30 to 8 p.m. (closed Monday morning)*
Credit Cards: AE, DC, V

Aldo di Castro is perhaps the best-known antique print dealer in Rome. There are racks and racks of high-quality prints and drawings dating from the 15th century onward. Of course, every corner of Rome is covered, from a single classical fragment to vast views of St. Peter's Basilica and Piazza. Prices begin at 15,000 lire for the common views and run into the millions of lire for the rare prints and drawings.

ARMANDO PERERA: see "Antiques"

CHIAMBRELLI
Via del Coronari 144 (tel. 656-0212)
Hours: *Monday through Saturday from 10 a.m. to 1 p.m. and 4 to 8 p.m. (closed Monday morning)*
Credit Cards: None

Chiambrelli is the only shop on Via dei Coronari that specializes in old, rare, and fine prints. They have an enormous selection of Italian themes, a large number of them hand-colored. It's a marvelous place to browse and the owner is extremely knowledgeable. Prices begin at about 20,000 lire.

RECORDS

RICORDI
Via Cesare Battisti 120 (tel. 679-8022)
Hours: Monday through Saturday from 9 a.m. to 1 p.m. and 4 to 8 p.m. (closed Monday morning)
Credit Cards: AE, DC, V
English Spoken.

It's no secret that the Italians love music, and while they enjoy foreign music, they vastly prefer their own home-grown variety, be it opera, bel canto, Neapolitan folk songs, or their own rocks stars like Mina, Vasco Rossi, Lucio Dalla, Pino Danieli, and Renato Zero (a transvestite rock-and-roller—something, you have to admit, you don't encounter every day). At Ricordi, an enormous record and sheet music store just around the corner from the central Piazza Venezia, you'll find them all.

RELIGIOUS ARTICLES AND VESTMENTS

The area around the church of Santa Maria Sopra Minerva (a few hundred yards from the Pantheon) is the center of the religious article industry. There are ecclesiastical outfitters where you can browse to see what the well-dressed cardinal is wearing these days. Don't think you can pick up a cardinal's biretta just for a laugh—the salespeople have been in this game a long time and they can spot an imposter a hundred yards away.

However, most of the shops stock religious objects and statuary which anyone can buy.

ANCORA
Via della Conciliazone 63 (tel. 656-8820)
Hours: Monday through Saturday from 9:30 a.m. to 1 p.m. and 4 to 7 p.m. (closed Monday morning)
Credit Cards: AE, MC
English Spoken.

At Ancora you'll find earnest seminarians and ancient learned clerics poring over editions of Thomas Aquinas in Swahili, and the writings of Dionysius the Areopagite in ancient or Demotic Greek. However, if you are in the market for religious articles, Ancora also has a large department given over to rosaries, crucifixes, missals, medals, and figures of the Holy Family and the saints.

If you want to buy religious articles at the head office, so to speak, i.e., at the Vatican, ignore the gaudy and tawdry stands and souvenir shops clustered around the colonnade and head for the best shop in the neighborhood of St. Peter's.

MARIA GAUDENZI
Piazza della Minerva 69A (tel. 679-431)
Hours: *Monday through Saturday from 9 a.m. to 1:30 p.m. and 4 to 7:30 p.m. (closed Monday morning)*
Credit Cards: None
English Spoken.

Gaudenzi has been supplying religious items to the Holy See and to pilgrims for decades and is probably the best-known name in the business. Their selection of rosaries, medals, statues, and crucifixes is huge, the salespeople are courteous, and the prices are reasonable. A specialty of the store are the ceramic Della Robbia–type reliefs of the Madonna, the Holy Family, and Saints. They are characterized by the traditional white-glaze figures on a beautiful blue background with a few splashes of bright-colored garlands, flowers, and fruit. A small figure of the Madonna and Christ child with a lovely colored swag is 75,000 lire. The larger figures cost 100,000 lire and up.

Smaller items, like rosaries and medals can be had for a few thousand lire, although it is possible to pay a great deal of money for rosary beads in silver and gold.

SHOES (see "Leather Goods")

STATIONERY SUPPLIES

PINEIDER
Via Due Macelli 68 (tel. 678-9013)
Metro Stop: *Spagna*
and
Via della Scrofa 7A, in the Piazza Cardelli (tel. 654-8014)
Hours: *Monday through Saturday from 9:30 a.m. to 1:30 p.m. and 4 to 8 p.m.*
Credit Cards: AE, DC, MC, V
English Spoken.

The Pineider on Via Due Macelli has just had a facelift and has become even more elegant than it was before. The whole place has been done over in brown marble and walnut paneling and looks magnificent. The quality of the Pineider products, of course, has not changed in 100 years. At both locations in Rome (the Via della Scrofa store is the larger of the two) you'll find Pineider's exceptional rag paper. There are small sets of lustrous paper in beige, white, pale blue, and pale yellow (each set named for a different Italian city) containing 20 sheets of writing paper and 12 envelopes. A set costs 35,000 lire. The larger gift boxes, which have a larger variety of paper and envelopes, as well as gift cards, cost 85,000 lire. This might seem like quite a lot to spend for paper, but remember that you'll be paying about twice the price at Pineider's only Stateside location, in the Trump Tower in New York City.

Pineider is based in Florence, the paper capital of Italy, so the shop there is even more impressive than the two here, but the prices are the same. However, if you want to see where the tradition was born, wait for Florence.

VERTECCHI
Via della Croce 70 (tel. 678-3110)
Metro Stop: *Spagna*
Hours: *Monday through Saturday from 9:30 a.m. to 1:30 p.m. and 4 to 8 p.m. (closed Monday morning)*
Credit Cards: AE, DC, MC, V

Vertecchi is always crowded with artists buying paints and other supplies, but it also has a vast selection of fun, cheap Italian notebooks and pens. A lot of the pens, like the famous snap-out pen, look as if they were something that a Memphis designer knocked off in his spare time. A few thousand lire will buy you ballpoints the likes of which you've never seen before. There is also an entire room devoted to expensive fountain pens—Waterman, Mont Blanc—and the like—but the prices are no lower than in their countries of origin, and in some cases more expensive than in the United States. Vertecchi is the kind of place where the less you spend, the more unusual the item.

TOYS

LA CITTA DEL SOLE
Via della Scrofa 65 (tel. 655-404)
Hours: *Monday through Saturday from 9 a.m. to 1 p.m. and 3 to 8 p.m. (closed Monday morning)*
Credit Cards: AE, DC, MC, V
English Spoken.

There are a number of these marvelous toy shops in Italy, but this is the largest. It specializes in educational (but not boring) toys, kites, books, and puzzles (which will drive adults to distraction, never mind children). There are lots of little stocking stuffers like tops, whistles, dolls, and yo-yos.

L'ERBAVOGLIO
Vis del Fiume 5 (tel. 360-6714)
Metro Stop: *Flaminio*
Hours: *Monday through Saturday from 10 a.m. to 1 p.m. and 3:30 to 7:30 p.m. (closed Monday morning)*
Credit Cards: *None*
English Spoken.

L'Erbavoglio is a tiny, cluttered store which specializes in new and antique mechanical toys. It's rare to see such a collection of new and reasonably priced toys of this type in this age of high-tech and macho-oriented toys. These are honest-to-goodness clockwork windup playthings. A ferris wheel, for example, is 45,000 lire. A clockwork set of tiny cars mounted on their own tracks—wind it up and let it go—is 20,000 lire. Some of the toys are downright peculiar: for 25,000 lire you can get a windup toy which consists of two bunny rabbits fighting over a carrot—they're trying to saw it in half, but don't seem to be getting anywhere.

WALKING STICKS

LA GAZZA LADRA
Via dei Banchi Vecchi 29 (tel. 654-1689)

"The Magpie" sells eclectic antiques as well as walking sticks

THE SERIOUS SHOPPER'S GUIDE TO ITALY

Hours: *Monday through Saturday from 10 a.m. to 1 p.m. and 3:30 to 7:30 p.m. (closed Monday morning)*
Credit Cards: *None*
English spoken.

The young proprietor of La Gazza Ladra ("The Magpie") knows more about walking sticks than anyone you are ever likely to meet. He has searched throughout Italy and the rest of Europe (many come from England) for the rarest and finest antique walking sticks. There are sturdy alpenstocks, malacca canes with silver tips, delicate carved ivory pieces, even 19th-century sticks in glass (from Venice, of course). Prices begin at 150,000 lire for the least ornate object, and top out at 650,000 lire for a silver and ivory-headed ebony stick from the English Regency period.

WINES

ENOTECA AL PARLAMENTO
Via dei Prefetti 15 (tel. 679-5156)
Hours: *Monday through Saturday from 9 a.m. to 1 p.m. and 5 to 8 p.m. (closed Thursday afternoon)*
Credit Cards: *None*

One of the best-known wine dealers in Rome, the Enoteca al Parlamento is an elegant vendor of wines and spirits, much patronized by the Italian members of Parliament (the Lower House is just around the corner). Here you'll find the great Italian wines—the barolos, barbarescos, and brunellos—at prices much lower than in the United States. A bottle of Renato Ratti barolo, from a great year like 1979, is 45,000 lire—it will cost more next year, though. The Enoteca al Parlamento has a small counter where you can have a refreshing glass of wine or champagne—everything from Mumm's to Veuve Cliquot—as well as small caviar or salmon snacks.

VINI E OLII
Via della Croce, at the corner of Via Mario dei Fiori (no phone)
Metro Stop: *Spagna*
Hours: *Monday through Saturday from 9:30 a.m. to 7:30 p.m. nonstop (closed Thursday afternoon)*
Credit Cards: *None*

This typical old wine and oil shop is one of the last of its kind in the heart of Rome. Virtually any kind of Italian bottled wine or liqueur can be bought here, but the real thrill is to have them draw a glass of their own wine from the cool,

18th-century marble tanks. The apprentices still wear the traditional long white apron and refer to the elderly proprietor as "maestro." Sadly, there is talk of tarting the place up into a London/Paris/New York–style wine bar. Doubtless, neither the quality nor the selection will suffer, but the atmosphere will. It seems that Rome isn't quite as eternal as we all thought it was.

INDEX

STOCKINGS

GENERAL INFORMATION

Access card, 17
Adami shipping, 19
Airmail, 18
Airport information: see Florence, Milan, Rome, Venice
Alimentari (grocery store), 24
American Express, 10; *see also* Florence, Milan, Rome, Venice
Asta auction house (Rome), 11
Auctions, 11
Availability of products in U.S., 10

Banking, 11; *see also* Florence, Milan, Rome, Venice
Bolliger Transport shipping, 19
Brerarte auction house (Milan), 11
Bruta and *bella*, 6
Business hours, 11–12; *see also* Florence, Milan, Rome, Venice

Cambio: *see* Currency Exchange
Ceramics, shopping for, 24–5
Chain stores, 12; *see also* names of specific stores in "*Establishments*" index
Cheeses, shopping for, 24
Chocolates, shopping for, 24
Christie's, 11
Comparison shopping, 10
Complaints: *see* Consumer complaints
Consulates, 14
Consumer complaints, 12
Credit cards, 17
Currency, 16
Currency Exchange, 11
Customs and duties, 13

Design, shopping for, 23
Detasse (rebate), 21
Direct-dial telephone codes, 22
Discount shopping, 14; *see also* names of specific stores in "*Establishments*" index
DOC wine designation, 29
DOCG wine designation, 29
Domus magazine, 23
Duties: *see* Customs and duties
Duty-free shops, 14

Embassies and consulates, 14
English spoken, 15

Faenza, 24
Faïence pottery, 24
Fashion, shopping for, 23–4
Fashion magazines, Italian, 10
Finarte auction house (Milan), 11
500-lire note, 16–17
Florence, 147–215; across the river and into the Pitti stroll, 164–8; airport, getting from, 149, 152; American Express, 153; banking hours, 153; Baptistery, 161, 163; Boboli Gardens, 167; business hours, 153; bus service, 152; Church of Santa Maria Novella, 171; Duomo, 161, 163; establishments listing, 173–215; getting around, 152; heart of Florence stroll, 157–64; high-fashion Florence stroll, 169–72; holidays, 153; *Il Porcellino*, 158; map of, 150–1; markets, 154; Museo degli Argenti, 167; orientation, 149–53; Palazzo Pitti, 166–7; Palazzo Vecchio, 161; pedestrian information, 152; Pitti collection, 166–7; post office, 154; restaurants and bars, 163–4, 167–8, 171–2; sales, 154; shopping strolls, 156–72; sightseeing, 160–3, 166–9, 171; taxes, 154; taxis, 152; tourist information, 152; Uffizi gallery, 160–1; weather, 152–3
Florentine stitch, 25
Food, shopping for, 24

Gettone telephone slugs, 21, 22
Gettoni telephone slugs, 21, 22
Glass, shopping for, 24–5
Guasto (broken) telephones, 21

Holidays, 15; *see also* Florence, Milan, Rome, Venice

Il Mercato Antiquario di Massimo Gelardini auction house (Rome), 11
Insurance for mailed packages, 19
IVA tax, 21; rebate, 21

Lace, shopping for, 25–6
Lake Cuomo silk production, 28
Leather goods, shopping for, 26–7
Legatori de libri, 27
Leonardo da Vinci duty-free shop, 14
Linate duty-free shop, 14
Lira, 16

INDEX

Lira pesante, 16
Long-distance phone calls, 22

"Made in Italy" shops, 14
Mailing of packages, 17–18
Mail orders, 15
Majolica pottery, 24
Markets, 15–16; *see also* Florence, Milan, Rome, Venice
Mazoni Finarte auction house (Milan), 11
Memphis-Milano studios, 23
Metric measurements, 9
Metric weights and measures, 16
Museums and sightseeing: Accademia (Ven.), 231–2; Baptistery (Flor.), 161, 163; Baths of Diocletian/Museo Nazionale Romano (Rom.), 305; Boboli Gardens (Flor.), 167; Brera Museum (Mil.), 50, 53; "Bridge of Sighs," 236; Church of Santa Maria Novella (Flor.), 171; Correr Museum (Ven.), 235, 236–7; Doges' Palace (Ven.), 235–6; Duomo, 161, 163 (Flor.), 54, 57 (Mil.); Galleria Vittorio Emanuele (Mil.), 54–5; Il Porcellino (Flor.), 158; La Scala Opera House (Mil.), 51; Museo degli Argenti (Flor.), 167; National Gallery of Art (Rom.), 294–5; Palazzo Barberini (Rom.), 294–5; Palazzo Ducale (Ven.), 235; Palazzo Pitti (Flor.), 166–7; Palazzo Vecchio (Flor.), 161; Poldi Pezzoli Museum (Mil.), 49–50; Saint Mark's Basilica (Ven.), 235, 236; Sistine Chapel (Rom.), 298; Teatro La Fenice (Ven.), 237; Uffizi Gallery (Flor.), 160–1; Vatican museums (Rom.), 297–8
Milan, 31–145; airport getting from, 36; American Express, 37; bank hours, 37; bargain shopping, 58–9; Brera area stroll, 50–4; Brera Museum, 50, 53; Corso Buenos Aires stroll, 58–9; Duomo, 54, 57; Duomo area stroll, 54–58; establishments listing, 60–145; Galleria Vittorio Emanuele, 54–5; getting around, 36–7; holidays, 38; La Scala Opera House, 51; map of, 34–5; markets, 38; metro system, 36; Monte Napoleone stroll, 40–50; orientation, 33–7; pedestrian information, 37; Poldi Pezzoli Museum, 49–50; post office, 37; restaurants and bars, 50, 53–4, 57–8; sales, 38; shopping hours, 38–9; shopping strolls, 40–59; sightseeing, 49–50, 53, 57, taxes, 39, taxis, 36–7; tourist information, 37; weather, 37
Misura, 19
Money matters, 16–17
Mosaics, shopping for, 27

Numero (size), 19

Olive oil, 24
Outdoor markets: *see* Markets

Packages, mailing, 18, 19
Paper goods and fine bindings, shopping for, 27

Pastries, shopping for, 24
Pazienza, 7
Phone orders, 15
Piazza Navona (Rome), 6
Piazza Vittorio (Rome) market, 15
Pineider stationer, 27
Piranesi prints, 27
Ponte holidays, 15
Postalmarket, 15
Post office, 17–18; *see also* Florence, Milan, Rome, Venice
Pottery, shopping for, 24–5
Prints and engravings, shopping for, 27–8
Punto firenze (Florentine stitch), 25

Ravenna mosaics, 27
Religious objects and vestments, shopping for, 28
Repairs policies, 18
Restaurants: *see* Florence, Milan, Rome, Venice
Returns policies, 18
Rome, 275–399; airport, getting from, 280–1; American Express, 283; Baths of Diocletian/Museo Nazionale Romano, 305; buses, 281–2; business hours, 283; discount house, 305; establishments listing, 307–99; getting around, 281–2; heart of Old Rome stroll, 299–303; holidays, 283; map of, 278–9; markets, 284–5; National Gallery of Art, 294–5; orientation, 277, 280–3; Palazzo Barberini, 294–5; pedestrian information, 282; Piazza di Spagna and north stroll, 289–91; Piazza di Spagna stroll, 286–96; post office, 285; restaurants and bars, 295–6, 298, 302–3, 305–6; Rome map, 300; sales, 285; shopping strolls, 286–306; sightseeing, 294–5, 297–8, 305; Sistine Chapel, 298; Spanish Steps area stroll, 293–4; subway, 281; taxes, 285; taxis, 281, 282; tourist information, 283; Vatican museums, 297–8; Via Cola di Rienzo stroll, 296–8; Via Condotti and south stroll, 288–9; Via del Corso stroll, 291–2; Via Nazionale stroll, 303–6; weather, 283

Salamon Augustoni and Algranti auction house (Milan), 11
Saldo (sales), 18
Sales, 18
Santa Maria Sopra Minerva religious objects, 28
Sconti (discount), 18
Sconto (discount), 21
Seamail, 18
Senior citizens discounts, 18
Servizi intercontinentali, 22
Shipping, 19
Shopping strategies, 9–22; American Express, 10; auctions, 11; banking and currency exchange hours, 11; before you go, 9; business hours, 11–12; chain stores, 12; comparison shopping, 10; consumer complaints, 12; customs and duties, 13; discount shopping, 14; duty-free shops, 14; embassies and consulates, 14; Eng-

GENERAL INDEX

lish spoken, 15; holidays, 15; mail orders, 15; markets, 15–16; metric weights and measures, 16; money matters; post office, 17–18; returns and repairs, 18; sales, 18; senior citizen discounts, 18; shipping, 19; sizes, 19; size conversions, 19–20; student discounts, 18; taxes, 20; telephones, 20–1; what to buy, 23–9

Shopping strolls: see Florence, Milan, Rome, Venice
Sightseeing: see Museums and sightseeing
Silk, shopping for, 28
SIP (phone company) long-distance phone centers, 22
Size conversions, 9, 19–20
Sizes, Italian, 19
Sotheby's, 11
Stamps, 17
Standa chain stores, 12
Strategies for shopping: see Shopping strategies
Student discounts, 18
Studio Alchemia, 23

Taglia, 19
Taxes, 21
Telephones, 21–2
Three-fire work, 25
Time difference between U.S. and Italy, 22
Tourist information: see Florence, Milan, Rome, Venice
Traveler's checks, 17

Upim chain stores, 12
U.S. size conversion chart, 9, 19–20

Vendita promozionale (promotional sale), 18
Venetian glass, 24–5
Venice, 217–74; Accademia, 231–2; airport, getting from, 223; American Express, 226; bank hours, 227; "Bridge of Sighs," 236; business hours, 227; Correr Museum, 235, 236–7; dining, 227; Doges' Palace, 235–6; establishments listing, 241–74; getting around, 223–5; gondolas, 224; holidays, 227; map of, 220–1; markets, 228; the Mercerie and the Ruga Rialto stroll, 237–40; *motoscafi*, 223; orientation, 219–26; Palazzo Ducale, 235; pedestrian information, 222–3, 225; Piazza San Marco and the Frezzeria stroll, 233–7; post office, 228; restaurants and bars, 232–3, 239–40; Saint Mark's Basilica, 235, 236; sales, 228; San Marco to Campa Morosino stroll, 229–33; sightseeing, 231–2, 235–7; shopping strolls, 229–40; taxes, 228; Teatro La Fenice, 237; telephones, 228; tourist information, 225; *traghetti*, 225; *vaporetti*, 223–4; water-bus service, 223; water-taxi service, 223, 224; weather, 225–6
Venice lace production, 25

What to buy, 23–9; *see also* individual items
Wines, shopping for, 28–9

ESTABLISHMENTS

&C (Florence), 169, 212
Accademia (Milan), 52, 72
Adriana Chelini (Florence), 165, 173
Adrianamode (Milan), 42, 82, 114
Ai Tre Cedri (Venice), 237, 246
Alberta Ferretti (Milan), 43–4, 82
Alberto Pierini (Florence), 170, 173–4
Al Campidoglio restaurant (Florence), 163
Aldo di Castro (Rome), 291, 393
Al Duca d'Aosta (Venice), 237
Alex (Florence), 170, 184
Alexander Nicolette (Milan), 44, 124
Alfieri (Rome), 292, 371
Alfonso Garlando (Milan), 52, 124
Algani (Milan), 68
Aliani (Venice), 238, 254–5
Alicia Rosas (Rome), 288, 334
Allo Scudo restaurant (Milan), 58
Alma (Milan), 48, 82–3
Al Mercante restaurant (Milan), 58
American Bookstore, The (Milan), 68
Ancora (Rome), 394–5
Angela Caputi: Florence, 166, 185, 200; Milan, 51, 83, 119
Anglo American Bookshop (Rome), 316
Annuciata gallery: see Galleria Annuciata
Antichita Lorena (Florence), 165, 174
Antico Martini restaurant (Venice), 233
Antonella Bensi (Milan), 48, 144
Antonini, Clara: see Clara Antonini
A Piu A (Rome), 292, 334
Araba Fenice (Venice), 235, 246
Archimede Seguso (Venice), 234, 255
Arform (Milan), 53, 115–16
Armando Perera (Rome), 291, 307, 393
Armando Pollini (Milan), 42, 124
Armani, Giorgio: see Giorgio Armani
Arte Antica (Milan), 48, 60
Arte Filatelia (Venice), 234, 241
Artstudio (Florence), 165, 174
A. Soligo (Rome), 291
A. Ugolini & Figli: see Ugolini e Figli
Avagolf (Milan), 46, 83
Avolio (Milan), 55–6, 72

Babington's Tea Rooms (Rome), 295
Baby House (Rome), 297, 317–18
BAC Art Studio (Venice), 231, 273
Baccani, Giovanni: see Giovanni Baccani
Baci e Gioe (Rome), 297, 369
Baila (Milan), 42, 83, 125
Barbara: Milan, 59, 125; Venice, 231, 246
Barba's (Milan), 48, 72–3
Bar Giamaica (Milan), 53

Bar La Pace (Rome), 302
Bar Santa Trinità (Florence), 168
Bar Signoria (Florence), 163
Bartolozzi, Guido: see Guido Bartolozzi
Basta: see Roberta e Basta
Battiston (Venice), 230
Bauer Grünwald Hotel (Venice), 230
Beccaria, Luisa: see Luisa Beccaria
Bellini, Tino: see Tino Bellini
Beltrami: Florence: Via dei Calzaiuoli, 157, 185–6; Via dei Pecori, 158, 202–3; Milan: 44, 84, 126; Rome, 288, 371
Beltrami Junior (Florence), 158, 202–3
Beltrami Spa (Florence), 170, 203
Benetton: Florence, 186; Milan: 44, 84; Rome: Via Condotti, 288, 318, 321, 334–5; Via Nazionale, 304
Benetton 0–12 (Milan), 69
Bensi, Antonella: see Antonella Bensi
Bergamini gallery: see Galleria Bergamini
Bernabei (Rome), 291, 321–2
Bernasconi (Rome), 360
Betta Scarpa (Venice), 235, 246–7
B. Finzi (Milan), 55, 84
Biagiotti, Laura: see Laura Biagiotti
Bice restaurant (Milan), 50
Biffi Scala café (Milan), 57–8
Bijoux Cascio (Florence), 169, 200
Biki (Milan), 45, 84–5
Bises (Rome), 357–8
Bisonte: see Il Bisonte
BM Bookshop (Florence), 179–80
Böhm, Osvaldo: see Osvaldo Böhm
Bomba de Clercq (Rome), 292, 335–6
Boni (Venice), 231, 261
Bonne Nouvelle restaurant: see Ristorante Bonne Nouvelle
Books on Italy (Rome), 302, 316–17
Borsalino (Milan): 55, 73, 115
Bortolozzi, Guido: see Guido Bartolozzi
Bottega del Artigiana del Libro (Florence), 170, 213–14
Bottega Delle Stampe (Florence), 211
Bottega San Felice (Florence), 165, 174
Bottega Veneta: Florence, 170, 203–4; Milan, 41, 126; Venice, 230, 261–2
Boutique Biki: see Biki
Box (Rome), 304, 336
Bramani (Milan), 57
Bresciani, Giusy: see Giusy Bresciani
Brighenti (Rome), 289, 336
Brioni (Rome), 294, 322–3
Brocca Rialto (Venice), 238, 244
Brucoli, Mauro: see Mauro Brucoli

ESTABLISHMENTS INDEX

Brugnoli (Rome), 292, 372
Brummell, Lord: see Lord Brummell
Bruna Soletti (Milan), 66
Brunelli (Milan), 61
Bruno Magli: Milan, 56, 126–7; Rome: Via Barberini, 294, 372; Via Coladi Rienzo: 297, 372; Via Veneto, 293, 372; Venice: Frezzeria, 234, 262–3; San Moisè, 230, 262–3
Bruno Rizzato (Venice), 235, 270
Buccellati, Mario: see Mario Buccellati
Buenos Sport (Milan), 59, 73, 85
Bulgari (Rome), 288, 370
Burchi (Florence), 164, 201

Cacharel (Milan), 56, 69, 73, 85–6
Caffè Alegmena (Milan), 107–8
Caffè Greco (Rome), 295
Caffè Moda (Milan), 56, 74, 86, 140
Caffè Resentin (Milan), 53
Caffè Vittoria (Rome), 295
Calderai (Florence), 158, 195
Calderoni (Milan), 45, 120
Calzaturificio di Parabaigo (Milan), 59, 127
Cammillo restaurant (Florence), 168
Campana Coen (Milan), 42, 61
Campanile (Rome), 372–3
Canelli, Paolo: see Paolo Canelli
Capodarte (Rome), 294, 373
Caponi, Loretta: see Loretta Caponi
Caputi, Angela: see Angela Caputi
Carlo Bises & Figli (Rome), 302
Carlo Tivoli: see Tivoli
Carrano (Milan), 48
Casadei (Florence), 169, 204
Casa del Formaggio (Milan), 109
Casa del Guanto (Florence), 159, 204
Casa dello Sport (Florence), 158, 180, 181, 186
Casa di Hogg (Florence), 169, 186
Casagrande (Rome), 297, 373
Casalini (Florence), 170–1, 204
Casanova Grill restaurant (Milan), 50
Casellati (Venice), 230, 242
Cashmere Cotton and Silk (Milan), 51, 74
Cassini (Venice), 230, 242
Castroni (Rome), 297, 298, 361 (bar)
Celine (Rome), 289, 373–4
Celleno (Rome), 297, 323
Cellerini (Florence), 170, 204–5
Cennini bar (Florence), 168
Cesare Paciotti (Milan), 46, 127
Cesari: Florence, 169, 209; Rome, 294, 389
Chelini, Adriana: see Adriana Chelini
Chiambrelli (Rome), 299, 393
Children's Club (Rome), 290, 318–19
Chiwawa (Rome), 336
Cima (Venice), 237, 247
Cinzia (Florence), 166, 186–7
CIR (Rome), 294, 370
Cirri (Florence), 158, 180, 201–2
Citta Del Sole (Milan), 144

Cittone, Elio: see Elio Cittone
Clan (Milan), 74
Clara Antonini (Milan), 48, 86
Clemente (Florence), 205
Clemente, G.: see G. Clemente
Colombo (Milan), 127
Colombo, David: see David Colombo
Companile (Rome), 288
Contemporaneo (Florence), 169, 181–2
Conti (Milan), 42, 86
Controbuffet (Milan), 52, 116
Controcorrente (Venice), 234, 247–8
Coppola & Toppo (Milan), 42, 128
Corner, The (Florence), 166, 194
Coronari gallery: see Galleria Coronari
Corrado Irioné (Milan), 48, 112
Corte Sconta restaurant (Venice), 239–40
Coruzzi (Milan), 56, 74
Cose (Milan), 41, 86–7, 114
Cose del '900 (Florence), 166, 174–5
Costa: see Melegari and Costa
Cova (Milan), 45, 108
Coveri, Enrico: see Enrico Coveri
Crisci, Tanino: see Tanino Crisci
Cromo (Milan), 52, 61, 119
Cruz, Miguel: see Miguel Cruz
Cucci (Rome), 288, 323, 337
Cusi (Milan), 43, 120

Dabbene, Roberto: see Roberto Dabbene
Da Luciano restaurant (Milan), 58
Dal Vecchio (Milan), 43, 120–1
Danieli Terrace restaurant (Venice), 239
Da Quinta (Rome), 359–60
Dario Ustino (Venice), 233, 270
Darsena (Milan), 59, 74–5, 87
Datti (Rome), 323–4
David Colombo (Milan), 44
Davoli Antichita (Rome), 301, 307–8
De Bernardi (Milan), 55, 87
De Pietri (Milan), 46, 128
Desart (Milan), 59
Desiré (Venice), 233, 259
Diana Due (Milan), 56, 128
Dickinson (Rome), 297, 374
Diego (Milan), 59
Diego della Valle: Milan, 42, 128–9; Rome, 289, 374–5
Discount System (Rome), 305, 356
Di Varese (Milan), 56, 129
Dodo (Florence), 164, 180
Dominici (Rome), 292, 375
Donèl (Rome), 297, 375–6
Doney restaurant (Florence), 171
Donini (Milan), 45, 87
Don Lisander restaurant (Milan), 50
Donna (Venice), 237, 248
Drogheria Solferino (Milan), 52, 87–8
Duca d'Aosta (Venice), 244, 248

INDEX

Ducci (Florence), 170, 196, 211–12
Duvet (Florence), 166, 187

Economy Book Center, The (Rome), 317
Eddy Monetti (Rome), 289, 337
Eli Colaj (Rome), 291, 337–8
Elio Cittone (Milan), 61
Élite (Venice), 238, 248
Eliza (Rome), 293, 338
Ellesse (Florence), 159
Ellesse Spa (Florida), 182
El Toulà restaurant (Milan), 58
El Tumbun de San Marc bar (Milan), 53
El Vaquero (Milan), 41, 129
Élysée (Venice), 235, 248–9
Élysée 2 (Venice), 234, 248–9
Emanuel Zoo (Rome), 289, 338
Emilio Pucci: see Pucci
Emporio Armani: Milan, 56, 75, 88, 132; Rome, 291, 319, 324, 338–9
Enny (Milan), 45, 129–30
Enoteca al Parlamento (Rome), 398
Enoteca Cotti (Milan), 145
Enrica Massei (Venice), 230, 249
Enrico Coveri (Milan), 56, 89
Ercoli (Rome), 290, 361–2
Ermenegildo Zegna (Milan), 48, 75
Erreuno (Milan), 41, 89
Eskenazi (Milan), 44, 62
Étienne Aigner (Rome), 291, 376
Eve (Milan), 56, 130
Excelsior hotel (Florence), 170, 171

Fallaci, Rudolfo: see Rudolfo Fallaci
Fallani Best (Florence), 170, 175
Falzone (Milan), 105
Fantasie del Passato (Florence), 166, 175
Faraone (Milan), 45, 121
Femme Sistina (Rome), 294, 339
Fendi: Florence, 169, 205; Milan: Via della Spiga, 41, 89, 130; Via Sant'Andrea, 48, 112; Rome, 288, 289, 339, 376–7; Venice, 230, 249–50, 255, 263
Ferdin (Rome), 297, 377
Ferragamo, Salvatore: see Salvatore Ferragamo
Ferrari, Gian: see Gian Ferrari
Ferrario, Valeriano-Natale: see Valeriano-Natale Ferrario
Ferrario, Francesca: see Francesca Ferrario
Ferré, Gianfranco: see Gianfranco Ferré
Ferretti, Alberta: see Alberta Ferretti
Ferré Uomo (Rome), 289
Ferrini Firenze (Florence), 158, 209–10
F.G.B. (Venice), 231, 270–1
Fiera de Senigallia (Milan), 38
Figli: see A. Ugolini & Figli
Fimar (Milan), 55, 89–90
Finzi, B: see B. Finzi
Fioretto, Giampaolo: see Giampaolo Fioretto
Fiorucci (Rome), 304, 324, 339–40

Firenze, Ferrini: see Ferrini Firenze
Firenze Ricama (Rome), 304, 340
Florian's café (Venice), 239
FMR bookshop (Rome), 289, 317
Foccaci (Rome), 290, 362
Fontana (Milan), 42, 90
Forma e Memoria (Rome), 302, 363–4, 366
Fossi, Mario: see Mario Fossi
Francesca Ferrario (Milan), 42, 130–1
Franceschi, Kolligian: see Kolligian Franceschi
Franchi (Rome), 297, 298 (bar), 362–3
Francis Model (Venice), 238, 263–4
Franco il Contadino restaurant (Milan), 54
Franco Rizzo (Florence), 157, 187
Franco Sabetelli (Milan), 51, 62
Frascati restaurant (Rome), 305–6
Fratelli Recchia (Milan), 105
Fratelli Rosetti: Milan, 49, 131; Rome, 289, 377; Venice, 230, 264
Frette (Rome), 305, 389–90
Frezzati (Venice), 230, 242
Furla (Venice), 237, 265
Furs Bazaar (Milan), 46–7, 112–13

Gabrielli, Nazareno: see Nazareno Gabrielli
Galleria Annuciata (Milan), 66
Galleria Antiquaria dell'Arco (Rome), 301, 308
Galleria Bergamini (Milan), 66
Galleria Coronari (Rome), 299, 308
Galleria del Toro (Milan), 56
Galleria Giulia (Rome), 299, 301, 315
Galleria Lorenzelli (Milan), 66–7
Galleria Machiavelli (Florence), 165, 210–11
Galleria Romana (Rome), 299, 308–9
Galleria San Carlo (Milan), 56
Galleria Vittorio Emanuele (Milan), 54–5, 56, 57
Gallori Turchi (Florence), 165, 175
Galtrucco (Milan): Via Monte Napoleone, 43, 75–6; Piazza del Duomo, 54, 90, 106–7
Garlando, Alfonso: see Alfonso Garlando
Gastronomia Peck (Milan), 109
Gattegna Junior (Rome), 297, 377–8
Gattinori (Rome), 294, 340
Gaultier, Jean-Paul: see Jean-Paul Gaultier
Gazelle (Rome), 292, 378
G. Clemente (Florence), 157
Galateria Da Quinto bar (Rome), 303
Genni (Florence), 171, 187, 210
Gente (Rome), 291, 340–1
Gherardini: Florence, 170, 205–6; Milan, 41, 56, 131; Rome, 288, 378
Gherardini Uomo (Florence), 158, 205–6
Giachi (Florence), 166, 206
Giacosa bar (Florence), 171
Giampaolo Fioretto (Florence), 170, 176
Gianetti (Milan), 62
Gian Ferrari (Milan), 67
Gianfranco Ferré: Milan: Via della Spiga, 41, 90–1, 131–2; Via Sant'Andrrea, 47, 76; Rome, 289, 324–5, 341

ESTABLISHMENTS INDEX

Giannetti (Milan), 48
Gianni Versace: Florence, 169, 182, 187–8; Milan: Via della Spiga, 41, 91–2, 132; Via Pietro Verri, 77; Rome: Becca di Leone, 341; Via Borgognona, 288–9, 325, 378–9; Venice, 234, 244, 250, 265
Gilli bar (Florence), 163
Ginocchi (Rome), 294, 379
Ginori: *see* Richard-Ginori
Giofer (Rome), 289
Giolitti (Rome), 360
Gio Moretti (Milan), 41, 77, 92
Giorgio Armani: Florence, 169, 182, 188; Milan, 47, 77, 132; Rome, 291, 325–6, 341–2
Giovacchino restaurant (Florence), 164
Giovanni Baccani (Florence), 170, 212
Giovanni Pratesi (Florence), 165, 176
Giulia Carla Cecchi (Florence), 170, 188–9
Giulio Giannini e Figlio (Florence), 165, 214
Giusy Bresciani (Milan), 49
Glamour (Florence), 166, 189
G. Lorenzi (Milan), 44
G. Preattoni (Milan), 116
Gran Caffè Doney (Rome), 295
Grand Hotel (Florence), 170
Granna Market (Florence), 159, 195–6
Grasso (Milan), 110
Gregg (Rome), 290, 342
Grispini (Rome), 294, 379
Grosetti: *see* Studio Carlo Grosetti
Guarda Roba (Milan), 52, 92
Gucci: Florence, 169, 189, 206; Milan, 45, 46, 78, 92, 121, 132–3; Rome: Via Borgognona, 289, 379–80; Via Condotti, 288, 326, 342, 379–80; Venice, 237, 250, 265–6
Guerra (Rome), 290, 363
Guido Bartolozzi (Florence), 165, 176–7
Guido Pasquali (Milan): Via Gesù, 48; Via Sant'Andrea, 46, 133
Guisy Bresciani (Milan), 92–3, 114
Gulp!!! (Milan), 42, 93

Happy Jack (Florence), 170, 182–3
Harper (Rome), 294, 342–3
Harry's Bar: Florence, 172; Venice, 232–3
Hassler Hotel (Rome), 294
Hermès (Rome), 288, 343, 380–1
Herzel (Rome): Via Propaganda, 291, 381; Via Sistina, 294

I Cervone (Rome), 292, 381
I Giorni di Carta (Milan), 52, 143
Il Baco da Seta (Rome), 343
Il Barrino restaurant (Florence), 163
Il Bisonte: Florence, 169, 206–7; Milan, 51, 133
Il Cantinone (Florence), 215
Il Cenacolo (Rome), 299, 309
Il Cestello restaurant (Florence), 171
Il Drug Store (Milan), 59, 93
Il Forno del Ghetto (Rome), 360

Il Gabbiano (Rome), 315
Il Maggiolino (Florence), 165, 177, 198
Il Matriciano restaurant (Rome), 298
Il Narcisco (Rome), 316
Il Papiro (Venice), 231, 274
Il Ponte (Rome), 316
Il Prato (Venice), 234, 271
Il Salotto café (Milan), 57
Il Salumaio di Monte Napoleone (Milan), 44, 109–10
Il Salvagente (Milan), 105–6
Impianti Elettrici (Rome), 290, 309
Industrie Veneziane di Battiston (Venice), 255–6
Innsport (Rome), 301, 326, 343
I Nomi (Florence), 159, 189
International Bookshop, The (Milan), 68
Iraci Sport (Rome), 297, 319, 326, 343–4
Irene Perini (Rome), 319–20
Irioné, Corrado: *see* Corrado Irioné
Ivana Zanini (Milan), 42, 93–4

James (Rome), 302, 326–7
Jacqueline (Rome), 297, 344
Jean-Paul Gaultier (Milan), 42, 94
Jesurum: Milan, 44, 123; Venice, 233, 259–60

Kashiyama (Milan), 41–2, 94
Kenzo (Milan), 48
Kolligian Franceschi (Florence), 166, 177–8
Krizia: Milan, 42, 69, 94–5, 114; Rome, 291, 344; Venice, 231, 250–1
Krizia Poi (Milan), 56

La Bauta (Venice), 237, 266
La Bella Napoli (Rome), 361
La Bottega di Nino (Venice), 237, 244–5
La Bricola restaurant (Milan), 54
La Buccia (Venice), 237, 251
La Calza (Venice), 297, 344–5
La Carriola (Milan), 52, 69–70
La Casa Abitata (Florence), 165, 196
La Casa delle Stampa (Florence), 166
La Chimera (Rome), 299, 310
La Chiocciola (Rome), 299, 309–10
La Cicogna (Rome): Cola di Rienzo, 297, 320; Via Frattina, 289, 320
La Citta Del Sole (Rome), 396
La Coupole (Venice): Frezzeria, 234, 245, 251, 266; Via 22 Marzo, 230, 266
La Fenice (Venice): San Marco, 273; Via 22 Marzo, 230, 266–7
La Gazza Ladra (Rome), 302, 397–8
La Libera restaurant (Milan), 54
Lancetti (Milan), 41, 95
La Pinacoteca di Via Giulia (Rome), 301, 310
La Porcellana Bianca (Rome), 299, 392
La Porta Blu (Milan), 56, 119–20
La Ragazzeria (Milan), 56
La Rinascente: Milan, 54, 103–4; Rome, 292, 355

INDEX

Lario 1898 (Milan), 43, 133-4
La Ruga (Venice), 237-8, 267
Larusmiani (Milan), 44, 78
La Scrittura (Milan), 49, 143
L'Atelier Saletti (Rome), 291, 345
Laura Biagiotti: Milan, 49, 95-6; Rome, 289, 327, 345
Legatoria Artistica (Milan), 52, 143
Lello Calia (Rome), 293, 327
L'Équipe (Venice), 235, 245
L'Erbavoglio (Rome), 397
Leri (Rome), 294, 320
Leuce (Milan), 106
Liberty Deco (Rome), 299, 310-11
Libri e Roba (Milan), 53
Linealui (Rome), 292, 327-8, 346
Lineasport (Rome), 292, 328, 346
Lionello Ajô (Rome), 289, 346-7
Lisander, Don: see Don Lisander restaurant
L'Isola (Venice), 230, 256
L'Ixa (Venice), 231, 242
Longari (Milan), 62
Lord Brummell (Florence), 170, 183-4
Lorena, Antichita: see Antichita Lorena
Lorenzelli gallery: see Galleria Lorenzelli
Lorenzi (Milan), 116-17
Lorenzi, G.: see G. Lorenzi
Loretta Caponi (Florence), 170, 189-90, 210
L'Oriuolo (Rome), 302, 311, 368-9
L'Oro dei Farlocchi (Milan), 52, 62-3
Lo Scritoio (Rome), 299, 311-12
Lo Stipo (Florence), 166, 178
Luca (Milan), 43, 134
Luciano Lozzi (Rome), 289, 381-2
Luciano Soprani (Milan), 48, 96, 134
Luisa (Florence), 190
Luisa Beccaria (Milan), 51, 70, 96
Luisa Spagnoli: Milan, 55, 96-7; Rome, 294, 347; Venice, 237, 251
Luisa Via Roma (Florence), 158
Lulu (Milan), 59, 97

Macel (Florence), 165, 190
Machiavelli gallery (Florence), 165
Mada (Rome), 290, 382
Maghenzani (Milan), 44
Magli, Bruno: see Bruno Magli
Maiuccia Mandelli's Krizia (Milan), 42
Mama Noel (Milan), 59, 70, 71
Manager (Rome), 297, 328
Mannelli (Florence), 166, 207
Mantelassi (Florence), 158, 184, 190
Mara (Rome), 289, 366
Marcella Neroni (Rome), 291, 347
Marcello Rubinacci (Milan), 48, 97
Marforio (Venice), 237, 267
Maria Gaudenzi (Rome), 395
Maricla (Venice), 231, 243
Marina Rinaldi (Florence), 157, 191

Mario Buccellati: Florence, 169, 201; Milan, 45-6, 121-2
Mario Fossi (Rome), 294, 347-8
Mario restaurant (Rome), 296
Mario Valentino: Florence, 169, 207; Rome, 289, 382; Venice, 229, 267
Marisa (Milan), 46, 97
Martignetti (Milan), 44, 122
Mary Pavan (Florence), 166, 178
Masliz (Rome), 297, 382
Match (Rome), 297, 383
Mattolini (Florence), 170, 191
Maurizio (Rome), 294, 329
Maurizio Righini (Rome), 290, 383
Mauro Brucoli (Milan), 63
Max Mara: Florence, 158, 191; Rome, 288, 348; Venice, 237, 251-2
Mazzoleni (Milan), 43, 63-4
MC (Rome), 290, 348
Melegari (Milan), 115
Melegari e Costa (Milan), 45, 113
Melli (Florence), 164, 198-9
Memphis (Milan), 42, 111
Menegatti (Florence), 159, 211
Menghenzani (Milan), 64
Merù (Milan), 52, 122
Metamauco (Venice), 234, 257
Metastasio Casa D'Arte (Rome), 299, 312
Mia (Milan), 59
Michelle Mabelle/Milano Monamour (Milan), 42, 97-8
Miguel Cruz (Venice), 230, 252
Mila Schön: Florence, 170, 191-2; Milan, 45, 46, 78, 98; Rome, 288, 329, 348-9
Mirella Piselli (Florence), 165
Missoni: Milan: Caffè Moda, 56; Via Monte Napoleone, 46, 98; Rome: Via Borgognona, 288; Via del Babuino, 291, 349; Venice, 230, 252
Missoni Uomo (Rome), 291, 329
Modastock (Milan), 106
Momento (Rome), 301, 329-30
Mondo Antico (Rome), 302, 365
Monetti (Rome), 301, 312-13
Monitor (Milan), 106
Moretti, Gio: see Gio Moretti
Moriondo and Gariglio (Rome), 359
Mortarotti (Milan), 43, 134-5
Moscatelli bar (Milan), 53
Mujer (Florence), 159, 192
Mutinelli (Milan), 59, 115

Naj Oleari: Florence, 170, 181, 192-3; Milan, 51, 70, 98; Rome: Via dei Greci, 349; Via di San Giacomo, 292, 320-1, 358, 366-7
Nara Boutique (Venice), 230, 252
Nazareno Gabrielli: Milan, 57, 135; Rome, 291, 383
Neuber (Florence), 158, 193
Nia (Rome), 290, 349-50

ESTABLISHMENTS INDEX

Nicolette, Alexander: see Alexander Nicolette
1900 (Rome), 290–1, 313
Nino restaurant (Rome), 296
Noè Giocattoli (Milan), 42, 144

Odette (Rome), 304, 384
Oro dei Farlocchi: see L'Oro dei Farlocchi
Osé (Rome), 305, 350
Osteria Ar Galletto (Rome), 303
Osteria del Cinghiale Bianco restaurant (Florence), 168
Osvaldo Böhm (Venice), 230, 273

Paciotti, Cesare: see Cesare Paciotti
Palloni (Florence), 170, 178
Paola Romano (Florence), 170
Paola Ventura (Florence), 170, 179
Paoletti, Paolo: see Paolo Paoletti
Paoli restaurant (Florence), 163–4
Paolo Canelli (Milan), 48, 64
Paolo Paoletti (Florence), 165, 178–9
Paolo Romano (Florence), 179
Parfums-Bijoux (Florence), 166, 200–1
Pasini (Milan), 42, 70
Pasquali, Guido: see Guido Pasquali
Pauly (Venice), 257–8
Pavan, Mary: see Mary Pavan
Pegna (Florence), 159, 196, 215
Pellegrini (Milan), 46, 113–14
Pellux (Milan), 56–7, 135
Pennisi (Milan), 42
Perera, Armando: see Armando Perera
Pettinaroli-Raimondi (Milan), 142–3
Piazza Vittorio Emanuele market (Rome), 284–5
Piccadilly (Rome), 294, 321
Piccarda (Florence), 166, 193
Piccinilli Antichita (Rome), 299, 313
Picone (Rome), 292, 350
Pier (Venice), 234, 252–3
Pierini, Alberto: see Alberto Pierini
Piero Fornasetti (Milan), 51, 117
Pietri: see De Pietri
Pineider: Florence: Piazza della Signoria, 157, 214; Via dei Tornabuoni, 169, 214; Rome: Via della Scrofa, 302, 395–6; Via Due Macelli, 291, 395–6
Pino e Dino restaurant (Rome), 303
Pin Up (Rome), 301, 350–1
Pirovano (Milan), 46, 99
Piselli (Florence), 179
Pitti (Rome), 292, 364, 367, 392
Piva (Milan), 46, 64
Poldi Pezzoli Museum (Milan), 49–50
Polidori (Rome), 289, 358
Polidori Uomo (Rome), 289, 330
Pollini (Milan), 56, 135
Pollini, Armando: see Armando Pollini
Poltrona Frau: Milan, 111–12; Rome, 291, 364
Pomellato (Milan), 56, 122–3

Pon Pon (Rome), 304, 369–70
Pozzi (Milan), 111
Pradi (Milan): Galleria Vittorio Emanuele, 55, 136; Via della Spiga, 40, 136; Rome, 304, 351
Pratesi: Florence, 170, 210; Milan, 43, 139; Rome, 291, 390
Pratesi, Giovanni: see Giovanni Pratesi
Preattoni (Milan), 42
Prima Donna (Venice), 238, 253
Primizie (Milan), 43, 70–1
Principe (Florence), 158, 193
Provera (Milan), 145
Pucci (Florence), 159, 193–4
Puer (Rome), 304, 351

Quadri's café (Venice), 233, 239
Quaglia & Forte (Florence), 165, 199–200
Quel Quelcosa (Rome), 299, 313

Raimondi (Milan), 46, 118
Ramirez (Rome), 297, 384
Rampone (Rome), 384
Raphael Junior (Rome), 293, 384–5
Raphael Salato (Rome), 293, 385–6
Raspini (Florence), 158, 207
Ravasi (Rome), 291, 330
Reale (Milan), 59, 79, 99
Regal (Rome), 304, 386
Remi (Rome), 297, 386
Rene (Venice), 237, 268
Ribot (Florence), 157, 194
Richard-Ginori: Milan, 59, 141–2; Rome: Via Condotti, 288, 392–3; Via Cola di Rienzo, 297, 392–3
Ricordi (Rome), 394
Rinaldi, Marina: see Marina Rinaldi
Ringo bar (Florence), 168
Ristorante Bonne Nouvelle (Rome), 306
Rizzo, Franco: see Franco Rizzo
Roberta di Camerino: Florence, 169, 207–8; Venice, 234, 268
Roberta e Basta (Milan), 51, 64
Roberto Dabbene (Milan), 52, 65
Robin (Rome), 301, 386
Roeckl (Rome), 294, 387
Romana gallery: see Galleria Romana
Romani (Rome), 291, 351–2
Romano (Florence), 158, 208
Romano, Paola: see Paola Romano
Rosetti, Fratelli: see Fratelli Rossetti
Rubinacci, Marcello: see Marcello Rubinacci
Rudolfo Fallaci (Florence), 164, 199
Ruggeri (Milan), 59, 79–80
Runci (Rome), 288, 352

Sabetelli, Franco: see Franco Sabetelli
Sabry (Rome), 305, 352
St. Andrew's restaurant (Milan), 50
Salvatore Ala (Milan), 67

INDEX

Salvatore Ferragamo: Florence, 169, 194, 208; Milan: men's, 44, 80, 136–7; women's, 46, 100, 136–7; Rome, 288, 330–1, 352–3, 387
Salviati (Venice), 258
San Felice bottega: *see* Bottega San Felice
Savelli: Il Mosaico Arte e Tradizione (Rome), 391
Savini restaurant (Milan), 58
Scarabeo (Florence), 158, 208
Scarpa (Venice), 230, 242–3
Schostal (Rome), 292, 331
Scrittura: *see* La Scrittura
Sebastian (Milan), 49, 137
Sebastiana Perez (Venice), 234, 258–9
Seguso, Archimede: *see* Archimede Seguso
Sermoneta (Rome), 291, 387–8
Shit Shop (Milan), 56, 100
Silva (Milan), 46
Simone Donna (Rome), 289, 353
Sinigs (Milan), 49, 142
Sistina Uomo (Rome), 294, 331–2
Sogaro (Milan), 59
Soleiado (Rome), 292, 358
Soletti, Bruna: *see* Bruna Soletti
Solferino: *see* Drogheria Solferino
Soligo (Rome), 314
Soluzioni (Florence), 165, 197
Soprani, Luciano: *see* Luciano Soprani
Sorelle Negri (Milan), 59
Spaghetteria da Emilio restaurant (Milan), 54
Spagnoli, Luisa: *see* Luisa Spagnoli
Spazio Sette (Rome), 302, 364–5, 367–8
Spelta (Milan), 52, 137–8
Spiga 31 (Milan), 42, 100
Stationery (Milan), 52, 145
Stefanel: Milan, 56, 71, 100; Rome: Via Cola di Rienzo, 297, 353; Via Nazionale, 304, 353
Studio C&T (Rome), 299, 314–15
Studio Carlo Grossetti (Milan), 67
Studio Interni (Rome), 299, 315
Surplus (Milan), 52, 102

T&J Vestor (Milan): Corso Buenos, 59, 107; Via Alessandro Manzoni, 42, 107, 140
Tacconi (Milan), 48
Taf (Florence), 158, 181, 202
Tagliacozzo (Rome), 302, 356–7
Tamar (Rome), 304, 353–4
Tanino Crisci: Milan, 46, 138; Rome, 289, 388
Tauper (Milan), 59, 102
Taveggia (Milan), 108
Terre di Tuscia (Florence), 164, 211
Testa (Rome), 289, 332
"Things of the 1900s" (Florence), 166
Tincati (Milan), 59, 80
Tino Bellini (Milan), 65
Tivoli (Milan), 48, 114
Tokatzian (Venice), 233, 260
Tomassini (Rome), 294, 390–1

Top Sport (Milan), 59, 80, 102
Top Ten (Venice), 243–4
Touche (Rome), 291, 354
To You Uomo (Rome), 297, 332
Trattoria dell'Angelo restaurant (Milan), 58
Trattoria Scanderberg al Piccolo Arancio restaurant (Rome), 296
Trevisan (Venice), 260
Trois (Rome), 230, 243
Trussardi: Florence, 169, 208–9; Milan, 46, 138; Rome, 290, 389; Venice, 238, 268
Turchi, gallori: *see* Gallori Turchi
Tusseda (Rome), 289, 391

Ugolini, A.: *see* A. Ugolini e Figli
Ugolini e Figli menswear (Florence), 157, 158, 184, 195
Umberto (Florence), 165, 209
Ungaro: Milan, 43, 102; Rome, 289, 354
Uomo, Gherardini: *see* Gherardini Uomo
Uomo, Valentino: *see* Valentino Uomo
Uomo In (Rome), 297, 332–3
Urrah (Milan), 52, 80–1, 102

V&V Boutique (Venice), 234, 254
Vainio (Florence), 165, 214–15
Valentino: Florence, 170, 195; Milan, 48, 103; Rome, 288, 354–5; Venice, 230, 253
Valentino, Mario: *see* Mario Valentino
Valentino Piu: Milan, 142; Rome, 288, 368, 393
Valentino Uomo: Milan, 56, 81; Rome: Via Frattina, 289; Via Mario dei Fiore, 288, 333
Valeriano-Natale Ferrario (Milan), 45, 138–9
Valese Fonditore (Venice), 238, 271–2
Valextra (Milan), 49, 139
Vecchio Canneto restaurant (Milan), 54
Veneziartigiana (Venice), 238, 272
Venini: Milan, 45, 114; Venice, 259
Ventura, Paola: *see* Paola Ventura
Vera bar (Florence), 168
Verri Uomo (Milan), 81
Versace, Gianni: *see* Gianni Versace
Versace Donna (Rome), 289
Versace Uomo (Rome), 289
Vertecchi (Rome), 290, 396
Vestor, T&J: *see* T&J Vestor
Vice Versa (Florence), 159, 197–8
Vini e Olii (Rome), 398–9
Visconti (Rome), 292, 333–4
Vogini (Venice), 229, 268–9
Volpe (Venice), 234, 245, 253

Xavier (Rome), 302, 355

Zanini, Ivana: *see* Ivana Zanini
Zebedia (Milan), 56, 81–2
Zegna, Ermenegildo: *see* Ermenegildo Zegna
ZFW (Venice), 238, 274

PRODUCTS AND SERVICES

Antiques, 42, 48, 50, 52, 53, 165, 166, 170, 230, 231, 234, 290–1, 299, 302; eccentric, 62; gadgets, 290, in Florence, 173–9; in Milan, 60–6; in Rome, 307–15; in Venice; 241–3; *see also individual items*
Antiques fair, 38
Art, 46, 48, 61, 62, 64, 165, 174, 299, 301; Oriental, 62
Art deco, 64, 165, 174, 290–1, 310
Art galleries, 66–7, 315–16

Bags, 40, 41, 42, 45, 51, 158, 166, 262, 264, 265, 288, 289, 292, 294, 297, 304, 373, 379, 381, 382, 383, 386, 387; *see also* Leather goods
Bars, 53, 168, 295, 298, 302–3
Bed linens: *see* Linens
Books, 53, 289, 302; antique, 230, 242, 291, 302; in Florence, 179–80; in Milan, 68; in Rome, 316–17
Bracelets: *see* Jewelry
Bric-a-brac, 51, 234, 243, 307; antique, 63, 175

Cafés, 57–8, 171–2, 231, 239
Cameos, 165, 199; antique, 311; *see also* Jewelry
Candy, confectionary, chocolates, and pastries, 107–8, 359, 360–1
Carpets: *see* Rugs
Carnival masks, 231, 233, 234, 235, 238, 269–72
Ceramics, 24–5, 49, 51; antique, 170, 179, 299, 309
Cheeses, 24, 44, 196; *see also* Food shops
Children's clothes, 42, 43, 51, 52, 56, 59, 69–71, 164, 180–1, 231, 243–4, 289, 290, 292, 294, 297, 317–21; embroidered, 244
China, 297, 299; antique, 48, 62
Clocks, antique, 63, 309
Clothing: avant-garde, 42, 59, 92, 94, 102, 245; cashmere, 46, 49, 74, 78, 105, 166, 187, 230, 249; casual, 78, 80–1, 86, 99, 191, 194, 237, 290, 292, 302, 321, 327–8, 346, 350, 354; denim, 248; "different," 82, 86, 187, 246; discount, 104–6, 299, 305, 356–7; eccentric, 48, 52, 72–3; knitwear, 41, 42, 46, 56, 97, 166, 181, 186, 187, 235, 237; men's, 72–82, 181–4, 244–5, 321–34; women's, 82–103, 166, 184–95, 246–54, 289, 290, 291, 304, 334–55; new-wave, 56, 98, 100; no-name, 103; outerwear for men, 72, 73; secondhand, 52, 53, 102, 244; shirts (men's), 56, 59, 72, 79–80, 81–2, 244; silk, 28, 41, 74, 106, 159, 193, 234, 288, 343; skiwear, 326, 343; sportswear, 59, 73, 80, 85, 102, 158, 181, 186, 292, 297, 299, 301, 326, 336, 338–9, 343, 344, 346; stockings, 87, 297, 345; suedes, 42, 45, 51, 266; swimwear, 289, 294, 334, 336, 348; for teenagers, 292, 336, 351; ties and neckwear, 41, 56, 72, 74, 77, 289; for preppies, 74, 327, 330; wedding dresses, 291, 337; for yuppies, 328; in Florence, 180–95; in Milan, 69–103; in Rome, 317–55; in Venice, 243–54
Coffee and tea: *see* Food shops
Crafts: *see* Handcrafts
Crystal, antique, 170, 178
Curiosities, antique, 62–3
Cutlery, 42, 44, 53

Department stores, 54, 79, 90, 103–4, 292, 355
Design studios, 23, 52, 292, 302
Desks, 299, 310, 312
Discount shopping, 104–6, 299, 305, 356–7
Dolls, 302; antique, 166, 308
Dresses: *see* Clothing

Eccentric items, 165
Embroidery, 44, 158; antique, 165, 179; children's clothes, 244
Evening wear, 41, 42, 95, 100, 246–7, 288, 334

Fabrics, 42, 51, 59, 106–7, 169, 170, 230, 289, 292, 302, 357–8; antique, 165
Faience pottery, 24
Fillet lace, 25
Flea market, 38; *see also* Markets
Food shops, 24, 44, 158, 159, 238, 290, 297, 301; candy, confectionary, chocolate, and pastries, 107–8, 359, 360–1; cheese, truffles, and specialty foods, 108–10, 361–3; coffee, 297; ice cream, 110–11, 359–60; in Florence, 195–6; in Milan, 107–11; in Rome, 359–63; in Venice, 254–5
Frames, antique, 51, 62
Furniture, 42, 48, 111–12, 165, 170, 196, 291, 292, 301, 302, 363–5; antique, 44, 46, 48, 51, 60, 61, 62, 64, 165, 170, 173–7, 241, 242, 243, 299, 301, 302, 309, 310, 312, 313; art deco, 313; art nouveau, 64, 313; handsome, 364; in Florence, 196; in Milan, 111–12; in Rome, 363–5; Renaissance, 178; secondhand, 301

INDEX

Furs, 45, 46, 48, 113–14, 250, 261, 288; secondhand, 46

Gadgets, antique, 309
Games, 42
Garden supplies, 51
Glass, 24–5, 45, 53, 114, 230, 234, 235, 238, 255–9; antique, 166, 174, 175, 178, 310; blown, 257
Gloves, 159, 204, 387; *see also* Leather goods
Gold jewelry: *see* Jewelry
Gourmet foods: *see* Food shops

Handbags, 55, 207, 208, 229, 231, 238, 261; *see also* Bags, Leather
Handcrafts, 52, 235, 365
Handkerchiefs, 56
Hats, 55, 59, 114–15, 292, 302, 366
Hosiery, 55; *see also* Clothing
Housewares, 49, 56, 115–18, 159, 165, 196–8, 292, 366–8

Ice cream, 110–11, 359–60; *see also* Food shops

Jeans, 42, 82, 191; *see also* Clothing
Jewelry, 42, 43, 44, 45, 52, 55, 59, 119–23, 164, 169, 288; antique, 44, 52, 61, 63, 64, 119, 198–9, 308, 311, 368–9; costume, 41, 51, 56, 83, 119–20, 166, 169, 185, 200–1, 304, 369–70; handmade, 297; precious, 120–3, 201, 370; in Florence, 198–201; in Milan, 119–20; in Rome, 368–70

Kitchenware, 46, 159, 165; *see also* Housewares
Knives, 42, 44

Lace, 24, 25–6, 44, 45, 123, 158, 201–2, 232, 259–60, 299, 304, 370; antique, 260, 299, 313
Lamps, 51; antique, 310–11
Leather goods, 26–7, 40, 41, 42, 43, 44, 45, 46, 48, 49, 51, 56, 57, 83, 84, 86–7, 100, 157, 165, 166, 169, 170, 186, 194, 231, 234, 235, 237, 249, 250, 288, 289, 290, 291, 292, 293, 294, 304; accessories, 46, 48, 128, 130, 170; boots and shoes, 124, 130, 133, 134, 135; boxes, 204; discount, 170; handbags and luggage, 125, 127, 130; jewelry boxes, 379; luggage, 131, 139; shoes, 127, 129, 130; in Florence, 202–9; in Milan, 123–39; in Rome, 371–89; in Venice, 261–9
Linen, 42, 43, 44, 59, 139–40, 158, 169, 170, 209–10, 294, 305, 389–90
Lingerie, 45, 55, 59, 84, 87, 170, 187, 196, 237, 246, 247, 289, 294, 304, 305, 336, 340, 390–1
Luggage, 45, 49, 55, 56, 57, 59, 157, 170, 229, 269, 288, 289, 297, 373, 381, 383, 387; *see also* Leather goods

Magazines, 68, 317; *see also* Books
Majolica pottery, 24, 159; antique, 170, 175; *see also* Pottery
Malls, 140
Maps, antique, 230
Markets, 38
Masks: *see* Carnival masks
Maternity wear, 59, 71; *see also* Clothing
Militaria, 291, 314
Mosaics, 27, 391
Musical instruments, antique, 311

Newspapers, 68

Objets d'art, 48, 64, 165, 307, 308; *see also* Antiques
Olive oils, 24, 44, 195; *see also* Food shops
Oriental carpets, 42, 61
Orientalia, 44, 62, 165

Paintings, antique, 165, 170, 174, 175, 299, 301, 308, 309, 310, 313, 315; oil, 242
Paper goods, 27, 52, 165, 170, 231, 238; *see also* Stationary supplies
Pastries, 24, 45; *see also* Food shops
Perfume, 56, 86, 166
Pictures, antique, 51, 62
Porcelain and pottery, 48, 141–2, 210–11, 299, 392–3; antique, 165, 174, 179, 308
Postcards, 238, 274; antique, 274
Pottery, 24, 53, 159; antique, 48, 62, 170, 175
Prints and engravings, 27–8, 166, 170, 230, 231, 238, 299; antique, 230, 273, 391; in Florence, 211–12; in Milan, 142–3; in Rome, 393; in Venice, 273–4
Punto Firenze (Florentine stitch) lace, 25; *see also* Lace

Records, 394
Religious objects and vestments, 28, 394–5
Restaurants, 50, 54, 56, 58, 163–4, 166, 168, 171–2, 232–3, 239–40, 295–6, 298, 305–6
Rugs, 44; antique, 42, 61, 62
Russian icons, antique, 43, 64

Sculptures, 44, 48; antique, 46, 62, 64, 175
Sheepskin clothing, 237–8, 267; *see also* Clothing
Shoes, 40, 41, 42, 43, 46, 48, 49, 51, 52, 56, 57, 59, 158, 166, 169, 207, 208, 229, 230, 264, 266, 267, 288, 289, 290, 292, 297, 301, 351, 373, 374, 375, 376, 377, 378, 381, 382, 383, 384, 387, 388; children's, 385; *see also* Leather goods
Silver, 45–6, 165, 166; antique, 52, 65, 313
Stamps and coins market, 38
Stationery supplies, 49, 157, 169, 170, 290, 291, 302; in Florence, 212–15; in Milan, 143; in Rome, 395–6; in Venice, 274
Straw market, 158

PRODUCTS AND SERVICES INDEX

Tailor, men's, 294, 323; *see also* Clothing
Tapestries, antique, 61, 65, 164, 177, 179
Textiles, 1667, 357–8; *see also* Fabrics
Tombolo (pillow lace), 25; *see also* Lace
Toys, 42, 52, 53, 144–5, 396–7; antique, 48
Truffles, 44; *see also* Food shops
Tuscan antiques, 178
Tuscan foods, 195
Tuscan furniture, 174
Tuscan pottery, 164, 165

Umbrella, 51

Vinegar, 44; balsamic, 24; *see also* Food shops
Vinyl goods, 46, 130, 132

Walking sticks, 302, 397–8
Wallets, 55, 379, 382, 386, 387; *see also* Leather goods
Watches, antique, 177; *see also* Jewelry
Wines, 28–9, 44, 145, 215, 398–9

DESIGNER AND OTHER PROMINENT NAMES*

Alessi, 196, 198
Alma-Spazio, 346
Armani, Giorgio, 23, 24, 46, 56, 75, 88, 90, 105, 123, 234, 235, 245, 249, 253, 297, 323, 324, 342, 348, 356

Bailey, William, 315
Balla, Giacomo, 179
Ballantyne, 245
Balthus, 315
Baretta, Anne-Marie, 346
Basile, 183, 230, 248, 252, 253, 305, 352
Belfe, 81
Beltrami, 23, 123
Biagiotti, Laura, 23, 305, 352
Blancpain, 120
Botero, 315
Brioni, 43, 76, 183
Brooks Brothers, 80
Burberry, 78, 320
Byblos, 184, 190, 305, 332, 350

Cacherel, 140
Callaghan, 346
Cappucci, 23
Carrà, Carlo, 66
Casadei, 377
Castroni, 363
Ceretto, 29
Cerruti, Nino, 245, 253, 292, 326, 333, 356
Chanel, 48, 97
Chia, Sandro, 66
Clemente, Francesco, 66
Conterno, Aldo, 29
Cotton, Henry, 140, 334
Coveri, Enrico, 140, 245, 251, 253, 292, 328, 334, 336, 343, 346, 356, 382
Cremona, Tranquillo, 310
Cucchi, Enzo, 66

Daks, 245
De Chirico, 66
De Nittis, Giuseppe, 310
Diego Della Valle, 266
Dior, Christian, 193, 320
Dominici, 375
Dunhill, 245

"Elle Erre" (L.R.), 104
Ellerre, 355
Ellesse, 57, 59, 102, 180, 182, 186, 292, 319, 326, 328, 343, 344, 346, 354
Emporio Armani, 336
Erreuno, 348, 356

Fantoni, Giovanni, 310
Fendi, 23, 105, 261, 292, 346, 350, 356
Ferragamo, Salvatore, 23, 27, 123, 266
Ferré, Gianfranco, 23, 89, 105, 140, 292, 320, 328, 333, 343, 347, 348, 356, 373
Ferroni, Tommasi, 315
Fila, 57, 59, 73, 80, 85, 180, 181, 186, 292, 319, 326, 328, 343, 344, 346
Flying Cross, 245
Foppiani, Gustavo, 316
Fornesetti, Piero, 367
Fossati, 174
Frizon, Maud, 190, 230, 249, 266-7

Gaggia, 118
Gaultier, Jean-Paul, 184, 190, 346
Genta, Gerald, 120
Gherardini, 140
Giannini, 214
Gigli, Romeo, 184
Ginori, Richard, 49, 140
Girmi, 196
Gucci, 23, 28, 238, 248
Guttuso, Renato, 66, 316

Hechter, Daniel, 320
Hermès, 48, 97, 193
Hershey, Nona, 316

Iacomucci, Giancarlo, 316
Iceberg, 191

Kappa, 180, 186, 292, 336, 346
Kenzo, 190, 251
Klein, Calvin, 97
Koshino, Junko, 346
Krizia, 42, 46, 55, 90, 118, 248, 352, 356, 379
Krizia Poi, 105, 140, 305, 338, 343, 352

Lacoste, 181
Lagerfeld, Karl, 89, 205

*See also ESTABLISHMENTS index for individual designer boutiques

INDEX

Lancetti, Pino, 41
Lancetti, Roman, 246
Les Copains, 183, 320
Lloyd, Henry, 81
Longobardi, Nino, 316
L. R. ("Elle Erre"), 104

Mandarina Duck, 269, 381-2, 386
Mandelli, Mariuccia, 23, 95
Mani, 245
Mara: see Max Mara
Martini, Artuao, 67
Matsuda, 190
Max Mara, 55, 90, 356
Mendini, Alessandro, 23
Meroni, 174
Missoni, 23, 59, 107, 140, 238, 248, 292, 297, 323, 333, 346, 356
Missoni Uomo, 328
Miss V, 90, 190, 338, 343
Miyake, 190
Montana, Claude, 184, 190
Morandi, Giorgio, 66, 315
Moretti, Carlo, 256
Moschino, 190, 346
Mugler, Thierry, 184, 235, 249
Murano, 114, 256, 258, 259

Paciotti, Cesare, 332
Pauly, 258
Pfister, Andrea, 385-6
Pierre Deux, 358
Pitti, 266
Pucci, 23, 373

Raedelli, Carla, 351
Ratti, Renato, 29
Reeboks, 129
Ricci, Franco Maria, 317
Richard-Ginori, 142

Romagnoli, Luisa, 390
Ronchi, Graziella, 89, 348
Rossetti, Fratelli, 351, 373, 385-6
Rykiel, Sonia, 346

St. Juste, Jacque, 384
Santini, 375
Santini e Dominici, 249
Schön, Mila, 105
Sitbon, Martine, 184
Smith, Paul, 81
Sopriani, Luciano, 248, 332, 347, 352
Sottsass, Ettore, 111

Tacchini, Sergio, 57, 186, 343, 344
Tacchino, 319, 326
Tarlazzi, Angelo, 190, 346
Tiel, Vicky, 346
Timberland, 129
Titolo, 248
Tivoli, Carlo, 114
Topsider, 129
Tornabuoni, 249
Trussardi, 23, 49, 143, 292, 297, 334, 356
Trussardi Uomo, 328

Valentino, 23, 55, 87, 90, 105, 190, 208, 249, 253, 292, 293, 297, 318, 320, 323, 327, 328, 333, 345, 346, 356, 358, 373, 382, 386
Valentino Uomo, 183, 328
Venturi, 245, 251
Verri, 235
Verri Uomo, 245
Versace, Gianni, 23, 48, 83, 105, 123, 207, 323
Vietti, 29

Yves Saint Laurent, 230, 252

Zegna, Ermenegilda, 245
Zileri, 323

THE $35-A-DAY TRAVEL CLUB

The $35-A-Day Travel Club—How to Save Money on All Your Travels

In this book we'll be looking at how to shop in Italy, but there is a "device" for saving money and determining value on *all* your trips. It's the popular, international $35-A-Day Travel Club, now in its 26th successful year of operation. The Club was formed at the urging of numerous readers of the $$$-A-Day and Dollarwise Guides, who felt that such an organization could provide continuing travel information and a sense of community to value-minded travelers in all parts of the world. And so it does!

In keeping with the budget concept, the annual membership fee is low and is immediately exceeded by the value of your benefits. Upon receipt of $18 (U.S. residents), or $20 U.S. by check drawn on a U.S. bank or via international postal money order in U.S. funds (Canadian, Mexican, and other foreign residents) to cover one year's membership, we will send all new members the following items.

(1) *Any two* of the following books
   Please designate in your letter which two you wish to receive:

   Frommer's $-A-Day Guides
   Europe on $30 a Day
   Australia on $25 a Day
   Eastern Europe on $25 a Day
   England on $40 a Day
   Greece including Istanbul and Turkey's Aegean Coast
     on $30 a Day
   Hawaii on $50 a Day
   India on $25 a Day
   Ireland on $30 a Day
   Israel on $30 & $35 a Day
   Mexico on $20 a Day (plus Belize and Guatemala)
   New York on $50 a Day
   New Zealand on $40 a Day
   Scandinavia on $50 a Day
   Scotland and Wales on $40 a Day
   South America on $30 a Day
   Spain and Morocco (plus the Canary Is.) on $40 a Day
   Turkey on $25 a Day
   Washington, D.C. and Historic Virginia on $40 a Day

Frommer's Dollarwise Guides
   Dollarwise Guide to Austria and Hungary
   Dollarwise Guide to Belgium, Holland & Luxembourg
   Dollarwise Guide to Bermuda and The Bahamas
   Dollarwise Guide to Canada
   Dollarwise Guide to the Caribbean
   Dollarwise Guide to Egypt
   Dollarwise Guide to England and Scotland
   Dollarwise Guide to France
   Dollarwise Guide to Germany
   Dollarwise Guide to Italy
   Dollarwise Guide to Japan and Hong Kong
   Dollarwise Guide to Portugal, Madeira, and the Azores
   Dollarwise Guide to the South Pacific
   Dollarwise Guide to Switzerland and Liechtenstein
   Dollarwise Guide to Alaska
   Dollarwise Guide to California and Las Vegas
   Dollarwise Guide to Florida
   Dollarwise Guide to the Mid-Atlantic States
   Dollarwise Guide to New England
   Dollarwise Guide to New York State
   Dollarwise Guide to the Northwest
   Dollarwise Guide to Skiing USA—East
   Dollarwise Guide to Skiing USA—West
   Dollarwise Guide to the Southeast and New Orleans
   Dollarwise Guide to the Southwest
   Dollarwise Guide to Texas
   (Dollarwise Guides discuss accommodation and facilities in all price ranges, with emphasis on the medium-priced.)

Frommer's Touring Guides
   Egypt
   Florence
   London
   Paris
   Venice
   (These new, color illustrated guides include walking tours, cultural and historic sites, and other vital travel information.)

Arthur Frommer's New World of Travel 1988
(From America's #1 travel expert, a sourcebook with the hottest news and latest trends that's guaranteed to change the way you travel—and save you hundreds of dollars. Jam-packed with alternative new modes of travel that

will lead you to vacations that cater to the mind, the spirit, and a sense of thrift.)

A Shopper's Guide to the Caribbean
(Two experienced Caribbean hands guide you through this shopper's paradise, offering witty insights and helpful tips on the wares and emporia of more than 25 islands.)

Beat the High Cost of Travel
(This practical guide details how to save money on absolutely all travel items—accommodations, transportation, dining, sightseeing, shopping, taxes, and more. Includes special budget information for seniors, students, singles, and families.)

Bed & Breakfast—North America
(This guide contains a directory of over 150 organizations that offer bed & breakfast referrals and reservations throughout North America. The scenic attractions, and major schools and universities near the homes of each are also listed.)

Dollarwise Guide to Cruises
(This complete guide covers all the basics of cruising—ports of call, costs, fly-cruise package bargains, cabin selection booking, embarkation and debarkation—and describes in detail over 60 or so ships cruising the waters of Alaska, the Caribbean, Mexico, Hawaii, Panama, Canada, and the United States.)

Dollarwise Guide to Skiing Europe
(Describes top ski resorts in Austria, France, Italy, and Switzerland. Illustrated with maps of each resort area plus full-color trail maps.)

Guide to Honeymoon Destinations
(A special guide for that most romantic trip of your life, with full details on planning and choosing the destination that will be just right in the U.S. [California, New England, Hawaii, Florida, New York, South Carolina, etc.], Canada, Mexico, and the Caribbean.)

Marilyn Wood's Wonderful Weekends
(This very selective guide covers the best mini-vacation destinations within a 175-mile radius of New York City. It describes special country inns and other accommodations, restaurants, picnic spots, sights, and activities—all the information needed for a two- or three-day stay.)

Motorist's Phrase Book
(A practical phrase book in French, German, and Spanish designed specifically for the English-speaking motorist touring abroad.)

Swap and Go—Home Exchanging Made Easy
(Two veteran home exchangers explain in detail all the money-saving benefits of a home exchange, and then describe precisely how to do it. Also includes information on home rentals and many tips on low-cost travel.)

The Candy Apple: New York for Kids
(A spirited guide to the wonders of the Big Apple by a savvy New York grandmother with a kid's eye view to fun. Indispensable for visitors and residents alike.)

Travel Diary and Record Book
(A 96-page diary for personal travel notes plus a section for such vital data as passport and traveler's check numbers, itinerary, postcard list, special people and places to visit, and a reference section with temperature and conversion charts, and world maps with distance zones.)

Where to Stay USA
(By the Council on International Educational Exchange, this extraordinary guide is the first to list accommodations in all 50 states that cost anywhere from $3 to $30 per night.)

(2)   A one-year subscription to *The Wonderful World of Budget Travel*
This quarterly eight-page tabloid newspaper keeps you up to date on fast-breaking developments in low-cost travel in all parts of the world, bringing you the latest money-saving information—the kind of information you'd have to pay $25 a year to obtain elsewhere. This consumer-conscious publication also features columns of special interest to readers: **Hospitality Exchange** (members all over the world who are willing to provide hospitality to other members as they pass through their home cities); **Share-a-Trip** (offers and requests from members for travel companions who can share costs and help avoid the burdensome single supplement); and **Readers Ask... Readers Reply** (travel questions from members to which other members reply with authentic firsthand information).

(3)   A copy of *Arthur Frommer's Guide to New York*
This is a pocket-size guide to hotels, restaurants, nightspots, and sightseeing attractions in all price ranges throughout the New York area.

(4)   Your personal membership card
Membership entitles you to purchase through the Club all Arthur From-

mer publications for a third to half off their regular retail prices during the term of your membership.

So why not join this hardy band of international budgeteers and participate in its exchange of travel information and hospitality? Simply send your name and address, together with your annual membership fee of $18 (U.S. residents) or $20 U.S. (Canadian, Mexican, and other foreign residents), by check drawn on a U.S. bank or via international postal money order in U.S. funds to: $35-A-Day Travel Club, Inc., Frommer Books, Gulf + Western Building, One Gulf + Western Plaza, New York, NY 10023. And please remember to specify which *two* of the books in section (1) above you wish to receive in your initial package of members' benefits. Or, if you prefer, use the last page of this book, simply checking off the two books you select and enclosing $18 or $20 in U.S. currency.

Once you are a member, there is no obligation to buy additional books. No books will be mailed to you without your specific order.

PURCHASES IN ITALY

DATE OF PURCHASE	STORE & PRODUCT	GIFT FOR	COST	DATE & PLACE MAILED	AIR OR SURFACE

PURCHASES IN ITALY

DATE OF PURCHASE	STORE & PRODUCT	GIFT FOR	COST	DATE & PLACE MAILED	AIR OR SURFACE

PURCHASES IN ITALY

DATE OF PURCHASE	STORE & PRODUCT	GIFT FOR	COST	DATE & PLACE MAILED	AIR OR SURFACE

PURCHASES IN ITALY

DATE OF PURCHASE	STORE & PRODUCT	GIFT FOR	COST	DATE & PLACE MAILED	AIR OR SURFACE

PURCHASES IN ITALY

DATE OF PURCHASE	STORE & PRODUCT	GIFT FOR	COST	DATE & PLACE MAILED	AIR OR SURFACE

NOW!
ARTHUR FROMMER LAUNCHES HIS SECOND TRAVEL REVOLUTION
with

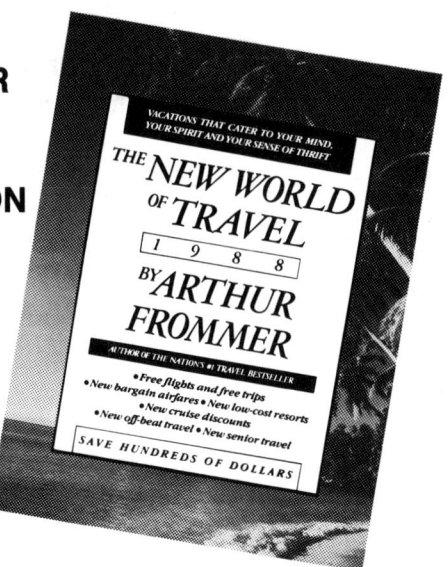

The New World of Travel

The hottest news and latest trends in travel today—heretofore the closely guarded secrets of the travel trade—are revealed in this new sourcebook by the dean of American travel. Here, collected in one book that is updated every year, are the most exciting, challenging, and money-saving ideas in travel today.

You'll find out about hundreds of alternative new modes of travel—and the many organizations that sponsor them—that will lead you to vacations that cater to your mind, your spirit, and your sense of thrift.

Learn how to fly for free as an air courier; travel for free as a tour escort; live for free on a hospitality exchange; add earnings as a part-time travel agent; pay less for air tickets, cruises, and hotels; enhance your life through cooperative camping, political tours, and adventure trips; change your life at utopian communities, low-cost spas, and yoga retreats; pursue low-cost studies and language training; travel comfortably while single or over 60; sail on passenger freighters; and vacation in the cheapest places on earth.

And in every yearly edition, Arthur Frommer spotlights the 10 GREATEST TRAVEL VALUES for the coming year. 384 pages, large–format with many, many illustrations. All for $12.95!

ORDER NOW
TURN TO THE LAST PAGE OF THIS BOOK FOR ORDER FORM.

NOW, SAVE MONEY ON ALL YOUR TRAVELS!
Join Arthur Frommer's $35-A-Day Travel Club™

Saving money while traveling is never a simple matter, which is why, over 26 years ago, the **$35-A-Day Travel Club** was formed. Actually, the idea came from readers of the Arthur Frommer Publications who felt that such an organization could bring financial benefits, continuing travel information, and a sense of community to economy-minded travelers all over the world.

In keeping with the money-saving concept, the annual membership fee is low—$18 (U.S. residents) or $20 U.S. (Canadian, Mexican, and foreign residents)—and is immediately exceeded by the value of your benefits which include:

(1) The latest edition of any TWO of the books listed on the following pages.

(2) An annual subscription to an 8-page quarterly newspaper *The Wonderful World of Budget Travel* which keeps you up-to-date on fastbreaking developments in low-cost travel in all parts of the world—bringing you the kind of information you'd have to pay over $35 a year to obtain elsewhere. This consumer-conscious publication also includes the following columns:

> **Hospitality Exchange**—members all over the world who are willing to provide hospitality to other members as they pass through their home cities.
>
> **Share-a-Trip**—requests from members for travel companions who can share costs and help avoid the burdensome single supplement.
>
> **Readers Ask . . . Readers Reply**—travel questions from members to which other members reply with authentic firsthand information.

(3) A copy of *Arthur Frommer's Guide to New York*.

(4) Your personal membership card which entitles you to purchase through the Club all Arthur Frommer Publications for a third to a half off their regular retail prices during the term of your membership.

So why not join this hardy band of international budgeteers NOW and participate in its exchange of information and hospitality? Simply send $18 (U.S. residents) or $20 U.S. (Canadian, Mexican, and other foreign residents) along with your name and address to: $35-A-Day Travel Club, Inc., Gulf + Western Building, One Gulf + Western Plaza, New York, NY 10023. Remember to specify which *two* of the books in section (1) above you wish to receive in your initial package of member's benefits. Or tear out the next page, check off any two of the books listed on either side, and send it to us with your membership fee.

Date_____

**FROMMER BOOKS
PRENTICE HALL PRESS
ONE GULF + WESTERN PLAZA
NEW YORK, NY 10023**

Friends:

Please send me the books checked below:

FROMMER'S $-A-DAY GUIDES™

(In-depth guides to sightseeing and low-cost tourist accommodations and facilities.)

☐ Europe on $30 a Day $13.95	☐ New Zealand on $40 a Day $10.95
☐ Australia on $25 a Day $10.95	☐ New York on $50 a Day............ $10.95
☐ Eastern Europe on $25 a Day $10.95	☐ Scandinavia on $50 a Day.......... $10.95
☐ England on $40 a Day............. $11.95	☐ Scotland and Wales on $40 a Day..... $11.95
☐ Greece on $30 a Day.............. $11.95	☐ South America on $30 a Day $10.95
☐ Hawaii on $50 a Day.............. $11.95	☐ Spain and Morocco (plus the Canary Is.) on $40 a Day $10.95
☐ India on $25 a Day $10.95	☐ Turkey on $25 a Day $10.95
☐ Ireland on $30 a Day.............. $10.95	☐ Washington, D.C., & Historic Va. on $40 a Day $11.95
☐ Israel on $30 & $35 a Day $11.95	
☐ Mexico on $20 a Day $10.95	

FROMMER'S DOLLARWISE GUIDES™

(Guides to sightseeing and tourist accommodations and facilities from budget to deluxe, with emphasis on the medium-priced.)

☐ Alaska......................... $12.95	☐ Cruises (incl. Alaska, Carib, Mex, Hawaii, Panama, Canada, & US) $12.95
☐ Austria & Hungary $11.95	☐ California & Las Vegas $11.95
☐ Belgium, Holland, Luxembourg $11.95	☐ Florida......................... $11.95
☐ Egypt.......................... $11.95	☐ Mid-Atlantic States $12.95
☐ England & Scotland $11.95	☐ New England.................... $12.95
☐ France......................... $11.95	☐ New York State $12.95
☐ Germany....................... $12.95	☐ Northwest...................... $11.95
☐ Italy........................... $11.95	☐ Skiing in Europe $12.95
☐ Japan & Hong Kong $12.95	☐ Skiing USA—East................. $11.95
☐ Portugal (incl. Madeira & the Azores) . $12.95	☐ Skiing USA—West $11.95
☐ South Pacific.................... $12.95	☐ Southeast & New Orleans.......... $11.95
☐ Switzerland & Liechtenstein $12.95	☐ Southwest...................... $11.95
☐ Bermuda & The Bahamas.......... $11.95	☐ Texas.......................... $11.95
☐ Canada $12.95	
☐ Caribbean $13.95	

TURN PAGE FOR ADDITIONAL BOOKS AND ORDER FORM.

THE ARTHUR FROMMER GUIDES™

(Pocket-size guides to sightseeing and tourist accommodations and facilities in all price ranges.)

☐ Amsterdam/Holland	$5.95	☐ Mexico City/Acapulco	$5.95
☐ Athens	$5.95	☐ Minneapolis/St. Paul	$5.95
☐ Atlantic City/Cape May	$5.95	☐ Montreal/Quebec City	$5.95
☐ Boston	$5.95	☐ New Orleans	$5.95
☐ Cancún/Cozumel/Yucatán	$5.95	☐ New York	$5.95
☐ Dublin/Ireland	$5.95	☐ Orlando/Disney World/EPCOT	$5.95
☐ Hawaii	$5.95	☐ Paris	$5.95
☐ Las Vegas	$5.95	☐ Philadelphia	$5.95
☐ Lisbon/Madrid/Costa del Sol	$5.95	☐ Rome	$5.95
☐ London	$5.95	☐ San Francisco	$5.95
☐ Los Angeles	$5.95	☐ Washington, D.C.	$5.95

FROMMER'S TOURING GUIDES™

(Color illustrated guides that include walking tours, cultural & historic sites, and other vital travel information.)

☐ Egypt	$8.95	☐ Paris	$8.95
☐ Florence	$8.95	☐ Venice	$8.95
☐ London	$8.95		

SPECIAL EDITIONS

☐ A Shopper's Guide to the Caribbean	$12.95	☐ Motorist's Phrase Book (Fr/Ger/Sp)	$4.95
☐ Bed & Breakfast—N. America	$8.95	☐ Swap and Go (Home Exchanging)	$10.95
☐ Guide to Honeymoons (US, Canada, Mexico, & Carib)	$12.95	☐ The Candy Apple (NY for Kids)	$11.95
☐ How to Beat the High Cost of Travel	$4.95	☐ Travel Diary and Record Book	$5.95
☐ Marilyn Wood's Wonderful Weekends (NY, Conn, Mass, RI, Vt, NH, NJ, Del, Pa)	$11.95	☐ Where to Stay USA (Lodging from $3 to $30 a night)	$9.95

☐ Arthur Frommer's New World of Travel (Annual sourcebook previewing: new travel trends, new modes of travel, and the latest cost-cutting strategies for savvy travelers) $12.95

ORDER NOW!

In U.S. include $1.50 shipping UPS for 1st book; 50¢ ea. add'l book. Outside U.S. $2 and 50¢, respectively.

Enclosed is my check or money order for $_____

NAME _____

ADDRESS _____

CITY _____ STATE _____ ZIP _____